100 Years
of British Naval Aviation

First published in 2009 by Haynes Publishing in association with the Royal Navy

A catalogue record for this book is available from the British Library

ISBN 978 1 84425 661 7
Library of Congress control no. 2008943647

Published by Haynes Publishing, Sparkford, Yeovil, Somerset BA22 7JJ, UK
Tel: 01963 442030 Fax: 01963 440001
Int. tel: +44 1963 442030 Int. fax: +44 1963 440001
E-mail: sales@haynes.co.uk
Website: www.haynes.co.uk

Haynes North America Inc.
861 Lawrence Drive, Newbury Park,
California 91320, USA

Designed by James Robertson

Printed and bound in the UK.

To convert from imperial to metric dimensions:
Feet to metres – multiply by 0.305
Inches to millimetres – multiply by 25.4
Miles to kilometres – multiply by 1.609
Gallons to litres – multiply by 4.546
Pounds to kilos – multiply by 0.454

100 Years
of British Naval Aviation

Christopher Shores

Foreword by Rear Admiral Simon Charlier

Haynes Publishing

in association with

CONTENTS

Glossary of Terms and Abbreviations   6

Foreword   7

Introduction and Acknowledgements   8

Chapter 1   **EARLY DAYS**   10
The Birth of Naval Aviation

Chapter 2   **AND SO TO WAR**   20
Naval Air Power in the Great War

Chapter 3   **GUARDING THE REALM**   30
The Air Defence of Great Britain

Chapter 4   **HEAT AND DUST**   34
War in the Middle East

Chapter 5   **WINGS OVER WATER**   38
North Sea Air Operations

Chapter 6   **KILLING FIELDS**   48
Over the Western Front

Chapter 7   **WAKE-UP CALL**   58
The Smuts Report

Chapter 8   **PER ARDUA**   66
The Royal Air Force Takes Over

Chapter 9   **SERVICE RIVALRY**   70
The Fleet Air Arm of the RAF

Chapter 10   **CALL TO ARMS**   88
The Second World War – the Opening Shots

Chapter 11   **WAR IN NORWAY**   96
First Blood to the Skua

Chapter 12   **BRITAIN ALONE**   110
Dunkirk and the Battle of Britain

Chapter 13   **IN THE MED**   116
Force 'H' and the Mediterranean Fleet

Chapter 14 **THE U-BOAT WAR** 152
The Battle of the Atlantic

Chapter 15 **ENTER THE JAPANESE** 162
Fighting a Fearless Foe

Chapter 16 **BACK TO THE MED** 170
Operations 'Pedestal' and 'Torch'

Chapter 17 **EAST OF MALTA** 176
Operations in the Med and the Far East

Chapter 18 **TURNING THE CORNER** 180
Gaining the Upper Hand in Atlantic Waters

Chapter 19 **UNFINISHED BUSINESS** 188
War of Attrition in the Far East

Chapter 20 **FLYING NUMBERS** 200
Aircraft for the Fleet

Chapter 21 **DIVE-BOMBING** 206
An Afterthought

Chapter 22 **PEACE DAWNS** 210
But Storm Clouds Gather

Chapter 23 **THE 38th PARALLEL** 214
War in Korea

Chapter 24 **FASTER AND FASTER** 222
The Coming of the Jets

Chapter 25 **BIGGER AND BETTER** 236
The New Carriers

Chapter 26 **END OF EMPIRE** 240
Operation 'Musketeer' and the Suez Debacle

Chapter 27 **AFTER SUEZ** 246
The World's Policeman

Chapter 28 **A VERTICAL SERVICE** 268
The Amazing Harrier

Chapter 29 **TASK FORCE** 276
Operation 'Corporate' and the Falklands War

Chapter 30 **NEW WORLD ORDER** 292
New Enemies, New Dangers

Bibliography 306

Index 307

GLOSSARY OF TERMS AND ABBREVIATIONS

AA	Anti-Aircraft
AACU	Anti-Aircraft Co-operation Unit
AEW	Airborne Early Warning
AFC	Air Force Cross
AMRAAM	Advanced Medium Range Air-to-Air Missile
AS	Anti-Submarine
ASAC	Airborne Surveillance and Area Control
ASH	US version of Air-to-Surface Vessel radar
ASV	Anti-Surface Vessel
ASW	Anti-Submarine Warfare
BoB	Battle of Britain
BPF	British Pacific Fleet
CAG	Commander, Air Group
CAM	Catapult Aircraft Merchant ship
CAP	Combat Air Patrol
CL	Carrier, Light (US only)
CO	Commanding Officer
CV	Carrier Vessel
CVB	Carrier Vessel, Large
CVE	Carrier Vessel, Escort
CVL	Carrier Vessel, Light
CV(N)	Carrier Vessel, Nuclear
DSC	Distinguished Service Cross
DSM	Distinguished Service Medal
DSO	Distinguished Service Order
ECM	Electronic Counter Measures
FAA	Fleet Air Arm
HMAS	His/Her Majesty's Australian Ship
HMS	His/Her Majesty's Ship
IFOR	Insertion Force
IJN	Imperial Japanese Navy
JAAF	Japanese Army Air Force
JSF	Joint Strike Fighter
LST	Landing Ship (Tank)
MAC	Merchant Aircraft Carrier
MDAP	Mutual Defence Assistance Programme
MET	Meteorological
MTB	Motor Torpedo Boat
MV	Motor Vessel
NATO	North Atlantic Treaty Organisation
NCO	Non-Commissioned Officer
NVG	Night Vision Goggles
OCU	Operational Conversion Unit
QFI	Qualified Flying Instructor
RAAF	Royal Australian Air Force
RAF	Royal Air Force
RCNVR	Royal Canadian Naval Volunteer Reserve
RFC	Royal Flying Corps
RM	Royal Marine
RN	Royal Navy
RNAS	Royal Naval Air Service
RNVR	Royal Naval Volunteer Reserve
ROK	Republic of Korea
SAR	Search and Rescue
SAS	Special Air Service
SBD	Scout Bomber, Douglas (US Navy designation)
SFOR	Stabilisation Force
Sqn	Squadron
STOVL	Short Take-Off and Vertical Landing
TAG	Telegraphist Air Gunner
TASS	Tactical Air Support Ship
TBF	Torpedo Bomber, Grumman (US Navy designation)
TBR	Torpedo Bomber Reconnaissance
TF	Task Force
TG	Task Group
TOW	Tube-launched, Optically tracked Wire-guided
UN	United Nations
UNPROFOR	United Nations Protection Force
USAAF	United States Army Air Force
USN	United States Navy
VC	Victoria Cross
VIFF	Vectoring in Forward Flight
WI	Warfare Instructor

FOREWORD BY REAR ADMIRAL SIMON CHARLIER

Chief of Staff (Aviation and Carriers) and Rear Admiral Fleet Air Arm

I highly commend Christopher Shores' eloquent and knowledgeable account of *100 Years of British Naval Aviation*. The author, with great care and diligence has, together with an enormous amount of research given us a full and fascinating insight into the remarkable history of Naval aviation and the grit, determination and unsurpassed bravery of the early aviators.

Naval aviation is an integral part of the Royal Navy. Naval aircraft are part of the ship's weapon system and the ship provides the operational infrastructure for the aircraft. The core business of the Fleet Air Arm has always been operating at sea and it is the unforgiving and extremely demanding nature of flying from ships at sea that has driven so many of the remarkable achievements of Naval aviation.

No sooner had the first four naval pilots completed their flying training at Eastchurch in 1911 than they were putting their new-found skills to use in the fleet. The first take-off from a ship underway anywhere in the world was carried out by one of those first four naval aviators, Lieutenant Samson, in May 1912. In the First World War the Navy carried out the first strategic bombing from the air; the first sinking of a ship by torpedo from the air; the first air-to-air kill and the first use of aircraft in a sea battle.

Naval aviators and engineers are well known for their pioneering spirit. The decades of carrier air power and fast jets generated a succession of innovative new technologies including the mirror landing sight; the angled flight deck; the steam catapult and the ski-jump – the take-off ramp used by Harrier jets – now standardised in navies around the world.

The aircraft, the technology and vivid personal accounts of operations make this a highly readable book, essential for anyone with an interest in our national Naval aviation heritage.

INTRODUCTION AND ACKNOWLEDGEMENTS

BELOW *HMS* Centaur *sails into Valletta's Grand Harbour, Malta, in August 1954. On her deck in the foreground are Sea Furies, while at the stern may be seen a pair of Grumman Avenger AS 4s.*

When setting out to prepare this work it rapidly became obvious to me that much of the information I felt it would be necessary and desirable to include had already been the subject of detailed coverage elsewhere. In consequence I have made much use of previously published works, some of which I have relied upon heavily. Nonetheless, I hope that I have been successful in producing something more than a simple 'cut-and-paste' job.

In the light of the above I would like to commence by setting out those works which I have used extensively, and to recommend them most wholeheartedly to any readers who may wish to delve deeper into this complex and multifarious subject. My two most particular 'bibles' have been, firstly, Norman Polmar's seminal work *Aircraft Carriers* (Macdonald, 1969), and secondly, *Carrier Operations in World War II, volume I: The Royal Navy* (Ian Allan, 1968 and 1974) by my greatly missed late friend, David Brown. For information related to the First World War I have used *Per Ardua* by Hilary St George Saunders (Oxford University Press, 1944) to a substantial degree, while of very great assistance have been the works of another recently departed friend, Ray Sturtivant. Principal amongst these was his *The Squadrons of the Fleet Air Arm* (Air-Britain, 1984) and *Fleet Air*

LEFT *Sea King HAS 1s transport underslung loads.*

Arm Aircraft 1939 to 1945 (with Mick Burrow, Air-Britain, 1995).

In regard to the operations of the Second World War, I have drawn heavily on my own earlier publications, including *Fledgling Eagles*; *Air War for Yugoslavia, Greece and Crete, 1940–41*; *Malta: The Hurricane Years, 1940–41*; *Malta: The Spitfire Year, 1942*; *Dust Clouds in the Middle East*; *Bloody Shambles*, volumes 1 and 2; and *Air War for Burma*. These were all published by Grub Street between 1987 and 2005. In preparing them I was greatly assisted in the research, particularly insofar as the operations of the Royal Navy were concerned, by my friend and co-author Brian Cull. For this period I also found *The Forgotten Fleet* by John Winton (Michael Joseph, 1969) of great help.

For the more recent operations over the Falklands, I sought guidance from *Air War South Atlantic* (Sidgwick & Jackson, 1983) by more friends, Alfred Price and another who has left us, Jeffrey Ethell. I also found the fantastically thoroughly researched *Falklands: The Air War* by five members of Air-Britain (Arms & Armour Press, 1986) to be of great value.

While these volumes have been of particular help and importance to me in preparing this work, there are also a wide range of aircraft carrier histories and personal biographies and autobiographies of RNAS and Fleet Air Arm personnel which can be recommended, and which I have appended in a Bibliography at the end.

Production of this book would not have been possible without the great support and encouragement of Graham Mottram, Director of the Fleet Air Arm Museum, Yeovilton, and of his dedicated staff. Particular thanks are due to Susan Dearing for her sterling work on my behalf in the photographic archive. Graham organised for me a session group with Admiral Sir Michael Layard, RN (Retd), Captains Mike Rawlinson and John De Winton, RN (Retd), and Commander Neill Thomas, RN (Retd). I was also greatly assisted by Rear Admiral Simon Charlier, RN, regarding the more immediate aspects of the Fleet Air Arm. To all these naval gentlemen I am deeply indebted.

Thanks are also due to my old friends Norman Franks and Squadron Leader Andrew Thomas, RAF, who came to the rescue with photographs of specific personnel, and to Wing Commander C.G. 'Jeff' Jefford, MBE, RAF (Retd), for preparing the maps. Finally, my thanks go to Jonathan Falconer of Haynes Publishing, himself a knowledgeable enthusiast for aviation subjects, who proved to be all that an author could hope for in a publisher; thank you Jonathan, your support and patience were great!

Publisher's note about the photographs
Most of the photographs that appear in this book are drawn from the archives of the Fleet Air Arm Museum, Yeovilton. These are uncredited. Those supplied from other sources, notably the Imperial War Museum, the Bundesarchiv, the US Naval Historical Center and the US National Archives, are credited as appropriate. Readers wishing to obtain copies of photographs for personal use should contact the archive in question and not the publisher.

CHAPTER 1

EARLY DAYS

The Birth of Naval Aviation

'Their Lordships instruct me to express to you their thanks for the demonstration to them of your flying machine. Regretfully, they perceive no practical use to the Naval Service.'

Reportedly, words of this nature were sent to the Wright Brothers following a demonstration given during 1907 of their 'Flier' to a collection of senior officers and civil servants from the Admiralty. Hardly a correct assessment of the future of aviation in the Royal Navy, one might surmise! Nor, perhaps, an appropriate one, given that the USA was already conducting the first tentative experiments in flying an aircraft from a cruiser of the US Navy. However, the Admiralty's decision was hardly surprising given the very limited endurance of such early aircraft. Nevertheless, the display did, apparently, awaken in certain admirals the thought that if it were possible to remain in the air for a considerably longer time than the 'Flier' had indicated as potentially possible, such devices might well prove of use for some forms of reconnaissance, and perhaps even for gunnery spotting.

Thus it was that in May 1909 Messrs Vickers, Son & Maxim, the armaments conglomerate, were commissioned to design and build a rigid

LEFT *One of the early types of aircraft employed by Samson's Wing was the Maurice Farman Shorthorn. An aircraft of this type is seen here in flight (although this is in fact an example operated by the Belgian Flying Corps).*

ABOVE *'She may fly
or she may not!' The
ill-fated rigid airship
Mayfly seen just before
she broke her back
while attempting to
make her first flight on
24 September 1911.*

OPPOSITE *Involved
in naval aviation from
the very start, Murray
Sueter, RN (seen here
as a rear admiral) was
considered by many
to be effectively the
'Father of the Royal
Naval Air Service'. He
certainly played a most
important part in its
early development.*

airship capable of carrying wireless equipment, of remaining in the air for a considerable period, and on occasion of remaining stationary in the sky. This was initially named 'No.1 Rigid Naval Airship'.

This was not necessarily a revolutionary idea, for balloons and airships had preceded heavier-than-air aircraft by some appreciable period. Indeed, Count Zeppelin in Germany was already developing and producing such machines.

Work commenced in Cavendish Dock, Barrow-in-Furness, in conditions of strict secrecy. Under the general direction of Captain Murray F. Sueter, RN, aided by two lieutenants, design and construction progressed for two years. Finally, the very large airship emerged from the dock for attachment to a mooring mast. She was some 512ft long, 48ft in diameter, and could contain around 700,000ft³ of gas. The rigid framework was constructed of a new alloy called duralumin, while she was powered by two Wolseley-built engines of 180hp each.

Unfortunately, with a complete lack of a sense of humour, she was christened *Mayfly* – and, needless to say, quickly became the butt of jokes along the

lines of 'She may fly, but then again, she may not!' She did not. Having spent four days at her mast, during which a 45mph wind buffeted her, she was moved back into the dock for repairs. It was considered that the craft had developed insufficient lift to become airborne, and that modifications were therefore necessary. When next exposed to the outside elements on 24 September 1911, her back broke as she was being pulled towards the mooring mast, and she became a total wreck. The Court of Inquiry which inevitably followed held all parties blameless, deciding that structural weakness had been the problem. In practice, she was simply too heavy. The consequence of this debacle was that the Admiralty lost all interest in airship development until the outbreak of war, nearly three years later.

Despite the earlier disregard of the aeroplane, development of this mode of flying had not been similarly pushed into the doldrums. This was not so much due to Admiralty rethinking or initiative as to developments elsewhere within the politico-military establishment. During 1909, as the order for *Mayfly* was being placed, R.B. Haldane, then

Secretary of State for War in the Liberal government of Herbert Asquith, directed Lord Rayleigh and Dr Richard Glazebrook, Chairman and Director respectively of the National Physical Laboratory, to prepare a scheme for a scientific inquiry into flight. Their brief required that this inquiry should, from the start, be prepared to undertake experiments of substantial size.

The scheme which was prepared gained the approval of the Prime Minister, and an Advisory Committee for Aeronautics was set up, its ten initial members including Rayleigh and Glazebrook. A balloon factory at Farnborough was taken over, and research commenced into many related subjects in aircraft design, construction and so forth.

From these beginnings the Royal Aircraft Factory at Farnborough was set up. Its birth was seen by private manufacturers as a great threat to their own nascent industry by the creation of a government monopoly, despite Farnborough refraining from building any standard government engines and leaving such work almost entirely to the private sector.

Individual enthusiasm for flight amongst officers of the Royal Navy had grown rapidly during the early years of experiment and development. During 1909 – the same year as *Mayfly* had been ordered, it will be recalled – the first RN officers were permitted to learn to fly. Two flying enthusiasts,

Francis McClean and George Cockburn, had made an offer to the Admiralty to train a number of naval officers how to fly. This offer was met with approval and volunteers were called for. More than 200 names were put forward, indicating the level of interest at more junior level, and four candidates were selected. All were to be taught by Cockburn. They included lieutenants C.R. Samson, R. Gregory and A.M. Longmore, who were joined by Lieutenant G. Wildman-Lushington, RM; when the latter became indisposed the group was joined by another Marine, Lieutenant E.L. Gerrard. In the event, all five had completed their training by September 1911, following which Samson, who had been the first to solo, managed to persuade the Admiralty to purchase the two aircraft on which they had been instructed, in order to allow them to continue to practise. Before the group had reached this stage, however, another officer, Lieutenant G.C. Colmore, had learned to fly at his own expense, gaining his aviator's certificate on 21 June 1910.

On 28 February 1911 the Air Battalion of the Royal Engineers was formed, comprising two companies, one with airships and one with aeroplanes – the predecessor of the Royal Flying Corps. Less than a year later, in December 1911, the first Naval Flying School was created at Eastchurch, staffed by the four recently qualified pilots already

mentioned, together with a dozen ratings. This was the first unit of what would soon become the Royal Naval Air Service.

Another pilot who joined them was Commander Schwann, who had also learned to fly at his own expense, aided by a little financial help from some of his fellow officers. An aircraft fitted with floats, rather than the usual wheels or skids, was acquired by the group, and on 18 November 1911 Schwann made a take-off from water for the first time, although he then crashed as he attempted to land. (He would later change his Germanic-sounding name to the more simple 'Swann'.)

Shortly after this event, Lieutenant Arthur Longmore made a successful water landing in a Short S.27 on the River Medway. This was, however, effectively a ditching of a wheeled aircraft, supported in the water by flotation bags. Always to the fore with initiative, Samson then persuaded the Admiralty to allow him to take off from a platform built on the bow of the battleship HMS *Africa*. Again using an S.27, he made a successful take-off, then ditched with the aid of flotation bags. This allowed the aircraft to be recovered undamaged and for a second such flight to be made on 10 January 1912, following which he landed ashore at Eastchurch.

Eight days later the leading British aeronautical magazine, *The Aeroplane*, included an editorial which stated:

'It must not be thought for a moment that alighting with a large biplane in still harbour water, or getting a biplane off a large and clumsy platform built on the bows of a battleship, has any direct relation to naval aviation proper. …As has already been pointed out in The Aeroplane *with considerable emphasis, the only possible naval aeroplane for use at sea is one which is launched from the ship by auxiliary power, and on returning alights on the water as near the ship as may be.'*

Fair comment, and a truly prescient description of the form naval aviation was soon to follow. But it had been a start, and developments were now proceeding quite fast.

Three months after his experiments from HMS *Africa*, Samson made a similarly successful first flight in the first proper seaplane which had been constructed by the Short brothers, who had set up a factory at Sheerness on the Isle of Sheppey during the previous year. At much the same time another pioneer, T.O.M. Sopwith, constructed the first flying boat.

Samson then took the opportunity to fly off the ramp, transferred from *Africa* to the forecastle of the battleship HMS *Hibernia*, while the ship was steaming at more than ten knots during a review of the fleet held at Weymouth in May 1912. He was to repeat this feat from HMS *London* two months later.

In June 1912 the technical sub-committee of the Committee of Imperial Defence despatched Captain Sueter and Mervyn O'Gorman (a Member of the Advisory Committee for Aeronautics) to France, Austria and Germany to investigate progress in airships in those countries. In Germany they discovered that 30 were already in service, and obtained a flight in one of these. The report which they presented on their return stated percipiently:

'…that German airships have, by repeated voyages, proved their ability to reconnoitre the whole of the German coastline on the North Sea. In any future war with Germany, except in foggy or stormy weather, it is probable that no British war vessels or torpedo craft will be able to approach within many miles of the German coast without their presence being discovered and reported.'

The problem facing the sub-committee was that without a nucleus of trained aircrews, the immediate acquisition or construction of large rigid airships was not possible. At once they reconstructed the Naval Airship Section, which had been disbanded after the *Mayfly* disaster, and attached it to the airship company of the Military Wing of the new Royal Flying Corps.

Attempts were made to purchase some Zeppelin airships, but such sales were prohibited by the German government. These restrictions did not, however, apply to the non-rigid airships manufactured by the Parseval concern, and one of these was subsequently purchased. Also, during 1913 an Astra-Torres non-rigid airship was acquired from France, and Winston Churchill, then First Lord of the Admiralty, obtained Treasury funds to order two rigid and six non-rigid craft. While several of these were to be built by Vickers and Armstrong Whitworth, part of the order was placed abroad. Consequently, in 1914 two of the latter were retained by Germany and Italy. Of the others under construction in Great Britain, none had been completed by August of that year.

Meanwhile, however, at the end of 1913 the airships of the RFC's airship squadron were ordered to be handed over to the Navy. By this time considerable experimentation with wireless

ABOVE AND RIGHT
The Parseval non-rigid airship (above) which became His Majesty's Airship No 4, was acquired in 1913, as was an Astra-Torres of French manufacture (right). Both were employed escorting vessels carrying the British Expeditionary Force across the English Channel during August 1914.

formation of a British Aeronautical Service to be known as the Flying Corps. It would contain two Wings, one Military and the other Naval, together with a common Central Flying School. A permanent Air Committee should also be formed to deal with all related matters affecting both the Admiralty and the War Office.

A technical sub-committee, headed by the Right Honourable J.E.B. Seely, worked out the details; interestingly, its members included Lieutenant Samson and Mr O'Gorman. Amongst the evidence collected by this sub-committee which was found to be the most compelling was that provided by Captain Sueter, RN, and Captain B. Dickens of the Army. Sueter claimed that there was 'sufficient intellect' in both Services to produce, with the advisory committee and the manufacturers, an organisation with which Great Britain could attempt the command of the air. He believed this to be as vital for the country as its command of the sea. 'I think it will come to that. I do not say that we wish to do so, but I think we shall be forced to do so.' Dickens' advice was equally compelling. He maintained that fighting in the air would be inevitable, since during the next war each side would have large numbers of aircraft and would each be trying to discover the movements of the other's land forces. The result would mean inevitable conflict. The consequences, he believed, of introducing a new element into warfare were therefore of the greatest importance to a people such as the British who lived on an island. We had been compelled to become masters of the seas in order to be masters of ourselves. Now that the air had been conquered, that task was doubled.

The sub-committee's recommendations were approved by the Committee for Imperial Defence and on 13 April 1912 the Royal Flying Corps came into existence by Royal Warrant. In May the Air Battalion and the Naval Air Organisation were absorbed into the new force.

Only three months before the formation of the RFC, the authorities had come to the realisation that only 19 officers – eight RN and eleven Army – had actually completed pilot training. To create a nucleus of pilots was thus clearly the initial aim, the Central Flying School being set up at Upavon Down on Salisbury Plain as swiftly as possible. The Military Wing alone would require 364 trained pilots. Consideration was given to the question of rank. Should all pilots be officers, or might some be NCOs? For a variety of reasons the initial suggestion was favoured in the first instance, and when war broke out in 1914 nearly all pilots were of commissioned rank.

An early problem arose relating to the status of

telegraphy had been undertaken by this unit, which was put into effect from the very commencement of the First World War when the Astra-Torres and Parseval craft patrolled over the shipping carrying the British Expeditionary Force to France.

The little Naval Flying School at Eastchurch (located adjacent to the Royal Aero Club) continued to seek to develop naval flying, greatly assisted by the constant efforts of Captain Sueter, who spent much time and effort urging the formation of a naval air service equipped with both airships and aeroplanes. Indeed, in the view of this author Murray Sueter may fairly be considered as much the 'Father' of the RNAS as Hugh Trenchard would later be seen as the founder of the RAF.

The Government now moved with some speed and resolution, having become convinced of the importance of aviation. Late in 1911 the Committee for Imperial Defence instructed its sub-committee to report on the future development of aerial navigation for both naval and military purposes, and to advise what measures might be taken to obtain an efficient aerial service for the country.

The sub-committee recommended the

this unproven upstart as anything approaching its equal. From the start, therefore, the Navy began to go its own way.

The headquarters of the new Naval Wing was set up at Eastchurch, alongside the Naval Flying School. All personnel of the latter were put under the orders of the Captain of HMS *Actaeon* and held on that vessel's books. Soon the term Royal Flying Corps, Naval Wing, became replaced in practice by 'Royal Naval Air Service', this resulting in the RFC soon being seen only as relating to the Military Wing. Originally it had been intended that all pilots should be trained initially at the Central Flying School, those for the Naval Wing then going on to the Eastchurch School for specialised naval training. In the event the Navy trained its pilots at Eastchurch almost from the outset, and continued to do so throughout the First World War.

Why, one may well ask, did the Royal Navy see fit to behave in this somewhat cavalier fashion, effectively sabotaging the wishes of the Committee of Imperial Defence? Here it is necessary to bear in mind the sheer speed of events. In 1912 it was only ten years since the first powered flight by an aeroplane had been accomplished, and the predominant role of aircraft was still seen as one encompassing reconnaissance and little else. For the Military Wing that made matters easy. The Army could be expected to operate abroad as an expeditionary force; the Military Wing would accompany it to undertake the reconnaissance activities required. Its role was therefore already apparent.

But what were aircraft – in either aeroplane or airship form – actually to do in defence, or with the fleet at sea? A Service steeped in naval tradition and experience of seaborne warfare had had little more than two years to arrive at a view regarding what these basically unproven new assets might actually be able to offer, either tactically or strategically. The degree of scepticism which existed in a basically conservative environment is therefore all too easy to understand.

An early decision, made in October 1912, was that those aircraft available to the RNAS might most profitably be employed from a succession of airfields located within flying distance of each other around the coasts of the United Kingdom, thereby replacing the coastguard service. The first such base, not surprisingly, was Eastchurch. This was followed by the Isle of Grain, and by June 1913 bases had been established at Calshot, Felixstowe, Yarmouth and Cromarty.

All these new bases were short of aircraft, but the youthful Service was much inspired by the enthusiasm of Murray Sueter, now appointed

the new Service. Should it be a separate branch of the armed forces of equal status to the Army and the Navy? Certainly, the initial recommendation of the sub-committee had intended that this should be the case. This proved to be anathema to the Navy. While Great Britain maintained only the smallest standing Army possible, this was definitely not the case for the Royal Navy, which for centuries had been seen as the bulwark of the defence of the kingdom. It had been awarded the title 'Royal' by Henry VIII and was not well disposed to consider

Director of the Air Department. He was greatly aided and encouraged by the First Lord, Winston Churchill, who had himself made his first flight in a seaplane in 1912.

At the end of 1912 an old light cruiser, HMS *Hermes*, was converted to become a seaplane carrier. Two seaplanes – then termed 'hydroaeroplanes' – could be launched on trolleys from a short deck constructed over the bow. So successful did this expedient prove to be that, towards the end of 1913, the Admiralty acquired a partly built merchant vessel to be completed as a carrier for ten aircraft. This initiative was supported by Churchill, who, however, took exception to the name 'hydroaeroplane' and pressed for this to be changed to the more succinct 'seaplane'. Samson was subsequently to test an aircraft with folding wings from this carrier.

As early as June 1912, experiments had been undertaken to see if submarines could be detected from the air. The results were heartening – in clear weather a periscope could be seen from quite a considerable distance away.

Less than a year later newly promoted Commander Samson and Lieutenant E.A. Clark-Hall undertook experiments in dropping bombs and other missiles – partly to test the effectiveness of this form of attack, but also to ascertain its effects on the aircraft. During December 1913 floating charges were exploded beneath Maurice Farman seaplanes flying at a variety of heights to see what the effects might be from an explosion below. These showed that a 100lb bomb containing 49lb of explosives could be dropped from 350ft without damage to the aircraft.

Lieutenant H.A. Williamson produced a paper at this time, suggesting that an air-dropped bomb of about 50lb weight, designed to explode 20ft below the surface of the sea, could be a suitable weapon for combating submerged submarines. Effectively, he had sown the seeds of the first depth charge.

The dropping of weapons was also deemed to be the most likely way to respond to the unwelcome presence of Zeppelins. Consequently tests were also made with towed explosive grapnels and with the dropping of small grenades. The latter tests appeared so promising that by August 1914 200 grenades with especially sensitive fuses were available.

In July 1913, when the annual naval manoeuvres took place, two seaplanes were flown off launching platforms on HMS *Hermes*, by then the headquarters of the Naval Wing when at sea. Due to the difficulty of taking off from anything other than very smooth water, this was rapidly becoming the favoured manner of getting airborne.

On 26 October that year Churchill issued a Minute recommending that three types of aircraft should be developed for naval use. These were 'an oversea fighting seaplane to operate from a ship as base, a scouting seaplane to work with the fleet at sea, and a home service fighting aeroplane to repel enemy aircraft…and to carry out patrol duties along the coast'. The First Lord continued with an exposition of his views of the correct manner to attack a Zeppelin, then seen very much as the most dangerous opponent in the air. He described how an aeroplane should attack from an oblique angle, dropping small bombs or fire-balls so that a string of them 'would be drawn like a whiplash across the gas bag'. Matters had progressed a long way in just four years.

As the year ended the Naval Wing, with its HQ now moved to Sheerness, had some 100 pilots on hand, while its aircraft had flown some 131,000 miles during the preceding 12 months. It was well in advance of the Military Wing in the dropping of bombs, and was permitted by the Admiralty to make available to the latter the fruits of its labours.

Despite this co-operation, the two Wings had drawn so far apart that this became officially recognised (despite some reluctance in Government circles in Whitehall), and on 1 July 1914 the Naval Wing formally became the Royal Naval Air Service and a separate entity under direct RN control. A few days later, with international tension in Europe growing apace, Churchill mobilised the Fleet. Five days of review and manoeuvres at Spithead followed, during which, on the 20th, all available RNAS aeroplanes, including 17 seaplanes and two flights of landplanes, led by the indefatigable Commander Samson, flew in formation over the ships. Some of those watching were reported to be impressed, while others considered it to be 'an acrobatic exhibition useless for the purposes of war'. The aircraft, the doubters claimed, flew low because they could not get any higher.

Thus it was that at the beginning of August 1914, on the threshold of one of the greatest conflicts in history, the fledgling Naval Air Service possessed some 95 aircraft, 57 of which were seaplanes; only 50 per cent of these were serviceable but 46 more were on order. Personnel strength amounted to 104 officers and 550 ratings. The RNAS would soon be tested to the full.

(Note: In subsequent years the terms 'seaplane' and 'floatplane' both became used, and were in fact interchangeable. However, 'floatplane' has become the more widely used in recent years, and will therefore be employed hereafter.)

CHAPTER 2

AND SO TO WAR

Naval Air Power in the Great War

Due to the impending departure of the whole of the RFC to France with the British Expeditionary Force, the Admiralty was requested to take over the air defence of Great Britain. At this stage the existing available floatplanes lacked the range to operate adequately from airfields on the coast. The carrier already ordered would not be completed for some time, so in the interim the Admiralty acquired two cross-Channel steamers, *Engadine* and *Riviera*, which were converted each to carry four floatplanes. These ships were perceived from the start to have insufficient range and speed for all likely requirements, so at the same time an old Cunard liner, *Campania*, was also purchased, and was fitted with a 120ft-long flying-off deck over the bow. The 18,000-ton vessel could carry up to ten aircraft. During 1916 she would be further modified, her funnel being divided in two and the deck thereby extended to 200ft, which rendered her considerably more suitable for operations at sea.

Although the main duty of the RNAS at this stage was perceived very much as being related to the defence of the British seaboard, at the opening of the conflict a squadron was despatched to Ostend in Belgium under the command of Charles Samson

RIGHT *The splendid Felixstowe F.2A flying boat, one of the most successful British aircraft of the First World War. N4297 is seen in flight on 20 August 1918. This aircraft and two others had engaged four Brandenburg W.29 seaplanes on 4 July 1918; it had been forced down, but had subsequently been repaired.*

ABOVE *The family of Sopwith floatplane scouts served in the North Sea and English Channel area for much of the war. Sopwith Schneider 3788 of 2 Wing is lowered by crane from a seaplane carrier during the early days of the war. This aircraft served in the Eastern Mediterranean for many months.*

(now bearing the new-style RNAS rank of Squadron Commander, introduced in 1914), to support a Royal Marine brigade which was operating there. On arrival the nine aircraft (of seven different types!) commenced reconnaissance flights for the Marines, to which Samson soon added ground reconnaissance by the unit's motorcars, some of which he had armed with machine guns.

The German advance through Belgium drove the Marines out of Ostend, but Samson persuaded the Admiralty, in his usual manner, that the retention of his squadron on the Belgian coast would be of considerable value to the war effort. The unit therefore continued its air and ground reconnaissance work, adding some limited patrolling. Involvement in the latter caused Samson to have some of the unit's motorcars fitted with armour. This led to actual armoured cars being supplied, and subsequently to the formation of the Royal Navy Armoured Car Force. Samson also received 250 Marines to provide the ground defence of his unit's airfield. Throughout this period Samson was much aided by the enthusiastic personal support he received from Churchill as First Lord, and now very much his mentor.

The opening weeks of the war brought no attacks on Britain by Zeppelins or aircraft, but the potential for such raids was very obvious. (Though the crew of a German Friedrischaven seaplane claimed to have bombed Dover on 14 October 1914, but no record of such an attack exists in British sources; the first officially recorded incursion by a hostile aircraft over England

to release any form of missile occurred on 21 December of that year.)

Churchill therefore acceded to another Samson plan, to undertake raids on the sheds where the Zeppelins were known to be housed. Consequently three aircraft were flown up to an advanced base at Antwerp on 12 September, before the port had fallen into German hands. Unfortunately an outbreak of bad weather caught the aircraft in the open on the airfield, and all were destroyed. A further attempt was made on 22 September, two aircraft heading for Cologne and two for Dusseldorf, each carrying three 20lb bombs. Fog intervened, and three of the aircraft returned to Antwerp, but the fourth pilot continued to Dusseldorf, found his targets and released his bombs. He was, however, flying too low for the fuse safety device to unwind sufficiently, and two of the bombs failed to explode. The third exploded near a shed, killing two or three soldiers and marking the first British air raid on German soil.

Greater success was achieved on 8 October when two aircraft set off, one for each location. Fog again intervened, causing one pilot to bomb a railway station instead, but Flight Lieutenant R.L.G. Marix dropped two bombs on a shed at Dusseldorf, destroying both the structure and an Army airship, *Z.IX*, which was moored inside; an adjacent machine shop was also written off. Anti-aircraft fire hit Marix's aircraft, causing fuel to leak out. As a result he force-landed 20 miles from Antwerp, but was able to complete his journey back on a borrowed bicycle.

These raids, the first to be undertaken by any nation away from the battlefield, may be considered the first seeds of strategic bombing. Marix's success led to plans being laid for a raid on Zeppelin sheds near Cuxhaven on the North Sea coast. There were now three converted cross-Channel steamers, *Empress*, *Engadine* and *Riviera*, which set off on 24 December 1914 covered by two light cruisers, ten destroyers, and ten submarines. Early on Christmas Day morning the aircraft were lifted out when 12 miles north of Heligoland; seven of the nine available aircraft were able to take off from the water and head for their target. German radio traffic was then heard to increase considerably, following which a Zeppelin and a single aircraft appeared and dropped bombs near the ships, although no damage was caused.

Three of the raiding force then returned, landing alongside the carriers and being lifted aboard, but of the other four there was no sign. After a further wait, the surface vessels turned for home, leaving the submarines to continue keeping watch. One further British aircraft then appeared and after landing was taken in tow by submarine *E.11*. At that point two more floatplanes approached, apparently accompanied by a Zeppelin. They were in fact more of the British contingent, landing swiftly as the Zeppelin, which had followed them, prepared to attack. *E.11* took aboard all the crews and shot-up the three aircraft before submerging, with bombs from the Zeppelin falling around her. The seventh aircraft had come down close by a Dutch trawler, the crew being interned in Holland.

Low clouds over the target area had caused the crews of these aircraft to miss the airship sheds and instead they had to bomb port installations and any vessels in harbour. No worthwhile damage was achieved, but the raid was believed to have had the very satisfactory result of causing the German Navy to move a part of its fleet through the Kiel Canal to the Baltic Sea coast, where they were less of a threat; in fact this was not the case.

However, the senior flying officer, Squadron Commander Cecil L'Estrange Malone, had correctly identified the future promise of such operations. In his report he concluded:

'I look upon the events which took place on 25 December as a visible proof of the probable line of development of the principles of naval strategy. One can well imagine what might have been done had our seaplanes, or those which were sent out to attack us, carried torpedoes or light guns. Several of the ships in Schelling Roads would have been torpedoed, and some of our force might have been sunk as well.'

The raid had indeed been a precursor of the Taranto attack which followed some quarter of a century later.

While these early bombing raids were being undertaken, three more ships had been acquired by the Royal Navy for conversion to floatplane carriers. These were the more substantial merchant

ABOVE *The Fairey F.17 Campania was designed in 1916 specifically to operate from the floatplane carrier, HMS Campania. The aircraft served during the rest of the war, both in this role and with several of the coastal patrol flights. This is N2366, seen here at Dundee in January 1918.*

vessels *Ben-My-Chree*, *Manxman* and *Vindex*. The ship purchased before the war had now also been completed, becoming HMS *Ark Royal*. The latter was the first vessel to actually be completed for the task, rather than converted for it. She was 366ft long and displaced 7,020 tons, but had a top speed of only a little over ten knots. At this time typical Fleet speed was well in excess of 20 knots, rendering it effectively impossible for the new vessel to remain with the main body.

The Royal Navy and, indeed, the Government, received a shock on New Year's Day 1915 when a German submarine – a U-boat – torpedoed and sank the battleship *Formidable* in home waters off Devon. RNAS aircraft were at once given the added assignment of undertaking anti-submarine patrols around the coastline. This occurred just before the commencement of the Dardanelles operation far away in the Middle East, and the start of Zeppelin raids on targets in England, all of which brought additional calls on the fledgling Service's slender resources.

By the end of November 1914 floatplane bases had been established at Dover and Dunkirk (Dunkerque) to cover the Channel, but clearly much more was required. At the end of February 1915 the First Sea Lord ordered Wing Commander E.A.D. Masterman and Commander N.F. Usborne to produce a small, fast airship specifically to hunt U-boats, and to do so *at once*. In the incredibly

short period of three weeks the SS (Submarine Scout) Class airship was ready for service. The simple expedient had been employed of hanging the fuselage and empennage of a standard BE 2C aircraft beneath a non-rigid gasbag, which was produced by a raincoat manufacturing company. This remarkable 'lash-up' could fly at 40–50mph, and remain in the air for up to eight hours while carrying both a wireless and 160lb of bombs.

Patrols were at once commenced, both over the Straits of Dover and the northern and southern entries to the Irish Sea. These sorties were typically long, cold and boring. Rarely was anything seen. Whilst in the clear waters of the Mediterranean or Baltic Seas submarines could clearly be seen at depths down to 80ft , that was certainly not the case in the murky North Sea. U-boats could readily be seen on the surface, but once submerged they were much more difficult to spot, even when their periscopes were breaking the surface. However, the very presence of the airships, which could be anticipated to call up surface vessels when a sighting had been made, had the effect of keeping the U-boats submerged, which rendered their movements much slower and substantially reduced their range. By the end of July 1915, airship bases had been added at Folkestone and Polegate in Britain, and at Marquise, near Calais, on the French coast. Within a few weeks a fourth station had opened on the Isle of Anglesey, off north-west Wales.

BELOW *The SS class of non-rigid airship was developed in just three weeks to meet the new menace of German U-boats late in 1914. These aircraft featured the fuselage and engine of a BE 2C aeroplane hung beneath the gasbag. This is SS 14A.*

ABOVE The most numerous of the RNAS's floatplanes was the Short 184 which gained fame by achieving the first successful torpedo attack from the air on 12 June 1915. Powered by a variety of engines, the type saw widespread service until the end of the war, much of it on coastal patrol work. This is N2987 which was based at Lee-on-Solent during 1918.

LEFT The larger 'C'-Class airship was developed towards the end of 1915. Capable of remaining aloft for 11 hours at a time, C 23A is seen here in its typical escort role.

Towards the end of 1915 a larger 'C'-class airship had been designed, which could stay aloft for 11 hours, and these gradually took over from the SS, 27 having been built before the end of 1916 to add to some 50 SS class. New bases had been added at Pembroke in South Wales, Pulham in Norfolk, Howden in Yorkshire, Peterhead in Scotland and Mullion in Cornwall. Further development continued, the SS-P (Pusher) appearing around the start of 1917, which was capable of 17 hours in the air at 43 knots.

Up to this time the U-boat war had fluctuated in its intensity. The initial phase had included the sinking of the liner *Lusitania* on 7 May 1915, when 1,198 men, women and children lost their lives, many of them US citizens. The sinking of the White Star liner *Arabic* on 19 August 1915 was again accompanied by heavy loss of life, including a high percentage of American citizens. This brought the USA and Germany close to war, and while the German Admiralty was convinced that unrestricted U-boat war would bring certain victory, their opposite numbers at the German Foreign Office were determined not to bring the US into the war at this stage. Consequently, on 27 August 1915 the Kaiser issued an order that any vessel in the 'prohibited zone' was not to be sunk until everyone aboard had been safely removed. The effect of this was to greatly restrict the action of most U-boats in British home waters, causing them to divert their attentions instead to the Mediterranean and the Aegean, where such restrictions did not apply.

Unrestricted action was resumed in March 1916, but halted again within a month. Attacks on shipping along the British coast started again in September, the position quickly becoming serious. The RNAS formed floatplane bases at Calshot, Portland and Bembridge, Isle of Wight, in an effort to counter these operations. However, on 1 February 1917 the final unrestricted campaign commenced which was to continue unabated for months, bringing Great Britain close to starvation and to surrender. At that point, therefore, it may be said that the undersea war commenced an entirely new phase. By this time the German Navy had 111 such vessels in service: 49 of these were based in North Germany, 33 at Zeebrugge and Ostend, 24 at Pola in the Adriatic, two at Constantinople and three in the Baltic. About 40 would be at sea at any one time.

During the first week of February 1917, 35 ships were sunk in the English Channel and Western Approaches, indicating that the situation was becoming critical. While in due course the convoy system would go far to ameliorate the situation, this would take time to set up. In the first instance

a considerable increase in RNAS presence around the coasts of Great Britain would be essential.

One problem which the Service had initially faced was that its floatplanes were not really seaworthy, and in consequence had to be used in conjunction with surface vessels. A much more robust aircraft was clearly needed, and here the answer was fortuitously to hand. As early as 1909 Sopwith had endeavoured to design and build such a craft, but it was 1914 before the company's 'Bat' became the first flying boat to be constructed in England. In the USA, however, a somewhat larger and more practical flying boat had been built by Glenn Curtis, and it was this aircraft, the H-4 – soon to be known as the 'Little America' – which provided the inspiration for one of the RNAS's greatest pioneers. This was Commander J.C. Porte, an ex-Royal Navy man who had become the test pilot of the White & Thompson Company of Bognor, Sussex, which had become the British agent for Curtiss. When Porte returned to the Navy on the outbreak of war he was given command of the Naval Air Station at Felixstowe on the Suffolk coast in 1915, and quickly persuaded the Admiralty to purchase two H-4s, which were tested at Felixstowe. Although requiring a calm sea to operate from, they were deemed satisfactory and 62 more were ordered, eight of which would be constructed in Britain.

Here, under Porte's guidance, a series of improved planing hulls were designed and tested, the results of these being provided to Curtiss and to the subsequent manufacturer of flying boats at Felixstowe. His initial design proved to be too slow and vulnerable, but meanwhile a larger and more powerful development of the H-4, the H-12 'Large America', powered by two Rolls-Royce Eagle engines, was also developed, and orders were placed for 71, which entered service during the spring of 1917. The H-12 was operated both as an anti-submarine reconnaissance aircraft and an anti-Zeppelin fighter. These aircraft were to gain considerable success; on 14 May 1917 Flight Lieutenant C.J. Galpin and his crew, flying from Great Yarmouth, were despatched after a Zeppelin airship was reported near the Terschelling Light Vessel, north-north-west of Texel Island. Arriving soon after dawn they spotted *L.22* 2,000ft below them, and, diving to attack, shot it down in flames. This was the first airship to be brought down by a flying boat. Flight Sub-Lieutenant B.D. Hobbs repeated the feat on 14 June, when his Felixstowe-based aircraft accounted for *L.43* off Vlieland. Following these losses, Zeppelin crews abandoned low patrols, operating only at much higher altitude where the flying boats could not catch them.

Meanwhile, on 20 May 1917 Flight Sub-Lieutenants C.R. Morrish and Boswell sank U-boat *UC-36* on the surface of the North Sea, the first sinking of a submarine by air action alone, while *UB-20* was destroyed by another H-12 on 29 July. *UC-72* was destroyed by an H-12 operating from Dunkirk on 22 September 1917, while Hobbs and Flight Sub-Lieutenant R.F. Dickey claimed *UC-6* six days later.

To maximise the use of these new aircraft, a system was designed known as the 'Spider's Web'. The centre of the first such web was the North Hinder Light Vessel, and from this eight radial arms were projected, each 30 miles long. These were joined by cords, placed at intervals of ten, 20 and 30 miles from the centre. This system allowed about 4,000 square miles of sea to be searched by Felixstowe-based aircraft. Any U-boat spotted would be reported to Felixstowe, where the sighting could be plotted on the web with a high degree of accuracy. Similar web patrols were instituted at Plymouth, Newlyn, the Scilly Isles and Fishguard. The system stood the test of time and would form the basis of much larger, more complex patterns employed by RAF Coastal Command during the Second World War.

In the following 12 months the flying boats would sight 68 U-boats and attack 44 of them with bombs. Two more were sunk in July, these successes causing the Germans to bomb Felixstowe twice in an effort to reduce the activity of the aircraft based there. During 1918 the Admiralty acquired 75 improved H-16s from Curtiss, this type of flying boat also being operated by a number of US Navy units based in Great Britain during the final months of the war.

Porte had meanwhile 'married' an improved hull to the wings and tailplane of an H-12 to produce the Felixstowe F.2, and the F.2A which followed. Of considerably greater seaworthiness than the Curtiss boats, it was at once put into production. The F.2A was delivered from late in 1917 onwards, 160 being ordered, although somewhat less than 100 were in fact delivered as production was switched to the later – though less successful – F.3.

Powered by two Eagle VIII engines of 345hp

BELOW *Curtiss H.12 'Large America' flying boat being carried out to sea on a towed lighter in order to extend its radius of action.*

each, the F.2A particularly proved manoeuvrable enough to fight German floatplanes, and could be armed with up to seven Lewis guns. It could also carry bombs of 230lb, which airships could not, and which could damage a submarine seriously even with a near miss. They were employed widely in the 'Spider's Web' patrols and also hunted Zeppelins, as had the H-12s. On 10 May 1918 Captains T.C. Pattinson and A.H. Munday, operating from Killingholme, were to shoot down *L.62* over Heligoland.

German naval floatplanes also sought to intercept the flying boats, but these were soon found to be formidable opponents, well able to defend themselves on most occasions. During one flight, Flight Commander N. Sholto Douglas and (now promoted) Flight Lieutenant Hobbs were engaged in a 30-minute fight with two floatplanes, and were ultimately forced down on the sea. When their attackers withdrew, the British crew were able to get the engines running again and taxied the aircraft across the surface for nine hours until they reached Orfordness.

On 4 June 1918 occurred a most notable fight. Four F.2As and an H-12 from Great Yarmouth and Felixstowe, led by Captain R. Leckie, became involved in an engagement with a formation of German floatplanes reported to be 14 strong. Despite the fact that one F.2A had been forced down near the Dutch coast by a blocked fuel line prior to the engagement, the remaining four crews claimed six of their opponents shot down. A second F.2A was brought down by a broken fuel pipe, but was

repaired and got off again, three F.2As returning safely although the H-12 had been lost.

Due to the continued danger of coming down on the sea because of fuel line problems, the Great Yarmouth and Felixstowe boats had their fuselages painted with a series of stripes and squares, etc., in various colours to render them more visible to search parties. When operating as far away as Heligoland, flying boats were on occasion towed to the area on specialised lighters by destroyers.

An air station was established at Cherbourg in July 1917, and from here, on 18 August, a Wright flying boat sank *UB-32* with a single 100lb bomb which achieved a direct hit just forward of the periscope.

The Germans now constructed a second base for their seagoing aircraft at Ostend, and commenced a counter-attack which for a time allowed them to gain local superiority over the Continental coastal area. At Dunkirk six French flying boats were shot down, but nine Sopwith 'Baby' floatplanes were sent to the area to resume patrols. These were soon followed by Sopwith Pups, and then by Camels, which redressed the balance. Large Americas then operated from this base for a time.

Occasionally the U-boats elected to remain on the surface and fight back, but on most occasions they chose to submerge, thus reducing their potential cruising time and range.

The Felixstowe F.3, which supplanted the F.2A, was ordered in quantity by March 1918. Slower and less manoeuvrable than its predecessor, but with a greater range, it was less able to combat the German floatplanes which it might encounter, and was consequently employed generally at those bases from which anti-submarine patrols were the main duty and where aerial opposition was less likely to be met. It was also widely used in the Mediterranean, and 18 of them were actually built in the dockyards at Malta.

By mid-July 1917 the convoy system was in full use, convoys proving considerably easier for floatplanes, flying boats and airships to escort. The most active airship base during this period was that at Mullion, Cornwall, the airships from which flew a total of 2,845 hours in 1917 alone. No ships were lost while in the care of this base's aircraft. As an example, airship *C.9*, commissioned in July 1916, covered more than 70,000 miles by the war's end. On 3 October 1917 an increasing gale caused all airships, *C.9* included, to return to Mullion. On the way home Flight Commander J.G. Struthers saw an Italian ship burst into flames some six miles away. He turned downwind and quickly reached the vessel, which had been torpedoed by a U-boat which was still close by, but beneath the water. All the airship's bombs were dropped on this, and help from surface vessels was called for, these arriving and attacking with depth charges. *C.9* then had to be flown directly into the gale, which was now approaching 60mph, six hours being needed to cover the 40 miles to Mullion.

By June 1918 Allied shipping losses in home waters had been halved. The U-boat commanders were also finding it difficult to engage convoys in the open seas, so were increasingly laying their vessels in coastal waters in order to attack individual merchant ships as they broke away from their convoys to head for specific ports. This required increased local air patrols, and to cope with this further demand quantities of DH.6 trainer aircraft were issued to newly formed coastal flights based at airfields from the Humber to the Irish Sea.

The efforts of the RNAS units, and their successors of the RAF after 1 April 1918, had been considerable. During 1917, 864,497 miles had been covered by patrolling aircraft, while in 1918 this figure rose to 3,504,435 miles. Thirteen attacks on U-boats were made by airships and 117 by aeroplanes, in the course of which six were sunk and 25 damaged. Despite this undoubted achievement, however, the greatest contribution of aircraft to winning the U-boat war had been the number of such vessels that were forced to submerge, and to remain submerged, by their presence, which reduced considerably the time they could stay at sea and the distance over which they could patrol.

BELOW *In order to achieve a rapid increase in the number of patrol flights around the British coastline the de Havilland DH 6 trainer was pressed into quite widescale use, although it was far from being an ideal aircraft for this task. C5194 is seen here at Padstow with 250 Squadron, RAF. In the background is Short 184 N1754, which would bomb a U-boat on 11 August 1918.*

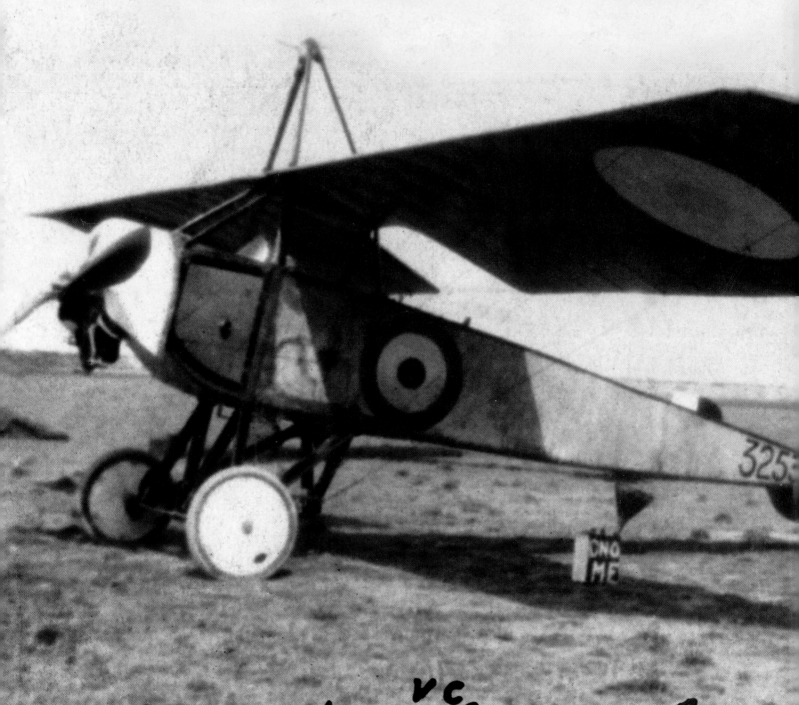

325

VC
Lt Warneford. ∧ Morane. Bomb
which he dropped. bombs. from & de
6/6/15

CHAPTER 3

GUARDING THE REALM

The Air Defence of Great Britain

It will be recalled that in 1914 it had been agreed that the primary duty of the RNAS was to provide the air defence of the mother country. Not until January 1915 was any attack made, but then the picture changed radically. The main reason for the delay in such attacks commencing was the early Zeppelin losses suffered by the Germans, for there had been strong support from the populace of that country for air attacks to be visited upon the English. On their first operational flight, three of the six available Army airships were shot down, while two naval Zeppelins were lost in operational accidents. By January 1915, however, nine new airships were ready. On the 15th of that month the Kaiser gave permission for London to be attacked provided great care was taken not to hit any historic buildings or private property. It was a different concept of war in those early days of the conflict!

The first incursion occurred on 19 January when a raid was made on Norfolk, although little damage was done. London became the target for the first time on 26 May, when it was raided by Army Zeppelin *LZ.36*. Ten days later *LZ.37*, together with some naval airships, raided Hull and Grimsby, where quite substantial damage was inflicted. As *LZ.37* returned to her moorings she passed over southern Belgium, where she was intercepted by

LEFT *This Morane Saulnier MS 3 monoplane No 3253, is the very aircraft in which Flt Sub Lt Warneford shot down Zeppelin LZ.37 during the night of 26 May 1915.*

Flight Sub-Lieutenant R.A.J. Warneford, who was operating from the RNAS base at Dunkirk. Climbing above the huge airship in his Morane Saulnier MS 3, he then flew diagonally across, as had been suggested to be a suitable method of attack, dropping a string of small bombs. These hit home, splitting the gasbag which exploded violently in flames. *LZ.37* then fell burning onto a convent where, sadly, a number of Belgian nuns were killed. With his aircraft at first rendered uncontrollable by the force of the explosion, Warneford regained control but then had to force-land behind German lines. Undeterred, he repaired a fractured oil pipe, then single-handedly swung the propeller to restart the engine before racing round from the nose in order to jump into the already moving aircraft and take off to return to Dunkirk. On 11 June 1915 he was awarded the RNAS's first Victoria Cross for this action, but a few days later was killed in a crash.

This would prove to be the only success over a Zeppelin gained by the RNAS during raids on Britain. As the pace of attack quickened, public reaction and Press agitation demanded a more orderly defence, calling for one person to be made responsible for a co-ordinated effort. Bowing to pressure, the Admiralty appointed Admiral Sir Percy Scott, but friction between the RNAS and RFC increased, the latter force initially refusing to aid in the matter as it was deemed to be a naval responsibility.

Eventually, during 1916, the RFC became more involved, and all further successful interceptions of airships over home territory were achieved by pilots of that Service. By the end of the year the defence forces had got the measure of the Zeppelins, and while 22 raids were made during 1916, these reduced to only seven in 1917 and four in 1918.

During 1917, however, attacks by German bombing aeroplanes began, and became a considerable concern to the public. Again, with pressure to maintain the maximum number of squadrons at the front in France, the defence was sporadic and achieved little success. Both RFC and RNAS pilots engaged in attempts to intercept the raiders, but with little organised early warning available nothing much was achieved. Only on a few occasions were RNAS pilots able to shoot down a raiding aircraft. Flying in a Sopwith Pup from Walmer on the Kent coast on 12 August 1917, Flight Sub-Lieutenant H. Kerby attacked one Gotha which was lagging behind its formation, forcing it down on the sea. Kerby was to gain further success a few days later, shooting down another Gotha off Margate on 21 August. Next day three Gothas were brought down during a raid on Ramsgate, two by the AA guns and one by Flight Sub-Lieutenant J. Drake. These successes, although coming within a short period, were rare, however.

It would be mainly the controversy occasioned by these attacks and the indifferent response to them that would lead to the amalgamation of the RNAS with the RFC to form the Royal Air Force in 1918. It has to be said that of all the duties undertaken by the RNAS during the First World War, the defence of the home country was probably the least effectively undertaken.

OPPOSITE *The first RNAS recipient of the Victoria Cross was Flt Sub Lt R.A.J.Warneford, who shot down Zeppelin LZ.37 over Belgium on 26 May 1915.*

BELOW *A German Gotha G.IV of the type attacked by Flt Sub-Lt H. Kerby on 12 August 1917.* **Philip Jarrett**

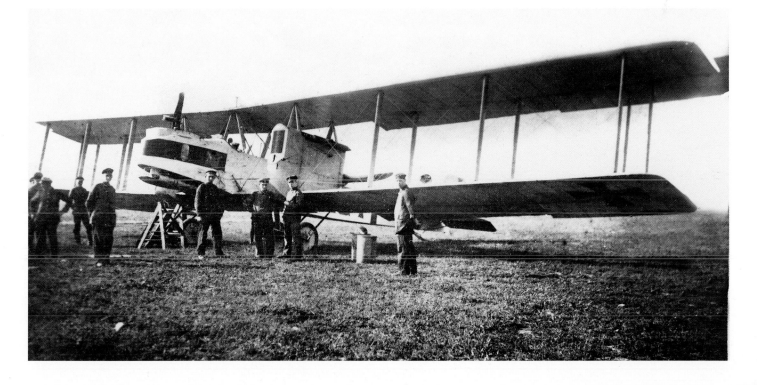

CHAPTER 4

HEAT AND DUST

War in the Middle East

The newly commissioned *Ark Royal* with her eight floatplanes had been sent to the Eastern Mediterranean in February 1915 prior to the commencement of the naval action which began the ill-fated Dardanelles/Gallipoli campaign. She moored at the island of Tenedos, 15 miles from the entrance to the Dardanelles, and her aircraft were soon in action, undertaking reconnaissance and spotting missions for naval gunfire. However, the performance of the float-equipped aircraft she had brought was worse than that of wheeled machines, and was considered insufficient for operations over land, even without the presence of opposing aircraft. Consequently Wing Commander Samson, newly promoted, was sent out by sea with his squadron to operate from the same island in co-ordination with *Ark Royal*'s aircraft. He and his unit arrived at the end of March.

Samson's aircraft bombed targets ashore, spotted for guns and reported troop concentrations. Flight Lieutenant C.H. Butler operated daily over the Turkish positions, personally taking some 700 photographs of the

LEFT *When called upon to provide support to the RFC on the Western Front during the latter months of 1916, the RNAS initially employed Sopwith Pups and Nieuport Scouts. However, these particular Nieuport 12s of 2 Wing were about to depart for a different destination – Rumania – in October of that year. The three aircraft seen in this photograph are Nos 8514, 8524 and 8525.*

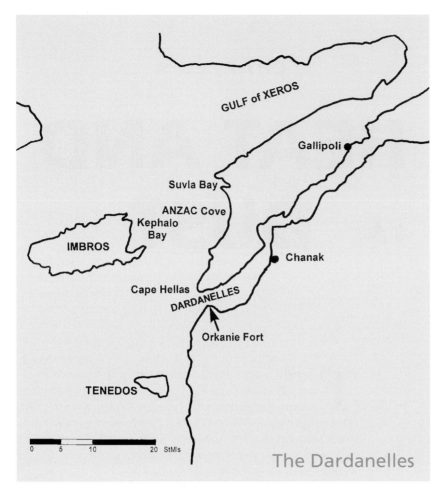

The Dardanelles

the air war so far. He also attacked and damaged a car carrying Mustafa Kemal Pasha, who was later to become the founding father of modern Turkey.

By June 1915 it had become obvious that *Ark Royal*'s limited speed rendered her vulnerable to submarine attack, and she was replaced by *Ben-My-Chree*, which was capable of more than twice her speed. Amongst the new arrival's air contingent were two Short 184 floatplanes, each capable of carrying a 14in diameter, 810lb torpedo. This aircraft had been developed following the first dropping of a torpedo from an aircraft by Lieutenant Longmore just prior to the outbreak of war.

On 11 August a Turkish vessel was spotted on the north side of the Sea of Marmara, and just before dawn next morning Flight Commander C.H. Edmonds took off in one of the Shorts, carrying a torpedo. He spotted a 5,000-ton vessel in the reported area and glided in to attack. As he cut in the engine and climbed away, he saw the torpedo strike the ship, which at once began to settle. As luck would have it, this could not be claimed as the first sinking by an air-launched torpedo, for the commander of a British submarine claimed that his vessel had torpedoed the target vessel just before Edmonds' attack.

Edmonds was not to be denied this honour, however, for just five days later he and Flight Lieutenant G.B. Dacre, both flying Shorts, took off to attack another supply vessel just above the Gallipoli narrows. Edmonds' attack this time left the vessel in flames and sinking, while

whole area. Samson himself on one occasion undertook a sortie in an aircraft carrying a 500lb bomb, by far the heaviest weapon employed in

RIGHT *The seaplane carrier HMS* Ben-My-Chree *was the most effective of the Royal Navy's earliest carriers of aircraft. She served for many months with the forces in the Dardanelles and Eastern Mediterranean area.*

Dacre suffered engine failure, coming down on the sea. Here he spotted a Turkish tug which he taxied towards, releasing his torpedo towards it. Incredibly, it struck home, sinking this vessel as well. His engine then began to pick up, and without the weight of the torpedo he was able to take off and return to the *Ben-My-Chree*.

By now, however, the position at Gallipoli was a stalemate. In October Bulgaria entered the war on the side of the Central Powers (Germany, Austro-Hungary and Turkey). This secured for the Turks the rail link from Constantinople to Berlin, which was no longer under immediate threat from the Serbians, thereby securing the supply route from Germany. The Allies consequently needed to interfere with this line of communication if at all possible, and also the line to Salonika. On 8 November 1915, therefore, Samson led the first of a series of attacks on an apparently vulnerable bridge at Ferejik, which was 15 miles from the Gulf of Xeros and a round trip of 180 miles from Tenedos. For this mission Samson flew in a Maurice Farman, carrying two 112lb bombs, and was accompanied by two Shorts from *Ben-My-Chree*, piloted by Edmonds and Dacre. Samson's bombs missed, but hit one of the piles supporting the bridge, which delayed traffic for two days. The floatplane crews hit the track. The bridge would be attacked five more times by day and once by night, but was never hit.

On 19 November Flight Sub-Lieutenant G.F. Smylie in a Henri Farman sought to attack a station on the line, escorted by a Nieuport 12 Scout (N3172) flown by Flight Commander R. Bell Davies. As he attacked, rifle fire hit Smylie's aircraft and he had to land near the target and set fire to his machine. The Nieuport then landed close by on rocky ground. Seeing this, Smylie fired his revolver at the Farman's remaining bomb, which exploded, completing the destruction of the aircraft. He then ran to the Nieuport, which although normally a two-seater, had one cockpit faired over. Wriggling beneath the instrument panel and around the controls, he managed to wrap his tall frame around the fuel tank as Bell Davies took off again and flew back to Tenedos. There, Bell Davies (later to become an Air Commodore in the RAF) reported: 'Returning saw H-5 burning in marshes. Picked up pilot.' He became the second (and last) member of the RNAS to be awarded a Victoria Cross; Smylie received a DSC for his part in this action.

These activities were brought to a close by the Allied withdrawal from Gallipoli. Following the departure from the immediate area, the RNAS became involved in other actions against the Turks.

Samson had by now been promoted to command *Ben-My-Chree*, together with two companion vessels which had come out from England to join her. These were *Anne* and *Raven II*, both of which had been cargo steamers, taken as prizes from the Germans. Each had been modified to carry four floatplanes, providing the little force with 14 aircraft in total.

Operations continued over the Eastern Mediterranean and the Red Sea, above the Sinai, Palestine and Arabian deserts, the flotilla being usually escorted by French warships. In January 1917 *Ben-My-Chree* moored by the island of Castelorizzo, just off the southern coast of Turkey. Here, however, a well-camouflaged Turkish battery opened fire from the mainland, its fourth shell hitting the hangar where the ready-fuelled aircraft quickly caught fire. More shells hit home and the vessel soon became a total loss, sinking in shallow water.

Samson was next appointed commander of British naval air operations in the Middle East, and in April 1917 went aboard *Raven II* to lead a hunt for the German surface raider *Wolf* in the Indian Ocean; their quarry was not to be found.

The force's final major involvement in the area occurred early in 1918 when *Ark Royal* and *Manxman* joined RFC aircraft for attacks on a Turkish battlecruiser, the *Yaviz* (the ex-German *Goeben*), which had run aground during January and became the target of the First World War's greatest and most sustained attack on a warship by aircraft. The two air services rained 15 tons of bombs onto the vessel, but the 65lb and 112lb missiles of that period were not capable of inflicting serious damage on an armoured vessel of this type, even when hits were obtained. Bad weather and heavy seas prevented the aircraft carrying torpedoes – which would probably have been much more effective – from taking off.

ABOVE *Flt Cdr R. Bell Davies (front, lower left) was involved in a dramatic rescue of a fellow pilot brought down during a bombing raid on a railway station on 19 November 1915. For this exploit he became the second RNAS pilot to be awarded the Victoria Cross.*

CHAPTER 5

WINGS OVER WATER

North Sea Air Operations

While the Admiralty remained unconvinced that aeroplanes were the most appropriate form of defence against Zeppelins, their use at sea in support of the fleet remained of potentially greater promise. Following the acquisition of a growing number of floatplane carriers, experiments to get higher performance aircraft into the air above the waves continued. On 3 November 1915 Flight Commander Lieutenant B.F. Fowler managed to take off from *Vindex*'s launching platform in a wheeled Bristol Scout C.

Meanwhile, receipt of growing numbers of the reliable Short 184 – of which 650 would ultimately be built for the RNAS – meant that more suitable aircraft were now available to be launched from the carriers for operations in hostile skies. Late in March 1916, therefore, *Vindex* crossed the North Sea to launch five aircraft to attack Zeppelin sheds at Hoyer and Tondern on the German North Sea coast. In poor weather the sheds were not spotted, but the presence of the formation of British aircraft over their territory brought out a number of German floatplanes, and word was received that the German High Seas Fleet was putting to sea. The Royal Navy's Grand Fleet at once prepared to

RIGHT *Intended to serve on HMS* Argus *was the Royal Navy's first carrier-borne torpedo bomber, the Sopwith Cuckoo. The ship and aircraft arrived just too late to participate in operations before the Armistice of November 1918. This is N6954 of 155 Squadron, RAF, seen here at East Fortune.*

join action, but the Germans then withdrew back into port.

The possibility of bringing out the German battlefleet in such a manner caused a further incursion to be planned, and on 3 May 1916 *Vindex* returned, this time with *Engadine* and a total combined strike-force of 11 floatplanes. A force of fast RN battlecruisers stood ready for any German sortie.

In the early hours of 4 May all the floatplanes were hoisted out onto the water, but misfortune then struck. A high sea rendered eight immediately unserviceable, either with broken propellers or flooded carburettors. Of the three that managed to get airborne, one collided with the radio mast on a nearby vessel and crashed and one suffered engine trouble and had to turn back. The sole aircraft which reached Tondern found the Zeppelin sheds shrouded in mist. The German fleet did not put to sea, but a Zeppelin came to investigate and was shot down by gunfire from submarine *E.11*.

Towards the end of May the German High Seas Fleet did put out, the British Grand Fleet immediately preparing for action. To accompany the latter, the floatplane carrier *Campania* also prepared to sail. A separate fast battlecruiser force was again formed, and this was to be joined by *Engadine*. The British warships sailed from Scapa Flow during the night of 30/31 May, but *Campania*, moored on the far northern side of Scapa Flow adjacent to an island where the floatplanes were prepared for flight, failed to receive the message at the same time and sailed late, failing to catch up with the Grand Fleet.

Engadine got away on time with the battlecruisers, and early in the next afternoon was ordered to launch a reconnaissance when smoke was seen in the distance. A Short 184, flown by Flight Lieutenant F.J. Rutland with Assistant Paymaster G.S. Trewin as observer, was launched safely and a number of German light cruisers and destroyers were soon spotted. Rutland radioed a

report back and continued to shadow the enemy ships until a broken fuel line forced him to land on the water. He was able to repair this and take off again. However, there had been a delay in the information being passed by *Engadine*, as a result of which the force commander did not request further information.

The problem was exacerbated by *Engadine*'s slow speed, which prevented her from keeping up with the battlecruisers while operating her aircraft. Consequently this operation – the sole air involvement in what became the Battle of Jutland – was not particularly successful or significant. It was, however, another 'first' – the first occasion when an aircraft communicated with ships during a fleet action. Jutland turned out to be a cautious battle, for it was later described by Churchill as the one occasion on which the war could have been lost in an afternoon had it gone badly. Although subsequently claimed as a British victory, the Grand Fleet had actually lost double the tonnage that the German High Seas Fleet suffered.

The High Seas Fleet returned to harbour and never came out again – but the Grand Fleet was held in readiness for the rest of the war, in case it did, tying down huge resources that might have been employed elsewhere. It has been suggested that had 'proper use' been made of

Campania's and *Engadine*'s air components, a comprehensive British victory might have been achieved. But it was early days and the full potential of such aerial involvement was still by no means fully understood, so such a view is clearly one of hindsight – undoubtedly the most accurate, but surely the most useless of all sciences.

The year 1917 was to see renewed efforts to get wheeled aircraft – particularly fighting scouts – to sea. Rutland, after his service aboard *Engadine*, was promoted and posted as senior flying officer to the larger *Manxman*, from which he was able to take off in a Sopwith Pup with a run of only 20ft. By now *Campania* and *Manxman* were carrying 15 Pups between them and 14 reconnaissance aircraft, but more fighters were needed by the fleet, and ideally in much faster vessels. Rutland's flying skills were exceptional at this time, and most pilots required 35–45ft to get Pups into the air.

Rutland was convinced that one of the answers was to get Pups aboard capital ships, and with this in mind the light cruiser *Yarmouth* was ordered into Rosyth dockyard to have a flying-off platform installed, from which Rutland felt aircraft could take off in less than 45ft. While these works were in hand, *Manxman* put to sea, Rutland and another pilot taking off on an anti-Zeppelin sweep. The

second pilot came down at once due to engine failure and was picked up by a destroyer, but Rutland was forced to land in Denmark. He was able to leave this neutral country, making his way back to Britain via Sweden and Norway in time to undertake tests from *Yarmouth* during June.

The results were very promising, Rutland getting his Pup into the air in less than 20ft, a second pilot also achieving the same. Back aboard *Manxman* he soon had all the scout pilots taking off in one-third of the 60ft flight deck. In consequence orders were issued for all cruisers that could take the additional weight to be fitted with 20ft flying-off platforms, and then to be issued with Pups. *Yarmouth* then put to sea with her Pup aboard for a sweep of the Danish coast. Early on 21 August Zeppelin *L.23* appeared, shadowing the British vessels. Having lured the airship somewhat further from its base, the Pup was launched, Flight Sub-Lieutenant B.A. Smart climbing above before diving to attack with incendiary ammunition. His second pass sent the Zeppelin down in flames, Smart then landing safely in the water, from where he was rescued by a destroyer.

Twenty-two light cruisers were fitted with flying-off platforms, but the Commander-in-Chief of the Grand Fleet still refused to have these fitted to battleships and battlecruisers, since he feared that

BELOW *Newly promoted Sqn Cdr Rutland subsequently became much involved in tests to operate the Sopwith Pup from aboard warships such as cruisers. He is seen here in N6431 taking off from a platform mounted on* HMS Yarmouth *on 28 July 1917.*

the need to turn into the wind to launch aircraft would be unacceptable to warship commanders during an engagement. Commander Rutland, now senior flying officer on the new carrier *Furious*, felt that the answer was to place the platforms on the turrets of the main battery, as this would require only the turret, not the whole ship, to be turned into the wind. To test this theory a platform was fitted to the second forward 15in turret on the battleship *Repulse*, and on 1 October 1917 Rutland flew a Pup from this with great ease. Then, to ensure that the ship's superstructure would not create airflows which would interfere with a launch from the aft turret, he took off from this position on *Repulse* – again without a problem. Thereafter all British battlecruisers were fitted to carry two fighting aircraft, while light cruisers with a weight restriction were provided with a lighter revolving platform. In later tests even two-seat aircraft were flown off from turret platforms on battlecruisers.

All this development would soon prove redundant, however, since the first aircraft carrier in the modern sense of the word now made its appearance. Shortly after the outbreak of war three new light battlecruisers had been ordered, which were to be named *Glorious, Courageous* and *Furious*. These were to have a fairly shallow draft, rendering them capable of operations in the Baltic Sea. Started in

1915, the first two were completed towards the end of 1916, each mounting batteries of four 15in guns and 14 torpedo-launching tubes – a very high number. *Furious* was delayed by an intention to provide her with a pair of 18in guns – the largest calibre that had yet been fitted to a warship. She was also to have no less than 18 torpedo tubes.

Before *Furious* was completed, however, alterations were ordered on 17 March 1917 requiring the removal of the provision for the forward 18in gun and its replacement by a slanted flight deck 228ft long and 50ft wide, which formed a 'roof' over a hangar. The rear 18in gun was retained. This gun was extraordinarily – almost ludicrously – powerful, with a range of 20 miles and firing a shell weighing 3,320lb. One officer whose cabin was beneath the turret described the recoil as 'tremendous – every time she fired it was like a snowstorm in my cabin, only instead of snowflakes sheared rivet-heads would come down from the deckhead and partition'.

The complement of aircraft initially intended to be carried amounted to four floatplanes and six wheeled aircraft. A hydraulic lift was incorporated to move aircraft from the hangar to the deck. At this stage she was still only a 'flying-off' vessel; on completion of flights her aircraft would still have to land at an airfield ashore, or ditch nearby – not a very appealing idea for pilots of wheeled aircraft.

ABOVE *The magnificently controllable Sopwith Pup undertook many of the early trial launchings from flying-off platforms above gun turrets. It became the first fighting scout to go to sea. Here N6453 is mounted above 'B' Turret on the battleship HMS* Repulse.

ABOVE *The first aircraft carrier to enter service was HMS* Furious, *seen here in her initial form featuring just a flying-off platform on her bows. She would later be modified on several occasions, ultimately with an all-through launching and landing deck. In this final configuration she was to continue to serve throughout the Second World War.*

The ship's initial senior flying officer, Squadron Commander E.H. Dunning, a veteran of the Dardanelles campaign, was convinced that landings could be made aboard, and on 2 August, after less than a month at sea, he approached in a Pup as the ship steamed at 26 knots into a 21-knot wind. As this was virtually equivalent to the scout's landing speed, it was possible to hover over the deck. He therefore flew along the starboard side of the vessel, side-slipped to port and cut his engine, whereupon several sailors grabbed strategically placed straps and brought it to a stop. It was the first landing of a warplane on a warship under way.

Five days later he tried again, but this time there was a stronger headwind which actually caused the aircraft to be blown backwards against the lift hatch. Climbing into another Pup, Dunning tried again, waving the crew away as he obviously wanted to try the approach a further time before landing. As he opened the throttle, the Pup stalled, and while men rushed to grab the straps it was blown over the side, crashing into the sea. Although a boat got to the wrecked Pup, which was held up by a flotation bag at the tail, Dunning was dead, apparently knocked unconscious and drowned.

Experiments then stopped, and the ship briefly joined *Glorious* and *Courageous* for offensive operations with the Home Fleet. In November 1917 *Furious* again returned to the dockyard,

this time for a landing-on deck to be installed. The remaining 18in gun and one battery of 5.5in weapons were removed and a second deck (287ft long and 70ft wide) was placed behind the funnel. A second hangar was provided beneath this, allowing a further ten aircraft to be carried. Thus 12 Pups and eight Short floatplanes could now be accommodated.

Trackways were now included round each side of the funnel and bridge so that aircraft which had landed could be wheeled round on special 'dollies' to the flying-off deck. A sandbag arrester gear was provided to catch a hook under the aircraft. Additionally, small v-shaped hooks on the wheel axles were designed to catch fore-and-aft wires. It was hoped that these various devices would halt the aircraft before it reached the heavy hawsers that were stretched across the end of the landing deck.

Though the arrester system worked satisfactorily when tested ashore, it was not so successful aboard ship. It was nevertheless retained until 1925, after which British carriers maintained no arresting facilities for some years, relying instead on headwind and low speed to stop the aircraft on landing.

Furious, as delivered after these works in March 1918, was still only useable as a take-off vessel, since gasses emanating from the funnel had a very bad effect on the airstream over the landing deck, making its use extremely dangerous.

LEFT *Sqn Cdr E.H.Dunning, a veteran of the Dardanelles campaign, became Senior Flying Officer on HMS* Furious. *He undertook the initial trials involved with landing a Sopwith Pup on this vessel, but on 7 August 1917 his aircraft stalled and crashed into the sea, leading to his death.*

By now the Pup had been replaced by the more potent Sopwith Camel, a special version of which, the 2F1, was being built for use at sea. The RNAS was also becoming a part of the new RAF at this time. On 19 July 1918 *Furious* and a force of light cruisers and destroyers sought to attack the old enemy – the airship sheds at Tondern. Seven Camels were launched, the first three of which bombed one large shed successfully. Of the other four, one came down in the sea due to engine failure, one crashed soon after take-off, and one had to force-land in Denmark. The fourth reached Tondern and also obtained a direct hit on a shed. In the two sheds which had been bombed, two Zeppelins (*L.54* and *L.60*) were destroyed. However, only two Camels made it back to the

LEFT *The Sopwith 2F1 Camel was a specially adapted version of this fighting scout for shipboard use. One of the two nose-mounted Vickers guns was replaced by a Lewis on the top wing which could be tilted back by the pilot to fire into the underside of a Zeppelin. These aircraft replaced the Pups for use over the North Sea during 1918, and on 19 July of that year were responsible for destroying the Zeppelins L.54 and L.66 during a raid on airship sheds at Tondern. N7149, named 'Swillington', was serving with the Test Flight of the ARS at Turnhouse when photographed.*

ABOVE *Just too late to see service during 1918, HMS* Argus *was the Royal Navy's first carrier to feature a clear flight deck. Even the funnels and control superstructure were at the rear and below deck level, although a small island structure could be raised hydraulically when flying was in progress.*

ship, both having to ditch because of the problems with the landing deck. Nonetheless, four of the other five pilots eventually reached Denmark.

Due to these losses, the Admiralty decided not to employ *Furious* for further offensive sorties and she completed the war flying captive balloons for reconnaissance purposes. However, the Tondern raid had a severe impact on the Germans, who were so concerned that a further raid might follow that the base was used only as an emergency landing ground for the rest of the war.

Samson, now holding the initial RAF rank of Colonel, had taken command of Yarmouth naval air station on his return from the Middle East, and had sought to investigate further use of towed platforms for aircraft. These had been used before, but had usually been cut loose when within range of the aircraft's destination, the flying boats involved then being transferred to the sea for take-off. However, since these flying boats did not have the performance or range to allow for the interception of Zeppelins, Samson's plan was to employ a fighter on a barge towed by a destroyer at high speed, the aircraft taking off when the speed had reached 30 knots. The barge being about 60ft in length gave about the same amount of take-off room as the platforms on cruiser turrets.

Samson's first trial used a Camel fitted with skids instead of wheels, the aircraft being held back by a releasable cable until the pilot was ready to go. This attempt failed, as it seemed that the skids had fouled a cross-piece, causing the aircraft to topple forward off the barge, which then passed over it, forcing both the Camel and its pilot underwater. Samson survived this rather traumatic experience and was rescued. Photographs of the attempt were then studied, and it was decided to make a second attempt, this time using a wheeled aircraft. The flight deck was modified so that it could be horizontal when the barge was moving at high speed, and a tail-guide kept the aircraft parallel with this. Following these modifications, the next test was flown by Flight Sub-Lieutenant S. Culley on 1 August. Towed by HMS *Redoubt* at 35 knots, Culley got into the air successfully and subsequently landed ashore.

Having shown that it could be done, immediate use was made of this new facility. *Redoubt* set off towing the barge and Camel across the North Sea, accompanied by four light cruisers, each carrying on its deck a motor torpedo boat, and by a dozen other destroyers. Three of these towed barges carrying floatplanes for reconnaissance and rescue work.

Next morning, 11 August, this force arrived off the Dutch coast, lowering the MTBs into the water. The sea was running too much of a swell to allow the floatplanes to be prepared for flight, but by prearrangement three more then flew over from England, and these spotted a Zeppelin at high altitude. As before, this airship (*L.53*) was lured further out to sea while *Redoubt* built up speed, allowing Culley to take off in the Camel. He spent the next hour climbing as high as the aircraft would go, and searching for the Zeppelin. Finally, he suddenly came out of cloud to see it close by and about 200ft higher. Unable to climb any further, he positioned himself below *L.53*, pulled the fighter into a near-vertical position and then opened fire. The Vickers gun jammed after a few rounds, but he managed to get a full double pan of incendiaries from the above-wing Lewis into the gasbag, which quickly caught fire and went down in flames into the sea. Only one man survived, baling out from what must then have been a record 19,000ft.

Culley's Camel then stalled, but he regained control and subsequently was able to ditch close by the flotilla. He was picked up safely, the Camel also being recovered. For this sortie he was awarded the DSO.

By now a new generation of ships was nearing service. HMS *Vindictive* had been commenced as a light cruiser, but was launched during 1918 as an aircraft carrier similar in arrangement to *Furious*. As such, she did not prove to be a great success, and would be reconverted to a cruiser during the mid-1920s.

However, during 1916 an unfinished Italian liner, the *Conte Rosso*, had been purchased and was completed as a carrier with a flight deck stretching from bow to stern, uninterrupted by superstructure or funnels. Given the name *Argus*, she was completed with a deck length of 550ft and a width of 68ft. Of 14,450 tons displacement, she was able to reach 20.75 knots and to carry 20 aircraft. A hangar was situated below the deck, accessed by two lifts, while her engine exhausts were carried to the stern via trunking, thereby avoiding any discharge over the landing-on portion of the deck.

Just as she was ready to commence operations a new single-seat torpedo-bomber, the Sopwith Cuckoo, also became available, and in October 1918 a squadron of these went aboard. However, the war ended during the following month before any use could be made of this revolutionary pairing.

Two further aircraft carriers were also under construction as the war ended, although these differed from *Argus* in having their superstructure and funnels in a streamlined 'island' on the starboard side of the deck, preserving the all-through facility of the latter. *Eagle* had begun life in 1913 as the battleship *Almirante Cochrane* for Chile, but with the outbreak of war in 1914 work had been halted. She was therefore purchased by the Admiralty for conversion during 1917, being launched in June 1918 and commissioned in April 1924. Longer than *Argus* and with a displacement of 22,600 tons, she was also faster at 24 knots and could carry 21 aircraft.

The second vessel was *Hermes*, the first to be built from the start as an aircraft carrier. Commenced in January 1918, she was launched on 11 September 1919, but with no urgency – as the war was over – would not be commissioned until 1923. Although displacing only 10,850 tons, she was almost as long as *Eagle*. She could steam at 25 knots and could carry 25 aircraft. The position of the 'island' on the starboard side of each of these ships was dictated both by the natural torque of most rotary aero engines, which pulled to port, and the rule of the sea whereby ships passed on the starboard side.

BELOW *A battleship under construction for the Chilean government as the* Almirante Cochrane *was taken over by the Royal Navy and completed as the aircraft carrier HMS* Eagle. *Launched in June 1918, she was commissioned in 1924, serving until April 1935, when she was placed on the Reserve. She was then reconditioned and resumed operational use in January 1937. Active early in the Second World War, the vessel was sunk by torpedoes from U-73 during a convoy to Malta on 11 August 1942.*

CHAPTER 6

KILLING FIELDS

Over the Western Front

From the outset the RNAS had established an excellent relationship with the Sopwith concern, and was to reap great benefits from the aircraft which were born on the drawing board of Herbert Smith, the company's brilliant premier designer. After the initial little floatplanes – the Tabloid, Schneider and Baby – early in 1916 Sopwith produced a classic two-seat fighting scout which came to be known unofficially as the 'One and a Half Strutter' due to its unusual arrangement of interplane struts. Of superior performance to nearly all other aircraft at the front when it first appeared in the spring of that year, the 1½ Strutter was able to considerably outperform the German Fokker Eindekker aircraft.

Delivered to 5 Wing at Coudekerque during April, the aircraft featured a forward-firing Vickers machine gun synchronised to fire through the propeller arc – the first such fitting to a British production aircraft – while in the rear seat the observer was armed with a Lewis gun for rearward defence.

Initially the aircraft was employed as an escort for the Wing's Breguet and Caudron bombers, but

LEFT *The excellent Sopwith Triplane appeared over the Western Front early in 1917 and soon equipped several RNAS squadrons. It was to gain an early ascendancy over its German opponents, but with only one machine gun, was somewhat under-armed. N5454, N5475, N5472 and N5387 are here serving with 1 Squadron at Bailleul in October 1917, by which time this was the last unit still equipped with these aircraft.*

RIGHT *One of the main bombing aircraft used by the RNAS on the Franco-Belgian frontier area was the Caudron G.IV. This particular aircraft was serving with 5 Wing when photographed.*

a single-seat version, capable of carrying 65lb of bombs within the fuselage, soon began arriving. In May 1916 Captain W.L. Elder was tasked with setting up 3 Wing as a strategic bombing force – the first such to be formed. His new unit was to be equipped with 15 Short aircraft, 20 1½ Strutter bombers, and 20 more two-seaters as fighting escort. The unit was anticipated to grow further to a strength of 100 aircraft.

At this stage, however, the British Army was deeply involved in the huge Somme offensive, and the RFC was suffering heavy casualties to increasingly aggressive German scout units. Indeed, it was considered to be 12 squadrons under strength in the numbers thought necessary to fully support the ground forces. Very few aircraft of good performance were available with units at home, so General Hugh Trenchard issued an

urgent plea for help. As the great air historian Sir Walter Raleigh wrote in *The War in the Air*, volume II:

> *'The Admiralty could only respond at the expense of their new bombing wing. Anxious as they were to strike a blow at German munitions centres, they realised the urgency of the Flying Corps demands and agreed to hand over at once a number of Sopwith two-seaters; by the middle of September 1916 they had transferred no less than sixty-two of this type.'*

This greatly slowed down the launch of 3 Wing's activities, which did not get fully under way until 12 October. On that date 13 1½ Strutters and six Breguets took off with 12 Farmans and

RIGHT *The Sopwith 1½ Strutter was built for the RNAS and later also acquired by the RFC. With a fixed forward-firing machine gun in the nose and a Lewis gun for the observer in the rear cockpit, this aircraft was widely employed both as a fighting scout and as a bomber. It proved very successful in both roles. This is N5107 of 3 Wing late in 1916, bearing the identification number '36'.*

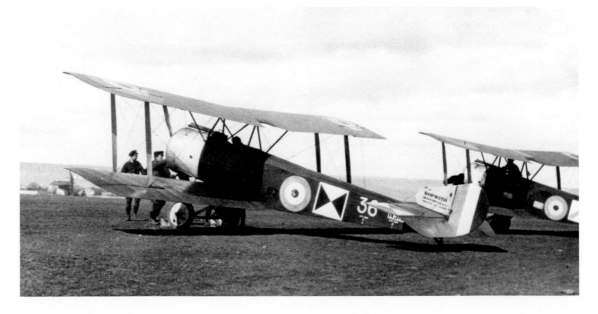

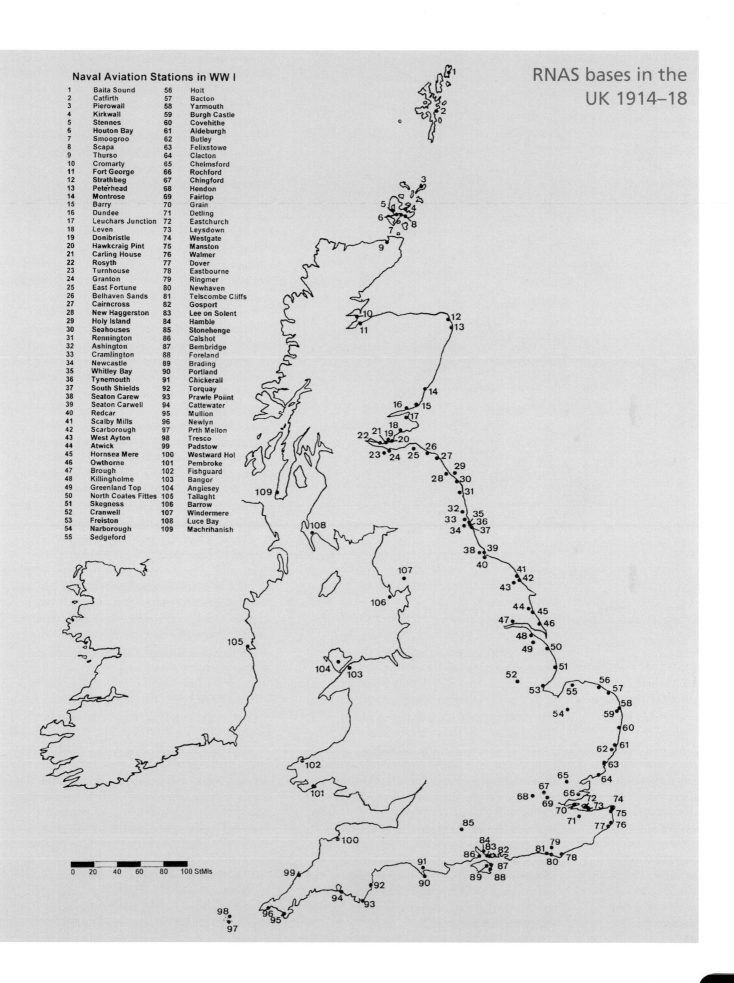

Naval Aviation Stations in WW I

1	Balta Sound	56	Holt
2	Catfirth	57	Bacton
3	Pierowall	58	Yarmouth
4	Kirkwall	59	Burgh Castle
5	Stennes	60	Covehithe
6	Houton Bay	61	Aldeburgh
7	Smoogroo	62	Butley
8	Scapa	63	Felixstowe
9	Thurso	64	Clacton
10	Cromarty	65	Chelmsford
11	Fort George	66	Rochford
12	Strathbeg	67	Chingford
13	Peterhead	68	Hendon
14	Montrose	69	Fairlop
15	Barry	70	Grain
16	Dundee	71	Detling
17	Leuchars Junction	72	Eastchurch
18	Leven	73	Leysdown
19	Donibristle	74	Westgate
20	Hawkcraig Pint	75	Manston
21	Carling House	76	Walmer
22	Rosyth	77	Dover
23	Turnhouse	78	Eastbourne
24	Granton	79	Ringmer
25	East Fortune	80	Newhaven
26	Belhaven Sands	81	Telscombe Cliffs
27	Cairncross	82	Gosport
28	New Haggerston	83	Lee on Solent
29	Holy Island	84	Hamble
30	Seahouses	85	Stonehenge
31	Rennington	86	Calshot
32	Ashington	87	Bembridge
33	Cramlington	88	Foreland
34	Newcastle	89	Brading
35	Whitley Bay	90	Portland
36	Tynemouth	91	Chickerall
37	South Shields	92	Torquay
38	Seaton Carew	93	Prawle Poiint
39	Seaton Carwell	94	Cattewater
40	Redcar	95	Mullion
41	Scalby Mills	96	Newlyn
42	Scarborough	97	Prth Mellon
43	West Ayton	98	Tresco
44	Atwick	99	Padstow
45	Hornsea Mere	100	Westward Hol
46	Owthorne	101	Pembroke
47	Brough	102	Fishguard
48	Killingholme	103	Bangor
49	Greenland Top	104	Angiesey
50	North Coates Fittes	105	Tallaght
51	Skegness	106	Barrow
52	Cranwell	107	Windermere
53	Freiston	108	Luce Bay
54	Narborough	109	Machrihanish
55	Sedgeford		

0 20 40 60 80 100 StMls

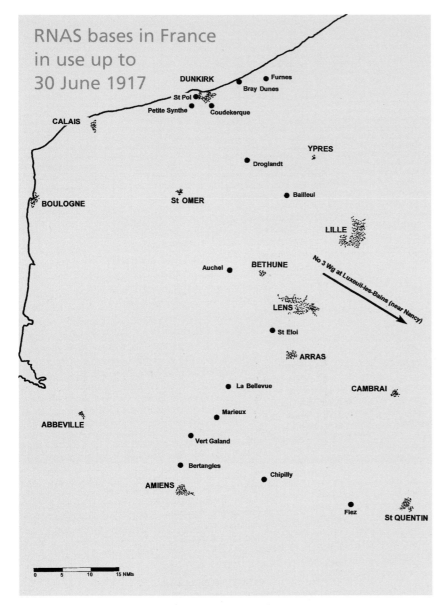

RNAS bases in France
in use up to
30 June 1917

DUNKIRK

Furnes

Bray Dunes

St Pol

Petite Synthe

Coudekerque

CALAIS

YPRES

Droglandt

BOULOGNE

St OMER

Bailleul

LILLE

Auchel

BETHUNE

No 3 Wg at Luxeuil-les-Bains (near Nancy)

LENS

St Eloi

ARRAS

La Bellevue

CAMBRAI

Marieux

ABBEVILLE

Vert Galand

Bertangles

Chipilly

AMIENS

Flez

St QUENTIN

0   5   10   15 NMls

eight Breguets of the French 4eme Groupe de Bombardement to attack the Mauser factory at Oberndorf. In the event 3 Wing would never reach its designated strength, while further calls were soon forthcoming from the RFC. It was in October 1916 that the first direct reinforcement of the Western Front by an RNAS fighting unit occurred.

At this time the RNAS remained established on the Franco-Belgian coast, mainly at airfields at St Pol and Furnes, the bases of the various elements of 1 Wing. The equipment of this unit included Nieuport 11s and 17s, and Bristol Scouts for fighting purposes, while bombing activities were undertaken by 1½ Strutters, Farman F 40s and a few Short types. The first examples of the new scout (to which reference has already been made above), known colloquially as the Sopwith Pup, were just arriving.

During October came an impassioned plea for

more help from Field Marshal Haig. Due to the level of losses recently suffered by the RFC, he was concerned that there was now a grave risk of air superiority being lost to the Germans. At once 'A' Squadron of 1 Wing was detached to help, led by Commander G.R. Bromet, and referred to initially as 'Detached Squadron, RNAS'. On 3 December this unit would be renamed 1 (Naval) Squadron, operating from Furnes.

A rapid expansion of the RNAS in France was under way at this time. 'B' Squadron of 1 Wing became 2 (Naval) Squadron on 5 November at St Pol, equipped with a mixed bag of Pups, 1½ Strutters and Farman F 40s, while 'C' Squadron became 3 (Naval) Squadron, also at St Pol, wholly equipped with a variety of fighting scouts. At the end of December 4 (Naval) and 5 (Naval) Squadrons were both formed from elements of 5 Wing, and each was equipped with 1½ Strutters.

Meanwhile, 'A' and 'B' Squadrons of 4 Wing provided the nuclei for 6 (Naval) and 7 (Naval) Squadrons as bomber units, while at St Pol a new 8 (Naval) Squadron had been created from elements provided by all three wings; on 26 October this unit had already moved to Vert Galant with Nieuport 17s, Pups and 1½ Strutters. This was in fact the first unit to move away from the coast to operate over the area of the Somme battles. The 1½ Strutters were already becoming outclassed by this time, and were replaced by more Pups by mid-November.

The Pup, probably another Herbert Smith design, had reached 1 Wing at Dunkirk during September. From here on 24 September Flight Sub-Lieutenant S.J. Goble shot down an LVG two-seater near Listelles. During the next month the Wing's Pups and Nieuports were to claim eight German aircraft destroyed.

No 8 (Naval) Squadron undertook its first patrol on its new duties on 3 November 1916, and by the end of the year the unit's Pup pilots had claimed 20 victories. They were then withdrawn at the end of January 1917 to re-equip with the new Sopwith Triplane. Meanwhile, the Pups continued to serve with 3 (Naval) Squadron, and on 11 April 1917 Flight Sub-Lieutenant J.S.T. Fall claimed two Albatros scouts and a Halberstadt scout shot down during a single sortie near Cambrai. No 4 (Naval) Squadron also replaced its 1½ Strutters with Pups during the spring, and continued to operate along the coastal area from Bray Dunes, becoming involved in a big fight over Zeebrugge on 12 May 1917 when seven Pup pilots claimed five Albatros scouts shot down.

The naval scout units particularly had by now become a very important part of British aerial activity over the Western Front, enjoying the advantage of having generally a better-performing set of aircraft than those with which RFC units were equipped at that time.

The 1½ Strutter was also now in service with some of the RFC's squadrons following the transfer of the large batch of these aircraft already referred to. This force now also followed the Navy's lead in acquiring the Pup. By this time, however, the former aircraft was beginning to prove inferior to the latest Albatros scouts, indicating an early need for a more potent fighting aircraft. Here the RNAS was already in a good position, for the new Sopwith Triplane was about to be introduced into service with some of its units.

In fact both the RNAS and RFC had ordered examples of this aircraft, both also ordering a British-built version of the French Spad S.VII. In one of the few pieces of sensible co-operation to occur at this juncture, the two Services agreed that all the Triplanes should go to the Navy and all the Spads to the Army.

The first Triplanes appeared over the front early in 1917 in the hands of pilots of 1 (Naval) Squadron, which moved to Chipilly during February. In that same month 3 (Naval) became fully equipped with Pups, which it took to Vert Galant before moving on to Bertangles at the end of the month. The new 8 (Naval) Squadron, following its initial actions over the Western Front, also received Triplanes, moving with these to Furnes where it quickly made its presence felt in no uncertain manner.

The month also saw the formation of two more units, both of which quickly became equipped with fighting scouts. No 9 (Naval) Squadron was formed at St Pol at the start of the month from a nucleus provided by 8 (Naval), and 10 (Naval) followed 12 days later at the same airfield. Both began life with a variety of Nieuports and Pups, but soon replaced these with more Triplanes – an aircraft which had swiftly gained the respect of its German opponents.

During March 1917, 4 (Naval) Squadron replaced the last of its now-obsolescent 1½ Strutters with Pups, while during that month 2 (Naval) received DH 4 bombers – previously issued only to RFC squadrons. No 5 (Naval) Squadron undertook a similar re-equipment during the following month, moving to Petit Synthe. April saw 4 (Naval) Squadron move to Bray-Dunes, 8 (Naval) to Auchel, and 7 (Naval) to Coudekerque where it was to receive new twin-engined Handley Page O/100 heavy bombers. To provide an element of 'operational training' for the first time, 12 (Naval) Squadron was formed at St Pol, while 11 (Naval) was formed as an operational unit at Dunkirk, receiving further DH 4s.

While the Pup and the Triplane were proving

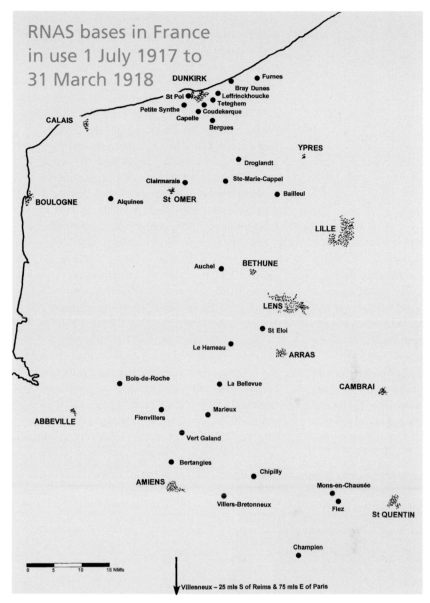

RNAS bases in France in use 1 July 1917 to 31 March 1918

formidable opponents for the German fighting scout units (*Jastas*) by virtue of their superior manoeuvrability, they still demonstrated one major inferiority to their opponents: each had only a single machine gun firing forward, whereas the Albatros and Pfalz scouts which they faced were equipped with two. To rectify this situation, design and development in England were close to bringing forward a pair of new two-gun aircraft. For the RFC the Royal Aircraft Factory was producing the SE5, while Sopwith, long the favoured manufacturer for the Royal Navy, was about to introduce the Camel. The latter would prove to be one of the most successful fighting aircraft of the war (as, indeed, would the SE5 when developed into its SE5A version); the Camel would soon also become the recipient of large RFC orders.

Nonetheless, it was the RNAS which first employed the Camel in combat, the initial unit so equipped being 4 (Naval) Squadron which took delivery of the first examples during June 1917. Its first engagement with hostile aircraft took place on 4 June when Flight Commander A.M. Shook attacked a German aircraft 15 miles off Nieuport, last seeing it disappear into sea haze near Middlekerke. Next day he spotted 15 aircraft between Nieuport and Ostend and attacked, causing one German scout to crash on a beach, while a second was claimed 'out of control'. On 25 June Shook and Flight Sub-Lieutenant Chadwick encountered a mixed formation of scouts and two-seaters, Chadwick shooting down one of the latter in flames. Gotha bombers were engaged for the first time on 4 July, Shook leading five Camels to attack 16 of these aircraft north-west of Ostend. At least four were claimed to have been hit, although post-war research indicated that no losses had actually been inflicted on this occasion. For these early successes, however, Shook was awarded a DSC.

Meanwhile, the spring of 1917 had seen a serious escalation of the war which impacted on the RNAS to a considerable degree. Previously the Germans had been to an extent circumspect in their use of U-boats against international shipping in the Atlantic for fear of so enraging the United States as to bring that major power into the fighting on the Allied side. Now, with the war in the East

approaching a conclusion likely to be favourable to Germany, they resolved to unleash unrestricted U-boat warfare upon their Western opponents in an effort to strangle imports of food and strategic materials to Great Britain in particular.

This, of course, resulted in a substantial increase in the anti-U-boat activities of the Royal Navy and of the British-based coastal flights, and also of the RNAS's bomber units now in France. Initially raids on U-boat pens in the Belgian coastal ports were undertaken by day by 1½ Strutters, with Caudrons and Shorts operating by night. As soon as the new DH 4s and Handley Page O/100s became available, these were also thrown into the attack on Ostend and Zeebrugge. The Shorts were able to carry bombs of 520lb weight, at that time the largest such missiles in the world, while the O/100 proved capable of releasing 14 bombs, each of 112lb. These big aircraft were employed initially by day, but vulnerability to defending interceptors soon led to their use only by night, as they were deemed too valuable to risk losing in any numbers. The day effort then devolved onto the DH4s. The use of monitors (armoured shallow-draught vessels armed with large-calibre guns) was also attempted, RNAS aircraft being used to spot for the fall of shot from such ships.

As the ground campaign launched in Flanders

BELOW *Introduced to service by the RNAS, the Handley Page O/100 equipped three squadrons by the time the RAF was formed on 1 April 1918. Here aircraft of 14 (N) Squadron are seen at Dunkirk during that same month, just as the unit became 214 Squadron of the new air force.*

at this time also gathered pace, the efforts of the RNAS bombers were on occasion deployed here too, particularly by 5 (Naval) Squadron with its new DH 4s, and by the O/100s of 7 (Naval). As more of these latter aircraft became available 7 (Naval) performed as 'Adam's Rib', being split into two squadrons – 7 (Naval) and 7a (Naval). The bombers were also supported at times by the scouts of 3 (Naval) Squadron.

During the night of 16/17 August 1917 fourteen O/100s dropped more than nine tons of explosives on the railway system at Thourot. They also bombed airfields being used by Gotha twin-engined bombers which were undertaking attacks on London and south-eastern England at this time. These were effective in forcing the German units to be withdrawn eastwards but brought an immediate response, as the Gothas retaliated by attacking the RNAS airfields in France. One lucky bomb did great damage to the main depot at St Pol, while further heavy raids followed.

An effort was made during this period to bomb lock gates at Zeebrugge, but no success was achieved. In general it must be admitted that the bombing attacks launched from the general Dunkirk area proved to be a failure. During the latter three-quarters of 1917, 344 tons of bombs were dropped without in fact hitting any important targets.

Happily, the efforts of the scout units had been considerably more successful. The Camel having taken over Sopwith's production line from the Triplane, the latter were fazed out of service with remarkable rapidity once the new aircraft became available in numbers. Following 4 (Naval) Squadron, 3 (Naval), 9 (Naval) and 10 (Naval) all re-equipped during July, while 8 (Naval) received the new aircraft in September. Only 1 (Naval) soldiered on until the end of the year, when it returned to England for a rest. In February 1918 it returned to the Continent, taking its new Camels to Teteghem.

Meanwhile, a unit which had operated as the St Pol Defence Flight, but which had grown to full squadron status as 13 (Naval) during January 1918, moved with its Camels to Bergues on the 25th of that month.

By the end of March 1918 nearly 100 RNAS scout pilots had been classed as 'aces' after taking part in five or more victories over enemy aircraft. While these victories did not necessarily mean the destruction of an opponent's aircraft, this was, nonetheless, a most important contribution to the war effort, and one which makes clear the enormous debt that the RNAS owed to the Empire – and to Canada in particular, since no less than 35 of these pilots, including many of the most

successful, hailed from that Dominion. Canada had proved a particularly fruitful recruiting source for the Service. Many of these pilots, of all nationalities, were to continue to add to their tallies of successes following their incorporation into the new Royal Air Force on 1 April 1918.

Amongst the other units, 6 (Naval) Squadron had been disbanded in August 1917 following a relatively brief spell as a fighting scout unit, but was re-formed at Dover from the Walmer Defence Flight at the start of November, now equipped with DH 4s. In January 1918 this new unit moved to Petit Synthe to commence bombing operations, being reinforced in February by the arrival of DH 9 aircraft. No 11 (Naval) Squadron's fortunes had followed a somewhat similar course, with disbandment in August 1917. A new squadron of this number was formed at Petit Synthe on 10 March 1918, also equipped with DH 4s and 9s.

The production of the big Handley Page bombers meanwhile allowed the formation of four more new RNAS squadrons. No 7a (Naval) was renumbered 14 (Naval) in December 1917, while during the next month 16 (Naval) was formed; this unit would receive the first of the more powerful O/400s during March. The latter month also saw the formation of 15 (Naval) from a nucleus provided jointly by 7 (Naval) and 14 (Naval) Squadrons. No 17 (Naval) – the last numbered RNAS squadron – was formed with DH 4s in January 1918 from the RN Seaplane Base.

Now, at the end of March, everything was about to change – and yet in many ways stay exactly the same (for the time being anyway).

ABOVE *Originally designed for the RNAS, the Sopwith Camel became the most widely used fighting scout of the British forces during the First World War. Extremely manoeuvrable, its pilots claimed more victories than those of any other type on the Allied side. It was, however, something of a handful for inexperienced pilots, and training fatalities were high. Although employed mainly on the Western Front, some of these aircraft became involved in home defence duties. This particular Camel, B3834, named 'Wonga Bonga', was usually flown by Flt Sub Lt A.F. Brandon at the RNAS War School at Manston, Kent. Flying from here, it was successfully employed to join in shooting down a raiding Gotha G.IV bomber on 22 August 1917.*

TOP-SCORING RNAS SCOUT PILOTS AS AT 31 MARCH 1918

The numbers in brackets indicate as follows: individual claims for aircraft destroyed + shared claims for aircraft destroyed; individual claims for aircraft 'out of control' + shared claims for aircraft 'out of control'; individual claims for aircraft forced to land in Allied lines and captured; shared claims for aircraft forced to land in Allied lines and captured; observation balloons shot down.

Name	Nationality	Squadron	Victories as at 31.3.18	Final Score
R. Collishaw	Canadian	3W, 3 (N), 10 (N), 13 (N)	39 (15+1; 21+2)	61 (28+2; 29+2)
R.A. Little	Australian	8 (N)	38 (10+3; 21+2; 1+1 capt)	47 (17+5; 21+2; 1+1 capt)
J.S.T. Fall	Canadian	3 (N), 9 (N)	36 (11+2; 10+3)	36
R.J.O. Compston	British	8 (N)	25 (2+4; 11+6; 0+5 capt)	25
C.D. Booker	British	8 (N)	23 (2+3; 12+4; 0+2 capt)	29 (6+4; 12+5; 0+2 capt)
R.S. Dallas	Australian	1W, 'A', 1 (N)	23 (9+0; 13+0; 1+0 capt)	32 (15+0; 15+1; 1+0 capt)
S.W. Rosevear	Canadian	1 (N)	22 (14+1; 6+1)	25 (16+1; 7+1)
R.F. Minifie	Australian	1 (N)	21 (10+1; 8+1; 1+0 capt)	21
E.V. Reid	Canadian	10 (N)	19 (10+1; 7+1)	19
W.L. Jordan	British	8 (N)	18 (0+4; 4+10)	39 (6+5; 14+14)
W.M. Alexander	Canadian	10 (N)	18 (2+0; 15+1)	23 (5+0; 17+1)
S.M. Kinkead	South African	3W, 1 (N)	18 (2+1; 11+1; 3 other)	35–40 (5+2; 21+3; 1+0 capt; 3-8 other)*
H.F. Stackard	British	9 (N)	15 (0+6; 3+6)	15
L.H. Rochford	British	3 (N)	14 (1+3; 6+4)	29 (6+7; 11+5)
A.T. Whealy	Canadian	3 (N), 9 (N)	14 (2+1; 8+2; 1+0 capt)	27 (12+4; 8+2; 1+0 capt)
F.C. Armstrong	Canadian	3 (N)	13 (4+2; 4+3)	13
W.A. Curtis	Canadian	10 (N)	13 (1+3; 8+1)	13
J.A. Glen	Canadian	3 (N)	13 (2+5; 2+4)	15 (3+6; 2+4)
R.M.N. Keirstead	Canadian	4 (N)	11 (3+3; 5+0)	13 (3+3; 6+0; 0+1 capt)
A.W. Carter	Canadian	3 (N)	10 (2+0; 8+0)	17 (4+1; 9+1; 1+0 balloon; 1+0 capt)
A.J. Enstone	British	4 (N)	10 (6+1; 2+1)	13 (9+1; 2+1)
E.G. Johnstone	British	8 (N)	10 (0+3; 2+5)	17 (1+3; 5+8)
H.T. Mellings	British	2W, 10 (N)	10 (6+0; 4+0)	15 (10+0; 4+1)
O.W. Redgate	British	9 (N)	10 (1+5; 1+3)	16 (3+5; 4+4)

* Kinkead's total includes an indeterminate number claimed over South Russia during 1919. His initial three claims were made during the very early days of air fighting.

The most successful naval fighting scout pilots prior to the amalgamation of the RNAS with the RFC to form the RAF on 1 April 1918, were:

1 Sqn Cdr Raymond Collishaw (Canadian), who had claimed 39 victories prior to this date and would end the war with 61, being awarded the DSO & Bar, DSC and DFC

2 Flt Cdr Robert Little (Australian), claimed 36 by 1 April 1918, increased subsequently to 47. Died of wounds, 27 May 1918; awarded the DSO & Bar, DSC & Bar.

3 Flt Cdr Joseph Fall (Canadian), claimed 36 victories; awarded the DSC & 2 Bars.

4 Flt Cdr Robert Compston (English), claimed 25; awarded DSO, DSC & Bar.

5 Sqn Cdr Charles Booker (Australian), claimed 23 by 1 April 1918, subsequently increased to 29, but killed in action 13 August 1918. Awarded the DSC and Croix de Guerre.

6 Sqn Cdr Roderic Dallas (Australian), claimed 23 by 1 April 1918, increased subsequently to 32, but killed in action 1 June 1918; awarded the DSC & Bar.

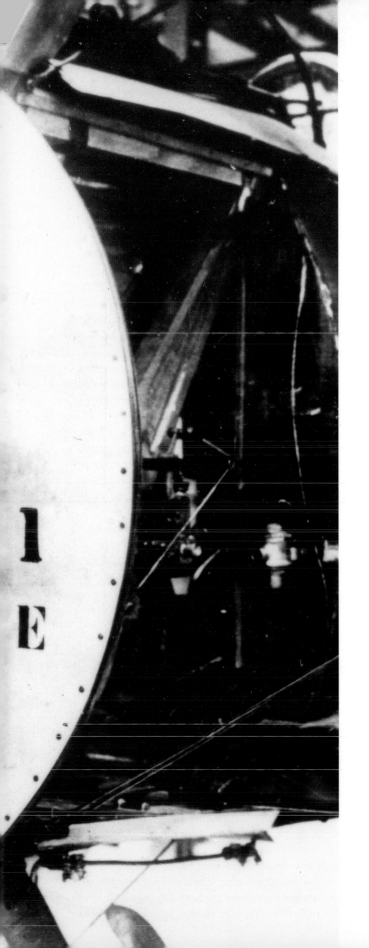

CHAPTER 7

WAKE-UP CALL

The Smuts Report

During the opening months of the First World War, the nascent aviation industry in Britain was quite incapable of producing the numbers of aircraft and aero engines required by the armies at the front. Initially, it was to France that the authorities turned to make good the deficit. However, the French were also short of various strategic materials required for the manufacture of engines particularly, while their aircraft constructors had to meet the needs of their own service and of Russia, as well as those of Britain, and subsequently, Italy.

The greatest problem soon became that of engines, and before long airframes were languishing, incapable of completion as aircraft since no suitable – and above all, reliable – engines were available. Increases in the number of squadrons were blithely approved by the government of the day, as yet unaware that the means with which to achieve these targets simply did not exist.

The Joint Air Committee initially worked satisfactorily in connection with the design and development of aircraft, but disappeared soon after the start of the war. The War Office then formed a Military Aeronautics Directorate under Brigadier-General David Henderson, which in many ways contained the origins of the later Air Ministry. It was semi-independent and was able to enter into contracts directly with outside firms. The RNAS,

LEFT *A Le Rhone rotary engine fitted in a Sopwith Pup.* Philip Jarrett

examples of an improved Hispano-Suiza engine to be constructed in France in specially built factories. Incredibly, this brought a riposte at Government level from Lord Curzon, Lord President of the Council of Ministers, who had come to believe that every country involved in the war would be exhausted by the end of 1917, and that the fighting would then just peter out. He advised that should this happen, 'to be left with a large number of aeroplanes would be highly inconvenient'. Nothing, at the time, could have been further from the truth!

While the Government was not ignorant of the problems that existed, and even the general public were becoming aware that all was not well with the country's air services, it was the commencement of daylight bombing raids on the south of England by Gotha aircraft which brought matters to a head. The first raid on London on 13 June 1917 caused the Government to double the size of the air services – on paper.

Another result was the setting up of an urgent inquiry by Lieutenant-General Jan Christian Smuts, the South African. He shocked the Cabinet on 18 September when he reported that even earlier and more modest targets had yet to be met. In contrast the Cabinet had believed that by 1918 there would be a surplus of both aircraft and engines. 'I consider that the Cabinet have really no option, but must give the fullest and most complete priorities necessary not only to carry it [the smaller programme] into effect, but even to accelerate it. If this is not done we will run risks which may well prove disastrous.' Horrified, the Cabinet at once set up the War Priorities Committee to push through Smuts' recommendations.

Earlier, as a result of public concern, a permanent Joint War Air Committee had been set up on 15 February 1916 to ensure collaboration and co-operation between the Services. Unfortunately, the naval representatives on this board, not being members of the Board of Admiralty, could not agree to anything without reporting back to the supreme body in naval affairs. Worse, the committee had no executive powers. The consequence was, unsurprisingly, that it collapsed after just two months.

When the committee's failure was reviewed by Lord Curzon, he quickly analysed its shortcomings and suggested that an Air Board should be created as a preliminary to the formation of an Air Ministry. He even hinted that a separate air service might well be the appropriate solution. This brought an immediate response from Lord Kitchener, Chief of the Imperial General Staff, who felt that useful as

however, was less well served at this stage as it was not even directly represented on the Board of Admiralty.

Initially, the requirements for engines differed between the two Services, but as the War Office increasingly began placing orders haphazardly throughout the industry in an effort to meet its increasing needs there arose a growing situation where the Services were competing with each other in their efforts to acquire the necessary equipment.

The Internal Combustion Engine Sub-Committee of the Advisory Committee for Aeronautics began ordering large quantities of new and unproven engines into production without adequate initial testing, with disastrous results. Most of these turned out to be little better than useless, while many engines acquired from France were poorly manufactured, and gave many problems in service.

As a consequence, the Admiralty had encouraged Rolls-Royce to develop and produce aero engines of good quality, and more than 6,000 were ultimately produced by this company. At the end of 1916 the Admiralty also called for 8,000

such a Board might be, its decisions should not be allowed to bind either the Board of Admiralty or the Army Council, which he insisted should remain free to decide questions of policy. Arthur Balfour, who had succeeded Churchill as First Lord of the Admiralty, commented on behalf of the Royal Navy that 'a fighting department should, as far as possible, have the whole responsibility…of the instruments it uses, the personnel it commands and the operations it undertakes…the Navy should not have to consult any outside department…it should be autonomous'. Subsequently, he added '…unless some dramatic change may be forced on them [the Government] by the House of Commons'.

On 11 May 1916 an Air Board was formed under the chairmanship of Lord Curzon, with wider powers than the defunct Joint War Air Committee. Again, though, it was not provided with any executive authority, and despite having the Third Sea Lord and the Director-General of Military Aeronautics as members, it was nearly as impotent as its predecessor.

Following the Air Board's formation, a Court of Inquiry into the Royal Aircraft Factory at Farnborough by Mr Justice Bailhache praised the factory's design work, but was critical of the way in which it dealt with supply – a view shared by Curzon. Immediately after this, Curzon became aware that the Admiralty had obtained Treasury sanction to spend £3 million on aircraft and engines without reference to the Air Board. A formal protest was made which met with a formal denial of the Board's right to protest, which almost led to the work of the Board grinding to a halt. On 24 October 1916 *The Times* published a leading article calling for the replacement of the Board with an Air Ministry with appropriate powers.

The Board, meanwhile, had urged that there should only be one supply department, responsible to the Board alone, and that the Board should be supreme in all matters of supply, design and finance. It also sought that the RNAS should be placed under a single officer who should be a member of the Board, thus placing the RNAS on an equal footing with the RFC.

Balfour was quick to respond, making it very clear that the Admiralty considered the Air Board to be a hostile department with 'the right to criticise, the power to embarrass, but with no direct responsibility for military or naval action'. While, he felt, the Admiralty might possibly consent to a unified air supply department, they would never agree to a system under which they did not fully control the number and design of the aircraft to be used with the fleet.

The position again appeared hopeless as Curzon and Balfour, both highly respected figures of great gravitas, squared up to each other. Now onto the scene came Colonel Bares, representing the French Air Service. He stressed the importance of long-range bombing. This struck a chord with the Admiralty, who were setting up their own force in the Dunkirk area for just such a purpose, as has already been outlined. Immediate support for Bares' suggestion was forthcoming, and equally immediate provision was sought of 1,000 engines to maintain 200 aircraft for this purpose.

Now it was the turn of General Sir Douglas Haig, Commander-in-Chief of British forces in France, to protest. If the Navy were to pre-empt all available engines, thus interfering with the supply of aircraft to the RFC, his land operations on the Western Front would be adversely affected. Until enough aircraft were available to meet all the requirements of the army in the field, the bombing of Germany should be considered a luxury. To hammer home his point, he ended by demanding 20 more fighting squadrons.

In November 1916 the Asquith government fell, and a new one was formed under David Lloyd George with a smaller War Cabinet. This at once widened the powers of the Air Board and transferred the responsibility for the design and supply of aircraft from the Admiralty and the War Office to the Ministry of Munitions. The composition of the Board was also changed, Lord Cowdray taking the chair. This almost proved to be the start of the Air Ministry, for the Board quickly grew as it took on substantial staff, moving into the Hotel Cecil with the Aeronautical Department of the Ministry of Munitions. Here the two bodies worked together unofficially, but in close harmony.

The repercussions of the time lost in quarrels and confusion during 1916 began to have an extremely deleterious effect upon the RFC during the spring of 1917, which led to the urgent pleas for RNAS assistance described earlier. This effectively ended Admiralty plans to commence a long-range bombing offensive of a strategic nature.

The Gotha raids of June 1917, also referred to earlier, now had an immediate effect upon the Air Board, which on the 21st recommended that the Government increase the size of the RFC from 108 to 200 squadrons, 40 of which were to be long-range bombing units. This again upset Haig, who feared that it would prevent his required increase in the number of front-line squadrons to 76. Although assured that his needs would be given priority, he remained sceptical. Bombers, he advised, should be used primarily against the enemy's airfields: 'In this way alone, is it possible to

RELATIVE RANKS OF OFFICERS OF THE ROYAL NAVY, ARMY

ROYAL NAVY

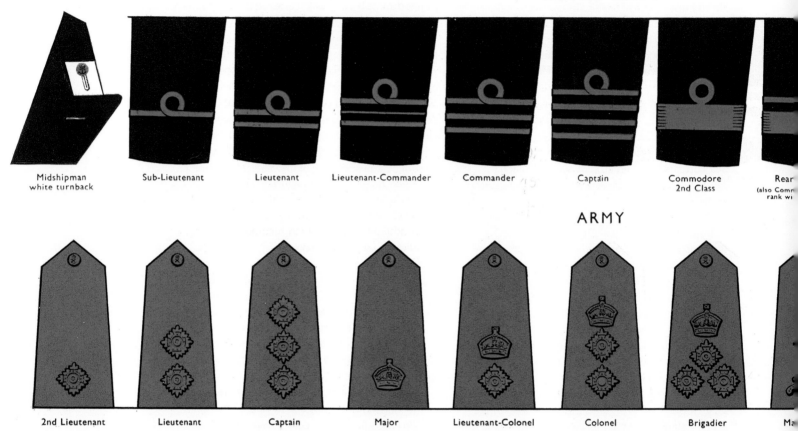

Midshipman white turnback	Sub-Lieutenant	Lieutenant	Lieutenant-Commander	Commander	Captain	Commodore 2nd Class	Rear (also Comm rank wi

ARMY

2nd Lieutenant	Lieutenant	Captain	Major	Lieutenant-Colonel	Colonel	Brigadier	Ma

ROYAL AIR FORCE

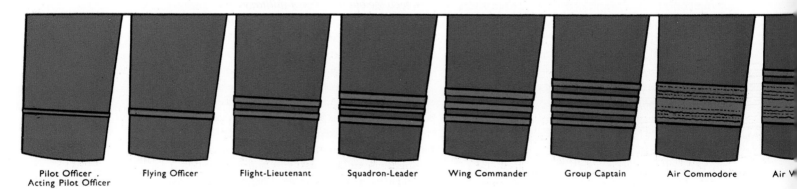

Pilot Officer . Acting Pilot Officer	Flying Officer	Flight-Lieutenant	Squadron-Leader	Wing Commander	Group Captain	Air Commodore	Air V

ROYAL AIR FORCE

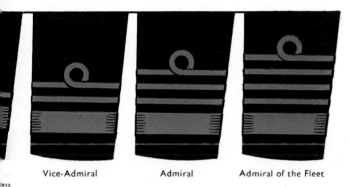

Vice-Admiral   Admiral   Admiral of the Fleet

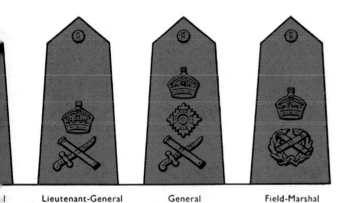

Lieutenant-General   General   Field-Marshal

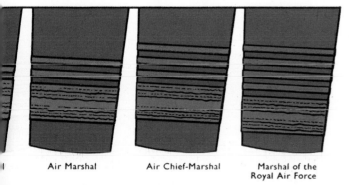

Air Marshal   Air Chief-Marshal   Marshal of the Royal Air Force

compel the enemy to fight on his side of the line at a distance from the battlefront.'

At a meeting of the Air Board a few days after an attack on London on 7 July, Lord Cowdray stated that a consistent, vigorous and intelligent air policy could not be pursued by calling occasional conferences between representatives of mutually antagonistic services. Indeed, the disagreements between the Admiralty and the War Office which had been such a prominent feature of the Home Front during 1916 had not diminished. Some members of the Board expressed the view that they would not disappear until the Board was able to exercise its proper function and state what aircraft should be allocated to each service. However, they were sure that in such circumstances the heads of the two Services would at once combine to seek ways in which to sabotage any such decision.

The Cabinet, however, was taking forthright action at last, for on 11 July 1917 it set up a Special Committee to consider how the Air Board might deal with policy as well as supply. Once more the running of the committee was placed in the capable hands of Smuts. On 17 August he produced a report which recommended the creation of an Air Ministry,

> 'to control and administer all matters in connection with air warfare of every kind and that the new Ministry should proceed to work out the arrangements for the amalgamation of the two air services and for the legal constitution and discipline of the new Service.
>
> 'The day may not be far off when aerial operations with the devastation of enemy land and destruction of industrial and populous centres on a vast scale may become the principal operations of war, to which the older forms of military and naval operations may become secondary and subordinate.'

Thus advised Smuts.

The Government gave consideration to the likely wrath of the Admiralty and War Office, but decided that it was more important to placate the rising anger of the general public at the continual bickering of the admirals and generals. On 24 August an Air Organisation Committee under David Henderson was set up to begin the huge task of forming a completely new Ministry and Service. However, this was all kept secret for the time being in order to prevent the Germans from attempting to take advantage of it.

Surprisingly, no particularly violent opposition

LEFT *Relative ranks of officers of the Royal Navy, Army and Royal Air Force.* Jonathan Falconer

was initially met with from the Admiralty, while the War Office simply passed a copy of the report to Haig in France. The latter's reaction was as might have been expected, since his prime concern was for the immediate requirements and support of his troops at the front. He was apprehensive regarding the 'grave danger of an Air Ministry…assuming control with a belief in theories which are not in accordance with practical experiences'. (How right he would prove to be in the next great conflict.) He then presented a reasoned statement regarding the shortages still affecting the RFC. The repeated failure to make them good, he said, made him 'somewhat sceptical as to the large surplus of machines and personnel which the Air Organisation Committee hoped to have shortly available'.

The War Cabinet then precipitated matters on 21 September by forming an Aerial Operations Committee to be chaired by Smuts and to include Winston Churchill, to decide the whole question of priorities in regard to all war equipment and munitions. The name of the committee was soon changed to War Priorities Committee, and it continued under Smuts' impartial and intelligent guidance throughout the rest of the war.

On 15 October 1917 the House of Commons was advised that a Bill to 'coordinate the Air Services and provide for the eventual setting up of an Air Ministry' was being prepared. Seven weeks later, on 29 November, the Air Force Bill, soon to be known as the Air Force (Constitution) Act, received the Royal Assent. At this stage Lord Rothermere replaced Cowdray as President of the Air Board, and on 3 January 1918 he became Secretary of State for the Air Force. After a search for a suitable building to house the new Ministry, it was decided that it would remain at the Hotel Cecil, alongside the Ministry of Munitions.

Discussions regarding the ranks for the new Service continued for months, the War Office complaining that the initial suggestions provided military ranks for the junior personnel and naval ranks for the commanders. The Admiralty restricted itself to the rather sour statement that the use of any naval title was objectionable. In consequence, military titles were initially adopted and it would be 27 August 1919 before an Air Council order set out the ranks finally adopted for the RAF.

There was similar lack of agreement regarding uniforms, both the RFC's double-breasted khaki 'maternity jacket' and the RNAS blue reefer jacket being rejected in favour of a slate-blue tunic. All stars, crowns and gold rings of rank gave way to simple rings of braid. These and many other decisions took time to resolve, and thus it was not

until 1 April 1918 that the Royal Air Force formally came into existence.

In the circumstances pertaining at the time, particularly the ongoing hostility between the two main Services, it is difficult to see how the previous situation could have continued to exist. However, the results were by no means favourable to either of the older Services in the longer term. The RAF, anxious after the war to sustain its new independent existence with all the advantages that conferred on its personnel, did indeed concentrate its efforts and activities upon the very theories that Haig had feared it might. Highly developed systems of support and co-operation with the ground forces which had arisen during the closing months of the war, were swiftly set aside and forgotten with the coming of peace. When war broke out again some 20 years later it would take many months before

they could again be developed to the same degree, or the appropriate aircraft could be acquired and put into service to sustain them.

For the Royal Navy the results were worse. Just as Balfour had feared, the Navy lost much of its ability to select and procure the appropriate aircraft and personnel for its purposes. Much of the RNAS's original role in convoy and coastal protection, anti-submarine activity, and even training was lost to the RAF forever. What remained was a poor shadow of the once-comprehensive Service which would be replicated as a near-ideal model by the naval services of the world's other great fleets.

It would be wrong to suggest that the effects of the RAF on the other Services were actually malignant. However, in the atmosphere of economic stringency and hostility to armaments budgets that prevailed between the wars, it remained in the RAF's interests – and was therefore understandable – for it to stress the things that it alone could do, even where these were as yet unproven theories. To highlight instead the excellent support that it might offer to the Army or the Navy would have made the new Service a hostage to fortune, at risk of being subsumed back into either or both of those older bodies.

BELOW *The Imperial War Cabinet in the garden of No 10 Downing Street. Front row left to right: Mr Arthur Henderson, Lord Milner, Lord Curzon, Mr Bonar Law, Mr Lloyd George, Sir Robert Borden, Mr W.F. Massey and General Smuts. Middle row: Sir S.P. Sinha, Sir James Meston, Mr Austen Chamberlain, Lord Robert Cecil, Mr Walter Long, Sir Joseph Ward, Sir George Perley, Mr Robert Rogers, and Mr J.D. Hazen. Back row: Capt L.S. Amery MP, Admiral Jellicoe, Sir Edward Carson, Lord Derby, Major General F.B. Maurice, Lt Col Sir M. Hankey, Mr Henry Lambert and Major Storr.* TopFoto

CHAPTER 8

PER ARDUA

The Royal Air Force Takes Over

As at 1 April 1918, on amalgamation with the Royal Flying Corps, the RNAS had an establishment of 55,000 officers and men, 2,900 aircraft and 103 airships, and control of 126 air stations – quite a dowry to bring to the marriage! Immediately following the merger all the existing RNAS squadrons were renumbered by the simple expedient of adding the number 200 to each. Thus 1 (Naval) Squadron became 201 Squadron, RAF, and so on. This arrangement covered squadrons 1 (N) to 17 (N) at once, while a few days later a new unit – 218 Squadron – was formed equipped with DH 9 bombers.

At the same time a process was commenced whereby the RNAS's coastal flights were grouped by twos or threes to form further squadrons. 219–228 Squadrons came into being immediately, but to incorporate all flights into squadrons in this way would take some time and reorganisation.

LEFT *Developed from the DH 9A bomber, the Westland Walrus was a 'stop-gap' spotter-reconnaissance aircraft, produced during the austerity years immediately following the First World War. Its service was limited, the two flights operating these aircraft being re-equipped with Blackburn Blackburns and Avro Bisons in 1925. This is N9500.*

Consequently the others followed at a somewhat more leisurely pace:

May 1918	250–252 and 254 Squadrons
June 1918	253–256 Squadrons
July 1918	244, 255, 258 and 272 Squadrons
August 1918	228–243, 245–248, 257, 260, 268 and 273 Squadrons
September 1918	263–264, 266–267 and 271 Squadrons
October 1918	269 Squadron

Squadron numbers 259, 261, 265 and 274 were also allocated, but the formation of these units seems never to have been completed, while the number 262 appears not to have been allocated at all.

In practice, operations by all squadrons and flights continued very much as before, at least until hostilities ended with the 11 November 1918 Armistice.

As soon as peace terms had been settled, the RAF, together with the other armed forces of the combatant nations, underwent a very rapid reduction in strength. Commencing in February 1919, within just 12 months 62 of the 73 ex-RNAS units had been disbanded.

206 Squadron was renumbered 47, and went on to see service in South Russia in support of the White Russian forces there. It was commanded by the RNAS's most successful scout pilot, Major Raymond Collishaw.

214 Squadron was absorbed into 216 Squadron, which was itself retained within the RAF, initially as a heavy bomber unit, while 232 Squadron was absorbed into 4 Squadron, which became

a communications unit. Inside 12 more months this squadron re-established 230 Squadron at Felixstowe, equipped with Felixstowe flying boats and Fairey IIIC floatplanes.

Meanwhile, at Alexandria in the Middle East, 270 Squadron was absorbed by 269 Squadron, which itself was 'swallowed' by 267 Squadron. The latter then found itself equipped with a melange of Felixstowe flying boats, Short 184 floatplanes and a variety of other types. During 1920 Fairey IIIDs were received, the unit subsequently maintaining detachments on the seaplane carrier HMS *Ark Royal* in Kilya Bay during 1922, a posting occasioned by the possibility of renewed hostilities with Turkey, where revolution was creating an uncertain political situation.

Thus it was that by the middle months of 1920 the RAF appeared to be left with no worthwhile residue of the RNAS at a time when, in spite of the peace, the Royal Navy was taking on a growing number of aircraft-carrying vessels. HMS *Argus* was already in service, as was HMS *Furious*, despite still featuring fore and aft flying-off decks. Nevertheless, it was already planned that she would be modernised and converted to full-deck status in the near future. Her recommissioning would take place on 1 September 1925.

Similarly, HMS *Eagle*, launched in June 1918, was due for somewhat delayed commissioning in April 1920; and HMS *Hermes*, which had been launched in September 1919, would be commissioned on 1 May 1923. Thus the Navy would soon own four carriers. Furthermore, while HMS *Vindictive* had been converted back into a standard cruiser she now featured catapult gear for the launch of aircraft

BELOW
HMS Hermes *was the first aircraft carrier to be constructed as such from the time when the keel was laid. The vessel is seen here off Wei-Hai-Wei on the China Station in 1932.*

for spotting and reconnaissance duties. Although she was the first British cruiser to be provided with such a facility, it would soon become available to others of her class too, as well as to battleships and battlecruisers – thus placing further demands on the RAF's resources.

The cutback in the number of ex-RNAS squadrons had not been a unique event, however, and the original RFC squadrons had suffered similar swingeing reductions. However, the need to provide air groups for the growing number of aircraft carriers was obvious even to a cash-strapped Treasury, and even as the cutbacks were under way efforts were put in hand to ameliorate the situation.

So it was that three new squadrons were formed during the opening months of 1920, using the numbers of ex-RNAS units already disbanded. The first such was 210 Squadron, formed at Gosport on 1 February by the simple expedient of renumbering 186 Squadron. The latter unit had a rather unusual history, however. In October 1918 185 Squadron had been formed from a nucleus provided by 31, 33, 39 and 49 Training Depot Squadrons, equipped during the following month with Sopwith Cuckoo torpedo-carrying biplanes. In April 1919 this unit was disbanded, although volunteers from its personnel went to serve on HMS *Argus* for an

intended anti-shipping operation in the Caspian Sea from Baku. These proposed activities were then cancelled and the squadron was put ashore at Gosport to re-establish a torpedo-dropping development unit, for which it too was equipped with Cuckoos prior to its renumbering as 210 Squadron.

One month later 203 Squadron was re-established at Leuchars in Scotland, equipped initially with now decidedly elderly Sopwith Camels. In August 1922 these would be replaced with Nieuport Nightjars, the squadron going aboard HMS *Argus* for the detachment to Kilya Bay already mentioned. On return the unit was landed back at Leuchars at the start of January 1923.

The third new unit was 205 Squadron, formed on 15 April 1920, also at Leuchars, and equipped with Parnall Panther spotter aircraft. In October 1921 a flight from this squadron was detached to join the nucleus of 3 Squadron at the same airfield, this new unit initially receiving DH 9As. These were supplemented and gradually replaced by Westland Walrus aircraft (not to be confused with the Supermarine Walrus which would appear a decade or so later). The Walrus was itself a modified DH 9A for spotter-reconnaissance work. In November 1922 this new unit moved south to join 210 Squadron at Gosport.

ABOVE *The first fighter to be acquired for use by the naval aviation arm of the RAF post-war was the Nieuport Nightjar, which was to serve aboard* Hermes *and* Furious. *The English Nieuport Company was subsequently taken over by the Gloucestershire Aircraft Company which thereafter built the aircraft as the Gloucestershire Mars.*

CHAPTER 9

SERVICE RIVALRY

The Fleet Air Arm of the RAF

At this stage a complete reorganisation took place, the four existing squadrons being disbanded on 1 April 1923 to create a number of flights, each nominally of six aircraft, for a more orderly creation of mixed air groups to serve aboard the growing carrier force. This was due in part to the limited size of such groups that the existing aircraft carriers were able to accommodate. Flights were to be numbered in the 400 range, as follows:

401–419	Fleet fighter flights
420–439	Fleet spotter flights
440–450	Fleet reconnaissance flights
460 onwards	Fleet torpedo flights

401 and 402 Flights were formed from 203 Squadron. 401 was at first equipped with Nightjars and was allocated to HMS *Argus*. 402 Flight, which was destined for HMS *Eagle* initially, was just receiving the first examples of a new fighter designed specifically for shipboard use – the Fairey Flycatcher.

420, 421 and 422 Flights, all equipped with Walruses, sprang from 3 Squadron. 420 and 421 were allocated to HMS *Furious*, while 423 joined 402 with HMS *Eagle*. 205 Squadron, meanwhile, gave birth to 440, 441 and 442 Flights; these units

RIGHT *The fleet fighter for more than ten years, the Fairey Flycatcher served widely on all the Royal Navy carriers and with all nine fighter flights during its relatively long life.*

took the Panther to sea, 440 with *Eagle*, the other two with *Argus*. Finally, from 210 Squadron came 460 and 461 Flights, both now equipped with the new Blackburn Dart torpedo-bomber; 460 went to HMS *Eagle* and 461 to HMS *Furious*.

More flights soon followed, these being formed from scratch rather than out of existing squadrons. 403 and 404 fighter flights came into being on 1 June and 1 July respectively, while 443 Flight was created on paper on 21 May, although it would not actually come into being for a further 24 months. Then on 21 November 423 Flight was formed with Walrus and Blackburn Bison spotters.

The two new fighter units received mixed equipment, due in part to a shortage of Nightjars (only 22 had been built). These were supplemented by Parnall Plovers. 403 Flight was allocated to HMS *Hermes* and 404 to HMS *Furious*. The Plover had been constructed to the same requirements as the Flycatcher, but proved less successful and only about half a dozen were built. They were employed only until more Flycatchers became available. Within a year all remaining Nightjars and Plovers had been replaced with Flycatchers, which became the standard fleet fighter for almost a decade.

Exactly one year after the creation of this new force, on 1 April 1924 it formally became known as the Fleet Air Arm of the Royal Air Force. It continued to be known as the Fleet Air Arm thereafter – sometimes officially, sometimes unofficially – right up to the present day. It would not be correct, however, to assume that the Royal Navy, and through it the Admiralty, were satisfied or happy with the situation.

While the War Office had *de facto* accepted the creation of the RAF, the same cannot be said of the Admiralty, which remained implacably opposed to it, particularly insofar as the new Fleet Air Arm was concerned. Concerns regarding both the future use of aircraft, and of the potential expense of development and procurement for a force in which equipment employed appeared to become obsolete at an alarming rate, remained a major preoccupation. So too did the perception that separate control of the air could prevent the Navy from deriving the greatest possible degree of benefit from this still-new technology.

As far as the Fleet Air Arm was concerned, the Admiralty felt it had a different, and perhaps stronger, case than the Air Ministry. In fact both sides appeared to have a strong case. To remove the Fleet Air Arm from its parent body would, said the Air Ministry, cause constant difficulties and greatly increase expense in development, procurement and training – issues which had

OPPOSITE TOP
Blackburn became a major designer and constructor of aircraft for the Fleet Air Arm. Designed as a torpedo-dropper to replace the Sopwith Cuckoo, the Dart saw quite widespread service from 1923 until the early 1930s, serving with at least five flights. This is an aircraft of 460 Flight seen at Heliopolis, Egypt, during the late 1920s while forming a part of Eagle's *air component.*

OPPOSITE BOTTOM
A 'flying chartroom', the Avro Bison was the epitome of the naval requirement for a spotter-reconnaissance aircraft when it entered service in 1923. It served for some six years with several flights until superceded by the Fairey IIIF at the end of the decade.

LEFT *One of the first aircraft to be constructed specifically for carrier operations, the Parnell Panther served in the spotter-reconnaissance role with 406, 421, 441 and 442 Flights, these aircraft operating from both* Argus *and* Hermes. *N7426 is seen here during deck-landing trials on HMS* Eagle *in June 1920.*

played a large part in justifying the formation of the separate air service in 1918.

The Admiralty's major concern, however, centred on the fact that it was the Air Ministry which raised, trained and maintained the Fleet Air Arm, despite the fact that it was then operated by the Admiralty under its complete control when at sea in carriers which had themselves been designed and constructed by the Navy. The air element on which, it was pointed out, the safety and success of the Battle Fleet might well now depend, should not be undertaken by 'persons belonging to another Service imbued by different traditions and looking for support and promotion to a different Department'. It may fairly be said that these concerns transcended any issues of innate conservatism or inter-Service jealousy. They were also hammered home by the Admiralty at every opportunity – particularly at the time of each year's Services allocations in Parliament.

There is little doubt that the concerns expressed had probably been exacerbated by a report issued by the Select Committee on National Expenditure on 14 December 1921 relating to the maintenance of an independent air force, which stated that 'without a separate existence' the air force would not be able 'to work out developments which might in the next decade or so entirely revolutionise methods of attack and defence'. If these were successful, said the committee, 'very large economies in the cost of the fighting Services' might be made 'by substituting air for land and sea forces'. To the Admiralty this must have been pure anathema!

The consequence of all these arguments occurred in 1922 – just before the reorganisation

and the formation of the Fleet Air Arm as such – when a sub-committee of the Committee of Imperial Defence recommended that, as a compromise, at least 30 per cent of the officers of the Fleet Air Arm should be naval officers, and the proportion could be substantially increased if necessary. However, as a check on this, not less than 30 per cent must be RAF officers. In practice this devolved into a system where about 50 per cent of officers in the Fleet Air Arm were from the Navy and about an equal number from the RAF. For the time being all aircraft-related technicians of non-commissioned rank would continue to be supplied by the RAF.

Although this was undoubtedly a victory for the Admiralty, it would fail to solve the problems which they had sought to address, and left them still far from satisfied. Practically, since the RAF provided all flying training at this time, the majority of pilots remained members of that Service, while naval officers predominated as observers. The Admiralty would continue to lobby for a full separation at every opportunity, but for the time being this was the best they could get. It will be necessary to return to this contentious issue later in this chapter. It is worth noting at this juncture, however, that at the operational level aboard ship co-operation between the two Services seems to have been very good, and to have caused little deep-seated resentment.

Soon after the 1923/4 reorganisations there was a further increase in the size of the Royal Navy's aircraft carrier strength. The cruisers *Courageous* and *Glorious* were paid off in 1924, and work was undertaken to turn both into carriers of a fairly substantial size. *Courageous* would be completed

RIGHT *Almost a
completely new type
from the earlier IIID,
the Fairey IIIF was
to become one of the
classic Fleet Air Arm
aircraft of the interwar
years. Operated widely
on both wheels and
floats, the aircraft
served from 1928
almost until the
outbreak of the Second
World War, straddling
the period when flights
were combined to
form squadrons. Many
operated from the
catapults of cruisers as
well as from the decks
of all the Royal Navy's
carriers. Here a float-
equipped aircraft of
824 Squadron is
lowered to the water by
a crane aboard* Eagle.

first, commissioning occurring in February 1928,
with *Glorious* following some 18 months later in
October 1929.

The arrival of these significant new ships
required the formation of further flights, which
effectively doubled the size of the Fleet Air Arm by
the end of 1929. Four new fighter flights (405–408),
three spotter-reconnaissance flights (444–446)
and three new torpedo flights (462–464), plus
the delayed 443 Flight, all came into being during
this five-year period. Entry into service of the
very versatile Fairey IIIF also allowed the roles
of spotter and reconnaissance to be combined,

and in consequence the flight numbers in the
420–439 range were done away with, and the
440–459 range now encompassed the merged
spotter/reconnaissance role. To comply with this
adjustment, 420 Flight was renumbered 449, 421
Flight became 447, 422 Flight became 450, and
423 Flight became 448. The year 1929 also saw the
arrival of the Blackburn Ripon II in the torpedo-
bomber role, displacing the elderly Darts.

Most units were transferred at this point to
operate from the two new ships, which allowed the
now somewhat dated *Argus* to be transferred to
the reserve.

RIGHT *Serving with the
Fleet Air Arm during
the period 1924–30,
the Fairey IIID was
developed from the
wartime IIIA–IIIC
aircraft. It replaced
the Parnell Panthers in
441 and 442 Flights,
serving ultimately with
at least six flights and
operating at various
times from all the Royal
Navy cruisers and
the seaplane carrier
Vindictive. S1092 is seen
here, fitted with floats,
while serving with 441
Flight aboard* Argus.

FLEET AIR ARM ORDER OF BATTLE, LATE 1931

HMS *Courageous*

401, 404, 407 Flights	Flycatchers
445, 446, 450 Flights	Fairey IIIFs
449 Flight	Blackburn Is, Fairey IIIFs
463, 464 Flights	Darts

HMS *Glorious*

405, 406, 408 Flights	Flycatchers
441, 447, 448 Flights	Fairey IIIFs
460, 461, 462 Flights	Ripon IIs and IIas

HMS *Furious*

443 Flight	Fairey IIIFs
465, 466 Flights*	Ripon IIs and IIas

HMS *Eagle*

402 Flight	Flycatchers

HMS *Hermes*

403 Flight	Flycatchers
440, 442 Flights	Fairey IIIFs

2nd Battle Squadron

444 Flight (catapult aircraft)+	Fairey IIID and IIIF floatplanes

* These two flights had been formed during March/April 1933.
+ This flight had originally been formed to serve on the seaplane carrier HMS *Vindictive* until the latter was withdrawn for conversion to a cruiser.

ABOVE *Of remarkably similar (and equally unlovely!) appearance to the Avro Bison, the Blackburn Blackburn served during much the same period as its contemporary. The Mark II, one of which is seen here in service with 449 Flight, brought the production total to 62.*

ABOVE *Fairey IIIF of 444 Flight, serving at Wei-Hai-Wei, China, 1926–8.*

LEFT *The Blackburn Ripon succeeded the Dart as the standard torpedo-bomber in 1929, although its length of service was relatively brief. The aircraft served with five flights, and later with two squadrons of the Fleet Air Arm. Seen here is a Mark IIC.*

The long-serving Flycatcher was replaced by the beautiful Hawker Nimrod, which had been developed from the RAF's Fury. The aircraft, joined by smaller numbers of Osprey two-seaters, equipped the Fleet Air Arm's fighter squadrons, 801 and 802, until replaced by Skuas and Sea Gladiators just before the outbreak of the Second World War.

Given the circumstances of the 1920s, following the devastation of the Great War and the resultant public revulsion regarding military or naval issues, coupled with the financial constraints of the time, the growth and modernisation of the Fleet Air Arm and the Royal Navy's carrier fleet can be seen as little short of extraordinary. Development work had continued all the while, one of its fruits being the first successful night-time deck landings undertaken on HMS *Furious* during 1926.

Further progress was about to be made as the 1930s commenced, with the arrival of an exciting new generation of higher-performance aircraft. At the start of the decade the aircraft manufacturer Hawker had introduced a beautifully streamlined two-seat biplane bomber named the Hart. This aircraft, which utilised one of the new Rolls-Royce Kestrel water-cooled engines, demonstrated an outstanding performance, in particular by being faster than any fighter aircraft then in service. Hawker's design team, led by Sydney Camm, followed this with a strikingly similar single-seat fighter, soon named the Fury, which proved to be the first British service aircraft to exceed 200mph.

Both types were ordered for the RAF, and versions suitable for use by the Fleet Air Arm swiftly followed in the form of the Osprey and Nimrod, both of which would initially be issued to the various fighter flights. When fitted with hook and floatation gear, these aircraft proved to have performances only marginally below that of their land-based cousins, and maintained the Fleet Air Arm at a world-class standard at the time of their introduction. Although both could be fitted with floats for catapult operations, in practice it was generally only the Osprey that was so modified.

These aircraft brought with them a new problem that led to further developments in carrier landing. Previous biplanes had been able to glide down slowly to land, enabling the cushion of air between the deck and their wings to let them set down with no more than the guidance of the fore-and-aft wires standard on all carriers. However, this new generation of faster aircraft occasionally required something more substantial to slow them down to an acceptable landing speed. In consequence transverse arrester wires laid across the deck were introduced, initially on HMS *Courageous*, and these soon became standard aircraft carrier equipment.

By this time it had become desirable to regroup the flights into squadrons, in line with RAF practice ashore. This was occasioned by the new generation of carriers, which could carry considerably larger air groups, obviating the need for the multiplicity of command and administration required by the smaller units. Consequently on 3 April 1933 a further complete reorganisation of the Fleet Air Arm took place. The new squadrons, numbered now in the 800 range, were formed usually (though not in every case) from pairs of existing operational flights, as detailed in the accompanying sidebar.

FLEET AIR ARM REORGANISATION 1933–35

Fighter units

402 and 404 Flights became 800 Squadron, equipped with Ospreys and Nimrods.

401 Flight became 801 Squadron, with Flycatchers and Nimrods.

408 and 409 Flights became 802 Squadron, with Ospreys and Nimrods.

409 Flight became 803 Squadron, with Ospreys and Nimrods.

Spotting and reconnaissance units

445 (part) and 450 Flights became 820 Squadron, equipped with Fairey IIIFs, Baffins and Seals.

445 (part) and 446 Flights became 821 Squadron, with Fairey IIIFs and Seals.

442 and 449 Flights became 822 Squadron, with Fairey IIIFs and Seals.

441 and 442 Flights became 823 Squadron, with Fairey IIIFs and Seals.

460 Flight became 824 Squadron, with Fairey IIIFs and Seals.

Torpedo units

463 and 464 Flights became 810 Squadron, equipped with Darts, Ripons and Baffins.

465 and 466 Flights became 811 Squadron, with Ripons and Baffins.

461 and 462 Flights became 812 Squadron, with Ripons and Baffins.

Eighteen months later 825 Squadron was formed by renumbering 824 on HMS *Eagle*, this unit taking over 824's ubiquitous Fairey IIIF. On the same date 824 Squadron was re-formed with Seals for service with HMS *Hermes* on the China Station. In 1937 a new 813 Squadron was formed, but it would be nearly two more years before 814 Squadron came into existence. Thus by the end of 1938 the torpedo, bomber and reconnaissance force comprised 11 squadrons.

Immediately following this reorganisation, the remaining flights were allocated for catapult duties instead of continuing to operate from carrier decks. At the same time re-equipment with more suitable aircraft for these duties took place. Thus:

403 Flight was allocated to the 5th Cruiser Squadron, its Flycatchers being replaced by Osprey floatplanes in May 1934.

406 Flight also exchanged its Flycatchers for Ospreys in June 1934, having joined the 4th Cruiser Squadron in January 1933. The following year the flight also received a single Fairey IIIF.

407 Flight joined the 2nd Cruiser Squadron, similarly exchanging Flycatchers for Osprey floatplanes.

443 Flight was also allocated to the 2nd Cruiser Squadron, but was then split up to serve the 6th and 8th Cruiser Squadrons. In May 1935 this unit's Fairey IIIFs gave way to Ospreys.

444 Flight was allocated to the 2nd Battle Squadron and the 1st Cruiser Squadron in September 1931, being equipped for this role with a small number of Fairey IIIFs, Fairey Seals, Seagull Vs and Ospreys.

445 Flight was re-formed at the end of August 1935 for similar duties with the 3rd Cruiser Squadron, fully equipped with Ospreys.

447 Flight continued to served on HMS *Glorious* until March 1934, when it received a number of Ospreys to augment its IIIFs.

ABOVE *The Ripon was replaced by the Blackburn Baffin from 1934, the new aircraft ultimately equipping three torpedo-bomber squadrons. This was the heyday of colourful Fleet Air Arm aircraft paint schemes, each unit carrying brightly painted fuselage bands to indicate their identity.*

BELOW *When the Hawker Osprey joined the fleet, it introduced a new fighter-reconnaissance category to the service. Operated in conjunction with Nimrod single-seaters in the fighter squadrons, it also served widely as a floatplane on the catapults of a number of cruisers. Here one of the latter is seen serving with 407 Flight.*

RIGHT *Developed from the Fairey IIIF, the Seal was built as a spotter-reconnaissance aircraft serving at the same time as the Baffin torpedo-bomber. Both types were steadily replaced by the ubiquitous Fairey Swordfish from 1938 onwards. This is K3481.*

BELOW *The last of the line of Blackburn biplane torpedo-bombers, the Shark, was introduced into service in 1935. A good aircraft, later fitted with an enclosed canopy for the cockpit area, the type's first line service was brief as it was rapidly replaced by the Swordfish from 1938 onwards. It remained in use as a trainer for several years thereafter. Its performance was generally marginally superior to that of the Swordfish, and it was considered by some pilots to be a better aircraft. Here can be seen a formation of Sharks of 820 Squadron, operating from HMS Courageous.*

Even as these changes were under way, the rapid development of aviation was bringing new types of aircraft into service. 1933 saw the faithful Fairey IIIFs beginning to be replaced by the radial-engined Fairey Seal, which had been developed from it. The next year saw the Ripons being withdrawn to be refurbished and re-engined with radials, thereby becoming Blackburn Baffins. A more modern torpedo-dropping aircraft also appeared, the Blackburn Shark, first flying in May 1934. Ordered into production, it would re-equip 810 and 820 Squadrons on HMS *Courageous* and 821 Squadron on *Furious*. These aircraft would not remain in first-line service for long, however, for during 1935 orders were placed for the Fairey Swordfish, which had actually first flown in 1931 and would eventually take the place of all TBR (torpedo, bomber and reconnaissance) aircraft. Initially 86 examples were ordered.

Although in appearance an absolutely classic traditional open-cockpit, radial-engined biplane, the Swordfish was to prove supremely reliable and adaptable. Christened the 'Stringbag' by its crews, it would be built in larger numbers for the Fleet Air Arm than any other aircraft up to that time, and was to serve in many roles for the next ten years. Those initially delivered were supplied to the catapult flights as floatplanes.

Another aircraft which was to prove of considerable importance to the Fleet Air Arm (and, indeed, to the RAF as well) also started to enter service during 1936. This was the Supermarine Walrus, a small flying boat which was to play a prominent role from the catapults of the Royal Navy's big ships. Having first flown in 1933, the 'Shagbat', as it swiftly became known, just preceded into service another aircraft destined to fulfil a similar role, albeit in smaller numbers and during a considerably shorter time span. This was the Fairey Seafox, a biplane floatplane of which

BELOW *For much of the Second World War the Fairey Swordfish (affectionately named 'Stringbag' by its crews) remained the most numerous aircraft type with Fleet Air Arm units. Here a formation of these aircraft is seen in the torpedo-bombing role.*

CATAPULT FLIGHT RENUMBERING 1936

On 15 July 1936 the various catapult flights were all renumbered in the 700 range, as follows:

403 Flight became 715 Flight, 5th Cruiser Squadron.
406 Flight became 714 Flight, 4th Cruiser Squadron.
407 Flight became 712 Flight, 2nd Cruiser Squadron.
443 Flight became 716 Flight, 6th Cruiser Squadron, and 718 Flight, 8th Cruiser Squadron.
444 Flight became 702 Flight, 2nd Battle Squadron, and 705 Flight, Battlecruiser Squadron.
445 Flight became 713 Flight, 3rd Cruiser Squadron.
447 Flight was disbanded to provide the nuclei for 702 Squadron, 1st Battle Squadron, and 711 Flight, 1st Cruiser Squadron.

These units had all risen to squadron status by the early months of 1939.

BELOW *When fitted with floats, the Swordfish also saw service as a catapult-mounted spotter aircraft on board several major warships.*

64 were ordered during 1936 and started to enter service during the spring of the following year.

The biggest news of all at this time, however, was the ordering of a new state-of-the-art aircraft carrier in 1935. HMS *Ark Royal* (the same name as had been previously borne by the seaplane carrier) represented a major step forward in carrier development. All the earlier carriers acquired by the Royal Navy had been provided with two lifts to remove aircraft from the deck to the hangar below. *Argus*, *Hermes* and *Eagle* had also been too limited in size to accommodate much more than 20 aircraft. *Furious*, following her rebuild in 1925, had been able to embark 33, while *Courageous* and *Glorious* could each cope with 48. The new vessel, however, was to feature three lifts which allowed its aircraft complement to increase to 60 – or even 72 in an emergency. *Ark Royal* would be launched during 1937, commissioning taking place in 1938.

Another development which just preceded the arrival of *Ark Royal* was the introduction of the Deck Landing Control Officer (known colloquially as 'The Batsman'). It was the role of this individual to stand on one side of the deck at the stern of the ship when an aircraft was approaching to land. As it did so, he would indicate by a series of standard signals with the large 'bats' he held in each hand whether the incoming machine was too high, too low, not level, etc. Just before the aircraft was ready to touch the deck and was in the correct position to do so, he would cross his arms and the bats in front of himself, indicating that the engine should

be cut at that moment. If he was not satisfied that the aircraft was positioned to make a safe landing, he would give the 'wave-off' sign – which was just that, a wave off with his bats. This system of landing control would continue to be employed until well after the Second World War, and was adopted on the aircraft carriers of all navies which employed them.

At this time military aircraft design had taken another major leap forward, occasioned by a substantial increase in the power of the aircraft engines now becoming available. Monoplane designs with retractable undercarriages, enclosed cockpits for the crew, greatly enhanced armament and weapons-carrying capability, and all-metal stressed-skin construction, pointed the way ahead.

The first such monoplane for the Fleet Air Arm appeared in 1937. This was the Blackburn Skua dive-bomber/fighter, which was not dissimilar to aircraft being designed and constructed for the US and Japanese navies. With a top speed of 225mph and a forward-firing armament doubled from the traditional two machine guns to four, it seemed to have a performance sufficient to at least keep pace with any bomber aircraft which might threaten the fleet, and which it might potentially attempt

to intercept. The additional offensive capacity occasioned by its ability to dive-bomb must also have been welcome.

However, the Admiralty was concerned (very properly) that a machine more closely comparable in speed and armament to the Hurricane and Spitfire, which were also appearing at that time, ought to be made available to the Navy. Unfortunately, though, the Admiralty required a second seat in such aircraft for a navigator, to ensure a safe return to the parent carrier should adverse weather be encountered. This was clearly at variance with the years of successful flying experienced with the Flycatcher and the Nimrod, but a stated reason for their contrary decision has not been discovered.

The Air Ministry accordingly prepared and issued the necessary specification, but design and construction of prototypes would take some time. Despite the imminent availability of the Skua, therefore, the worsening political situation in Europe meant that something was required to fill the gap until a truly modern fighter could be made available. Even had a navalised version of the Hurricane or Spitfire been considered at that time, the urgent need for all such aircraft to re-equip the

BELOW *Introduced into service in 1938 in the new role of fighter/ dive-bomber, the Blackburn Skua was the Fleet Air Arm's first all-metal monoplane for carrier operations. It was to serve with some distinction during 1940, but was quickly outclassed by the opponents it might encounter. Here a formation of aircraft from 803 Squadron are seen in flight just before the outbreak of war in 1939. They would be the last fleet aircraft to be finished in bright peacetime colours, which would soon be covered by coats of camouflage paint.*

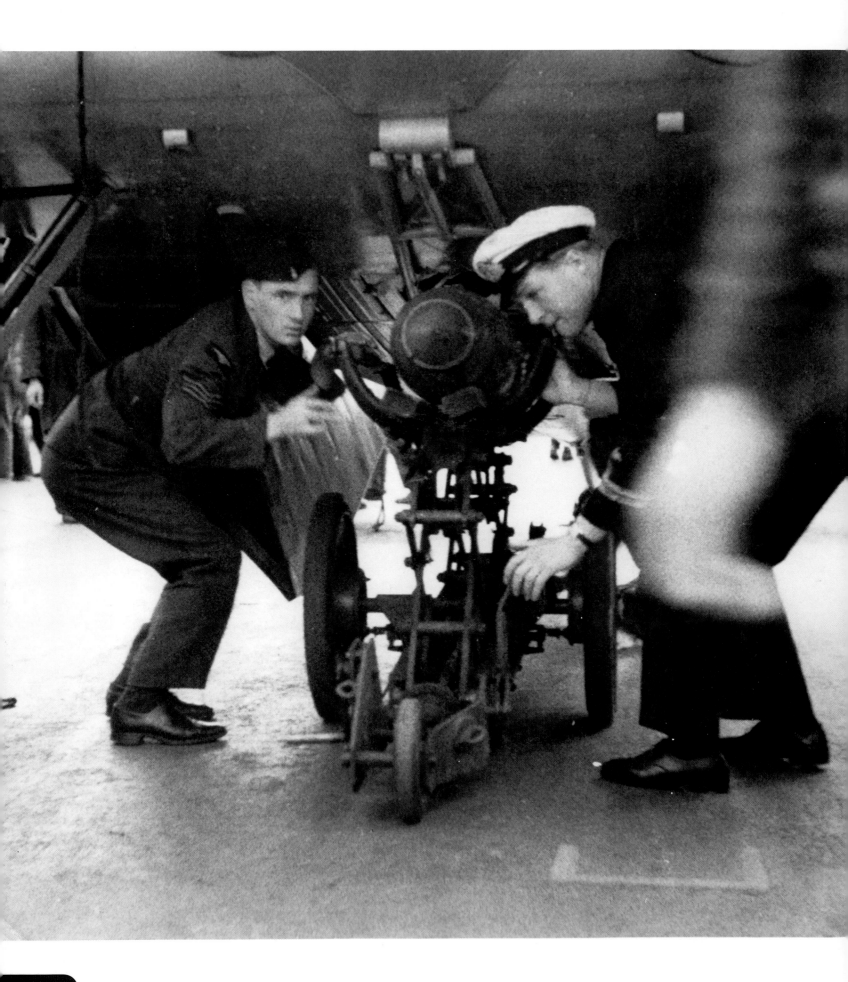

squadrons of the RAF's Fighter Command would undoubtedly have militated against the Air Ministry conceding such a possibility.

Consequently, 35 Gloster Gladiator II biplane fighters on order for the RAF were modified by the inclusion of an arrester hook, catapult points and a dinghy in a fairing beneath the fuselage, thereby becoming the Sea Gladiator. These additions resulted in a somewhat reduced performance when compared with the land-based Gladiator. However, a further 60 were ordered to be built to this standard from the start of production.

The Gladiator really was an interim type. In appearance it was a traditional biplane fighter with a fixed undercarriage. However, it did feature an enclosed cockpit and, like the Skua, an armament of four machine guns. It was also about 20mph faster than the latter, and was undoubtedly fast-climbing and extremely manoeuvrable.

In October 1938 the first Skuas became available for issue to squadrons, 800 becoming the initial unit to commence re-equipment with them. Its arrival required new skills to be learned by its crews, those associated with dive-bombing. Within a month 800's 'B' Flight was detached to allow a new 803 Squadron to be formed – initially with the former unit's old Nimrods and Ospreys. By the end of the year the Ospreys had given way to

Skuas, and as more were received the Nimrods departed too.

While these two units worked up preparatory to going aboard the new *Ark Royal*, which was to become the first British aircraft carrier to operate monoplanes, examples of both Skuas and Sea Gladiators were supplied to 801 Squadron early in 1939 for use on HMS *Courageous* as a Deck Landing Training Squadron for the new types.

During May 1939 Sea Gladiators re-equipped 802 Squadron, which had just returned to the United Kingdom aboard HMS *Glorious*. The carrier had come home for a refit, so the new aircraft were initially taken aboard *Courageous*, although the squadron would soon return to its parent vessel and accompany it to the Mediterranean.

During the 1930s there had been an opinion amongst certain elements of the RAF establishment that a fighter aircraft could well perform better against bombers if its pilot was able to fly below, or alongside, such aircraft. The pilot would thereby be able to concentrate his attention on maintaining the fighter in a suitable position whilst a gunner in a heavily armed powered turret behind him directed a sustained fire at the opponent. This tactic relied upon the presumption that Fighter Command would operate outside the range of any escorting fighters accompanying the bombers

OPPOSITE *Bombing-up a Skua. On the left is an RAF sergeant, typical of the ground crews of the RAF still aboard the carriers at the outbreak of the Second World War. His task is shared by a lieutenant of the Fleet Air Arm.*

BELOW *A navalised version of the RAF's Gloster Gladiator, the Sea Gladiator was the last of the British fighter biplanes. Entering service just before the outbreak of the Second World War, it was something of an anachronism and was already generally outclassed. However, it saw service during the Norwegian campaign and then briefly over the Eastern Mediterranean.*

coming from Germany (already the likely enemy at that time). The possibility of France and the Low Countries falling into hostile hands, thereby bringing the enemy's air bases much closer to the United Kingdom, was not considered.

In consequence an aircraft of similar size and configuration to the new Hurricane and Spitfire, and powered by the same Rolls-Royce Merlin engine, was developed by Boulton Paul as the Defiant. Because of the greater weight occasioned by the inclusion of a second crew member and the heavy turret, the performance of this aircraft was, not surprisingly, lower than that of its two stablemates. The turret contained only four machine guns, rather than the eight of the single-seaters – undoubtedly because it was deemed that in its intended role the gunner would be able to continue firing for a longer period than the pilot of a conventional aircraft.

Perhaps in order to save weight, no forward-firing armament was provided.

In practice the Defiant proved capable of undertaking its designated role with reasonable success – just so long as there were no enemy fighter aircraft present. When, after a few initial victories, the latter were encountered, the Defiant proved almost defenceless against them and was rapidly rendered incapable of further operational use by day.

After being ordered in 1937, the start of 1939 saw an aircraft of similar configuration being constructed for the Fleet Air Arm. Essentially, the Blackburn Roc was born by fitting a turret to a Skua and removing its fixed wing guns. Powered by a Bristol Perseus engine of 905hp, as opposed to the Defiant's more powerful and better streamlined Merlin, the resultant aircraft offered a quite substantially lower performance than the

BELOW *The Blackburn Roc turret fighter was introduced to very limited service during 1938. It proved to be totally unsuitable in its designed role and was rapidly relegated to training and target-towing duties.*

Skua – indeed, one similar to the now-obsolescent Nimrod. Incredibly, 136 of these aircraft were to be built, an initial trio joining 803 Squadron in April 1939, while three more went to 800 Squadron in May. More will be recounted regarding the Roc's lacklustre fortunes in due course.

By now Europe had suffered the trauma of the rise of Nazi Germany, culminating in 1938 in the Munich crisis, and the resultant fragile agreement reached between the British, French and German leaders, brokered by Italy's Benito Mussolini. With imminent war looming on the horizon, the Admiralty had renewed its representations insofar as the Fleet Air Arm was concerned. On 21 July 1937 Sir Thomas Inskip, the Cabinet Defence Co-ordinator, announced in Parliament that control of naval aviation would revert to the Admiralty with effect from 24 May 1939. Finally, therefore, on that date – just as 802 Squadron was receiving its Sea Gladiators – control was passed to the Admiralty.

Unfortunately, this resulted in all the RAF aircrews having to be released to their own Service forthwith. Only a few volunteered to transfer to the Royal Navy and remain with their squadrons. For the time being the groundcrews remained RAF personnel, continuing to serve with the Fleet Air Arm until sufficient replacements could be recruited and trained to take their places. (In practice, numbers of RAF ground personnel would still be serving with the Fleet Air Arm six years later!) Flying training also continued to be provided and maintained at RAF flying schools. The Fleet Air Arm – and, indeed, the Royal Navy as a whole – was left with virtually no substantial cadre of long-serving career naval aviators able to advise on procurement, tactics, etc., whereas by this time the US and Japanese navies enjoyed a hard core of such officers who had been serving for up to two decades.

RAF officers had generally served with Fleet Air Arm units only for relatively short 'tours' before moving on to other elements of their parent Service. Few could therefore be expected to have any long-term feeling of loyalty or 'belonging' to the naval service. Most had joined the RAF to fly – the Service's whole *raison d'être* being connected to the concept of air power. Their commanders were all committed to the same beliefs and practices. To expect such men willingly to transfer in substantial numbers to a relatively small part of a Navy still tied to traditional views regarding sea power, to find themselves under the orders of crusty old Admirals, many of whom undoubtedly still had great reservations regarding any form of air service, stretches credulity to a considerable degree. Human nature just does not work that way! A few did transfer, but they were a small minority.

But then what senior officer seriously believes that he needs to look to his juniors for guidance on how to run his service?

All in all the Admiralty's victory was not the one which it would ideally have preferred to achieve. It had obtained control of the Fleet Air Arm, but not of the other aspects of what had been the RNAS. Coastal Command of the RAF retained control of all the land-based coastal reconnaissance, anti-submarine and torpedo-carrying aircraft, and of the flying boats. The Fleet Air Arm would not be able to rebuild a strong land-based force for these duties, or of bombers and fighters to support expeditionary forces beyond the parent nation in the way that the Japanese, and to a somewhat lesser extent the Americans, had done.

Along with the changeover of aircraft and personnel, a considerable number of bases ashore now passed to the Navy, which immediately allocated them ships' names and operated them as though they were vessels at sea. Contrary to RAF practice, all training and support units were given squadron numbers.

Initially the numbers 700–749 were reserved for the catapult units, while 750–799 were allocated to second-line units. Since 801 Squadron was at this time involved in deck-landing training as has been described, and was consequently a non-operational unit, one of the Admiralty's first actions was to renumber it in the latter series as 769 Squadron. With its Sea Gladiators and Skuas now joined by a few Rocs, this unit continued its activities on HMS *Furious* prior to that vessel's withdrawal for a refit.

On 23 August 1939, immediately prior to the outbreak of war, 710 Squadron was formed for service with the seaplane carrier HMS *Albatross*, being equipped with Walruses. *Albatross*, which had been launched during 1928 for the Australian Navy, had been purchased by the Royal Navy during 1938 and was commissioned for use just before the outbreak of war.

With the Swordfish firmly entrenched in service, Fairey produced a new TBR aircraft which first flew during 1938. The Albacore was again a fixed undercarriage biplane, although it did feature an enclosed cockpit for the crew and was stressed for dive-bombing.

The outbreak of war with Germany on 3 September 1939 therefore found the Admiralty with a quite substantial carrier fleet, although less well endowed with operational aircraft than might have been hoped. The arrival of the first of a new class of armoured carriers, four of which had been ordered during 1937, was still awaited, as was a prototype of a new naval fighter to serve on it, and of production examples of the Albacore.

CHAPTER 10

CALL TO ARMS

The Second World War – the Opening Shots

O n the outbreak of war in September 1939, the Royal Navy still fielded the largest number of aircraft carriers of any navy in the world. The two other major navies, the US Navy and the Imperial Japanese Navy, had five and six respectively, while France had recently taken delivery of its first such vessel, the *Bearn*. Construction was under way on the *Graf Zeppelin* in Germany, and on the *Aquila* in Italy, though neither of these ships would be completed.

Of the seven carriers available to the RN, only one, HMS *Ark Royal*, could be considered completely modern, the others dating from 1917 to 1930. However, neither the Americans nor the Japanese were much better placed in this regard, and each nation still only had two new vessels under construction. By contrast, the Admiralty had been able to place orders for six new armoured fleet carriers by 1939, the first of which, HMS *Illustrious*, was rapidly approaching completion.

It was in concentration of vessels that the USN enjoyed some advantage, with most of her carriers based on the western seaboard of the United

LEFT *HMS* Ark Royal *(III) enjoyed much travel during the early months of the Second World War. Commencing the war with the Home Fleet, she then departed for Alexandria and the Mediterranean Fleet, but returned in early summer 1940 just too late to take part in the actions off Norway. She then sailed back to Gibraltar to join Force 'H' where she stayed until her loss in November 1941. She is seen here during these early months, launching a Swordfish.*

FLEET AIR ARM ORDER OF BATTLE, 3 SEPTEMBER 1939

HMS *Ark Royal* – North-Western Approaches, Atlantic

800 Squadron	Lt Cdr G.N. Terry, RN	Skua II, Roc I
803 Squadron	Lt Cdr D.R.F. Campbell, RN	Skua II, Roc I
810 Squadron	Capt N.R.M. Skene, RM	Swordfish I
818 Squadron	Lt Cdr J.E. Fenton, RN	Swordfish I
820 Squadron	Lt Cdr G.B. Hodgkinson, RN	Swordfish I, Walrus I
821 Squadron	Lt Cdr G.M. Duncan, RN	Swordfish I

HMS *Courageous* – South-Western Approaches, Atlantic

811 Squadron	Lt Cdr R.S. Borrett, RN	Swordfish I
822 Squadron	Lt Cdr P.W. Humphreys, RN	Swordfish I

HMS *Hermes* – South-Western Approaches, Atlantic

814 Squadron	Lt Cdr N.S. Luard, RN	Swordfish I

HMS *Furious* – In Dock, Home Fleet
No squadrons allocated

HMS *Glorious* – Mediterranean Fleet, Alexandria

802 Squadron	Lt Cdr J.P.G. Bryant, RN	Sea Gladiator
812 Squadron	Lt Cdr A.S. Bolt, RN	Swordfish I
823 Squadron	Lt Cdr R.D. Watkins, RN	Swordfish I
825 Squadron	Lt Cdr J.W. Hale, RN	Swordfish I

HMS *Eagle* – Far East Fleet, Singapore

813 Squadron	Lt Cdr N. Kennedy, RN	Swordfish I
824 Squadron	Lt Cdr A.J. Debenham, RN	Swordfish I

1st Battle Squadron, Home Fleet
HMS *Barham*, *Malaya* and *Valiant*

701 Squadron	Lt Cdr W.L.M. Brown, RN	Swordfish I floatplane

2nd Battle Squadron, Home Fleet
HMS *Nelson*, *Rodney* and *Resolution*

702 Squadron	Lt Cdr R.A.B. Phillimore, RN	Walrus I, Swordfish I floatplane

Battlecruiser Squadron, Home Fleet

705 Squadron	Lt P.E. O'Brien, RN	Swordfish I floatplane

HMS *Albatros*

710 Squadron	Lt Cdr H.L. Hayes, RN	Walrus I

1st Cruiser Squadron, Mediterranean Fleet

711 Squadron	Lt Cdr A.H.T. Fleming, RN	Walrus I

2nd Cruiser Squadron, Home Fleet

712 Squadron	Lt Cdr G.A. Tilney, RN	Walrus I

3rd Cruiser Squadron, Mediterranean Fleet

713 Squadron	Lt S.J. Hamilton, RN	Seafox I

4th Cruiser Squadron, East Indies Station

714 Squadron	Lt Cdr A.S. Webb, RN	Walrus I

5th Cruiser Squadron, China Station

715 Squadron	Lt P.J. Milner-Barry, RN	Walrus I

6th Cruiser Squadron, South African Station

716 Squadron	Lt A.J.T. Roe, RN	Walrus I, Seafox I

8th Cruiser Squadron, American and West Indies Station

718 Squadron	Lt Cdr J.C. Cockburn, RN	Walrus I, Seafox I

New Zealand Division

720 Squadron	Lt Cdr B.E.W. Logan, RN	Walrus I

LEFT *HMS* Glorious *prepares to leave Greenock, loaded with RAF Hurricanes of 46 Squadron for delivery to northern Norway.*

States for Pacific operations. In this regard the IJN was even better placed, with all its carriers able to combine their strength as necessary around the Home Islands and the South China Sea.

By contrast, with its traditional duty of protecting the routes of Imperial trade and Empire, the Royal Navy was obliged to spread its resources wider, and therefore more thinly. The splendid *Ark Royal*, initially with no less than six squadrons aboard, was patrolling in the Atlantic, covering the North-Western Approaches, while those in the South-Western zone were covered by HMS *Courageous* with two squadrons and HMS *Hermes* with just one. HMS *Furious* was in dock with no squadrons allocated, while the smallest and oldest vessel, HMS *Argus*, had been brought out of reserve, but was in use only for deck-landing and other training purposes. The remaining two carriers were far from home – HMS *Glorious* in the Mediterranean with her four squadrons temporarily ashore at RNAS Dekheila, near Alexandria in Egypt, while HMS *Eagle* with two squadrons was in the Far East.

It was in aircraft that the Fleet Air Arm was beginning to falter in comparison with other naval air forces. Both the USN and IJN were at this time starting to introduce into service modern all-metal, low-wing monoplanes of a performance at least equal, if not superior, to the ground-based air forces of their respective nations. With no caucus

of long-serving career naval aviators to draw upon, the Royal Navy appeared to be uncertain as to what was really needed and continued to order aircraft of obsolescent design and concept, or to seek what were effectively RAF leftovers.

Further, the other two naval air forces, modelled so faithfully upon the original RNAS, retained control of their coastal reconnaissance flying boats and floatplanes, while the Japanese in particular were building a substantial land-based arm to the IJN equipped with modern twin-engined bombers to attack shipping with both bombs and torpedoes. These latter units were being provided with their own fighter units for escort duties to the bombers, and high-performance reconnaissance aircraft to search for targets. The Royal Navy, by contrast, was still faced with all these functions being effectively outside its control and in the hands of the RAF. Even the relatively new French *Aeronavale* was based on the RNAS model, and was rapidly forming not only units for carrier service, but flying boat and floatplane squadrons, and units of bombers and fighters to operate from bases ashore.

The carrier-based units of the Fleet Air Arm were equipped, as has been described, predominantly with Fairey Swordfish biplane torpedo-bombers, which were also employed for reconnaissance, gunnery spotting and conventional bombing. Although exceedingly reliable and versatile aircraft, they offered no great advance over those of 1918.

BELOW *A Swordfish of 816 Squadron is brought up to deck level on the lift aboard HMS Tracker while engaged in convoy escort duties in the North Atlantic during the latter months of 1943.*

ABOVE *Blackburn Skua Mk IIs of 800 and 803 Squadrons onboard* HMS Ark Royal.

Twelve squadrons of these rather dated aircraft were available. *Glorious* included in her air group the single squadron of Sea Gladiator biplane fighters, while aboard *Ark Royal* were two squadrons of Skua two-seat fighter/dive-bomber monoplanes – the nearest thing to modern aircraft within the FAA. These squadrons had been supplemented in each case with a trio of Blackburn Rocs.

In October 1939 *Furious* would put to sea again, heading for the North Atlantic. As she did so, 818 Squadron aboard *Ark Royal* would transfer to this vessel. At the same time a new unit would form to complete her air group; this would be 816 Squadron, also with Swordfish aircraft, which would initially be commanded by Lieutenant Y. Dalyell-Stead.

In addition to its carrier-based units the Fleet Air Arm also had available 12 nominal catapult squadrons, all fairly small units which, as described earlier, had begun life as flights. All but one were based around the world to provide aircraft for use on the launching catapults of the Royal Navy's various battleships and cruisers; their equipment included Fairey Swordfish and Seafox floatplanes, or Supermarine Walrus amphibians. The twelfth unit was the newly formed 710 Squadron, which maintained six of its nine Walrus aircraft on the seaplane carrier HMS *Albatross*, which was heading

for Freetown, Sierra Leone, when war broke out, from where these aircraft were to undertake anti-submarine patrols off the West African coast.

Ashore were now a further five training squadrons, all numbered in the 700 series; another 11 would be formed before the end of 1939. The cadres for new operational units would be drawn from these as the need and opportunity arose.

Action for the RN carriers was not slow in coming, despite the general lack of activity along the Franco-German frontier which was to persist for the first eight or nine months of the war. On 9 September 1939 HMS *Ark Royal*, *Courageous* and *Hermes* sailed into the Atlantic with a screen of destroyers to undertake anti-submarine patrols. Five days later, on Thursday 14 September, *Ark Royal* was attacked by *U-39*, which was sunk by the destroyers of the escort only after it had near-missed the British carrier with torpedoes. Skuas of 803 Squadron were flown off in the afternoon to protect the ships from further such attack, and two of these found *U-30*, commanded by *Kapitanleutnant* Lemp, on the surface. They dive-bombed the submarine, but both aircraft came down in the sea. Royal Navy records indicate that they were brought down by the explosion of their own bombs, but the Kriegsmarine claimed that they were shot down by the U-boat's gunners.

U-30 survived the attack and picked up both pilots, although in each case the gunner perished.

Three days later HMS *Courageous* was 350 miles west of Land's End when *U-29* was able to approach unobserved and sink the carrier with great loss of life, despite the fact that some of her Swordfish were in the air at the time, on the lookout for just such an attack. Some 518 Royal Navy personnel, 26 members of the Fleet Air Arm and 36 RAF servicing crew were lost. It was then realised that such patrols were far too dangerous for the carriers and they ceased forthwith.

After a further 11 days more action ensued. The Home Fleet put to sea on a brief sortie in considerable strength, the vessels sailing towards Norway to cover the return to base of a damaged submarine. Included in the flotilla were the battleships *Nelson* and *Rodney*, the battlecruisers *Hood* and *Renown*, the aircraft carrier *Ark Royal* and three cruisers, plus a covering force of four more cruisers and six destroyers. In case German warships might put to sea to give battle, elements of RAF Bomber Command were also brought to readiness.

Meanwhile, the *Oberkommando der Marine* had organised a search for the British ships, 18 Dornier Do 18 flying boats from three units being sent out, followed by more from a further two units. One of these aircraft spotted the fleet through cloud at 1045

hours on 26 September in the Great Fisher Bank area, and reported its location, which was about 250 miles north-east of Heligoland.

No defending fighters were in the air at the time, but three Skuas of 803 Squadron were launched, Lieutenants S.B. McEwan, C.L.G. Evans and W.A. Robertson attacking Do 18 K6+YK (pilot *Leutnant zur See* Wilhelm Freiherr von Reitzenstein, aircraft commander/observer *Leutnant zur See* Ernst Koerner). All three British pilots fired, and finally the Dornier was driven down by McEwan and his gunner, Petty Officer B.M. Seymour, and forced to land on the water. The crew of four were picked up by the destroyer *Somali*, while a second Do 18 escaped unscathed. Somewhat later another flying boat approached, and this was driven off by three 800 Squadron Skuas. Nonetheless, 803 Squadron had achieved the first aerial victory of the war over a German aircraft by British-based units.

Following receipt of the sighting report from the Do 18, *Fliegerdivision* 10 of the Luftwaffe alerted its 'anti-shipping' bombers and at 1250 hours nine Heinkel He 111s of 1./KG 26 took off under *Hauptmann* Vetter, followed at 1305 by a detachment of four Junkers Ju 88As from I./KG 30 under *Leutnant* Walter Storp. Expecting such an attack, the Royal Navy demonstrated a crashing lack of confidence in its defending aircraft. Rather

ABOVE *The carriers* Glorious, Furious *and* Courageous *at sea at the outbreak of war in September 1939.*

than launch patrols of Skuas to intercept incoming raiders, all petrol was emptied from the tanks of these aircraft so that they would not burn easily, and they were stowed below decks. Any air attack would be met by the fleet's anti-aircraft defences, it had been decided, and the fighters would play no part!

The German bombers arrived overhead in heavy cloud, the Heinkels dropping their loads from low altitude but in level flight; the bombs missed their targets. The new Ju 88s then appeared and dived on the ships. *Leutnant* Storp scored a direct hit on HMS *Hood*, but the bomb bounced off the deck without exploding. *Gefreiter* Carl Francke dropped two SC 500 bombs aimed at *Ark Royal*, but achieved no more than a near miss, though he returned claiming that he might have hit the carrier. Later in the day further reconnaissance noted two battleships and covering forces heading west, but no carrier. At once the German propaganda machine leapt on this, announcing that Francke had sunk the *Ark Royal*. As darkness fell a Do 18 again spotted the fleet and reported the carrier present, but nothing was done to stop the story going out to the world's press.

Thereafter, little of note occurred for some months. However, frequent Luftwaffe reconnaissance flights over the Orkney Islands resulted in the formation during November of a new Fleet Air Arm fighter squadron. At Hatston airfield a number of Sea Gladiators were held in reserve, while the training squadron, No 769, was stationed at Donibristle in Scotland with several more of these aircraft. At the end of the month four Sea Gladiators were despatched to Hatston, led by Captain R.J. Partridge – one of the Navy's rare Royal Marine pilots – to form the nucleus of a new unit. Next day this officially became 804 Squadron under Lieutenant Commander J.C. Cockburn, while at Wick six more Sea Gladiators were taken from storage and put into service, flying over to Hatston to bring the new unit up to strength. It may be recalled that 801 Squadron had been renumbered 769 during 1939 as a training unit. On 15 January 1940, however, 801 Squadron was brought back into existence for operations, and re-formed at Donibristle with Skuas.

Luftwaffe intrusions over the northern parts of Britain continued fairly regularly, and a clash with such intruders on 20 March 1940 was to prove the first action involving a pilot who would soon become one of the most outstanding amongst the naval units. On that date, two Skuas of 803 Squadron were patrolling at about 1930 hours when Lieutenant W.P. Lucy spotted a single German aircraft being pursued by three RAF Coastal Command Lockheed Hudson patrol bombers.

Losing sight of these aircraft, Lucy then saw an He 111 attacking ships east of Copinsay Island while he was flying back to Wick. He attacked at once and fairly riddled the bomber, which made off with its undercarriage hanging down while oil and smoke streamed from the aircraft; he claimed a 'Probable'. This aircraft, from 2./KG 26, was indeed hard hit and had to crash-land near Duhnen, west of Cuxhaven, its radio operator having been killed during the engagement. The aircraft was classified as a complete write-off.

Prior to these events, Fleet Air Arm aircraft had been involved in a totally different type of operation, many, many miles away. One of the German surface raiders, the pocket battleship *Admiral Graf Spee*, had been spotted in the South Atlantic on 13 December 1939, and exchanged fire with three Royal Navy cruisers, HMS *Exeter*, *Ajax* and *Achilles*, at a range of ten miles. Although outgunning these ships, the captain of the *Graf Spee* was well aware that, once spotted, heavier elements of the British fleet would soon be called in, and he made for the shelter of the mouth of the River Plate at Montevideo, Uruguay. *Exeter* carried two Walruses of 718 Squadron, but in the opening exchange of fire both of these had been damaged by shell splinters and were jettisoned. *Achilles* was without her Walrus, which was ashore undergoing overhaul, but *Ajax* was carrying two Seafoxes, also of 718 Squadron, and one of these was launched from its catapult with Lieutenant E.D.G. Lewin as pilot, and Lieutenant R.E.N. Kearney as observer.

Exeter had taken several hits during the battle and fell back, but the other two cruisers maintained the chase, with the Seafox crew radioing the results of their fire back to them. At one point Lewin flew in close enough to estimate the damage caused, which he reported to include at least 30 hits. However, he then had to draw off as his aircraft was hit by AA fire.

Despite this, he landed successfully alongside *Ajax* and the aircraft was lifted back aboard and made ready for a further flight. The German warship, meanwhile, reached Montevideo, seeking refuge there. The cruisers stood off some 40–50 miles away to await reinforcements, and each day Lewin undertook further reconnaissance flights. On 17 December he suddenly saw a series of explosions around the vessel and was able to report that she was being scuttled. This proved to be a most useful victory for the Royal Navy, not least for propaganda purposes. Lewin was awarded a DSC for his part in this operation, Kearney receiving a Mention in Despatches; these were the first decorations to be given to members of the Fleet Air Arm during the Second World War.

NAVAL AIRCRAFT PERFORMANCE, 1939/40

A brief comparison of the performances of the main aircraft types employed by major naval air arms, and maritime aircraft employed by national air forces, in 1939/40.

FIGHTERS

US Navy
Grumman F3F (single-seat biplane)	264mph
Brewster F2A (single-seat monoplane)	301mph
Grumman F4F-3 (single-seat monoplane)*	330mph

Imperial Japanese Navy
Mitsubishi A5M (single-seat monoplane)	283mph
Mitsubishi A6M (single-seat monoplane)*	332mph

Aeronavale
Dewoitine D.376 (single-seat monoplane)	251mph
Grumman G-36A (single-seat monoplane)*	330mph
Dewoitine D.520 (single-seat monoplane)*	329mph

Fleet Air Arm
Gloster Sea Gladiator (single-seat biplane)	245mph
Blackburn Skua (two-seat monoplane)	225mph
Fairey Fulmar (two-seat monoplane)*	265mph

DIVE-BOMBERS

US Navy
Curtiss SBC-4 (two-seat biplane)	237mph
Vought SB2U (two-seat monoplane)*	250mph
Douglas SBD (two-seat monoplane)*	253mph

Imperial Japanese Navy
Aichi D3A 1 (two-seat monoplane)*	267mph

Aeronavale
Loire-Nieuport LN.401 (single-seat monoplane)*	236mph
Vought V.156F (two-seat monoplane)*	250mph

Fleet Air Arm
Blackburn Skua (two-seat monoplane)	225mph

TORPEDO-BOMBERS

US Navy
Douglas TBD (three-seat monoplane)	206mph

Imperial Japanese Navy
Nakajima B5N1 (three-seat monoplane)	229mph

Aeronavale
Loire-et-Olivier H.257bis (six-seat, twin-engine biplane)	143mph
Latecoere 29.0 (three-seat monoplane)	131mph
Latecoere 298 (two/three-seat monoplane floatplane)*	180mph

Fleet Air Arm
Fairey Swordfish (three-seat biplane)	139mph
Fairey Albacore (three-seat biplane)*	161mph

Royal Air Force
Vickers Vildebeeste (three-seat biplane)	156mph
Bristol Beaufort (four-seat, twin-engine monoplane)*	265mph

Luftwaffe
Heinkel He 59 (four-seat, twin-engine biplane floatplane)	137mph
Heinkel He 115 (three-seat, twin-engine monoplane floatplane)*	203mph

Regia Aeronautica
Cant Z.506B (five-seat, trimotor monoplane floatplane)*	217mph

FLYING BOATS

US Navy
Consolidated PBY	190mph

Imperial Japanese Navy
Kawanishi H6K (nine-seat, four-engine monoplane)	239mph

Aeronavale
Breguet 521 Bizerta (eight-seat, twin-engine biplane)	151mph

Fleet Air Arm
None

Royal Air Force
Saro London (six-seat, twin-engine biplane)	155mph
Short Sunderland (ten-seat, four-engine monoplane)*	213mph

Luftwaffe
Dornier Do 18 (four-seat, twin-engine monoplane)	165mph
Blohm und Voss BV 238 (three-engine monoplane)*	177mph

MARITIME PATROL BOMBERS

US Navy
None

Imperial Japanese Navy
Mitsubishi G3M (twin-engine monoplane)	258mph
Mitsubishi G4M (twin-engine monoplane)*	272mph

Aeronavale
Martin 167F (three-seat, twin-engine monoplane)*	304mph

Fleet Air Arm
None

Royal Air Force
Avro Anson (twin-engine monoplane)	188mph
Lockheed Hudson (twin-engine monoplane)*	246mph

Luftwaffe
Heinkel He 115 (twin-engine monoplane floatplane)	203mph

* Aircraft marked thus were the latest types available, and in many cases were just entering service at this time.

CHAPTER 11

WAR IN NORWAY

First Blood to the Skua

On 9 April 1940 German forces invaded Denmark and southern Norway. The almost immediate capitulation of the Danish left the British and French able to concentrate on giving aid to the Norwegians. Due to the distances involved, however, this meant that all air support would have to be provided by the RAF and the Fleet Air Arm. Southern Norway could be reached by bomber aircraft from northern England and Scotland, but fighter escort and protection was effectively impossible for the RAF unless airfields could be secured in Norway. Only the Royal Navy's carriers offered the prospect of any fighter cover in the first instance.

By this time, however, the RN was not in a good position to provide it. HMS *Furious* had gone into the Clyde for a refit, while *Ark Royal* was at Gibraltar without her Skua squadrons, engaged in training; *Glorious* was still based in the Mediterranean, and the first of the new fleet carriers was still not available. All three existing Skua units, 800, 801 and 803, were currently at Hatston in the Orkney Islands, from where they could just about reach southern Norway. The fourth squadron there, 804, could only provide local defence with its short-ranging Sea Gladiators.

LEFT *Narvik harbour showing the wrecks of German supply ships sunk or left derelict after the raid of the 2nd Destroyer Flotilla on 13 April 1940, the second British naval action off Narvik.* **IWM A42**

Nonetheless, the Skua units were about to gain a place in history, for, as news of the German landings came through, an attack on Bergen harbour was planned for 10 April. Early that morning Lieutenant W.P. Lucy led five Skuas of 800 and 11 of 803 Squadron to attack this maximum-range target. En route one of the 803 Squadron aircraft crashed into the sea with the loss of Lieutenant B.J. Smeeton and Midshipman F. Watkins, but the other 15 arrived over the target area without encountering any fighter opposition. They then undertook a classic dive-bombing attack on the light cruiser *Königsberg*, which was moored alongside a wharf. She had been damaged by return fire from Norwegian coastal batteries a day earlier while landing troops in the harbour.

At 0805 hours the *Königsberg* took three direct hits and two near misses by 500lb SAP bombs, the latter causing more damage than the former. As the hull ruptured, masses of water poured in, and at 1051 the vessel sank with the loss of 18 dead and 24 wounded; with her went her catapult Arado 196 floatplane of 1./BFl 196. This was the first major naval vessel ever to be sunk by air attack in time of war, the action being accomplished with the loss of a single Skua (apart from that lost en route), which crashed at Askoy, near the port. The crew (Sub-Lieutenant Faragut and Midshipman Owbridge) survived unhurt and, rescued by the Norwegians, served with the Norwegian Naval Air Service for the rest of the month.

Aerial action over the North Sea area now became heavy, and during the evening of 10 April six Sea Gladiators from Hatston's 804 Squadron engaged some German aircraft which the pilots identified as an He 111 and two Dornier Do 17s. The former was claimed to have been shot down east of Burray by Lieutenant Commander J.C. Cockburn, while one Dornier was damaged by three other members of the unit. In reality the Heinkel was only badly damaged, and succeeded in getting back with one wounded aboard. One Sea Gladiator crashed on landing and was written off.

On the same day HMS *Furious* joined the fleet at sea, having completed her refit a few days previously. Her air group still comprised only 816 and 818 Squadrons, her departure having been so hurried that no fighter unit could be embarked in time. As a result, for the first two weeks of the campaign urgently needed fighter cover for the Home Fleet and Allied Expeditionary Force was not forthcoming.

At dawn on 11 April *Furious* launched the first air strike of the war by carrier-borne aircraft when 18 Swordfish from the two squadrons took off to attack suspected cruisers in Trondheim Fjord – soon to be the scene of much RN effort. Lack of knowledge of the area caused incorrect depth settings to be made to the torpedoes and most grounded in shallow water, no hits being obtained. No cruisers had been found in any event, although three destroyers were present, together with *U-30* and a number of transport vessels. Two Swordfish returned to the area later in the morning to bomb these, but missed. This inauspicious result was somewhat ameliorated when HM Submarine *Spearfish* (Lieutenant Commander J.H. Forbes) managed to torpedo the cruiser *Lützow* as she was making for Kiel, severely damaging her rudder and propellers; the damaged ship was forced to head for Oslo instead.

On 12 April, while 19 Skuas from all three squadrons at Hatston made a repeat attack on Bergen – without, on this occasion, achieving any notable success – the Home Fleet, having headed northwards from Trondheim, reached a point 150 miles from Narvik. Here two waves, each of six Swordfish, were launched on a bombing strike. The second wave, led by Lieutenant Commander Gardner, became lost in a snowstorm and eventually returned to undertake the first wartime deck landings by night. The first wave, led by Lieutenant Commander P.G.O. Sydney-Turner, attacked the port, claiming direct hits on two destroyers. One bomb hit the *Erich Koellner*, one crew member being killed and five wounded, and a Norwegian fishery protection vessel was badly damaged. A blizzard of anti-aircraft fire shot down two 818 Squadron aircraft, but both crews were rescued by British warships. A third was set on fire, but Leading Airman J.G. Skeats, although wounded, managed to dowse the flames, a feat for which he subsequently received the DSM. A further attack by 816 Squadron next day was unsuccessful, and two more Swordfish fell victim to flak.

At noon on 13 April, however, an RN destroyer force led by the battleship HMS *Warspite* entered Ofotfjord to flush out a flotilla of German destroyers. *Warspite*'s catapult-launched Swordfish floatplane was sent up, flown by Petty Officer F.C. 'Ben' Rice, with Lieutenant Commander W.L. Malcolm Brown as observer. The pair spotted two destroyers, and then attacked *U-164* (*Kapitanleutnant* Wilhelm Scholz) with bombs. One of these scored a direct hit and the U-boat sank – the FAA's first victory over a submarine. During the remaining hours of daylight all seven German destroyers in the fjord were sunk (indeed, the bows of one can be seen protruding from the waters of the upper fjord to this day). The British warships also shot down a pair of Junkers 52/3m transport aircraft which overflew them as part of a force of a dozen aircraft carrying troops to the area. Most of the rest landed on the frozen Lake Hartvigvaan, where they became stuck in ice and snow and provided a ready target for the carrier aircraft over the coming weeks.

The Skuas returned to Bergen on 14 April, 15 of them sinking the troopship *Baerenfels* and damaging three more vessels. They also strafed moored seaplanes, at least one Heinkel 115 being destroyed. A further attack two days later did not achieve any success, however, despite some claims being submitted.

A somewhat unusual loss for the FAA occurred at dusk on 17 April. The cruiser *Suffolk* had been shelling the Stavanger area, her catapult Walrus from 700 Squadron having been launched to spot for the guns. While engaged in this duty the aircraft was shot down by a heavily armed *Zerstörer* (heavy fighter) version of the Ju 88, which had been pursuing an RAF Hudson but had lost sight of it in the gloom.

While covering the return to base of *Suffolk*, the Skuas gained further success, a trio of 801 Squadron aircraft shooting down a Do 18G and claiming damage to an He 111.

After more than a week of action, Allied troops both in the Narvik area and in central Norway were experiencing increasing pressure from Luftwaffe bombers. Indeed, on 18 April He 111s of II./KG 26 and Focke-Wulf 200s from I./KG 40 spotted an estimated 16 British ships in the Vaagsfjord–Tromso–Harstad area, the four-engined FW 200s gaining a near miss on HMS *Furious* which damaged her propellers.

Help was at hand, however, for HMS *Glorious* arrived at Scapa Flow the same day, having been despatched at full speed from the Mediterranean. Here she would shortly be joined by HMS *Ark Royal*, which had sped to the area from Gibraltar, taking aboard the Skuas of 800 and 801 Squadrons from Hatston as she arrived. 701 Squadron, meanwhile, flew to Harstad from *Glorious* to operate its Walrus amphibians there in both reconnaissance and bombing roles.

Glorious's first priority, however, was to try and deliver some land-based defence for the Expeditionary Force, 18 Gladiators of the RAF's 263 Squadron being loaded aboard before the carrier sailed on 22 April. The Gladiators were to operate from the frozen surface of a lake named Lesjaskog, located in the Dombas–Aandalsnes area. With *Glorious* went *Ark Royal*, carrying 18 Skuas and three Rocs, together with 23 Swordfish of 810 and 820 Squadrons. Further north, *Furious*'s Swordfish continued to operate, but suffered several losses to accurate German flak fire.

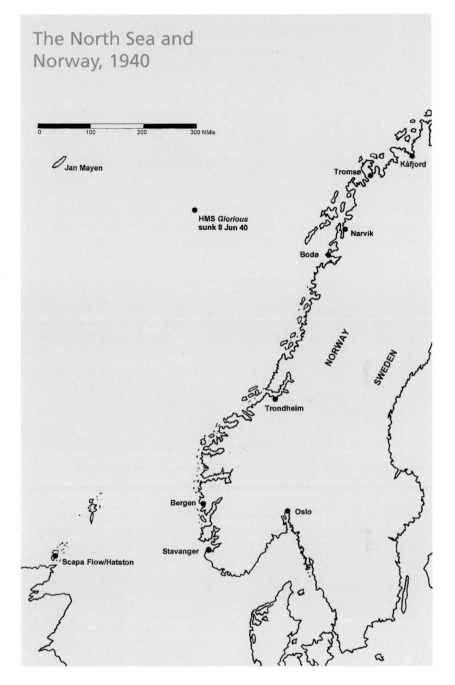

The North Sea and Norway, 1940

Fighter patrols over the central area commenced during the afternoon of 24 April, six Skuas from 803 Squadron (which was now aboard *Glorious*) undertaking the first successful interception over the Norwegian coast. Led by Lieutenant Lucy and Lieutenant L.A. Harris, RM, they shot down two bombers and damaged a third which was subsequently written off after its return to base. No Skuas were badly hit, but on return to the carrier two were so low on fuel that they had to come down in the water alongside, Sub-Lieutenant S. Lyver and his observer being lost.

Following this auspicious start, major carrier group activity was planned for the next day, the target being Vaernes airfield near Trondheim, which was being used by the Luftwaffe as its main reinforcement base. *Ark Royal*'s two Swordfish squadrons were first off at 0300. One crashed on take-off but the remaining 13 attacked with some success, although flak damage caused three Swordfish to force-land during their return flight.

Close behind came Skuas of 803 Squadron from *Glorious*, which dive-bombed moored floatplanes. They were followed in turn by more such aircraft from 800 and 801 Squadrons, and then by three more from 803 Squadron at 0430, led by Lieutenant G.R. Callingham. These intercepted and shot down an He 115 floatplane.

Altogether, 34 Fleet Air Arm aircraft had taken part in this series of attacks. Four Swordfish and two Skuas had come down in the sea while four more Skuas had force-landed in Norway, mainly due to fuel shortages. Norwegian sources reported that six German floatplanes had been destroyed or damaged beyond repair, and five other aircraft destroyed on Vaernes airfield. Actual losses to the Luftwaffe included seven Junkers 87 dive-bombers of 1./StG 1, which had just arrived, plus four He 115s destroyed and three damaged. Despite these actions, 42 Ju 52/3m transport aircraft managed to fly in more ground troops to Vaernes during the day.

For the rest of the month the carrier air groups were in almost constant action. Their presence was now needed more than ever, for the attempt

BELOW *A Royal Navy Swordfish of 818 Squadron, captured by German troops after crash-landing in Norway on 12 April 1940.* Author

to operate an RAF fighter squadron ashore had proved something of a disaster, nearly all the Gladiators being destroyed or damaged beyond repair by constant air attack, so that few sorties were actually flown.

Early on 26 April six 801 Squadron Skuas brought down He 111P 5J+CN of 5./KG 4, which crash-landed on a hillside. Many years later this aircraft would be recovered by enthusiasts and restored, the three surviving German aircrew and two of the Fleet Air Arm personnel meeting again at its roll-out at Gardermoen in 1979.

During the same morning 803 Squadron Skuas engaged a strong force of He 111s, shooting down one and damaging others. One Skua was hit by return fire and force-landed.

Next day a Luftwaffe reconnaissance aircraft spotted the carriers but was chased off and badly damaged by four Sea Gladiators launched by *Glorious*. Waves of bombers attacked during the afternoon, 800 and 803 Squadrons each managing to shoot down one aircraft. In a further raid which included Ju 88s, some confusion arose, and it was believed that four He 111s and a Ju 88 had been shot down. In fact only one Heinkel force-landed as a result of this engagement and one Ju 88 suffered slight damage.

While this fight was still in progress, three more 801 Squadron aircraft attacked a lone He 111, return fire from which shot down one Skua which fell vertically into the sea in flames, the crew being lost. The Heinkel was then shot down by the remaining British aircraft, the crew being picked up by a British warship. This hectic day was still not at an end, for a further raid was intercepted by a trio of 801 Squadron Skuas, and one more Heinkel fell victim to the defenders.

The He 111 shot down by 800 Squadron at the start of the afternoon's engagements had fallen victim to Captain R.J. Partridge, RM, and two other crews. The Heinkel – 1H+CT of 9./KG 26, flown by *Leutnant* Hans Schopis – force-landed south of Grotli, while Partridge, his Skua damaged by return fire, landed on a frozen lake nearby. As chance would have it, both crews found and took shelter in the same small shed.

Next day Partridge and Uffz Hauck set off together to try and find help for the German observer, who had been wounded, but they were discovered by a Norwegian patrol whose members shot Hauck before the situation became clear. The rest of the Heinkel crew were then taken prisoner and the two British airmen were assisted in returning to their carrier. Partridge's Skua eventually sank through the ice when the lake thawed, and went to the bottom of the fjord. From

here it was recovered during 1974, and its remains now form a panoramic exhibition at the Fleet Air Arm Museum, Yeovilton.

The situation on the ground in central Norway had meanwhile deteriorated to the point where the Army commanders were forced to order a withdrawal. In support of this *Ark Royal*'s Swordfish were directed to attack Vaernes again on 28 April. Twelve aircraft made the attack, destroying the last hangar there. Several Swordfish were hit by the intense flak which was encountered, but all returned safely. In the meantime six Skuas from 800 and 801 Squadrons attacked the slipway at Trondheim, and destroyed five more He 115 floatplanes anchored there.

The aircraft participating in the raids on British shipping now included not only He 111s and

BELOW *Captain R.J. Partridge, RM.*

Ju 88s, but also the recently arrived Ju 87 'Stukas', which on the 28th managed to sink an RN anti-submarine trawler, HMS *Siretoc*. This raid was intercepted by the trio of Rocs, but these could not catch the bombers, and were able to do no more than drive them off.

A little later six Skuas, including three from 803 Squadron which had landed on *Ark Royal* during the previous day when *Glorious* withdrew out to sea, set off on patrol. Lieutenant Lucy and Sub-Lieutenant Brokensha claimed one bomber shot down, identified as a Ju 88, and then shot down an He 111 of 4./KG 26 before pursuing other bombers which were attacked by a trio of 800 Squadron aircraft which had taken off at the same time. These shot down another He 111. Several more bombers were attacked and claimed to have been damaged, but all of the latter actually escaped unscathed. More Heinkels then approached and the 803 Squadron trio, with some ammunition still remaining, managed to shoot down yet another.

At this stage *Ark Royal* withdrew out to sea for two days to rest her tired aircrews and allow maintenance to be carried out on her depleted stock of aircraft. On 1 May the Home Fleet closed in again in three groups to provide escorts to departing convoys, completing the evacuation of central Norway. HMS *Glorious* now carried an air group composed entirely of fighters – nine Sea Gladiators of 802 Squadron, ten more of 804 Squadron, and 12 Skuas of 803 Squadron.

The approaching naval forces were spotted by Luftwaffe reconnaissance aircraft, and although these were driven off by Sea Gladiators, Ju 87s had already been launched to attack, led by He 115 'navigators'. The first wave attacked but missed, and the second was driven off by Sea Gladiators. During a third attack the Sea Gladiators gained their first concrete success when Lieutenant J.F. Marmont and his wingman shot down a dive-bomber from 2./StG 1. During the raid itself one bomb near-missed *Ark Royal*, but did no serious damage; on his return the German pilot claimed to have scored a hit on *Glorious*.

During the night of 30 April/1 May the last of the Allied troops in the Aandalsnes area were taken off, and the following night the evacuation of Namsos was completed. By 3 May operations over central Norway were at an end for the Fleet Air Arm – although the Norwegian campaign was by no means over.

Throughout the preceding period the FAA had not been alone in its actions over Norway. Although even the southernmost part of the country was beyond the range of RAF fighter aircraft from the UK, other than a handful of Blenheim bombers converted to a long-range fighter role, RAF Bomber Command had carried out a series of raids on targets in the south throughout this period. These had been undertaken without escorts and had frequently suffered heavy losses. With the evacuation of the Expeditionary Force from the central area, however, these attacks ceased and bomber units which had been operating from Scottish airfields were withdrawn south to their normal bases.

Driven out of central Norway, the Allies remained extremely anxious to try and retain a foothold in the north. From here at least, they would be able to control the supply of high-grade iron ore reaching Narvik from northern Sweden. This was the only viable route during the winter, when the upper reaches of the Baltic were frozen solid. Consequently, therefore, a new landing was made at Bodo, south of Harstad. Further landings followed at Mosjoen on 2 May and at Mo on the 4th. The King of Norway and his Ministers had been transported to this area aboard HMS *Glasgow* on 29 April, and a new seat of government had been established at Tromso.

Action against the German forces already in the area, and resistance to counter-offensives should Narvik successfully be captured, required air support. However, the Allied forces were now beyond the range of Bomber Command. Airfields for defending fighters at the least were therefore an urgent necessity, and would need to be constructed ashore. In the meantime all air support would have to come from the limited resources of the Fleet Air Arm. Ominously, the Luftwaffe was now moving fighter units into southern Norway, including both long-range Bf 110 and Ju 88C 'destroyers', and shorter-range Bf 109s for the defence of the more southerly ports and airfields. Most of these units were moving into the Trondheim area.

To maintain some level of attack on these southern areas, RAF Coastal Command despatched a unit of Beaufort torpedo-bombers to Lossiemouth to join Hudson patrol bombers and Sunderland flying boats in operations seeking to interdict German supply lines up the coast of Norway. In the north, work was swiftly put in hand to create airfields at Bardufoss, Elvenes, Banak and Skaanland. This required clearing snow and ice, levelling and draining the ground, and constructing blast pens for the aircraft and shelters for personnel. As a result of extraordinary effort, Bardufoss was completed in just three weeks, and Skaanland followed close behind. Banak, which had been intended for use by Blenheim bombers, was abandoned in the event, as was Elvenes. For the

ABOVE *HMS* Furious, *seen later in the war with Albacores on her deck.*

Royal Navy the main base area became Harstad and the Ofotfjord.

On 4 May, therefore, HMS *Ark Royal* departed Scapa Flow carrying 23 Skuas, mainly crewed by 800 and 803 Squadrons, but with some aircrews from 801 Squadron on board as well. There were also 21 Swordfish of 810 and 820 Squadrons. The carrier rejoined other fleet units in Ofotfjord on 6 May. Next day the Skuas had their first engagement in the new area of operations when five He 111 bombers approached. Two Skuas crewed by 801 Squadron personnel intercepted them first, claiming one of the Heinkels shot down, but when two more Skuas with 803 Squadron crews joined the action one of the British aircraft was hit and the pilot had to force-land in the fjord. The Skua crews reported that the German bombers' maintenance of formation and fire control seemed to have improved since the previous month.

On 9 May three 800 Squadron Skuas escorted Swordfish to attack bridges at Nordalen and Hudalen, the fighters then strafing the ten abandoned Ju 52/3m transports on Lake Hartvigvan, which had been disabled there since mid-April. One Skua crew became lost and force-landed, later walking to safety. After the remaining aircraft had been landed on, *Ark Royal* withdrew out to sea because of very adverse weather.

In Scotland, meanwhile, 804 Squadron had departed HMS *Glorious*, moving six of its Sea Gladiators to *Furious*. This move allowed space aboard *Glorious*, some replacement Skuas and Swordfish being taken aboard before she sailed for Greenock to embark the Hurricanes of 46 Squadron RAF, which she was to carry to Norway. Two days later 18 RAF Gladiator IIs, with which 263 Squadron had been re-equipped following the unit's somewhat disastrous first sojourn in Norway, were flown aboard *Furious* by Sea Gladiator pilots of 804 Squadron.

While the units of RAF Coastal Command continued to harass German shipping along the southern Norwegian coastline as far as their numbers allowed, on 10 May a newly formed Fleet Air Arm unit arrived at Hatston to supplement their efforts. 806 Squadron had been equipped with Skuas and Rocs at Worthy Down during February, and had now become operational. Immediately upon its arrival, the unit sent off its Skuas loaded with 500lb bombs to attack Bergen, escorted by six Blenheim IV fighters of 254 Squadron RAF. The crews returned claiming three hits on the training ship *Bremse*, but they had actually sunk the patrol boat *Jungingen*, killing three of the crew and wounding eight. One Skua crashed while landing back at Hatston.

British and French troops commenced an opposed landing near Narvik on 14 May, linking with Norwegian and Polish forces who approached from the north. These landings were covered by

patrols of Skuas. Later in the day Skuas returned to Lake Hartvigvan again, bombing the ice to break it up. Some He 111s were then seen and a chase commenced. Lieutenant Lucy and Lieutenant T.E. Gray inflicted damage on one, then pursued another down to low level, this Heinkel subsequently crash-landing at Vaernes on its return due to the damage it had sustained. They then sought to attack a further bomber, but as they did so Lucy's Skua was caught in a crossfire from this and another Heinkel and was seen to explode when only 60ft above the sea off Tranoy.

HMS *Whirlwind* was directed to the area and recovered Lucy's body, but no trace was found of his observer, Lieutenant M.C.E. Hanson, DSC. Meanwhile, Gray had force-landed when he ran out of fuel. Lucy was a considerable loss. One of the most experienced of Fleet Air Arm pilots, he had undoubtedly been that force's first true 'ace', having taken part in the destruction of five or six bombers, as well as leading the successful attack on the *Königsberg* at the start of the campaign, for which he had received the DSO.

That afternoon three more of 803 Squadron's Skuas returned to Lake Hartvigvan again to bomb the ice, which was now noted to be melting. Seven He 111s were then seen over the area, striking Allied shipping, and these were attacked, two being claimed damaged. In return one Skua was struck by machine-gun fire, both members of the crew being slightly wounded. By the end of the day, however, *Ark Royal* was down to 18 Skuas and 12 Swordfish still serviceable – and the Germans were strengthening their forces in the area.

On the morning of 16 May occurred the first engagement for the Skuas against superior German heavy fighters. A number of aircraft were encountered which the naval crews took to be Dornier Do 17s, but were actually Bf 110s and Ju 88Cs (a heavily armed fighter version of the high-performance Ju 88 bomber). In a fight which lasted a full 30 minutes, the Skua crews found their aircraft to be outclassed, Lieutenant L.A. Harris, RM, being forced down into Rombaksfjord, from where he and his observer were picked up by HMS *Matabele*.

During the afternoon it was the bomber version of the Ju 88 which appeared, with more satisfactory results for the defenders when three 803 Squadron crews shot down two of these aircraft. Three 800 Squadron fighters then became involved, the crews believing that they had brought down a third Junkers, which crash-landed in Bogenfjord, where the crew of five were seen to swim ashore. They had indeed dealt a further blow to the Luftwaffe, but in this case their victim had been another He 111.

Ark Royal withdrew to Tromso to refuel on 17 May, but as she did so *Glorious* and *Furious* arrived, bringing with them not only the RAF fighters and their own air groups, but also nine

ABOVE *The German battle cruiser* Scharnhorst.

Swordfish of 816 Squadron and six more Walruses to reinforce 701 Squadron at Harstad. These carriers joined the Home Fleet to the west of the Lofoten Islands, only to find that the airfields ashore were still not ready. However, the ground parties of the RAF units were able to go ashore from the transports to commence setting up ready for the arrival of their air parties in due course.

On this occasion, *Glorious* had left 823 Squadron behind at Hatston, and during the night of 17/18 May six Swordfish from this unit undertook a minelaying operation in the Haugersund area. An unusual loss was to be suffered on the 18th when a Walrus launched from the catapult of HMS *Devonshire* fell foul of reconnoitring He 111s, which shot it down. During the day, however, two Blohm und Voss Bv 138A flying boats, carrying a number of German mountain troops to Beisfjord, were spotted landing there by British troops, whose observation was reported to the Navy. Four 800 Squadron Skuas were launched at once, strafing these big aircraft so thoroughly that they had to be abandoned.

On 21 May, Bardufoss was at last reported to be ready to accept aircraft, although Skaanland still was not. 263 Squadron had been due to go to Skaanland, but was instead re-routed to Bardufoss. Two sections of Gladiators were each to be led to this destination by a Swordfish, but after the second section had got off a violent sleet storm intervened, all further launches being cancelled. The second section managed to land back on board, but the first continued on its way and became lost in the murk. As a result the two Gladiators and their guiding Swordfish all flew into some mountains at Torskenfjord, one of the fighter pilots being killed.

Due to these circumstances, delivery of the Hurricanes was postponed and *Glorious* returned to Scapa Flow with 46 Squadron's aircraft still aboard. Two days later, the weather having improved, all the remaining Gladiators got off *Furious* safely, making their way to Bardufoss under an 'umbrella' of Skuas from *Ark Royal*. One Gladiator pilot who had been wounded by bomb splinters during 263 Squadron's earlier service in Norway was, at the last minute, declared unfit, and his place was taken instead by a volunteer from 804 Squadron, Lieutenant Anthony Lydekker. Now, with 263 Squadron ashore at full strength, the main duty of local air defence devolved onto the RAF.

Their duty performed, the carriers now departed for Scapa Flow, where they arrived on 23 May. 804 Squadron flew off *Furious* to become land-based again, once more providing the air defence of the Orkneys from Hatston. Next day

806 Squadron, having undertaken several further raids on the Bergen area without loss, departed south for Worthy Down, leaving at Hatston the Skuas of 801 Squadron. At the same time 823 Squadron also left Hatston, returning aboard HMS *Glorious*.

Glorious, still with the Hurricanes aboard, slipped out of Scapa Flow in thick fog on 24 May, to return across the North Sea to Norway, where on the 26th she prepared to launch the RAF fighters. Initially it was feared that there was insufficient wind to allow a safe take-off, but the commanding officer having made the first attempt and got off with no trouble the first flight then headed for Skaanland. Here, on landing, one aircraft nosed-over on a patch of soft ground. After the next flight suffered a similar mishap the rest of the Hurricanes were diverted to Bardufoss, from where they would now operate.

Sadly, it was almost too late. German pressure – particularly from the Luftwaffe – had caused Mosjoen and Mo to be evacuated, and Bodo was about to be abandoned too, leaving only the immediate Narvik area in Allied hands, which was an untenable position. Nonetheless, the fighters at Bardufoss put up a spirited resistance during the next few days, achieving considerable success.

Aboard the carriers, meanwhile, the Sea Gladiators of 802 Squadron gained a rare victory on 28 May when three pilots intercepted a shadowing He 115 floatplane and despatched it into the sea. With the German *Blitzkrieg* successes in France and the Low Countries since 10 May having made any reinforcement of Narvik virtually impossible, evacuation of the remaining Allied forces there had become inevitable. On 30 May, therefore, *Ark Royal* and *Glorious* sailed again from Scapa Flow to aid in this operation. Both carriers had been able to bring their air groups up to strength in the interim, *Ark Royal* carrying 24 Skuas divided equally between 800 and 803 Squadrons, plus ten Swordfish of 810 Squadron and 12 of 820. *Glorious* had nine Sea Gladiators of 802 Squadron and nine Swordfish of 823 Squadron aboard.

The evacuation began on 3 June in conditions of great secrecy, and under cover of some adverse – but on this occasion, welcome – weather. *Glorious* was then detached to Tromso to refuel while *Ark Royal* launched a series of anti-submarine and fighter patrols. *Glorious* rejoined *Ark Royal* off Narvik on 5 June, where discussions commenced regarding how the bulk of the RAF fighters might be rescued, since the initial decision had been to destroy the remaining Hurricanes.

Having by now spotted the commencement of the Allied withdrawal from Narvik, on 6 June the German Navy despatched the battlecruisers

Scharnhorst and *Gneisenau*, supported by the cruiser *Hipper*, to intercept and destroy as much as possible of the retreating shipping.

On the same day two RAF Hurricanes escorted five of 701 Squadron's Walruses on a formation bombing attack in the neighbourhood of Sorfold – surely the only such operation ever undertaken by these little flying boats! Swordfish from *Glorious* bombed Sildvik railway station while Skuas from *Ark Royal* attacked German troops in the Fauske area – the last series of air support sorties to be undertaken during the ill-fated Norwegian campaign.

Meanwhile, *Glorious* had withdrawn out to sea to conserve fuel, but rejoined *Ark Royal* inshore again on 7 June, when four of her Swordfish flew to Bardufoss, ready to lead 263 Squadron Gladiators out to the carrier. Permission was given to try landing three Hurricanes aboard with the tail-end of their fuselages ballasted with sandbags; this was safely accomplished. Consequently the Swordfish and Sea Gladiators aboard were struck below, allowing the RAF Gladiators, their guiding Swordfish and all 701 Squadron's Walruses to be landed on, followed by the remaining seven Hurricanes, all of which came aboard successfully despite having no arrester gear (a lesson for the future).

At 0300 hours on 8 June *Glorious* was detached, escorted by destroyers HMS *Ardent* and *Acasta*, to sail to Scapa Flow at top speed. *Ark Royal* and the rest of the fleet followed at a more sedate pace,

allowing them to provide escort for the slower transport ships of the main convoy. This proved to have been a disastrous decision, however. At 1545 hours the German warships *Scharnhorst* and *Gneisenau* spotted *Glorious* and at 1630 opened fire at a range of 20,000yds. Their gunnery was excellent, the third salvo hitting the carrier's bridge. She returned fire, but was hopelessly outranged, and by 1720 was dead in the water and sinking fast.

Her attendant destroyers made suicidal attempts to defend her, but both were sunk – although not before *Acasta* had launched a fan of torpedoes, one of which hit *Scharnhorst* abreast of her after turret, inflicting serious damage. From the three British vessels, 1,519 personnel were lost, including 1,207 aboard the carrier. Included in these were 41 RAF ground tradesmen who were still serving with the Fleet Air Arm, and 18 RAF pilots. Two RAF officers – one of them the commanding officer of 263 Squadron – and 61 seamen got aboard a Carley float, but 25 of these died of exposure and exhaustion before the surviving 38 were picked up by a fishing vessel; the survivors included the two RAF men, who were the only aircrew from either service not to perish. Following this victory for the Germans, *Scharnhorst* made for Trondheim with all speed for emergency repairs to be undertaken.

Next day the main convoy came under attack by 19 Luftwaffe bombers during the afternoon. Skuas

BELOW *The German battle cruiser* Gneisenau.

from both of *Ark Royal*'s squadrons were put up, one He 111 being shot down with a second being claimed damaged. These were the last successes for the Blackburn Skua in northern skies.

RAF reconnaissance found *Scharnhorst* in Trondheim harbour on 11 June, and an attack was at once planned. By now, of course, it was the time of the 'Midnight Sun' over Norway, and attacks could be made in almost full daylight conditions at any time. For such an important target a co-ordinated attack would clearly be necessary, particularly as Trondheim was known to be heavily defended by the recently arrived Luftwaffe fighter units. The plan devised, therefore, was for Coastal Command Beauforts and Hudsons to attack Vaernes airfield to keep down the fighters, while Skuas from *Ark Royal*, escorted by Blenheim fighters, struck at the warship at the same time.

Two minutes after midnight on 13 June, 15 Skuas of 800 and 803 Squadrons began taking off from the carrier, each loaded with a 500lb semi-armour-piercing bomb. En route to the target, the Beauforts due to attack Vaernes lost formation in bad visibility and only four of them reached their target and attacked – but a few minutes before the

Skuas reached Trondheim at 0200 hours, not at the same time as had been planned. This allowed a substantial force of Bf 109s and Bf 110s to take off to pursue the bombers as they departed, and these ran straight into the incoming formation of Skuas. Even without their heavy bomb loads, the latter would have been hard-pressed by such opposition, but loaded as they were they were practically helpless. Within about ten minutes eight of them – more than half the formation, including both unit commanders – had been shot down. The survivors completed their dive-bombing attacks on *Scharnhorst*, but only one bomb hit home, and by great ill fortune for the intrepid crews this failed to explode.

The Blenheim fighter escort finally arrived at 0210, just too late to be able to do anything more than escort the seven survivors back to their carrier. Amongst the 16 missing aircrew, seven survived as PoWs.

No further raids were attempted – in the situation pertaining in mid-June 1940 there was little enough left with which to make any more attacks anyway. *Scharnhorst* was spotted at sea again on 20 June, making for her home port of Kiel. Next day six Swordfish drawn from 821 and

BLACKBURN SKUA CREWS INVOLVED IN THE ATTEMPT TO BOMB THE BATTLECRUISER *SCHARNHORST* IN TRONDHEIM HARBOUR ON 13 JUNE 1940

800 Squadron

Aircraft identification	Pilot	Observer
6A (L2995)	Capt R.J. Partridge, RM (PoW)	Lt R.S. Bostock (KiA)
6K	Lt K.V.V. Spurway	Pty Off R.F. Hort
6C (L3000)	Lt G.E.D. Finch-Noyes (KiA)	Pty Off H.G. Cunningham (PoW)
6G (L3028)	Mdspmn L.H. Gallagher (KiA)	Pty Off W. Crawford (KiA)
6H (L3047)	Mdspmn D.T.R. Martin (PoW)	L/A W.J. Tremeer (KiA)

803 Squadron

Aircraft identification	Pilot	Observer
7A (L2991)	Lt Cdr J. Casson (PoW)	Lt R.E. Fanshaw (PoW)
7B	Sub-Lt G.W. Brokensha	L/A F. Coston
7C	Pty Off T.F. Ridler	N/A H.T. Chatterley
7F (L2963)	Lt C.H. Filmer (PoW)	Mdspmn T.A. McKee (PoW)
7G	Mdspmn A.S. Griffiths	N/A F.P. Dooley
7L (L2992)	Sub-Lt J.A. Harris (KiA)	N/A G.R. Stevenson (PoW)
7P	Lt D.C.E.F. Gibson	Sub-Lt M.P. Gordon-Smith
7Q (L2955)	Sub-Lt R.E. Bartlett (PoW)	N/A L.G. Richards (PoW)
7R	Pty Off H. Gardiner	N/A H. Pickering

PoW = prisoner of war; KiA = killed in action. Those aircraft where the serial number is identified were shot down. Initially it was thought that only Captain Partridge, RM, had survived as a prisoner, but it was subsequently learned that nine other members of the missing crews had also been captured. However, it appears that N/A Stevenson had been seriously wounded, for he is reported to have died in a Norwegian hospital nearly a year later on 31 May 1941.

---

823 Squadrons at Hatston undertook what was the first land-based torpedo attack of the war on a capital ship at sea. They achieved no hits and lost two of their number in the attempt.

Subsequently, Coastal Command Beauforts managed to obtain three hits on the vessel, although little damage was inflicted; the cost was three Beauforts shot down.

There can be no doubt that the performance of the Royal Navy carriers and their Fleet Air Arm squadrons during the Norwegian operations had been little short of impeccable. Within the constraints of the number of vessels available and the quality and performance of the aircraft with which the carriers were equipped, the exercise had been a classic one. The ability of aircraft carriers to support an expeditionary force had been demonstrated convincingly, only the constraints already mentioned having allowed the Luftwaffe to gain the upper hand against the troops on the ground. Certainly what had been achieved – little as it was – would not have been remotely possible without the carriers.

It was therefore doubly sad that what had been done with relatively minimal loss should have ended with such disastrous consequences for both HMS *Glorious* and for *Ark Royal*'s Skua squadrons. The latter had performed so well in their mediocre aircraft that their end seems far from fitting. In one way, however, the real hidden cost of the Norway operations was the significant loss of so high a proportion of the Fleet Air Arm's quite small nucleus of highly trained and experienced aircrew personnel. It would take time to build up a new core of such men, and was doubly problematic at a time when the size of the Fleet Air Arm needed to be substantially increased in the shortest possible time.

The losses of Skuas over Trondheim, coupled with the current experience being gained by RAF Fighter Command regarding just how vulnerable dive-bombers were when faced with determined fighter opposition, was to put paid to any future such aircraft might have enjoyed in the British Services. Unfortunately, with the RAF's somewhat misplaced faith in the efficacy of level bombing, and, indeed, the Royal Navy's similar faith in the ability of aircraft to achieve hits with air-launched torpedoes, the one great advantage of the dive-bomber – its pinpoint accuracy – tended to be overlooked.

CHAPTER 12

BRITAIN ALONE

Dunkirk and the Battle of Britain

With the evacuation of the British Expeditionary Force from the coast of France commencing on 26 May 1940, the Fleet Air Arm was called upon to aid in providing cover for the shipping in the Channel, and to give some measure of assistance to the troops still holding back the advancing Wehrmacht. Consequently 806 Squadron, following its initial operations from the Orkneys, flew south to Detling on the 27th, as did 825 Squadron.

On 28 May a trio of Skuas took off on patrol, although one of these crashed on take-off. The other two were attacked over the Goodwin Sands, apparently by 24 RAF Spitfires which mistook them for German aircraft. Lieutenant Campbell-Horsfall's aircraft was hit and he ditched it in the sea, both he and his gunner being wounded; they were picked up by a destroyer. The second Skua, piloted by Midshipman G.A. Hogg, force-landed at Detling, wheels-up, with the air gunner, N/A Burton, dead. Immediately following this event, the French Air Attaché in London received a formal complaint indicating that the Skuas had been attacked by aircraft carrying French markings. This was met with a spurious excuse that the Germans

LEFT *HMS* Illustrious, *the first of the Royal Navy's new armoured deck aircraft carriers, entered action during 1940. Her air group gained much success over the Mediterranean during the latter part of that year and early 1941, including undertaking the very successful attack on the Italian Fleet at Taranto.* IWM FL2425

had captured '19 Curtiss Hawk 75A' aircraft, and that in consequence the British aircraft may have been attacked by German pilots flying these. While this was patently nonsense, no relevant claims by French fighters appear to have been made on this date, whereas claims for fighters shot down were submitted by both German and British units at approximately the right time and in approximately the right area. What actually happened has never been satisfactorily resolved, but there seems to have been inadequate aircraft recognition by everyone potentially involved.

Two days later two Skuas and a Roc encountered five Ju 88s near Ostend, all three fighters attacking the leading aircraft in a dive. All fired, and one bomber was seen to crash into the sea, while a second fell away and was last seen apparently limping towards the shore, losing height rapidly. This was to be the only confirmed victory in which a Roc took part, a share in this success being credited to N/A Newton, the turret gunner in Midshipman A.G. Day's aircraft.

On 31 May the units at Detling were joined by 801 Squadron, which immediately took its Skuas into action the same day, making a dive-bombing attack on a target near Nieuport. As the unit withdrew it was attacked by Bf 109s and two of the Skuas were shot down in flames, while a third was badly damaged and had to crash-land on return to base; both members of the crew had been wounded. However, the returning crews were able to claim one Messerschmitt shot down and a second as a probable. On the same day five Swordfish of 825 Squadron failed to return from a bombing raid, bringing to eight the losses suffered in the few days spent at the airfield.

Two days later, on 2 June, Lieutenant Commander Charles Evans, now commanding officer of 806 Squadron, attacked a Ju 88 head-on, but this spiralled into cloud. The crew of an RAF Anson subsequently reported seeing a Ju 88 with its port engine on fire trying to reach Dunkirk at about this time.

Other Swordfish units, notably 812 and 818 Squadrons, were attached to Coastal Command during this period, operating along the seaboard of France and the Low Countries. Following the evacuation they were to undertake bombing and mining activities against the fleet of barges which the Germans began to assemble for invasion purposes during the early summer of 1940.

While the fighting in France was still continuing, Prime Minister Winston Churchill had sought Admiralty agreement to loan the RAF a number of pilots to make good some of the losses suffered both on the Continent and over Dunkirk. Consequently during June 1940 some two dozen FAA pilots who had recently completed their flying training were transferred to Fighter Command on a temporary basis. They were rushed through conversion to Hurricanes or Spitfires, and were then posted to RAF squadrons. Several of these pilots were to make a significant contribution to the defence when the Luftwaffe's attentions were turned against Britain during July, notably A.G. Blake, R.J. Cork, R.E. Gardner, D.M. Jeram and F.D. Paul. However, attrition was high, nine of their number losing their lives during the Battle of Britain (including Blake and Paul), while six more were to succumb to combat or flying accidents by the end of the war.

Two of the Fleet Air Arm's fighter squadrons remained land-based in Scotland during the summer of 1940, providing air defence for the fleet bases there. Although neither of these units were to see actual combat during the period of the Battle, the 30 pilots involved were subsequently to receive the Battle of Britain Clasp, and qualified for membership of the Battle of Britain Fighter Association. While several of these pilots were to achieve much during the rest of the war, attrition amongst them was also heavy, 12 having been killed by the summer of 1945. Life as a Fleet Air Arm fighter pilot was indeed a high-risk occupation.

The Fleet Air Arm's part in the fighting throughout the summer months of 1940 mainly involved its TBR squadrons, which saw most of the action – and continued to pay the price. 815 Squadron was attached to Coastal Command during April, and operated from Detling during the Dunkirk evacuation, laying mines in the Channel. It was withdrawn in June to join the new carrier *Illustrious*. During the spring the new Fairey Albacore had become available, allowing 826 Squadron to be formed during March as the first unit equipped with these aircraft. On 31 May the squadron arrived at Detling at the same time as 801 Squadron. It went straight into action, undertaking a bombing raid on road and rail targets at Westende, and on E-boats off Zeebrugge. Subsequently moving to Bircham Newton to continue its operations under Coastal Command control, on 21 June the squadron despatched eight Albacores to attack merchant vessels at Texel. In the event the airfield at De Kooy was bombed as an alternative, as were Wilhelmsoord docks. Bf 109s appeared and shot down two of the big biplanes, but the gunners in the rest claimed one of the fighters in return.

On 2 September another Albacore was lost when four attacked an oil storage tank at Flushing,

FLEET AIR ARM FIGHTER PILOTS SECONDED TO RAF FIGHTER COMMAND DURING SUMMER 1940

Name	RAF Unit(s)	
Sub-Lt H.W. Beggs	151 Sqn	Killed in action during BoB
Sub-Lt A.G. Blake	19 Sqn	Killed in action during BoB
Sub-Lt H.G.K. Bramah	213 Sqn	
Sub-Lt G.G.R. Bulmer	32 Sqn	Killed in action during BoB
Sub-Lt J.C. Carpenter	46, 229 Sqns	Killed in action during BoB
Sub-Lt R.J. Cork	242 Sqn	Killed in flying accident, 1944
Sub-Lt R.E. Gardner	242 Sqn	
Sub-Lt H. la F. Greenshields	266 Sqn	Killed in action during BoB
Sub-Lt D.A. Hutchison*	74, 804 Sqns	Killed 1942
Sub-Lt D.E. Jeram	213 Sqn	
Sub-Lt I.H. Kestin	145 Sqn	Killed in action during BoB
Sub-Lt W.J.M. Moss	213 Sqn	Killed in flying accident during BoB
Sub-Lt F.D. Paul	64 Sqn	Killed in action during BoB
Sub-Lt G.B. Pudney	64 Sqn	Killed in action 1941
Sub-Lt D.H. Richards	111 Sqn	
Sub-Lt F.A. Smith	145 Sqn	Killed in action during BoB
Sub-Lt J.H.C. Sykes	64 Sqn	
Sub-Lt R.W.M. Walsh	111 Sqn	
Sub-Lt T.V. Worrall	111 Sqn	Killed in action 1941
Mdspmn M.A. Birrell	79 Sqn	
Mdspmn R.J. Gilbert	111 Sqn	
Mdspmn P.L. Lennard	501 Sqn	Killed in action 1942
Mdspmn P.J. Patterson	242 Sqn	Killed in action during BoB
Mdspmn O.M. Wightman	151 Sqn	Killed in action 1941

ABOVE *The most successful Fleet Air Arm pilot of those loaned to RAF Fighter Command in June 1940 was Sub Lt R.J. 'Dickie' Cork (left), who flew with 242 Squadron. He was later to gain considerable success during the Operation 'Pedestal' convoy to Malta in August 1942, when he claimed four aircraft shot down and a fifth shared in a single day. With nine individual and two shared victories, he was among the five most successful FAA fighter pilots of the war; in terms of individual rather than shared successes, he was in fact the top-scorer. Sadly, he was later killed in a collision between two Corsair fighters when flying from Ceylon. With him is Sub-Lt Arthur Blake who claimed four and one shared victories flying Spitfires with 19 Squadron. He was shot down and killed on 29 October 1940.*

FLEET AIR ARM SQUADRONS CONSIDERED TO HAVE TAKEN PART IN THE BATTLE OF BRITAIN

804 Squadron

Lt Cdr J.C. Cockburn	
Lt R.H.P. Carver	
Lt A. McL. MacKinnon	
Lt B. Paterson	
Lt G.F. Russell	Killed in flying accident 1940
Lt J.W. Sleigh	
Lt A.J. Wright, RM	
Sub-Lt S.H. Bunch	Killed in flying accident 1941
Sub-Lt P.C.H. Chilton	
Sub-Lt D. Grant	
Sub-Lt D.A. Hutchison *	Killed in action 1942
Sub-Lt R.R. Lamb	Killed in flying accident 1942
Sub-Lt W.R. Nowell	
Sub-Lt T.R.V. Parke	Killed in flying accident 1941
Sub-Lt N.H. Patterson	Killed 1941
Sub-Lt J. Reardon-Parker	
Pty Off T.J. Mahoney	
Pty Off F.J. Shaw	Killed in flying accident 1942
Pty Off W.E.J. Stockwell	

808 Squadron

Lt J.P. Coates	Killed 1940
Lt R.C. Cockburn	
Lt G.C.McE. Guthrie	
Lt R.C. Hay, RM	
Lt A.T.J. Kindersley	Killed 1940
Lt E.W.T. Taylour	Killed 1942
Lt R.C. Tillard	Killed 1941
Sub-Lt R.M.S. Martin	Killed 1940
Mdspmn P. Guy	Killed 1942
Mdspmn G.W. Roberts	Killed in flying accident 1946
Pty Off R.E. Dubber	
Pty Off D.E. Taylor	

*Hutchison served both with an RAF squadron, and then with 804 Squadron during 1940.

but the most memorable operation of this period occurred on 11 September when six Albacores, escorted by Blenheim fighters of the RAF's 235 Squadron, attacked a convoy five miles north-west of Calais. Near Cap Gris Nez the force was bounced by Bf 109s. The Blenheim pilots claimed two of these shot down, the Albacore crews adding a third. However, one Albacore ditched off Dover and one force-landed in Kent, while two more were badly shot-up but managed to struggle back to their base.

In all 826 Squadron spent five months with Coastal Command, suffering a final loss on 30 October. By that time the unit had undertaken 22 night attacks on coastal targets, laying seven tons of mines and dropping 26 tons of bombs. It had also escorted no less than 92 convoys, most of them during September, and had submitted claims

for five German aircraft shot down or damaged. Of the Swordfish squadrons also operating with Coastal Command at this time, 812 Squadron had suffered the loss of three aircraft during the Dunkirk operations, followed by another four during August 1940. As is thus shown, the Fleet Air Arm's contribution to both the Dunkirk evacuation and the Battle of Britain had been anything but small, particularly when the size of the force and its continued involvement further north is considered – as well as its rapidly growing involvement further south and east, as will shortly be recounted.

Following the attrition of the actions over and around Norway, by the middle of June 1940 the only aircraft carrier available to the Home Fleet at Scapa Flow was HMS *Ark Royal*. Following the fall of France, *Furious* had been despatched to the United States, where the British Purchasing

Commission had been hard at work, seeking to take over contracts for military aircraft which could no longer be fulfilled and delivered to countries which were now beneath the German heel. The new *Illustrious*, meanwhile, was still working up and was not yet ready for operations. However, demands in other quarters were now pressing. Consequently *Ark Royal* and the battleship HMS *Hood* were ordered to Gibraltar towards the end of June to join Vice-Admiral Sir James Somerville's new Force 'H' which had been formed there.

The duties of this force were to prevent a move towards the west by the Italian Fleet – Italy having become an additional enemy on 10 June. Coupled with this was the need to assume the local role previously undertaken by the French Navy, and, indeed, to ensure that major elements of their fleet were not taken over by the Germans or employed in any way hostile to British interests. As if these duties were not enough, the force also had to be vigilant against any attempt by German surface raiders to break out into the South Atlantic, and to take part in anti-submarine operations in this area.

Fortunately, the need for carriers with the Home Fleet was much reduced at this time, as the Kriegsmarine had recently lost three of its seven cruisers and a large number of destroyers as a result of its Norwegian operations. Also, one of its battlecruisers had been damaged and would not be available for some time.

Every cloud has a silver lining, so the old saying tells us, and in the case of the Fleet Air Arm the fall of France and the Low Countries did bring forward a golden opportunity to acquire some modern single-seat fighter aircraft. As already noted, immediately after the conclusion of operations in the Channel area *Furious* was despatched to the USA to bring back quantities of such aircraft taken over from now-defunct French and Belgian orders. The latter provided an initial 15 Brewster B.339 Buffalo aircraft, while from the former came a quantity of Grumman G-36As, soon to be known as Martlet Is. Testing of both types took place during the late summer, as soon as the carrier had delivered them to the UK. The Buffalo was swiftly relegated as suitable for service in the Middle East, the small numbers available militating against more widespread service. Most of the eventual total of 26 received from the Belgian orders were despatched to the Dekheila naval air base outside Alexandria in Egypt.

The Martlet was quite a different matter, and also had the advantage of becoming available in considerably larger numbers. In all, 122 were taken over from French orders, although 20 of these were to be lost when the SS *Ruprena*, carrying them to the UK, was torpedoed and sunk on 19 October 1940. Armed with four .50in Browning machine guns mounted in the aircraft's fixed wings, these were the export version of the US Navy's F4F-3 Wildcat. Its performance was at least equal to the RAF's Hurricane I.

The first unit to receive these new fighters as operational equipment was 804 Squadron, which received 12 during October. While a part of this unit was then removed to form a new 802 Squadron, similarly equipped, it was two of 804's pilots who were able to intercept and shoot down a reconnaissance Ju 88 over the Orkneys on Christmas Day 1940. Although the war still had many years to run, this proved to be the last Axis aircraft to be shot down by a UK-based Fleet Air Arm fighter.

No sooner had *Furious* off-loaded her cargo of fighters from the New World than she embarked 801 Squadron with its Skuas, together with the Swordfish of 816 and 825 Squadrons, and set sail to undertake anti-shipping attacks on Trondheim and Tromso during September and October, in which several more Skuas and Swordfish were lost.

During an attack launched on 9 September from Hatston, rather than from the deck of the carrier, one Skua was shot down by a Bf 109. A similar loss occurred on 2 October near Bergen, while next day two Skuas were damaged by five pursuing Messerschmitts while raiding Bjorne Fjord. These losses hammered home yet again that when faced with German fighters, the Skuas had small chance of survival. One further Skua had fallen to flak on 13 September.

The Swordfish of 825 Squadron, meanwhile, had launched the first night torpedo attack by a full squadron during one of these raids, but achieved no noteworthy results. It was the turn of their sister unit, 816 Squadron, to suffer grievous losses at this time, five of their Swordfish failing to return from one of the Trondheim attacks on 22 September.

Despite recent losses, 801 Squadron's Skuas continued to seek out targets off the coast of Norway. One of the last such sorties occurred on 27 December 1940, when five took off to attack shipping at Hagesund. One returned almost at once, but the other four, led by Lieutenant P.J. Connelly, completed the attack, returning safely to report damage to one ship.

While the Skua now disappeared as a first-line type in European skies, it is necessary to follow the fortunes of those units still flying these aircraft, and of much of the rest of the Fleet Air Arm, in the very different environment of the skies over the Mediterranean and North Africa.

OPPOSITE Designed to replace the Swordfish, the Fairey Albacore proved to be little better, although incorporating certain more modern features like an enclosed cockpit area. Equipping most of the new armoured carriers from 1941 onwards, the aircraft was not up to international performance standards, and in the event was actually outlived by the Swordfish. Here an aircraft of 820 Squadron from Formidable is seen in flight during the Operation 'Torch' landings in French North-West Africa in November 1942.

CHAPTER 13

IN THE MED

Force 'H' and the Mediterranean Fleet

With the reduction in activity in the North Sea and North Atlantic, most of the attention of the carrier force was now directed towards the Mediterranean, and to that part of the Atlantic relatively adjacent to Gibraltar commanding access to southern Europe, North Africa and the Middle East. It is necessary to do a little scene-setting first, however.

Upon re-equipment of her resident 802 Squadron with Sea Gladiators during 1939, HMS *Glorious* had off-loaded 18 spare aircraft in crates at Kalafrana, Malta, which could be drawn upon as replacements as necessary. When ordered urgently to the UK for operations over Norway in April 1940 she had picked up three of these, leaving 15 on the island.

To replace *Glorious* with the Mediterranean Fleet, HMS *Eagle* arrived through the Suez Canal, fresh from a refit in Singapore. With only TBR aircraft aboard, in the form of 18 Swordfish, and with Italian involvement in the war imminent, she drew four Sea Gladiators from stocks held in Egypt to provide some measure of air defence for the fleet. These were to be flown by a chosen group of Swordfish pilots serving with 813 Squadron and already aboard, led by Commander C.L. Keighley-Peach.

LEFT *HMS* Eagle *has her decks loaded with Spitfires for delivery to Malta. This will have been one of her last sorties prior to her loss on 11 August 1942.*

To replenish the stocks in Egypt, three of the crated Sea Gladiators on Malta were despatched to Alexandria forthwith. With the Italian declaration of war on 10 June, a further six of those remaining were released to the RAF, which maintained no fighters on this strategically important island. These became the initial equipment of an ad hoc fighter flight formed from flying boat and reconnaissance pilots; they were subsequently to gain considerable fame as the basis for the 'Faith, Hope and Charity' story which was later constructed around their activities.

Meanwhile, during November 1939 HMS *Argus* had delivered 767 Squadron to Poleyvestre, near Hyeres, in Southern France. Formed as a Deck Landing Training unit for TBR aircraft out of the surviving personnel of 811 and 822 Squadrons from the ill-fated *Courageous*, the squadron had been moved south to this location in order to allow training to continue without interruption by the winter weather in the UK. Immediately following the entry of Italy into the war, and the invasion by Italian forces of south-eastern France, nine of the unit's Swordfish had been armed with makeshift bombs and on 19 June had attacked targets in the Genoa area of northern Italy.

With the situation in France deteriorating rapidly, the 24 Swordfish on hand were flown to North Africa via Corsica. Here they were divided into two batches of 12, the more experienced crews then flying one batch to Hal Far on Malta, to become 830 Squadron, providing the island with a torpedo striking force. On arrival the few Swordfish floatplanes on the island with the RAF's 3 AACU (Anti-Aircraft Co-operation Unit) were incorporated into this new squadron, together with five RAF air gunners. The other 12 Swordfish were flown to Gibraltar for subsequent carriage home to England.

From their new base on Malta, 830 Squadron undertook its first sorties on 30 June, when a dive-bombing attack was undertaken against an oil refinery at Augusta, Sicily, albeit without any significant success.

Gibraltar was at this time becoming the base of the new Force 'H', which was formed under the command of Vice-Admiral Sir James Somerville on 28 June, following the arrival from the UK of HMS *Ark Royal* and the battlecruiser HMS *Hood*. Sadly, the first duty of this new fleet was to try and neutralise major elements of the French Fleet.

Here the Royal Navy faced a perplexing problem. Generally, the service possessed sufficient vessels to oppose the combined German and Italian Fleets adequately. However, should the French ships come under Axis control the balance of power would shift to the latter's advantage. Although most French ships had departed Metropolitan France to prevent just such a takeover, uncertainty as to the attitude and policies of the new Vichy government in France, together with strong suspicion that the Axis countries would not keep to their promise simply to decommission the French warships should they return home, as required by the terms of the Armistice, were matters of great concern to the British authorities.

In practice, quite a substantial proportion of the French Fleet had arrived either at the main British Mediterranean Fleet base at Alexandria, or at British ports, and it had proved possible for British forces to 'capture' all of these. However, the new 35,000-ton battleship *Richelieu* had left Brest and was making for Dakar in French West Africa, while her as yet uncommissioned sister ship, the *Jean Bart*, had got to Casablanca on the Atlantic coast of Morocco. All that remained in France were four heavy cruisers at Toulon. However, the bulk of the French Fleet was still in Algeria; this included six light cruisers at Algiers and, more importantly, two battlecruisers, two old battleships, six large destroyers, seven standard destroyers, four submarines and a seaplane carrier all at Mers-el-Kebir, near Oran. This represented a formidable force, about which it was considered that something had to be done. Thus it was that the first duty of the new Force 'H' was to deal with such elements of the French Navy as were in these North African ports.

On 3 July Force 'H', now increased in size by the arrival of two more capital ships, arrived off Oran, where the French vessels had not fired up their boilers. An attempt was made to try and persuade the Frenchmen to either come over to the British cause, or to sail to neutral ports where they could be decommissioned. These efforts failed, and action commenced accordingly. The French capital ships actually outgunned those of Force 'H', but the presence of *Ark Royal* appeared to swing the advantage in favour of the Royal Navy. Initially, therefore, Swordfish spotted for a dawn bombardment and laid mines at the entrance to Mers-el-Kebir to try and prevent any escape. The old battleship *Bretagne* blew up, while *Dunkerque* was damaged and was beached to save her. However, the fast modern *Strasbourg* and five of the large destroyers managed to slip past the mines and escape towards Bizerta in Tunisia. As they did so, two air strikes were launched against them, one by bomb-carrying Swordfish and one by six more armed with torpedoes. All achieved surprise, but nonetheless, no hits were obtained.

As *Dunkerque* showed no signs of significant damage despite her beaching, Somerville decided upon a torpedo strike against her, and consequently three days later on 6 July six 820 Squadron Swordfish undertook such an attack. Only one hit was obtained, and in this case the torpedo failed to detonate. However, one of the others had hit an armed trawler, the depth charges on which blew up violently, causing slight damage to the adjacent battleship.

Two follow-up strikes were launched, this time escorted by Skuas, one more hit on the *Dunkerque* being achieved. The Oran area was defended by the Curtiss Hawk 75A fighters of Groupe de Chasse II/5, pilots from this unit claiming Skuas shot down on each date, although the British aircrews reported that generally the French fighters – which considerably outperformed their own aircraft – did not press home their attacks. No Skua was in fact reported lost on 3 July, but on the 6th one was indeed brought down, although the crew was rescued.

While this melancholy action had been under way, HMS *Hermes* had been shadowing *Richelieu* for the past two weeks, hoping to capture her. As she reached Dakar, the British proposals were presented to her captain, but were refused. At dawn on 8 July, therefore, six Swordfish of 814 Squadron were launched to undertake a torpedo attack. This had to be delivered across two rows of moored merchant vessels and in the face of some fairly concentrated AA fire. Again, only a single hit was obtained, but in this case extensive damage was inflicted. *Richelieu*'s propeller shafts were twisted and the steering gear damaged, considerable flooding also occurring. With the limited repair facilities available at Dakar, *Richelieu* would be out of action for over a year, although her main 15-inch armament remained intact and useable.

At the eastern end of the Mediterranean, meanwhile, the first naval action against the new Italian foe began on 7 July when the Mediterranean Fleet sailed from Alexandria to provide cover for two convoys en route to Malta. These moves were quickly spotted by Italian reconnaissance aircraft next day, and air raids commenced at once.

In support of these moves, Force 'H' had sailed further into the Mediterranean from the west on 8 July, quickly coming under attack from *Regia Aeronautica* aircraft based in Sardinia. Following their rather uncomfortable encounters with the superior French fighters over Oran, the Skuas from *Ark Royal*'s two squadrons enjoyed more success against the multi-engined Italian aircraft, a trio from 800 Squadron shooting down a Cant Z.506B floatplane which was attempting to shadow the British vessels, while others from 803 Squadron shot down a Savoia S.79 from a bombing force which appeared later, also claiming damage to three more.

The successful crew comprised Acting Petty Officer A.W. Theobald and Naval Airman F. de Frias. The latter later recounted:

'Throughout the day the Italians had pressed home medium-level attacks on the Force; the Italians were pretty efficient and determined. They stayed in formation and were frighteningly good with their bombing. We took off at 1920, warned to expect a large formation. Fortunately we were able to get to 10–12,000 feet before they came in below us. Gibson [Acting Lieutenant D.C.E.F. Gibson] led the Section down in a diving turn to get at them and for some reason Theo didn't get a decent burst in. But we ended up flying straight and level with the enemy leader only 40–50 feet on our starboard beam. I could hardly believe it was happening as I opened up with the Lewis on a simple no-deflection shot using the nose of the enemy as an aiming point. After my first aiming burst the S.79 appeared to go nose down so I gave it the rest of the 100-round pan. Before I had finished, a side hatch opened and at least two people, perhaps three, baled out. The aircraft went into a dive and I caught a glimpse of it going into the sea before it went out of my vision behind the tailplane.'

De Frias was later awarded a DSM, mainly for this exploit.

The action now moved to the Mediterranean Fleet, nine Swordfish from 813 Squadron on *Eagle* making a night attack on Augusta harbour, Sicily, on 9 July, hoping to find elements of the Italian Fleet moored there. Only a few vessels were actually present, but the destroyer *Leone Pancaldo* was sunk. Two days later the British ships were again discovered, S.79s from both Sicily and Libya commencing a series of raids, 16 of which were recorded during the day. These provided *Eagle*'s little fighter flight the opportunity to achieve its first success, Charles Keighley-Peach being the pilot involved. As he and Acting Lieutenant L.K. Keith began a patrol during the early afternoon five S.79s were spotted approaching about 2,000ft below the fighters. Both dived vertically to attack, Keighley-Peach making three such passes on one bomber on the left of the formation. This dropped back, spewing black smoke which soon turned to flames.

It then went into a spin towards the sea, the crew being seen to bale out, although they were never found.

Lieutenant Lloyd Keith, the other pilot involved, was a Canadian, and one of the few RAF pilots who had transferred to the Fleet Air Arm in May 1939. This pair were airborne again next morning, when Keighley-Peach claimed another S.79 shot down. On a subsequent patrol, still before midday, they encountered three more S.79s south of Crete and obviously coming from Rhodes, and each claimed one of these shot down. In two days the Sea Gladiators had thus disposed of four bombers without loss, totally vindicating the decision to include them in *Eagle*'s air group.

Having undertaken so many raids during the past few days in both basins of the Mediterranean, the *Regia Aeronautica* had become convinced that it had reduced British naval power in the area by 50 per cent, but the *Regia Marina* – the Italian Navy – doubted it. They were right to do so, for in practice all that had been achieved during all these raids on the two British fleets had been a single hit

on a cruiser which had done no serious damage. Level bombing against naval vessels under way and defending themselves was proving to be a far less rewarding and effective form of attack than the proponents of aerial bombardment had anticipated!

Following this series of actions, *Eagle*'s Sea Gladiators were engaged again on 29 July whilst providing cover for a convoy approaching Alexandria. Two formations each of three S.79s were seen at 15,000ft and were engaged at once by Lieutenant Keith and Lieutenant P.W.V. Massy. Keith fired at two, but both broke away and escaped him. Massy, however, attacked the second trio and sent the right-hand aircraft flaming into the sea, two members of the crew baling out and being rescued by HMS *Capetown*. Massy had outrun his fuel supply during his pursuit of his quarry, and as a result was obliged to ditch near one of the destroyers escorting the convoy, HMAS *Stuart*, which picked him up safely.

Although Malta had been able to enhance its air defences with a handful of Hurricanes, which

had reached the island overland just before the fall of France, by the latter part of July it remained desperately short of fighter aircraft, and, indeed, of trained pilots to fly them. It transpired that a group of RAF NCO pilots had been trained for deck landing earlier in the year, but had declined an offer to transfer to the Fleet Air Arm and had joined fighter squadrons in the UK instead, their specialist skills unutilised. Now, however, they were called together and ordered to collect Hurricanes from a Maintenance Unit and fly them up to Glasgow, where they were to go aboard *Argus* for ultimate delivery to Malta. *Argus* departed Greenock on 23 July with 12 Hurricanes and two Skuas aboard – the latter to act as navigators on the flight to the island.

Arriving at Gibraltar, the carrier sailed into the Mediterranean escorted by Force 'H' to undertake this important delivery task. Initially, the pilots were ordered to take off on 1 August, but refused point-blank as the range was manifestly too great. However, Operation 'Hurry' was successfully achieved next day, two flights – each of six Hurricanes and one Skua – taking off to make the long flight. In the event all arrived safely, although one crashed on landing.

As Force 'H' and *Argus* turned back, 800 Squadron's Skuas intercepted two shadowers and claimed both shot down. One Z.506B floatplane was indeed lost, but a Z.501 flying boat escaped with severe damage. Fourteen Swordfish were launched by *Ark Royal* to attack Cagliari airfield on Sardinia; one 810 Squadron aircraft crashed into the sea on take-off, while a second failed to return from this sortie.

With Malta's defences thereby strengthened, its striking force resumed offensive operations. During the night of 13 August nine of 830 Squadron's Swordfish again attacked Augusta harbour, three of the raiders carrying torpedoes. This latter trio went in low, but were effectively wiped out: two aircraft were shot down over the target, one crew being killed and the other captured, while the third was badly damaged, and when it got back to the island its pilot was obliged to ditch in the sea off Hal Far.

Shortly after this raid the Mediterranean Fleet put out again, this time to undertake an attack on the important harbour at Bardia on the Libyan coast. During the return voyage to Alexandria a series of Italian bombing raids occurred during 17 August. On this occasion *Eagle*'s fighter flight had flown ashore to Sidi Barrani, from where a number of patrols were flown over the fleet in which the naval pilots were joined by Gladiators of the RAF's 112 Squadron.

When five S.79s approached at 1040 hours, Commander Keighley-Peach climbed to try and cut off their retreat but became separated from the other intercepting fighters. Realising that there was little to be gained by chasing the fast bombers, which could match the Sea Gladiator for speed, he headed back over the fleet just as two more formations appeared. Making three attacks on one of these, he saw it shed a variety of bits and pieces and go into a shallow dive as one member of the crew baled out. However, this opponent then disappeared into cloud and he was only able to claim it as a 'probable'. Meanwhile, the other two Sea Gladiators, flown by Lieutenants Keith and A.N. Young, together with an RAF pilot, had attacked another S.79 which was seen to burst into flames and crash into the sea, two members of the crew baling out. Other RAF pilots claimed five more Savoias, although on this occasion the total Italian bomber losses actually amounted to four shot down and eight damaged.

The fleet was sent out again on 22 August, to cover another convoy and hunt for the Italian Fleet, which had reportedly put to sea. No hostile warships were encountered, but on 31 August Commander Keighley-Peach was scrambled from *Eagle* with one other pilot to intercept a shadower near Kythera Island. Recalled Keighley-Peach:

> *'Off Crete I came across a Cant Z.506B – I think the crew must have been asleep as I was offered no opposition and felt I was almost committing murder – it was so easy. The Cant ditched off the coast of Crete and I saw the crew descend via parachutes and they must have landed close enough to land to be able to swim ashore.'*

This proved to be the fourth confirmed victory in which this pilot had been involved, all claimed while flying the same Sea Gladiator – N5517.

An exciting new development occurred on this same date with the entry into the Mediterranean of the new armoured carrier HMS *Illustrious*, accompanied by the battleship HMS *Valiant*, which was to depart Force 'H' and accompany the new carrier to join Admiral Cunningham's Mediterranean Fleet.

It will be recalled that the outbreak of war had found the Admiralty still without its new shipboard fighter, the Fairey Fulmar, available. The first prototype had flown in January 1940, the second following in April. There were no major teething troubles, and by June 12 production examples had been delivered. The following month 806 Squadron had become the first unit to receive them to replace its remaining Skuas and Rocs. The big two-seater carried eight .303in Browning

ABOVE *Fleet Air Arm pilots flew borrowed RAF Hurricanes on several occasions in the Middle East during 1941. Fully modified deck-landing Sea Hurricanes became available in growing numbers from early 1942, and a considerable number of naval squadrons were equipped with these aircraft. Already obsolescent, the type had generally been phased out of first line units by the end of 1943.*

machine guns in its wings, as did the RAF's Spitfires and Hurricanes at that time. However, its second seat, wing-folding mechanism, arrester hook and other deck-landing equipment amounted to a considerably greater load for the Merlin engine to haul around, so although rugged, reliable and surprisingly manoeuvrable, its top speed suffered. It could manage only 265mph at best – well below that of even the Mark I Hurricane or the Grumman Martlet. At least it was some 20mph faster than the Sea Gladiator, which would allow it to catch the majority of the Italian bombers it would meet.

806 Squadron, still commanded by Charles Evans, had taken the Fulmar aboard the new *Illustrious* for the first time in August 1940. Here it was joined by the 24 Swordfish of 815 and 819 Squadrons – the Albacores were still not available in sufficient numbers to allow them also to grace the new carrier.

Illustrious and *Valiant* were escorted by Force 'H' as far as the Sicilian Narrows, where they were to be met by the Mediterranean Fleet. Both vessels were also equipped with RDF (or radar,

as it subsequently became known), which would provide a further great and valuable advantage to the British fleet.

As the ships set off, *Ark Royal*'s Skuas were in action again, shooting down a Z.506B, followed two hours later by a Z.501. Next day, 1 September, the Fulmars got off to a bad start. Patrolling Skuas intercepted an intruder which, after an exchange of recognition flares, proved to be a long-range photo-reconnaissance Hudson of the RAF. At that moment, however, a trio of Fulmars appeared on the scene, the leading aircraft flown by Lieutenant Commander Robin Kilroy, formerly the commanding officer of 815 Squadron but now on his way to take command of the Dekheila naval air base at Alexandria. He had volunteered to fly one of the Fulmars, and unfortunately attacked the Hudson, inflicting substantial damage before realising his mistake and breaking away. The crippled Hudson, with two of the crew wounded, landed at Tunis, where all aboard were interned, although the wounded received immediate hospital treatment.

That night *Ark Royal*'s Swordfish undertook two attacks on Cagliari airfield as a diversion to the passage of the two warships, these raids being entitled Operations 'Smash' and 'Grab'.

Good progress towards the rendezvous with the Mediterranean Fleet, to the south of Malta, was being made on 2 September when Italian shadowers finally discovered *Illustrious* and her battleship escort. A trio of 806 Squadron's fighters, led by 'Crash' Evans, caught and shot down one Z.501 – the Fulmar's first victory of the war. However, their victim had been able to radio the position and composition of the British force, and raids by S.79s and Italian-flown Junkers Ju 87 'Stuka' dive-bombers were prepared.

The first S.79s to appear were met by nine Fulmars, one bomber being shot down and two damaged. Somewhat later more of these bombers appeared, four being claimed shot down and two more damaged, one of which was thought to have been finished off by the ships' AA guns. Actual Italian losses during these two attacks amounted to three shot down and two more damaged. One

Fulmar, the pilot of which subsequently claimed to have shot down two of the four bombers claimed, was hit and damaged. Lieutenant A.J. Sewell was then guided to Malta by a second Fulmar, both landing there. Sewell and his observer were later collected by a Swordfish and flown back to their carrier.

The arrival of *Illustrious* and these actions by her fighters led Admiral Cunningham to state: 'Seldom has a fleet had a greater boost to its morale, and from that moment on the whole picture changed.' It certainly did, for now the *Regia Aeronautica* found itself faced not by a tiny handful of elderly biplanes, but by a full squadron of much more modern aircraft – which the Italians initially identified as being carrier-borne Hurricanes.

Immediately after joining forces with the Mediterranean Fleet, the two carriers continued eastwards to launch an attack on Italian airfields on the Aegean island of Rhodes. At dawn on 4 September *Illustrious* launched her Swordfish to attack Calato airfield. *Eagle*'s 813 and 824 Squadrons followed, but became delayed, and arrived to find the defences fully alerted and a number of Fiat CR.32 and CR.42 biplane fighters in the air. Against these the Swordfish were nearly helpless and four of the attackers were shot down, two falling into the sea and one force-landing on the island of Scarpanto. One crew was picked up from the sea by an Italian submarine, but of the total of 12 aircrew involved four were killed and all the rest became prisoners. At Gadurra airfield 30 high-explosive and 20 incendiary bombs had destroyed two S.79s, damaging three more plus two Cant Z.1007 bombers, an S.81 and an S.82 transport. They had also destroyed a considerable quantity of fuel, oil and bombs.

Patrolling off the island, Fulmars shot down one S.79 and damaged three more, while Lieutenant Commander Kilroy – again flying one of 806 Squadron's aircraft – and Sub-Lieutenant S.G. Orr shared in shooting down a tri-motor transport which they identified as a Caproni 133 (it was actually another Savoia S.81).

The next sortie by the Mediterranean Fleet occurred on 17 September when a strike was launched against the Libyan port of Benghazi, where two destroyers and four merchant vessels were sunk and a fifth merchantman was badly damaged.

Thereafter, the carrier sorties were generally timed to coincide with the running of convoys to Malta to support the defence of that island. The first such operation took place on 28 September, when *Illustrious*, *Warspite* and *Valiant* put to sea with a force of cruisers and destroyers to cover two more cruisers which were carrying troops and supplies to the island. Many air attacks were launched by the Italians, but none were to gain any success. Next day a Z.501 was brought down by 806 Squadron Fulmars, though one of the latter was hit by return fire, Sub-Lieutenant Lowe ditching this aircraft a few minutes later; he was picked up by the ubiquitous HMAS *Stuart*. Three hours later another Z.501 fell to Sub-Lieutenant Stanley Orr, while on 1 October a third shadower fell victim to the CO, 'Crash' Evans.

In the meantime Force 'H' had sailed out into the Atlantic to take part in a new attempt to subdue the Vichy French. Unaware of the level of damage inflicted on *Richelieu* in July, Operation 'Menace' was to be an attempt to land Free French forces south of Dakar in the mistaken belief that the Vichy defenders would not fire on their fellow countrymen, and that the port might thereby be occupied unopposed. Indeed, it had been the intention of General Charles de Gaulle to set up the headquarters of his planned government in exile here. However, the authorities were swiftly disabused of these notions and the operation became a fiasco.

Force 'H' arrived off Dakar on 23 September. Swordfish from *Ark Royal* plus two Caudron Luciolle aircraft which were aboard then flew Free French representatives ashore, while leaflets were dropped. The French authorities ashore remained loyal to the Vichy regime, however, refusing to negotiate with the General. Coastal batteries and the battleship *Richelieu*'s guns opened fire, while French submarines left harbour in an attempt to torpedo some of the British and Free French ships. A trio of Curtiss Hawk fighters intercepted one of the Swordfish, their fire wounding all three members of the crew. The pilot, Lieutenant N.R. Corbett-Milward, managed to escape and crash-land on *Ark Royal*, the crew believing they had shot down one of their attackers. In fact it appears that the French pilot had pulled out of his attacking dive too low and had crashed into the sea.

Next day Skuas and Swordfish attempted to attack, but missed the main warships, although inflicting some damage on shore installations. The Curtiss Hawks were in evidence again, on this occasion shooting down two of 810 Squadron's Swordfish while a third was brought down by a Hawk and the crew of a Loire 130 amphibian.

Raids continued on the 25th, during which an 820 Squadron Swordfish was damaged by AA and fighters, the Curtiss Hawk pilots also shooting down a Walrus amphibian launched by HMAS *Australia*. By the 26th several British ships had been hit, including the battleship *Barham*, whilst one of the French submarines had put a torpedo into a second battleship, HMS *Resolution*.

In return, two of the Vichy submarines had been sunk. At much the same time one of the British battleships at last managed to gain a direct hit on *Richelieu*. However, neither she nor any of the three cruisers in harbour were seriously damaged, and Force 'H' withdrew, *Ark Royal* heading for the UK for some urgent repairs.

As it transpired, at the time of this departure the Governor of Dakar had been in the process of drafting his proposed conditions for a surrender. The operation did, however, teach the Royal Navy one salutary lesson – Swordfish would never again be despatched to undertake a torpedo attack on a defended location by the light of day.

The next convoy support operation for the Mediterranean Fleet, commenced on 12 October, brought out the *Regia Aeronautica* in force, 84 bomber and 38 fighter sorties being launched against the British ships. *Eagle* was near-missed by a dozen bombs, suffering some damage from their shockwaves. 806 Squadron's Fulmars were in the air constantly, shooting down two S.79s and a Z.501 shadower, and damaging another S.79. A fourth of these bombers then flew into a mountain during its return journey. Next day a lone S.79 was damaged by one of the Sea Gladiators still aboard *Eagle*. Early in November the fleet was out again, 806 Squadron's Sub-Lieutenant Sewell accounting for another Z.506B shadower.

It was the turn of Force 'H' next, escorting a convoy carrying troops to Malta from Gibraltar on 7 November. Three of 800 Squadron's Skuas were to shoot down yet another Z.506B, the victorious crews watching as the floatplane force-landed on the sea, the Italian crew then getting out and waving white cloths in surrender.

Next day a further convoy set out from Alexandria at the other end of the Mediterranean, some ships heading for Malta and others for Greece and Crete. For this sortie two of *Eagle*'s three remaining Sea Gladiators had been borrowed from the damaged carrier to reinforce *Illustrious*, and in the hands of Lieutenant Nicholls and Sub-Lieutenant Sewell these accounted for a Z.501.

More success followed that afternoon when three Fulmar pilots attacked seven bombers, claiming three damaged, Lieutenant Commander Evans then claiming one more shot down. Another Z.506B was shot down by Stanley Orr on the 9th, while on the 10th Lieutenant Barnes and Sub-Lieutenant Sewell (the latter back in a Fulmar) brought down a Z.501 and claimed damage to an S.79, which did actually fail to return to base.

While this was going on *Ark Royal* had returned briefly to Gibraltar, where 803 Squadron went ashore for return to the UK and was replaced by a new unit, the second to be formed on Fulmars; this was 808 Squadron, commanded by Lieutenant Rupert Tillard. The carrier then immediately put to sea again to launch a diversionary attack on Cagliari airfield in aid of a Mediterranean Fleet action by *Illustrious* which will be detailed below. Here on 8 November Lieutenant Tillard gained his new unit's first success, shooting down an S.79 south of Sardinia.

The following day's actions swiftly showed that this was no 'flash in the pan', for as Swordfish from 810, 818 and 820 Squadrons again attacked Sardinian targets, Tillard sent a Z.506B into the sea. A large formation of S.79s from Sardinia's Decimommanu airfield then attacked, and Tillard was successful in shooting down one of these too. The Skua pilots of 800 Squadron were not to be denied their share, joining the fight and claiming many hits; 18 of the 20 S.79s involved did indeed suffer damage on this occasion.

A photo-reconnaissance Martin Maryland from Malta's 431 Flight had meanwhile spotted that the greater part of the Italian Fleet was presently anchored in Taranto harbour in southern Italy. Alerted to this, *Illustrious* did not return from her sortie in support of the convoys on which she had embarked on 7 November, but instead headed out to strike at this tempting target. It was in support of this action that *Ark Royal*'s units had been engaged over and around Sardinia, as described above.

Thus it was that during the night of 11/12 November 1940, *Illustrious*'s Swordfish squadrons undertook what subsequently became the Fleet Air Arm's most celebrated achievement. Two waves of Swordfish undertook the attack, which went in by night to gain maximum surprise. They sank the battleship *Conte di Cavour*, caused *Caio Dulio* to be beached in sinking condition, and inflicted heavy damage on *Littorio*. The seaplane base was also wrecked, the whole raid being achieved for the loss of just two aircraft, one from each strike; only one crew lost their lives.

As soon as the returning aircraft had been landed on, the carrier and her escorts made all speed towards Alexandria in anticipation of massive air attacks with the arrival of daylight. But the Italians had to find the fleeing ships first, and shadowers were out searching all day. A very successful series of patrols by 806 Squadron's Fulmars made this a difficult task, shooting down three of the Italian reconnaissance aircraft before they could find anything, a fourth being brought down the next day. It was therefore some time before the first bombers appeared, and these failed to inflict any damage. Meanwhile, 431 Flight's

Maryland was out again to gather photographic evidence of the mayhem caused at Taranto.

Subsequently, Admiral Sir Andrew Cunningham recorded:

'Taranto and the night of 11–12 November 1940, should be remembered for ever as having shown once and for all that, in the Fleet Air Arm the Navy has its most devastating weapon. In a total flying-time of about six and a half hours – carrier to carrier – 20 aircraft had inflicted more damage upon the Italian fleet than was inflicted upon the German High Seas Fleet in the daylight action at the Battle of Jutland.'

This great victory for the Royal Navy was studied with immense interest by the naval staffs of other nations, not least by those of the Imperial Japanese Navy who were to glean lessons which proved of considerable assistance little more than a year later when their carrier fleet attacked the Americans at Pearl Harbor.

In the Mediterranean area there had been a significant development during October, when Benito Mussolini, the Italian dictator, launched his army from Albania into north-western Greece, anticipating an easy victory that would allow him to add that country to his new Roman Empire. In the event the Greeks responded with energy and courage, not only halting the invaders but actually driving them back across the frontier. It became imperative for the British to provide aid, and while the Greek government was anxious not to have Allied troops on their soil for fear of provoking a German reaction, the assistance of air force units was eagerly sought. This allowed the British access to the strategically important island of Crete, where bases were rapidly established on the north coast. It was for this reason that a proportion of the reinforcement and supply convoys now passing through Suez and heading north were making for this destination rather than Malta.

That latter island was now due some further reinforcement, and consequently on 17 November *Argus* – which had just arrived at Gibraltar carrying 12 Hurricanes and two guiding Skuas – headed into the Mediterranean escorted by Force 'H'. The fighters were launched at maximum range in two flights of six, each led by a Skua. However, the wind changed just as the first batch got under way, and by the time Galite Island was reached the Hurricanes were very low on fuel. Here they were joined by a Sunderland flying boat to escort them over the rest of the route. Two pilots were forced to bale out when their fuel level reached zero, but both were swiftly rescued by the Sunderland. The Skua and the four remaining fighters just made it to Malta.

The second flight was less fortunate. Firstly, the Sunderland with which they were to rendezvous did not appear. They then missed Galite Island and became hopelessly lost, all six Hurricanes ultimately going down into the sea with the loss of all the pilots. Though the Skua just managed to reach land this proved to be southern Sicily, and the crew were taken prisoner after they crash-landed.

A week or so later Force 'H' was out again, this time to escort a convoy of three transports carrying armoured vehicles and other supplies that were needed urgently by General Sir Archibald Wavell's army in Egypt, and were therefore sent directly through the Mediterranean rather than via the long route around the Cape and through Suez. The covering force was to meet strong elements of the Mediterranean Fleet which were despatched to the south of Sardinia. Operation 'Collar' commenced for Force 'H' on 25 November when it sailed from Gibraltar. Next day came news that the Italian Fleet had put to sea, and on the 27th battleships, cruisers and destroyers were spotted off Cape Spartivento, Sardinia, by Malta's ever-reliable reconnaissance aircraft. Fulmars from 808 Squadron shot down an early Z.506B shadower, but the crew of a Meridionali Ro 43 catapult floatplane from the cruiser *Bolzano* spotted the British ships.

Swordfish and Malta-based Sunderlands now began shadowing the Italian force, which comprised two battleships, three cruisers and 11 destroyers. At 1125 hours 11 Swordfish from 810 Squadron, led by Lieutenant Commander M. Johnstone, left *Ark Royal* to attack the Italians. An hour later they launched their torpedoes at the battleships, and believed that they had achieved a hit on *Vittorio Veneto*, whereas in fact all the torpedoes had missed. The leading British warships opened fire at 1220 at long range, as the Italians were now seeking to avoid Admiral Somerville's much stronger force. Despite the range, some damage was caused to the destroyer *Lanciere* which the British thought was a cruiser and for which *Ark Royal*'s aircraft were to search throughout the rest of the day.

At 1407 nine more Swordfish, this time from 820 Squadron, were preparing to take off when an incoming raid was detected. Seven Fulmars were on patrol and were directed to intercept as the Swordfish, led by Lieutenant Commander J.A. Stewart-Moore, got under way. They were ordered to search for the damaged Italian warship, which they failed to find. Instead they came upon the main force, launching torpedoes at a cruiser on which they believed two hits were obtained; again they were wrong – all the torpedoes had missed.

Above Force 'H', meanwhile, ten S.79s escorted by five CR.42 fighters were attacked by the Fulmars, the pilots of which claimed two or three bombers shot down. The S.79s held their formation and bombed the fleet, but missed. Lieutenant Tillard's section then attacked one flight of three Savoias, claiming one of these shot down, but at this point the escorting CR.42s struck. These had been mistaken for Sea Gladiators by the naval crews, most of whom had used up all their ammunition against the bombers in any event. In consequence one Fulmar was shot down into the sea with the loss of its crew. Eight of the S.79s had been hit, either by Fulmars or AA, but all managed to return to base on this occasion. However, a Vichy French four-engined civil Farman 223.4 (F-AROA, named 'Le Verrier') had somehow blundered into the fight and was shot down – apparently by fighters – with the loss of its crew of five and two passengers, one of whom was M. Jean Chiappe, the High Commissioner to Syria and the Lebanon.

Shortly after this engagement seven 800 Squadron Skuas set off, led by Lieutenant Smeeton, to try and dive-bomb the elusive damaged Italian destroyer. *Lanciere* was again not found, but three vessels identified as cruisers were spotted south-west of Sardinia and were dive-bombed, two near misses being claimed. On their return flight to *Ark Royal* the pilots did spot a lone Ro 43, the little float biplane having come from *Vittorio Veneto*'s catapult. It had run short of fuel and its crew were trying to reach Sardinia. It was now attacked by four Skuas and fell into the sea in flames.

Finally, late in the afternoon ten more S.79s attacked, this time without an escort. Fulmars and Skuas intercepted them and nine of the raiders were hit, of which two were badly damaged.

In support of Operation 'Collar', *Illustrious* undertook a diversionary assault on targets in the Aegean, for which purpose an additional six Fulmars had been embarked. These reinforcements came from 805 Squadron, which was being formed as a land-based unit at Dekheila for the defence of the Alexandria naval base. This was the squadron's second existence, for it had previously been formed at the naval base airfield at Donibristle in May 1940, where it had been intended to equip it with 18 examples of a floatplane version of the Blackburn Roc for operations over Norwegian waters. It was perhaps fortunate for the crews intended to serve with this unit that this proposal was swiftly abandoned, and it had been disbanded within a few days. Reportedly, it only re-formed in

The Mediterranean

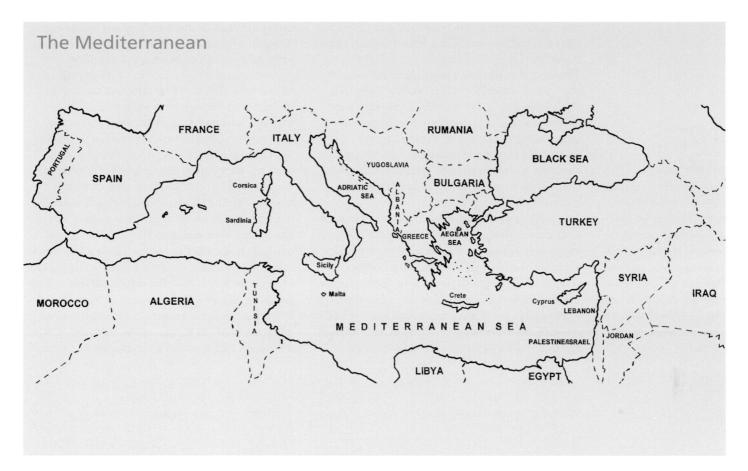

Egypt at the start of 1941, but there is no doubt that it existed at least as a flight some weeks earlier, commanded by Lieutenant Commander A.F. Black.

Three Fulmars from each squadron were on patrol when the carrier approached Malta on 28 November, when six CR.42s appeared on a reconnaissance. The 805 Squadron trio engaged, but the still-inexperienced pilots found the Fiats too manoeuvrable to hold in their sights. Not so the 806 trio which then appeared, Sub-Lieutenant Orr shooting down one 30 miles off the coast of Sicily, while the other two pilots claimed the other two damaged. One Fulmar was hit in return, its observer being slightly wounded.

The Italians remained very active as the 'Collar' convoy and Force 'H' approached, but the safe arrival of the ships in Egypt put the finishing touches to Wavell's plans to launch his first offensive in North Africa as Operation 'Compass'. The attack opened on 9 December 1940, gaining immediate success which was rapidly exploited. The Italian army was driven back across the border into Libya, having crossed it in the opposite direction during the previous September. Losing vast numbers of men as prisoners, together with large quantities of guns, tanks and other munitions, the Italians continued to fall back, allowing the Imperial force's assault to become a full-scale

offensive which occupied the whole province of Cyrenaica, including the ports of Sollum, Bardia, Tobruk and ultimately Benghazi.

In support of this offensive, *Illustrious* and *Eagle* literally went on a rampage. Bardia was bombed on 12 December, while the airfields on Rhodes and Stampalia were attacked on the 16th. On the 21st *Illustrious*'s Swordfish sank two cargo vessels off the eastern coast of Tunisia, near Sfax, as they were making for Tripoli, while next day 15 Swordfish raided Tripoli itself. The carriers finally returned to Alexandria on Christmas Day 1940, their only loss during this series of attacks having been a single Swordfish on the 21st.

The great successes gained by the Imperial forces in North Africa, coupled with the ill-fated Italian adventure in Greece – which had itself come as an unwelcome shock to Adolf Hitler, who was planning his assault on the Soviet Union – resulted in Hitler's decision to despatch a German 'rescue package' to the Italians. Elements of the Luftwaffe began flying into Sicily to start clearing the Mediterranean of British shipping, while troops prepared for shipment to Libya, where an *Afrika Korps* was to be formed under the command of General Erwin Rommel.

Against this ominous backdrop, instead of seeking to reinforce with all speed the exhausted troops who had just undertaken the great 'Compass' offensive, and now stood with little remaining heavy equipment on the Cyrenaican/Tripolitanian border, Winston Churchill – the British Prime Minister since May 1940 – insisted instead upon the despatch of all available units to Greece. Malta was now clearly identified as the key to interrupting the Axis supply routes to North Africa from southern Europe, and reinforcement of the island became of ever greater importance. Early in January 1941, therefore, a new convoy to the area was prepared under the codename Operation 'Excess'.

'Excess' got off to a bad start. Its vessels formed part of a much larger convoy which included the carriers *Furious* and *Argus*, and the cruiser *Berwick*. The two carriers were loaded with large numbers of Hurricanes for the Middle East, stowed below decks with the wings removed. On 25 December there was a brush with the German cruiser *Hipper* as the convoy approached Gibraltar, Force 'H' sailing immediately to hunt for the raider. At Gibraltar the 'Excess' ships left the rest of the convoy, turning towards the Mediterranean while the other ships headed towards West Africa. Because of the departure of Force 'H' into the Atlantic in search of *Hipper*, the five merchant vessels for the 'Excess' convoy were held at Gibraltar until an escort force became available.

Before proceeding with the story of Operation 'Excess', it is worth noting what was happening with the other part of the convoy. On arrival off Sierre Leone, two naval squadrons aboard *Furious* were flown off to Bathurst, both carriers then continuing south where on 9 January the Hurricanes were all flown off to Takoradi, Gold Coast. This was already a familiar duty for these two carriers, *Argus* having carried its first 30 Hurricanes to this area on 6 September, whilst during November *Furious* had delivered 73 Squadron's air party here. From Takoradi a long supply route had been established right across Central Africa to Sudan and Egypt, and would provide one of the

BELOW *Fairey Fulmars taking off from HMS* Ark Royal *with Force 'H' early in 1941. It is probable that these were aircraft of 803 Squadron, and that the Skuas at the stern were with 800 Squadron shortly before that unit also re-equipped with Fulmars.*

main routes for new aircraft to the Western Desert for the next two years.

Of the five vessels awaiting escort at Gibraltar, meanwhile, four were earmarked for the port of Piraeus in Greece, while the fifth was bound for Malta, carrying amongst its cargo 12 crated Hurricanes to make good the losses sustained during the November delivery by *Argus*. One of the former ships ran aground whilst at Gibraltar and was too badly damaged to continue.

The remaining four ships finally sailed on 6 January, with Force 'H' following the next day, *Ark Royal* included. At the same time the greater part of the Mediterranean Fleet sailed to meet them, *Illustrious* with 806 Squadron at its strongest yet in numbers of aircraft to hand, and with three 805 Squadron Fulmars again attached. Rumours of a German intervention in the area were rife, and indeed, the Junkers Ju 87 dive-bombers of three Luftwaffe *Gruppen* arrived in Sicily during the morning of 10 January, flying in to Trapani airfield. The Mediterranean had suddenly become a much more dangerous environment for the Royal Navy.

A day earlier *Ark Royal* flew off six Swordfish of a unit known as 821X Squadron to reinforce 830 Squadron on Malta. 821 Squadron had been disbanded a month earlier, but these six aircraft had been formed into an *ad hoc* operational flight and shipped down to Gibraltar on *Argus*. During the same day ten S.79s approached Force 'H', but 808 Squadron's Fulmars were ready for them and two were shot down by the indefatigable Lieutenant Tillard. For his recent run of successes, he and his observer, Lieutenant Somerville, would now be awarded DSCs. Three of 800 Squadron's Skuas were also in the air, and these encountered a trio of CR.42s. Not only were they able to avoid these fighters' attack without suffering damage, but one pilot was able to claim hits on one of them.

By 10 January Force 'H' had reached a point 25 miles north of Bizerta, and turned back. The 'Excess' convoy continued east, escorted by two cruisers, but already during the night the Mediterranean Fleet had made contact, and at dawn on the 10th all ships were west of Sicily – a point of considerable danger. Two groups of merchant ships had also sailed from Malta in order to gain the protection of the warships guarding the 'Excess' vessels. One group of two fast transports were to accompany the convoy to Piraeus, while six slower ships were to head for Alexandria.

During the morning Swordfish from *Illustrious* bombed an Italian convoy making for Africa, the aircraft then landing aboard. Other Swordfish were out on anti-submarine patrols and two sections of Fulmars totalling five aircraft were also on patrol.

The carrier was sailing between the battleships *Warspite* and *Valiant* – a position which provided good anti-aircraft and anti-submarine protection, but which restricted the carrier's ability to manoeuvre fast. At 1030 hours a single S.79 was encountered and shot down by Lieutenant R.S. Henley and Sub-Lieutenant Sewell, but the latter's aircraft was hit by return fire and he had to turn back to the carrier. Henley and the other remaining Fulmar pilot then engaged two S.79s, both of which he claimed to have damaged.

Two torpedo-carrying S.79sil aircraft then approached at very low level, well below the radar screen, and launched their missiles at *Illustrious*, but missed (these may have been the same two Savoias which Henley had just attacked). Sub-Lieutenants Orr and Hogg gave chase and claimed to have shot one down. In fact only one of this pair of bombers was hit during the attack, and this subsequently crashed while landing as a result of the damage it sustained.

By midday all of the available Ju 87s which had so recently arrived at Trapani were readied for operations. These included aircraft from *Hauptmann* Werner Hozzel's I./StG 1 and Major Walter Enneccerus's II./StG 2. Torpedo-carrying S.79sil of the *Regia Aeronautica*'s specialist 279 *Squadriglia* were also available at this airfield, and a few Italian-flown Ju 87s of 236 *Squadriglia* were on hand too.

At 1235 hours four more Fulmars were launched just as the force of Stukas, assessed as being 24–36 strong, appeared on the horizon. Efforts were at once made to get more Fulmars up on deck, but the first of these refused to start. A second – flown by Lieutenant Barnes with Lieutenant Vincent-Jones, the temporary CO, as observer – swerved past it and got into the air just as the attack began.

One of those which had already taken off was piloted by Sub-Lieutenant Sewell, back from his recent brush with the first S.79. His TAG, Leading Aircraftman Denis Tribe, recorded:

'We were at readiness on the flight deck and took off before Illustrious was into wind. Before we were at 2,000ft, the first bomb from a Ju 87 hit the ship. It went into the open lift well and exploded in the hangar – it was really horrific to watch as you realised how many would be blown to bits – also a very close escape. As we climbed to attack, the Stukas were diving to bomb. When we reached height the air seemed full of aircraft. From the rear seat I saw one go down and another was damaged. It wasn't long before we were out of ammunition and landed at Hal Far.'

Sub-Lieutenant Lowe was also seen to shoot down a Ju 87, but another got on his tail, fire from this killing his observer and disabling the aircraft. He ditched near HMS *Nubian*, but the aircraft sank almost at once and the destroyer's crew did not see him get out. Luckily, he was spotted half an hour later and picked up by HMS *Jaguar*. Two more Ju 87s were thought to have been shot down at this time, but climbing into the melee Lieutenant Barnes was faced with too many targets to concentrate on any one, so simply sprayed as many as he could get his sights on before also making for Malta. As he did so, over the radio came the order: 'All Fulmars proceed to Hal Far to refuel and rearm before returning over ship at best speed.' On arrival he found four other Fulmars which had landed there after pursuing the various Savoias, all ready to go, and his aircraft soon joined these.

The dive-bombing attack had been near perfect, the Ju 87s diving from 12,000 to 2,000ft. Six bombs hit the carrier, wrecking the flight deck and superstructure. Nine Swordfish and five Fulmars were destroyed and half the guns put out of action. The captain pulled the ship out of line and was ordered to make for Malta. However, it was three hours before she could be got under way, steering by the main engines as her steering gear had been put out of action.

Another aircraft to be lost was a Swordfish flown by Lieutenant Charles Lamb of 815 Squadron, who had been trying to land on as the attack commenced. Avoiding repeated attacks by Stukas, he continued to fly around the carrier until his fuel ran out, when he ditched and was picked up by HMS *Juno*. Attacks were not over, however, for seven S.79s then appeared and began to bomb from high level – missing, as usual. Thirteen Ju 87s returned at 1715 hours to attack again, and *Illustrious* suffered a further hit. 806 Squadron's Fulmars, now at Hal Far, took off again, six strong, but were only able to harass the Stukas as they departed, although the pilots believed that one or two fell from the formation. Finally a lone torpedo-carrying S.79 attacked when *Illustrious* was only five miles from Valetta, but this was driven off by AA fire.

By evening the stricken carrier had reached the comparative safety of Valletta's Grand Harbour, where she could shelter up against cliffs, protected to an extent by the harbour's legendary AA barrage and by the island's fighters. In all 126 members of her crew had been killed, including the crew of the Fulmar which had failed to take off, and eight members of the Swordfish squadrons. A further 91 personnel had been wounded. 805 Squadron's crews survived, but all their aircraft were amongst those destroyed during the attack.

It was believed at the time that 806 Squadron's Fulmars had accounted for about five Ju 87s shot down, but according to Luftwaffe records their losses during these attacks amounted to three, with a fourth crash-landing on return due to damage sustained from fighter attack. That night, in retaliation, six Swordfish from the resident 830 Squadron bombed Palermo harbour.

While these events had been unfolding, the 'Excess' convoy had proceeded on its way, while the ship destined for Malta had docked there and unloaded its precious cargo of Hurricanes.

Next morning 12 Ju 87s were led to the south-east of Malta by a 'pathfinder' He 111, to search for the convoy before it could pass out of range. The fast Piraeus-bound ships and their escorts were already well clear, but the six slower vessels were still just within range. Escorted initially only by the cruiser *York* and four corvettes, these had just been joined by two more cruisers, *Gloucester* and *Southampton*. None of these vessels had yet been fitted with radar and were thus taken completely by surprise as the Stukas, at maximum range, dived on them out of the sun. *Southampton* was hit three times and was badly damaged, but the one bomb to hit *Gloucester* passed right through her without exploding. By nightfall *Southampton* had to be abandoned and was sunk by torpedoes fired by HMS *Orion*, which had come to her aid.

When the attack occurred, one of *Gloucester*'s Walruses had been in the air on anti-submarine patrol. As the ship could not slow down during an attack, the pilot had landed instead adjacent to the destroyer HMS *Diamond*, the flying boat being abandoned after its crew had been picked up. *Gloucester*'s second Walrus, still aboard, was damaged by bomb splinters.

On 12 January HMS *Barham* and *Eagle*, the latter carrying three Sea Gladiators and two Skuas as 813 Fighter Flight, sortied from Alexandria to meet the incoming ships, but after receiving news of the virtual loss of *Illustrious* abandoned the sortie and returned to harbour.

On Malta 806 Squadron's Fulmar pilots now joined the island's defence force, taking part in interceptions as the Luftwaffe redoubled its efforts to complete the destruction of *Illustrious*. Heavy attacks were made on 16, 18 and 19 January, during one of which a Fulmar was shot down, its pilot being killed. Throughout these attacks *Illustrious* was not hit again, although she did suffer further damage from near misses. The dockyard team worked on urgent temporary repairs, and on 23 January she was sufficiently patched up to sail towards Alexandria. However, major works would be required to repair her, including almost complete rebuilding of her superstructure, and these could not be accomplished locally. Consequently she passed through the Suez Canal and commenced a long voyage to the Norfolk Navy Yard in the United States for these works to be undertaken. It would be more than a year before she could return to operations.

Despite the loss of *Illustrious*, the early months of 1941 were to prove an extremely active period for the Fleet Air Arm throughout the Mediterranean and Middle East. To replace the vital carrier, the second of the new armoured fleet carriers to be completed, HMS *Formidable* – which had been hunting surface raiders off St Helena in the South Atlantic – was despatched to the Mediterranean via the Cape and Suez Canal route almost at once. Commissioned at the end of October 1940, *Formidable* took aboard 803 Squadron, newly returned from service aboard *Ark Royal* with Force 'H' but now re-equipped with Fulmars and commanded by the very experienced Lieutenant J.M. Bruen. Thus the fighter squadron at least was composed mainly of experienced crews. The balance of her air group was made up of 826

and 829 Squadrons, equipped with a combined total of 21 of the new Albacores. It will be recalled that the former unit had already seen quite extensive action over the coasts of Western Europe while operating with RAF Coastal Command. It was commanded by Lieutenant Commander W.H.G. Saunt, while 829 Squadron was led by Lieutenant Commander J. Dalyell-Stead.

Formidable was needed in the Mediterranean doubly urgently, since *Eagle* was now in considerable need of a further refit, and was due to leave for the UK as soon as possible. In the meantime Crete had become available for at least some forward air support to shipping sailing between Greece and Egypt. The surviving Swordfish from *Illustrious* flew to the island to operate as 815 Squadron, while 805 Squadron at Dekheila continued to expand as more fighter aircraft became available, despite the loss of the unit's initial Fulmars on the carrier. Three Fulmars, led by Captain L.A. 'Skeets' Harris, RM, DSC, were to fly up to Maleme on 15 February, where they were attached initially to 815 Squadron.

In East Africa, Imperial forces had been building

BELOW *Tracers light up the night as anti-aircraft guns fire into the sky during an air raid over Grand Harbour, Valletta, Malta. The photograph was taken from the battleship HMS* **Warspite. IWM A19000**

up in the Sudan and Kenya ready for a two-pronged advance into Italian colonial territories that was planned to begin early in 1941. Those in Kenya headed into Italian Somaliland, which formed what is now often referred to as 'The Horn of Africa', while the Sudan-based columns entered Ethiopia. Eritrea was kept under regular air attack from Aden, on the Red Sea. Sailing up the coast of East Africa, *Formidable*'s air group began contributing to these operations on 2 February, when nine Albacores bombed Mogadishu on the Somaliland coast. Little damage was inflicted, but other aircraft from the ship were able to lay magnetic mines in the entrance to the harbour.

On this same date Force 'H' sortied into the Western Mediterranean again, where it was intended that *Ark Royal*'s Swordfish would attack Genoa. Due to bad weather this raid had to be cancelled and instead a night strike was made on a hydroelectric plant at the San Chiara Ula Dam on Lake Tirso in Sardinia. In wet weather, and in the face of heavy AA fire, four Swordfish launched torpedoes at this target, but with no success. One aircraft flew into a wire stretched horizontally above the lake to prevent just such attacks, and crashed into the water. The crew were rescued and became PoWs.

Off East Africa, HMS *Hermes* now entered action, her Swordfish attacking the port of Kismayu in the far south of Somaliland on 13 February as Imperial forces approached. Her aircraft also spotted for gunfire from the cruiser HMS *Shropshire*.

Formidable had by now reached the head of the Red Sea, ready to enter the Suez Canal, but the latter had been rendered impassable by air-laid mines, and until these had been cleared the carrier could go no further. During the night of 12/13 February, therefore, 14 of her Albacores raided the Eritrean harbour of Massawa, half carrying bombs and half with torpedoes. Low cloud reduced the attack to little more than a shambles, although the 5,723-ton steamer *Moncalieri* was damaged. However, two of the precious Albacores were shot down by the AA defences, and of their eight crew members two were killed and six taken prisoner. (Since the normal crew would have been three, it would appear that on this occasion each aircraft had taken along a 'passenger' to 'watch the show'.) This was bad news, for the air group had already lost two Fulmars in operational mishaps.

A repeat attack was nonetheless launched on 24 February, seven aircraft bombing the harbour in shallow dives. On this occasion four were hit by AA, but all returned to the carrier. One more such raid would be made on 1 March. This time five Albacores operated from a landing ground ashore at Mersa Taclai in Eritrea, but no notable results were achieved.

Over the Mediterranean land-based Swordfish remained active. During the night of 8/9 February eight 830 Squadron aircraft from Malta raided Tripoli, one of their number failing to return. Next day, a torpedo blew up while it was being loaded onto one of the unit's aircraft, wrecking the Swordfish and killing eight members of the groundcrew. During the night of 17/18 February three 815 Squadron Swordfish set off from Crete to join RAF Wellingtons in a bombing raid on Scarpanto.

Towards the end of the month *Eagle* sortied from Alexandria to meet and escort two fast merchant vessels approaching from the west. For this task she carried not only her little Sea Gladiator flight but also six Fulmars, drawn equally from 805 and 806 Squadrons – the latter was now arriving from Malta and re-forming at Dekheila. On the 21st two of the former unit's aircraft engaged a raid by five He 111s, shooting one down. Two 806 Squadron aircraft also took off, and their crews also claimed a Heinkel. It seems, however, that they may have attacked the same bomber, as only one loss was recorded by the Luftwaffe. Three days later, as the carrier returned to base, one of 805 Squadron's Fulmars with the flight in Crete, intercepted a reconnaissance S.79, which they claimed as probably shot down.

A British plan to obtain further bases in the Aegean was put in hand on 25 February under the name Operation 'Mandible', when a small force of Royal Navy personnel and Royal Marine Commandos were put ashore on the island of Castelorizzo. At first little resistance was met, but attacks from the air and shelling from destroyers, coupled with a counter-attack, forced the British to retreat, and by the 27th they had either surrendered or been evacuated, the operation having failed. Fleet Air Arm units were not involved on this occasion.

Despite this setback – or perhaps because of it – Crete became of increasing importance. From here 815 Squadron's Swordfish were now regularly flying up to Greece for operations over Albanian coastal waters. Refuelling and arming with torpedoes took place at Eleusis, after which the aircraft were flown on to the advanced airfield at Paramythia, from where RAF fighters were operating. Lieutenant Commander Jago led the first such operation, his aircraft carrying the normal crew of three, but each of the other five were fitted with extra long-range fuel tanks in the central cockpit, reducing the crew to two.

On 12 March the six crews set off to attack Valona harbour. Here the AA defences shot Jago's Swordfish down into the sea. Lieutenant Charles Lamb took over the lead, launching his torpedo after accidentally hitting the surface of the water with his undercarriage. Amongst the rest of the raiders, only Lieutenant F.M.A. Torrens-Spence was able to get his torpedo away, but the two which had been launched seem to have struck two vessels. The 3,539-ton *Santa Maria* was sunk, while the 7,289-ton *Po* – unfortunately a hospital ship – also went down. On return, command of 815 Squadron was taken over by Lieutenant Torrens-Spence.

Next day, while flying up to Paramythia again after being rearmed with a torpedo at Eleusis, Lieutenant Lamb was intercepted by two CR.42s. At once he jettisoned the torpedo and stood the aircraft on its tail, just as the fighters opened fire. Almost stalling, his aircraft then spun away as the two attackers, trying to keep the almost stationary Swordfish in their sights, both stalled and fell away. Recovering, they sought to attack again, at which Lamb threw his aircraft into a dive beyond the vertical. In trying to follow this manoeuvre the two Fiats collided and both crashed; one pilot managed to bale out, but the other was killed.

Due to shortages of Fulmars, 805 Squadron at Dekheila had been brought up to strength with the Brewster Buffaloes which had been taken over from the Belgian order, a separate flight of these aircraft

being formed. On 6 March six more Fulmars and three of the Buffaloes were flown up to Crete, led by Lieutenant Commander Black. Here the existing Fulmar flight was absorbed back into its parent squadron. Black would subsequently request that his unit be reinforced with Sea Gladiators, and because the Buffalo later gained a bad reputation following losses in Malaya and Singapore it became 'accepted wisdom' that this was because he had found these fighters lacking. He had indeed experienced problems with their serviceability, but was quick to defend their reputation:

'The Buffalo was a delight to fly – very manoeuvrable (compared with the Fulmar). It would have been an excellent fighter but the guns could not be fired because the ends of the wires which were part of the interrupter gear failed, and 805 did not have the necessary spares. At no time did I request that the Buffaloes be exchanged for Sea Gladiators but I do remember that in the light of the inadequacy of Fulmars against CR.42s I requested that the Sea Gladiators, if not required for other operations, should be sent to Maleme to reinforce 805.'

With the Suez Canal at last cleared, *Formidable* finally arrived at Alexandria on 10 March – and not, as it turned out, a moment too soon! Earlier in

the month the three remaining serviceable 806 Squadron Fulmars on Malta had flown to Egypt via El Adem, Libya, each carrying three members of the aircrew aboard. On arrival the unit was issued three additional aircraft, and prepared initially to fly up to Maleme to join 805 Squadron. While on Malta the squadron had suffered a sad and unnecessary loss. During the evening of 2 March a car carrying a group of the unit's pilots, including the very successful Lieutenant W.L.LeC. Barnes, DSC, was fired on by a Maltese sentry when it failed to stop (because the sentry's hand torch had failed to operate). The ricocheting bullet, which had hit a stone in the road, struck the back of the car, killing Barnes instantly.

On 16 March a pair of He 111 torpedo-bombers operating over the Dodecanese islands spotted the Mediterranean Fleet battleships *Warspite* and *Barham*, and launched attacks on both from quite close range. As the aircraft turned away, their crews spotted columns of water where hits might have been expected to be achieved, and – as torpedo-dropping pilots tended to – returned claiming damage to both ships.

This information was passed to the Italians by the German Naval Command, and would prove to have serious consequences for the former, who believed it and acted upon it. Intending to interfere seriously with the convoys now running on a regular basis to Greece, the battleship *Vittorio*

Veneto, eight cruisers and 13 destroyers put to sea from the main southern Italian ports. Unfortunately for the Italians, the British battleships had not, in fact, been hit.

On 18 March a large convoy of 13 ships left Alexandria for Greece, while on the 20th four fast merchant ships sailed for Malta, carrying vital supplies. The latter vessels were escorted by three AA cruisers and by *Formidable*, plus attendant destroyers. For so important a sortie the carrier had taken aboard six more Fulmars – the aircraft and crews of 806 Squadron, diverted from their intended move to Crete. She also carried *Eagle*'s three Sea Gladiators, although the intention was that these should be flown off to join 805 Squadron at Maleme during the return voyage.

Both convoys came under attack on 21 March, one of two Ju 88s being shot down over the Malta convoy by Lieutenant Bruen of 803 Squadron. Later in the day two of 805 Squadron's Fulmars from Crete came aboard to provide yet more fighter cover. However, the convoy bound for Greece was accurately bombed by more Ju 88s, a tanker being sunk. Next morning two more vessels were lost to He 111s, while S.79s sought to torpedo vessels in the Malta convoy, but without success. All these events tended to further convince the Italian Naval Command that opposition was currently muted.

With her duty to the Malta convoy completed, *Formidable* turned back for Alexandria on

23 March, the two 805 Squadron Fulmars and the three Sea Gladiators being flown off safely to Crete. Next day British Intelligence received and decrypted 'Ultra' intercepts which indicated that something big was afoot. The German Naval Liaison Officer in Rome now advised his allies formally:

'The German Naval Staff considers that at the moment there is only one British battleship, Valiant, *in the Eastern Mediterranean ready for action. It is not anticipated that heavy British units will be withdrawn from the Atlantic in the near future. Force "H" is also considered unlikely to appear in the Mediterranean. Thus the situation in the Mediterranean is at the moment more favourable for the Italian Fleet than ever before. Intense traffic from Alexandria to the Greek ports, whereby the Greek forces are receiving combat reinforcements in men and equipment, presents a particularly worthwhile target for Italian Naval Forces. The German Naval Staff considers that the appearance of Italian units in the area south of Crete will seriously interfere with British shipping, and may even lead to the complete interruption of the transport of troops, especially as these transports are at the moment inadequately protected.'*

Was there, perhaps, a degree of wishful thinking present here? The German High Command was in the process of committing troops and aircraft to North Africa, while also preparing for action in the Balkans against Yugoslavia and Greece to protect the southern flank of the forthcoming invasion of the Soviet Union. Italian naval action here might well reduce some of the risks associated with either of these moves. In any event, it proved to be a severely inaccurate assessment of the situation.

Further 'Ultra' intercepts next day convinced the British that a major operation directed from the headquarters in Rhodes was to commence in three days time, and Admiral Cunningham put his own plans in hand forthwith. A convoy heading for Greece on 26 March was ordered to reverse course after dark, while Force 'R', comprising four cruisers – two of which were fitted with radar – and four destroyers was ordered to assemble south of Gavdhos Island at dawn on the 28th; the 1st Battle Squadron would leave Alexandria after dark on the 27th. Meanwhile, the first sighting of the Italian Fleet was made by an RAF Sunderland on the morning of the 27th.

Formidable left harbour that afternoon, flying on her air group from Dekheila. 803 Squadron's ten Fulmars were again joined by three from 806 Squadron, while 826 and 829 Squadrons, with only ten serviceable Albacores between them, had been brought back to a degree of normal strength by the arrival of four Swordfish. At evening they were joined by *Valiant*, *Warspite*, *Barham* and nine destroyers. By first light on 28 March they were 150 miles south of eastern Crete, but not until noon were they spotted by Italian reconnaissance aircraft, when Admiral Angelo Iachino at last became aware of the strength of the forces opposing him.

Searches for the Italian vessels now began and anti-submarine patrols were put in hand, while Fulmars maintained patrols overhead. The searches were assisted by four 815 Squadron Swordfish from Maleme, all already armed with torpedoes. The first sighting was made by Albacore crews at 0720 hours, and confirmed soon afterwards. Shortly thereafter Force 'B' sighted Italian cruisers 18 miles to their north and an exchange of gunfire commenced, HMS *Gloucester* launching her Walrus to spot for the guns. The opposing force then withdrew westwards, shadowed by the Walrus.

Admiral Cunningham at once ordered *Formidable* to range a striking force, and six Albacores of 826 Squadron were prepared, all armed with torpedoes. Initially Maleme was ordered to send off its striking force first, but there was a delay in relaying the message and it was 45 minutes before the three Swordfish set out. *Formidable*'s strike took off meanwhile, escorted by two 803 Squadron Fulmars and a Swordfish to observe results.

By now *Vittorio Veneto* had come within range of Force 'B' and opened fire on the British cruisers, although an expenditure of 94 15in shells achieved no direct hits.

As 826 Squadron's formation passed Force 'B' it was fired on by the British ships and attacked at the same time by two Ju 88s. The escorting Fulmars at once dived to attack the bombers, claiming one shot down, although German records do not seem to confirm such a loss. Nonetheless, the Albacores were then able to commence their attack on the Italian battleship, the crew of which initially mistook them for an expected escort of CR.42s from Rhodes and were relieved to see all the torpedoes from the first flight miss. The second flight then attacked, but although they believed that they had got one or two hits they too had missed.

815 Squadron's trio then arrived and launched at the cruiser *Bolzano*; again, all missed. The 1st Battle Squadron was now close enough for *Warspite*'s two Swordfish floatplanes to be launched to make visual contact. A second strike was being prepared

on *Formidable*, but comprised only three Albacores and two Swordfish of 829 Squadron, to be led by Lieutenant Commander Dalyell-Stead. Once more a pair of Fulmars and a Swordfish accompanied them as escort. As they headed off, the first strike, a pair of patrolling Fulmars and *Gloucester*'s Walrus all came in and landed.

At around this time a Ro 43 from the Italian cruisers found *Formidable*, but as it could not be recovered during an action this aircraft flew to Rhodes to report. Consequently Admiral Iachino did not receive this news until two hours later.

Vittorio Veneto was then found and bombed twice by RAF Blenheims. As the second such attack was under way, the 829 Squadron strike arrived

BELOW *Lt Cdr W.H.G. Saunt, DSO, DSC, led 829 Squadron's Albacores to attack Italian cruisers during the Battle of Cape Matapan.*

and approached from head-on, while the Fulmars strafed the bridge and gun turrets to distract the aim of the gunners. Lieutenant Commander Dalyell-Stead closed to release his torpedo, but as he did so his Albacore was hit and crashed into the sea, he and his crew all being killed. The other Albacores and the Swordfish completed their attacks, believing that three hits had been obtained. In fact only one – probably that launched by Dalyell-Stead – had struck home, just above the outer port screw. *Vittorio Veneto*'s engines stopped as water flooded in and she began to list to port. Just at that moment the last of the Blenheims also achieved a bomb hit very close to the stern.

Learning that the Italian battleship had been damaged, Admiral Cunningham ordered a further strike and all available TBRs were sent off at 1730 hours, including six Albacores of 826 Squadron and two Swordfish of 829, the formation being led by Lieutenant Commander Saunt. Because darkness was approaching, they were ordered to land at Maleme after their attack. From this latter airfield 815 Squadron also sent two Swordfish at 1655 hours, led by Lieutenant Torrens-Spence, this pair finding four cruisers and six destroyers an hour later. As they flew round, Lieutenant Commander Saunt's force arrived and Torrens-Spence decided to join the rear of this formation. Unfortunately he and his companion were at first taken to be CR.42s and some avoiding manoeuvres ensued. However, at 1925 Saunt led the attack into thick smoke and searchlights, which tended to blind the pilots. Either the final Albacore to attack, or Torrens-Spence's Swordfish, gained a hit amidships on the cruiser *Pola* and she came to a halt. This was witnessed by the crew of one of *Warspite*'s Swordfish floatplanes, on its second sortie of the day. The Albacore which had made the final attack, flown by Sub-Lieutenant G.P.C. Williams, ran out of fuel during its return flight, but Williams was able to ditch in Suda Bay, close to HMS *Juno*, which picked up the crew.

Vittorio Veneto was shadowed through the night by 826 Squadron Albacores, one of which also had to ditch in Suda Bay; again the crew were saved. An assessment of the day indicated that 19 torpedoes had been dropped by *Formidable*'s aircraft and five by 815 Squadron. It was thought that five hits had been achieved. In fact there had been only two, one on *Vittorio Veneto* and one on *Pola*, but they effectively decided the ultimate outcome of the battle.

The Italian battleship's damage control party soon had two engines restarted, and she began her escape at 16 knots. By evening she was well on her way to Taranto, and was making 19 knots. However, three cruisers had been sent to aid *Pola*, and when the 1st Battle Squadron appeared on the scene, hoping to find *Vittorio Veneto*, it was these ships that they encountered. *Warspite* and *Valiant* opened fire, sinking the cruisers *Fiume* and *Zara* and the destroyer *Alfieri*. Italian destroyers tried to make a torpedo attack, but one was at once put out of action by two of the Battle Squadron's attendant destroyers. *Pola* was subsequently despatched with torpedoes after her crew had been taken off.

On this occasion, known subsequently as the Battle of Cape Matapan, the TBRs had done precisely what the Royal Navy had envisaged the Fleet Air Arm doing – slowing down the enemy by torpedo strikes to allow the main force's heavy ships to catch and despatch them – summarised as 'Find, Fix and Strike'. Appreciation was subsequently shown when 16 gallantry awards and 21 Mentions in Despatches were awarded to Fleet Air Arm personnel. These included DSOs to the two strike leaders, Saunt and Dalyell-Stead (despite the latter having been killed in action). Amongst recipients of DSCs were Lieutenant Bruen and the Albacore pilot, Grainger Williams.

The Albacores returned to the scene next morning to find only wreckage and survivors in the sea. The Battle of Cape Matapan was at a successful conclusion. As *Formidable* headed towards Alexandria, the retaliation that had been expected finally commenced during the afternoon, when the radar detected an approaching raid. Three Fulmars were boosted off to join two already in the air, and after climbing to altitude these attacked a formation of Ju 88s which had just dive-bombed the ships, narrowly missing the carrier with four bombs. Two of the Fulmars managed to shoot down one of the attackers, but its return fire hit one fighter, which crashed into the sea when its engine cut out; the crew were picked up by the destroyer *Hasty*. Somewhat surprisingly, no further attacks followed.

Shortly after this naval victory, matters turned decidedly grim for British Empire forces throughout the area. On 6 April 1941 a German 'Blitzkrieg' campaign was launched against both Yugoslavia and Greece, while at the same time Rommel's recently arrived units in Libya began to roll up the weak forces facing them.

This disastrous day was marked for the Fleet Air Arm by no more than the delivery of six 'almost new' Swordfish to 815 Squadron, which flew these reinforcements up to Paramythia. By this time *Eagle* was on her way home. Arriving at the northern head of the Suez Canal, her air party – now comprising just the 17 Swordfish of

813 and 824 Squadrons – flew off to Port Said, led by Commander Keighley-Peach, who had been awarded a richly deserved DSO. From this airfield on 2 April two Swordfish bombed and hit an Italian merchant vessel at Makra. In East Africa, the Italian forces were now in full retreat and facing imminent total defeat. Even as the Swordfish were undertaking this co-operative mission, six Italian destroyers had been ordered out of Massawa in a last desperate attack on Port Said and Suez. Warned of their approach by the British command at Aden, six Swordfish took off on 3 April to search for the approaching warships. At dawn Keighley-Peach, on a lone reconnaissance over the approaches to Port Said, spotted the Italian ships 28 miles to the east. He swiftly called up three more of the patrolling aircraft, then led an attack with 250lb bombs, several near misses being claimed.

While one Swordfish remained to shadow the destroyers, the rest returned to refuel and rearm. At 0813 hours Lieutenant A.G. Leatham led a second strike by seven aircraft during which Midshipman E. Sergent, RNVR, obtained a record six hits with six bombs on *Nazario Sauro*, which sank in less than a minute. The rest of the crews gained near misses which caused many casualties on the other vessels. Blenheims then attacked, but at 1010 a further Swordfish strike found the remaining destroyers 100 miles away, leaving the area fast. Sub-Lieutenant S.H. Suthers hit *Daniele Manin* between the funnels with two bombs, and she came to a halt, her crew abandoning her. Shadowing continued until 1100, by which time the remaining destroyers were getting out of range of the Swordfish, and further attacks were left to the RAF and to Royal Navy surface vessels. It had been a fitting last action for *Eagle*'s gallant air group and its outstanding commander, Charles Keighley-Peach. It brought an OBE for Keighley-Peach and DSCs for Sergent and Suthers.

Even as German activity throughout the Mediterranean rendered the area considerably more dangerous, a further attempt was put in hand to reinforce Malta's defences. As Operation 'Winch', *Ark Royal* took aboard 12 new Hurricane IIAs (the first such to reach the Middle East), which had just arrived at Gibraltar on board *Argus*. These were carried out into the Mediterranean and launched on 3 April, led by two Skuas; all arrived safely.

Ark Royal's own fighters were in action as she turned back for Gibraltar. Shadowers were reported and Petty Officer D.E. Taylor of 808 Squadron quickly intercepted a Z.506B, which he forced down on the sea in sinking condition; the crew were picked up by an RN destroyer.

Twenty minutes later another of these floatplanes was intercepted by Lieutenant R.C. Hay, RM, and driven off into cloud, apparently in a damaged condition. Searching destroyer crews reported finding it abandoned on the sea later.

Eight days after Operation 'Winch', one of Malta's reconnaissance Marylands spotted a convoy of freighters and three destroyers to the south-west of Pantelleria. 830 Squadron sent out a Swordfish to shadow this until seven more of the unit's aircraft, six of them with torpedoes, could be made ready to attack after dark. Just before 2100 hours they commenced their attack in the teeth of intense AA fire, which hit two of the Swordfish, obliging them to force-land near Hammamet on the Tunisian coast, where both crews were interned. The results of the attack could not be observed.

The Mediterranean Fleet commenced another major action on 18 April, sailing west to bombard Tripoli in an effort to assist the Army, now very hard-pressed in the Cyrenaican/Tripolitanian border area. As the vessels got under way they were spotted by two S.79sils from Rhodes. A Fulmar patrol from 803 Squadron pursued the intruders as they departed, but return fire hit Lieutenant Donald Gibson's aircraft which was in the lead. Wounded in one arm and almost completely blinded by hot oil, he attempted to land back on the carrier:

> '*I caught a wire very fast; this tore the bottom out of the aeroplane. I collided with the island and set fire to the petrol refuelling station; the tail folded forward over my head. I skidded on, hit "A" turret and somersaulted into the sea. I was run over by the whole length of the ship; had a great struggle to get out and was picked up in the wake by HMS* Hereward. *Alas, Peter Ashbrooke [Sub-Lieutenant P.C.B. Ashbrooke, the observer] was lost. I was very young and foolish, and should have ditched.*'

The second Fulmar continued to attack the Savoia, which force-landed in an extremely damaged condition at Gadurra, its torpedo still beneath the fuselage.

Because heavy air attack was deemed probable *Ark Royal* had taken aboard 15 Fulmars, including the six aircraft and crews of 806 Squadron, now once more led by Lieutenant Commander Charles Evans. After a stop in Suda Bay to allow the destroyers to refuel, the fleet departed for the target area on 20 April. On the way a single Cant Z.1007bis bomber was encountered flying between Sicily and Libya, and was shot down by Charles

Evans and Sub-Lieutenant 'Jackie' Sewell. Two hours later more hostiles were reported, two more sections of 806 Squadron Fulmars being launched to intercept. This proved to be not a bombing attack, but a formation of five Ju 52/3m transports on their way to Africa. These unfortunates were at once attacked, and while one escaped northwards, the other four were all claimed shot down, two of them exploding in mid-air, suggesting that they were loaded with fuel. One Fulmar was hit by return fire and spun into the sea with the loss of the crew. However, Luftwaffe returns list the loss of only two of their aircraft on this date, so it may be that there had been a degree of double-claiming by the FAA pilots.

That night *Formidable*, two cruisers and four destroyers broke away to provide air cover against any Axis attack, while the three battleships and *Gloucester*, covered by seven destroyers, headed inshore to bombard. Wellingtons from Malta also bombed, while flares were dropped by 830 Squadron Swordfish and by TBRs of 826 and 829 Squadrons. After a sustained bombardment with 15in and 6in guns, the fleet withdrew and headed east. Air attack next day was anticipated, but did not occur. Next morning a shadower approached, again in the form of a Z.1007bis, and this was attacked by two 803 Squadron Fulmars. One pilot returned, reporting that the Italian aircraft had been damaged, but of his wingman, Lieutenant Wright, there was no sign. Sub-Lieutenants Orr and Hogg of 806 Squadron were sent to try and find Wright and lead him back, but this pair met instead a German air-sea rescue Do 24N flying boat from Syracuse. Attacking this, they forced it down onto the sea. Twice it tried to take off again, but each time they strafed it, finally leaving it settling in the water. While they were so engaged, Lieutenant Wright arrived back on board, having found his own way to report that the Cant he and Sub-Lieutenant Simpson had attacked had indeed been shot down.

During the attack on Tripoli about 10 tons of bombs and 553 tons of shells had been expended. Air reconnaissance reported that some destroyer berths had been hit and one destroyer badly damaged, while five merchant vessels were burnt out and at least four others had been set on fire. The Mediterranean Fleet now headed for Alexandria. On 22 April, as the fleet approached its anchorage, an incoming raid was detected at 1724 hours. Two sections of Fulmars were on patrol, and others were at once launched until all 14 were in the air. The first pair of Ju 88s were intercepted by Lieutenant Bruen and Sub-Lieutenant Richards of 803 Squadron and by Lieutenant Henley and

Sub-Lieutenant Sparke of 806 Squadron. One bomber was forced to jettison its bombs and make off into clouds, while the second was shot down into the sea by Julian Sparke. Two more sections from 806 Squadron encountered a lone Ju 88, believed to be a reconnaissance machine, and this was claimed probably shot down by Lieutenant Commander Evans, Sub-Lieutenant Sewell and Sub-Lieutenant Orr. The fleet suffered no damage and was able to enter harbour safely next morning.

Ark Royal undertook a further sortie towards Malta on 27 April to launch 24 more Hurricanes to the island. Operation 'Dunlop' resulted in three groups, each of eight fighters led by a Fulmar, making the flight. These were met by three Marylands and a Sunderland, and although a lone He 111 appeared as the launch was taking place 23 of the aircraft landed safely on the island.

Two days later the Fleet Air Arm became involved in a completely different environment. Following the recent British reverses, a revolt had occurred in Iraq, where dissident elements hoping to take over the government threatened the British oil supplies and training bases in the country. While this would be a predominantly RAF matter to deal with, on 29 April HMS *Hermes* arrived at Basra in the south, with two RN cruisers. On 2 May 814 Squadron's Swordfish flew ashore to use Shaibah airfield as a land base, six of these aircraft undertaking a demonstration flight over the city. Operations commenced on 4 May when four Swordfish bombed a railway bridge over the River Euphrates.

During the night of 9/10 May the squadron undertook a series of attacks on Iraqi army barracks at Nazari, dropping First World War 112lb RAF bombs. Similar attacks were made subsequently, the eighth of these on barracks in the Basra area on 15 May, three aircraft attacking those at Samawa. Here one of the bombers was hit by fire from the ground and made a very heavy forced-landing. The aircraft was at once surrounded by local Arabs, but these fell back when the pilot offered them a one dinar note! Seeing the crew's plight, Lieutenant J.H. Dundas landed alongside and picked them up, just as Iraqi troops advanced on them and opened fire, hitting Dundas's aircraft in the fuel tank. Leading Air Mechanic Latham then engaged the Iraqis with

BELOW *Down inside the hangar deck on HMS* Argus.

his Lewis gun, allowing Dundas to take off despite the damage; he was subsequently awarded a DSC. Next day four Swordfish bombed petrol tanks at Amawa, following which they landed aboard *Hermes*, which withdrew, duty completed.

Elsewhere, however, matters had altered considerably in the meantime. In North Africa the Imperial forces had been driven right back across Cyrenaica and over the frontier into Egypt. The situation in the Balkans was even worse. Yugoslavia had swiftly fallen to the 'Blitzkrieg', while in Greece, despite reinforcement of that hard-pressed country by British, Australian and New Zealand troops, the Germans had driven all before them. Before the end of April the Allied expeditionary force had been evacuated to Crete, leaving the whole of Southern Europe in enemy hands.

'Ultra' transcripts now indicated that Crete was the next target for invasion, and there was concern that Cyprus might also be in danger as a 'stepping stone' towards Syria, Iraq and the Middle East's oilfields. In Greece 815 Squadron had continued to operate for as long as possible. Six Swordfish had flown up to Paramythia again in mid-April, ready to attack Albanian or Italian ports. Five flew back to Eleusis to exchange torpedoes for mines, then departed during the night of 11/12 April to attack Brindisi in south-eastern Italy, accompanied by one aircraft carrying a torpedo. The harbour was found to be crowded with shipping, against which torpedoes would have been a more suitable weapon. Nonetheless, the one available was

launched at a tanker while the mines were dropped close alongside anchored vessels in the hope of at least delaying them. Two nights later seven aircraft, all with torpedoes, made for Valona, where several ships were attacked, although in the darkness the crews somewhat overestimated the size and tonnage of their targets. The 3,329-ton *Luciano* and 1,228-ton *Stampalia* were both sunk, but one Swordfish hit the water and crashed, the crew surviving to become prisoners.

Since 13 March this single squadron, 815, had torpedoed ten Axis merchant ships, five of which had been sunk. Now, however, the unit began evacuating its Grecian detachment to Crete, initially flying the stock of mines and torpedoes at Eleusis to the island. It had been agreed that, now Crete was in imminent danger of air attack and possible invasion, 815 Squadron should be withdrawn to Egypt to free up dispersal room at Maleme for Hurricanes and Fleet Air Arm fighters.

Thus, just as the 1st Battle Squadron arrived back at Alexandria from its bombardment of Tripoli, 815 Squadron flew in to Dekheila on 22 April. The unit was soon followed by four non-combatworthy Fulmars from 805 Squadron which arrived at Aboukir, leaving at Maleme five Fulmars, seven Sea Gladiators (more of which had been flown over from Egypt in the meantime) and two totally unserviceable Buffaloes. Crete would suffer its first air raid before the end of April.

Determined as ever to try and maintain the offensive, Churchill was already pressing Wavell

BELOW *A Savoia S.79 bomber of 193°* Squadriglia *of the* Regia Aeronautica, *Sicily, 1941.* Author

to counter-attack in the desert once the retreat there had come to a halt. One attempt, codenamed Operation 'Brevity', had failed at once, but in order to facilitate an early repeat Churchill insisted that a major convoy carrying large reinforcements – comprising 295 tanks, 180 motor vehicles, and 53 Hurricane fighters – should be pushed through the Mediterranean direct to Alexandria. Codenamed 'Tiger', this convoy was to comprise five fast merchantmen supported to the full by both Force 'H' and the Mediterranean Fleet. The opportunity was also to be taken to send, with the latter fleet, four large merchant vessels and two tankers carrying fuel and supplies to Malta.

The 'Tiger' convoy departed Gibraltar on 6 May, Force 'H' in attendance, while on the same date *Formidable* and five cruisers put out from Alexandria. While at Gibraltar, *Ark Royal* had exchanged 800 Squadron and its Skuas for another new Fulmar unit, 807 Squadron, led by Lieutenant Commander J. Sholto Douglas. This had been formed on 15 September 1940 and had served aboard *Furious* for a short time, engaged in convoy escort duties in the Atlantic. In April it had become the first to re-equip with the Mark II version of the Fulmar.

There would be sustained aerial action over both fleets on 8 May, as the Axis responded to this new challenge. As day dawned aboard *Ark Royal*, only 12 Fulmars were fully serviceable. The morning remained quiet, but at 1345 hours the first incoming raid was detected and eight Fulmars

were launched, four from each squadron. Sixteen S.79s were spotted, all armed with torpedoes, but as the 808 Squadron quartet sought to intercept they were 'bounced' by 12 escorting CR.42s with disastrous results. Lieutenant Tillard's aircraft was shot down at once, he and Lieutenant Somerville being lost, and the other three Fulmars were all hit, each suffering some damage; in Lieutenant Taylour's aircraft his observer was hit, suffering a severe leg wound. One CR.42 overshot and Taylour was able to fire on this, believing that he had probably shot it down.

The four 807 Squadron aircraft now got through to the bombers, Lieutenant N.G. Hallett and his wingman attacking one. However, gunners in the Savoia hit the engine of Hallett's Fulmar and he had to ditch at once; he and his observer were rescued by the destroyer *Foresight*. The remaining pair of Fulmars, flown by Lieutenant R.E. Gardner (one of the successful Battle of Britain pilots) and Lieutenant K. Firth, managed to shoot down one bomber, but eight broke through to launch torpedoes at *Ark Royal* and *Renown* – all of which missed.

After a short lull, small formations of S.79s again began appearing and two 808 Squadron pilots were able to shoot down one of these. So far all these raiders had come from Sardinia, but at evening a further raid approached composed of Luftwaffe aircraft from Sicily. Just before dusk five 807 Squadron and two 808 Squadron Fulmars – these seven representing all the fighters that now remained serviceable – engaged a force of Ju 87s and Bf 110s, which at once attacked the Fulmars, Lieutenant Commander Sholto Douglas's aircraft being damaged. Petty Officer R.T. Leggott managed to fire on one dive-bomber, but was himself attacked by a Bf 110. Turning inside this, he claimed to have got some hits on it. Lieutenant Taylour, now flying with a replacement observer, claimed a Ju 87 shot down, but he too was then jumped by a Bf 110 and his aircraft was damaged, one undercarriage leg dropping down. Lieutenant Gardner claimed one Ju 87 and a second as a probable. Apparently the latter was confirmed when the film in the camera gun with which his Fulmar was equipped was developed. Return fire had shattered his windscreen.

All seven Fulmars managed to land back on board *Ark Royal*, but two were scrambled again almost at once as three more S.79s were seen approaching. They were unable to prevent the attack, and two torpedoes released by the raiders narrowly missed the carrier. During this raid the Luftwaffe actually suffered damage to one Bf 110, which crash-landed on return, while at least one Ju 87 was damaged, although none were actually lost.

Meanwhile, in the east, 803 Squadron Fulmars from *Formidable* started the day by intercepting two Italian Z.1007bis, which the pilots believed they shot down, although one Fulmar was also lost. Early in the afternoon a pair of 806 Squadron pilots encountered two He 111s, both of which were shot down. A section from 803 Squadron intercepted another Heinkel, which was shot down by Lieutenant Bruen, while two other 806 Squadron pilots accounted for a fourth. However, one of this latter pair, Lieutenant G.B. Davis, then crashed into the sea on return to the carrier, only the observer surviving. Of this engagement, 806 Squadron's Lieutenant MacDonald-Hall recounted:

'We came across two He 111s, the first of which I rather stupidly flew in formation with some 50 yards behind, but managed to blow up the Heinkel's starboard engine – the debris of which, being glycol and fuel, smothered my cockpit – and I watched it cartwheel down and hit the sea. I then rejoined [Lieutenant] Touchbourne and we harassed, attacked and shot down the other Heinkel prior to returning to Formidable. *My hydraulics had been damaged and the starboard wheel would not come down, and the port wheel was badly damaged by the rear gunner's fire, as was the port tyre. I landed with one leg down, the other retracted and the wheel deflated.'*

Later in the afternoon 806 Squadron aircraft were up again when a Ju 88 shadower was seen and attacked by Lieutenants Henley and Sparke, who claimed its destruction. It actually suffered heavy damage, but managed to regain its base nonetheless. Just before dark a further shadower was claimed shot down by Lieutenants MacDonald-Hall and Touchbourne, who reported that it crashed into the sea with no survivors following their attack. Bad weather during the day had saved the fleet from more sustained air attack, but resulted in two Albacores and a Fulmar being lost during patrols, only one Albacore crew surviving.

By 0800 hours on 9 May the 'Tiger' ships were still 90 miles west of Malta and the Mediterranean Fleet was 120 miles to the south. By 1515 the convoy to Malta from the east had reached the island, and at that stage Force 'H' turned back, regaining Gibraltar without further attack occurring. The weather was again rather poor on this date, with many fog patches – all of which was greatly to the Royal Navy's advantage. As *Formidable* reached its turning point, Lieutenants Hendry and Sparke of 806 Squadron intercepted a Ju 88 which they again claimed to have shot down; in reality it had been badly damaged and would crash as it attempted to land in Sicily.

Next day Axis reconnaissance aircraft were out in force, but in the weather conditions prevailing were generally unable to retain contact with the British vessels even when they managed to find them. This, however, made it equally difficult for the defending fighters to find any of these 'snoopers'. One He 111 was pursued by Lieutenants MacDonald-Hall and Touchbourne, but was lost amongst clouds. Somewhat later another was detected approaching, but as Lieutenant Touchbourne's Fulmar was boosted off by catapult for an interception the fighter crashed over the starboard side of the carrier, and both he and his observer were killed. This caused a crisis of confidence amongst the other crews regarding the use of the catapult, which was resolved when the Commander (Flying), Commander C.J.N. Atkinson, who had never flown a Fulmar before, allowed himself to be boosted off without any problems.

The last attacks occurred on 11 May when, as the fleet neared Alexandria, Lieutenants Henley and Sparke intercepted a formation of Ju 88s. Henley shot down one, but Sparke closed to very short range with another and the two aircraft were then seen to fall together. They had either collided, or shot each other down simultaneously; both crashed into the sea, Henley seeing only one parachute. Lieutenant Commander Evans demanded that a search be made at once, for the

ABOVE *Sea Gladiator with aircrew.*

sea was very calm, and if Sparke and his observer had baled out or force-landed it should be easy to find them. However, *Formidable*'s captain refused to allow such a search as he felt the dangers inherent in slowing the ship were too great, and the safety of the convoy was paramount. Thus the Fleet Air Arm lost another of its most successful fighter pilots.

'Tiger' convoy and the 1st Battle Squadron both docked at Alexandria next morning, 238 of the tanks and 43 of the Hurricanes having survived the voyage. On arrival Charles Evans, following his long period at the head of 806 Squadron, was rested, his place being taken by Lieutenant Commander J.N. Garnett, who had previously commanded the Sea Gladiator Flight on HMS *Eagle*.

While the 'Tiger' convoy had been the focus of attention, Crete had come under increasing attack from the numerous Luftwaffe units now based in southern Greece. 805 Squadron and newly arrived RAF fighters continued to intercept raids, but suffered rising levels of attrition. By 11 May 805 Squadron had just two Fulmars and four Sea Gladiators left; the pilots were beginning to share some of the RAF Hurricanes at Maleme. On 15 May one Sea Gladiator was flown to Egypt but suffered engine failure on the way and ditched. At Maleme another was in the process of taking off when

Bf 109s appeared and began strafing the airfield. The little biplane tipped over and was shot up immediately after the pilot had got clear. A second Sea Gladiator was also strafed, as were the already wrecked Buffaloes.

Next day, flying borrowed Hurricanes, three of the remaining pilots encountered a force of Bf 109s. Lieutenant A.H.M. Ash was at once shot down into the sea, while Lieutenant H.J.C. Richardson baled out of his stricken aircraft but died when his parachute failed to open. Lieutenant A.R. Ramsay, however, managed to shoot down two of the Messerschmitts before landing at Retimo with his aircraft badly damaged. It was effectively the end of the squadron as a fighting force, only three pilots remaining available. One of these, the commanding officer Lieutenant Commander Black, was flown out in a Sunderland to try and obtain replacements. None were forthcoming, and on 20 May, when the German airborne invasion of the island commenced, just three officers (including Lieutenant Ramsay) and 50 ratings remained there. Most would be evacuated in the coming days, including Canadian Lieutenant Lloyd Keith, who had been in hospital during most of this period with dysentery.

As fighting on the island swayed one way and the other, at midday on 25 May the 1st Battle

Squadron departed Alexandria to undertake operations around Crete. Two battleships – *Barham* and the newly arrived *Queen Elizabeth* – were accompanied by *Formidable* and eight destroyers. The carrier's air group now comprised 12 Fulmars, crewed equally by 803 and 806 Squadron personnel, although several of these aircraft were of distinctly dubious serviceability. They were accompanied by 15 Albacores and Swordfish of a now-composite 826/829 Squadron. The first task of the air group was to attack Scarpanto at dawn next day, as it was believed that airfields here were being extensively used in the assault on Crete. At 0330 hours on the 26th six Albacores, led by Lieutenant Commander Saunt, took off to begin this attack. Two returned early, but the other four reported finding the airfield lined with closely parked CR.42s and Ju 87s. Two of these aircraft were said to have been destroyed and several damaged. Four Fulmars then arrived, led by Lieutenant Bruen, and these claimed to have left 12 aircraft out of action by strafing. In fact there do not appear to have been any Ju 87s present, although the attack was successful in destroying six CR.42s, a S.81 and a Ju 88, with others damaged.

Reprisal air raids were now anticipated and the four Fulmars were swiftly refuelled, taking off again at 0710 with two other sections, just as raiders were detected. These proved only to be reconnaissance aircraft, and the Fulmars landed on again. More sections were launched throughout the morning, but only one of these engaged, around midday, when Lieutenant Commander Garnett and Sub-Lieutenant Sewell encountered two He 111s, one of which Sewell immediately shot down. A pair of Ju 88s then appeared, which Garnett attacked, joined by Sewell, and the aircraft went down into the sea. However, the rear gunner of one hit Garnett's Fulmar as it did so, and this too went down. The crews of both aircraft were picked up by HMS *Hereward*. Another 806 Squadron pair also reported meeting two Ju 88s, Lieutenant MacDonald-Hall and Sub-Lieutenant Hogg claiming both shot down. As the Luftwaffe recorded the loss of only two Ju 88s during this attack, it is possible that all four Fulmar pilots had in fact attacked the same pair of aircraft.

Lieutenant Bruen and Sub-Lieutenant Richards of 803 Squadron also exchanged fire with a Ju 88, but Richards' Fulmar was hit by return fire and, with his engine misfiring badly, he crash-landed on *Formidable*'s deck.

At 1310 the 1st Battle Squadron, which was by now steaming 150 miles from the Kaso Strait, was spotted by a formation of Ju 87s. These were not from Greece or Scarpanto, and were not engaged in operations around Crete, nor were they searching for the carrier or the battleships. They were based in North Africa, and were hunting for coastal shipping seeking to resupply the besieged port of Tobruk. Led by Major Walter Enneccerus of II./StG 2, who had been one of the leaders of the attack on *Illustrious* in January, the dive-bombers thus came upon *Formidable* purely by chance. The pilots took full advantage of this opportunity and attacked at once, gaining two direct hits on the carrier's flight deck plus several near misses, one of which created a large hole in the starboard side below the waterline. Casualties were light considering the severity of the damage, with only 12 men killed and 10 wounded.

Two Fulmars had just landed when the attack began, and two more had launched as the Stukas approached. Gaining height, these hit back as the raiders retired, each pilot claiming one Ju 87 shot down; in fact only one was lost in this action. Return fire hit one Fulmar, wounding the observer, but both fighters were able to land back on despite the damage. One of the escorting destroyers, HMS *Nubian*, had also been hit and had her bows blown off.

Damage to *Formidable* was not as serious as that suffered by *Illustrious*, and by 1800 hours it was already possible to launch and recover aircraft again. Patrols were therefore sent off, but no further raids occurred. It was necessary for *Formidable* to follow her sister vessel to the USA for repair, however, and she would be out of action for many months. In the meantime, the air group was flown off to Aboukir.

With no carrier remaining in the Eastern Mediterranean, and with the RAF hard-pressed in its operations over Crete – now all flown from Egypt following the loss of the airfields on the island – the Royal Navy's surface vessels came under almost constant air attack, and suffered severe losses. During a sustained series of raids on the cruisers and destroyers of Force 'B' on 28 May, Admiral Cunningham ordered a standby flight of Fulmars at Aboukir to be despatched to provide some cover. Two 806 Squadron aircraft took off, Lieutenant MacDonald-Hall recording that:

'We received a signal from the C-in-C to the effect that because of the evacuation and heavy losses of ships we were to provide the maximum air cover until relieved, and if not relieved, to ditch. As we were flying from shore the air gunner was strictly not necessary for navigational purposes, and in view of the signal we thought it prudent to discard all air gunners.'

On his arrival at the conclusion of a dive-bombing attack, he engaged a Ju 87, claiming it as a probable.

Patrols over the ships taking part in the evacuation of the defenders of Crete continued for several days. On 31 May, while on one such sortie from Aboukir, Lieutenant MacDonald-Hall and Sub-Lieutenant Hogg encountered a lone Ju 88 which they shot down into the sea, bringing to a close the Fleet Air Arm's involvement in the Cretan operation.

Following emergency repairs at Alexandria, *Formidable* passed through the Suez Canal on 24 July. With her went six Swordfish of 829 Squadron to provide anti-submarine protection en route to the USA. It was to be 38 months before any fleet carrier would again operate in the Eastern Mediterranean area and for the time being air cover would have to be provided by the RAF's 201 Naval Co-operation Group, of which disembarked naval squadrons became a part.

At the other end of the Mediterranean, following the 'Tiger' operation, Force 'H' put to sea on 19 May to support another major Malta supply run known as Operation 'Splice'. HMS *Furious* had sailed from the UK for this, carrying 48 Hurricanes and six Fulmar IIs of 800X Squadron. The latter was in fact a flight formed from the now-defunct

801 Squadron, which it had been intended should fly on to Egypt to reinforce 805 Squadron in Crete. On arrival at Gibraltar half of the Hurricanes were transferred onto *Ark Royal*, while that carrier's old Fulmar Is were exchanged for 800X's new aircraft. The Mark Is were now to be used as navigators to lead the Hurricanes to Malta prior to undertaking their own planned flight to join 805 Squadron. Commanding officer of 800X was Lieutenant Commander G. Hare, DSC, an observer, while senior pilot was Lieutenant R.M. Smeeton. Despite a number of mishaps, 46 of the Hurricanes and five of the Fulmars arrived in Malta, where, it transpiring that Crete had already fallen, the Fulmars would remain, being attached instead to 815 Squadron. They were subsequently employed for night intrusion sorties over southern Sicily.

Immediately upon return to Gibraltar, Force 'H' became involved in the hunt for the German battleship *Bismarck*, to be described in Chapter 14.

By this time the Luftwaffe in Sicily was being substantially reduced as units left to take part in the forthcoming invasion of the Soviet Union. It then became viable to fly more Hurricanes in by this route, not only to strengthen Malta's defences but in many cases to fly on to North Africa to reinforce

BELOW *One of the Grumman Martlet IIIs taken over from a Greek order which had reached Egypt in April/May 1941, is seen here serving with 805 Squadron land-based in the Western Desert later that year.*

BELOW *Torpedo-carrying Albacores of 828 Squadron leave Malta to support an incoming convoy under attack on 23 March 1942. As they departed, Messerschmitt Bf 109s attacked them and their Spitfire escort. The 109s were driven off but the escorting fighters had to turn back early, low on fuel. After two more hours the Albacore crews were ordered by Admiral Vian to return to base, as the presence of British aircraft over the battle zone 'might confuse the issue'. Vian's order almost certainly saved the lives of these crews.*

the forces in the Western Desert. As such it was both a faster and a safer route than that across the continent from Takoradi.

Consequently on 6 June Operation 'Rocket' ensued, *Ark Royal* and *Furious* flying off 44 more Hurricanes; one returned early to the carriers, but 43 arrived safely. A little over a week later, on 14 June, Operation 'Tracer' followed. This time HMS *Victorious*, fresh from the *Bismarck* operation, accompanied *Ark Royal*, carrying 28 Hurricanes while the veteran vessel brought in 20 more. Forty-five of these reached Malta, although one spun in on arrival. *Ark Royal* carried a further 22 on 27 June, all but one arriving to make Operation 'Railway I' another success. 'Railway II', launched just three days later, had more mixed fortunes. Twenty-six Hurricanes departed *Ark Royal* successfully, but after one aircraft had left *Furious*'s deck the next Hurricane crashed and a number of personnel were injured, including six of the pilots waiting to take off in the second batch of aircraft. Eight more of the first batch got into the air, but there were now no pilots available for the remaining six, and the carrier returned to Gibraltar with these still aboard. Of the 35 launched, all

but one arrived safely. They were accompanied by a number of Swordfish from 825 Squadron, which were to reinforce 830 Squadron. 825 had transferred from *Victorious* to *Ark Royal* after the 27 June run, allowing *Ark Royal*'s long-serving 820 Squadron to return to the UK for a well-earned rest. By now, of course, news had been received of the German attack on the Soviet Union, and Britain was no longer alone.

In the Eastern Mediterranean *Formidable*'s old air group had not remained idle, nor had the successful 815 Squadron. Following the end of the Cretan operations and the pacification of Iraq, efforts had been made to further secure the British position east of Egypt, in the rear of the forces facing the increasingly powerful *Afrika Korps*. It had become obvious during the Iraq situation that the Vichy administration in the French-mandated territories of Syria and Lebanon had co-operated with German and Italian efforts to influence the situation in Iraq to their advantage, allowing them facilities to pass through Syria to provide aid and advice to the dissidents. It was decided, therefore, to occupy these French territories in order to neutralise them.

An invasion was prepared under the title Operation 'Exporter', which commenced on 8 June 1941. Again, the British authorities underestimated the level of resistance likely to be offered by the local French forces, which in the event received reinforcement – particularly in air force units – from Metropolitan France and North Africa. To the French, the British action appeared to be an effort to steal French colonial interests. Consequently a hard-fought campaign followed, which took more than a month to bring to a successful conclusion. This resulted in the transfer of forces urgently needed in the Western Desert.

At the start of 'Exporter', Fleet Air Arm units allocated to take part alongside the RAF included:

815 Squadron at Nicosia, Cyprus, with six Swordfish
829 Squadron at Lydda, Palestine, with six Albacores
803 Squadron at Lydda, Palestine, with six Fulmars
806 Squadron at Aboukir, Egypt, with six (borrowed) Hurricanes

The initial invasion, undertaken along the coastal strip into the Lebanon, was provided with gunfire support by the 15th Cruiser Squadron. Patrols over the warships were seen as vital, given recent losses to Axis aircraft, and these were to be undertaken by the Hurricanes of 80 Squadron, RAF, and the Fulmars of 803 Squadron. On the first day while engaged thus, the latter were attacked by French Dewoitine D.520 fighters, which shot down three of them, damaged a fourth so badly that it had to be written off, and inflicted lesser damage on a fifth; only one escaped unscathed. The French incorrectly identified their opponents as Hurricanes. With 803 Squadron thus effectively destroyed, therefore, 80 Squadron was left to continue the duty alone, but likewise suffered heavily at the hands of the French fighters next day. Later in the month a composite RAF/FAA unit, 33/806 Squadron, moved to Lydda to assume responsibility for covering the 15th Cruiser Squadron. By this time, however, Australian-flown Curtiss Tomahawk fighters had proved to have the edge over the French Dewoitines, and had effectively cleared this part of the sky of their presence.

The main Fleet Air Arm involvement now moved to 815 Squadron, still led by Michael Torrens-Spence, now a Lieutenant Commander. On 10 June he led three of the unit's Swordfish to bomb destroyers in Beirut harbour. Two days later a similar attack was made on the port of Jounie, to the north of Beirut, where a tanker was torpedoed and caught fire.

Three large French destroyers were discovered to be on their way from Toulon, and as these approached the Syrian coast on 16 June, 815 Squadron attacked, Sub-Lieutenant D.A. Wise torpedoing *Chevalier Paul*, which sank. Three more Swordfish also attacked, but one was shot down into the sea by AA, the crew being captured. Six members of the destroyer's crew were killed and nine wounded, the rest all being rescued.

At the end of the month five Albacores of 826 Squadron arrived at Nicosia to join 815 Squadron. This unit had been operating a detachment of aircraft at Fuka in the Western Desert for the past month, dropping flares for night-bombing Wellingtons of the RAF's 205 Group, pioneering 'pathfinding'. At this stage French reinforcements began to arrive by sea, and at 0700 hours on 4 July Albacores of 829 Squadron from Lydda torpedoed the transport *Saint-Dizier*. Further attacks followed, but all the torpedoes were avoided. Finally, at 1700 four more aircraft attacked. The first torpedo launched missed the ship and hit a jetty at the little port of Adalia, just across the Turkish border, which brought a protest from the Turkish government. However, the other three aircraft all obtained hits on the damaged vessel, which sank with the loss of 52 of those aboard. A second steamer was then ordered to turn back.

On 11 July 33/806 Squadron left Lydda for Amiriya, task completed, and next day an armistice with the Vichy authorities came into force.

From the midsummer months of 1941 onwards, the little night-striking force on Malta, which 830 Squadron represented, had begun to achieve a higher rate of success during its attacks on Axis supply ships crossing the Mediterranean either to east or west of the island. By this time 'Ultra' intercepts were providing the high command on Malta with quite accurate information on the sailing, route and content of these convoys. However, great care had to be taken to maintain the absolute secrecy of their source. A charade therefore had to be gone through whereby reconnaissance aircraft had first to search all routes which might be used, and to 'find' the convoy under way before strikes could be launched. If the reconnaissance crews failed to spot the ships, no strike could be sent out. Of course, the Swordfish were by no means alone in the work they were undertaking. Whenever circumstances on Malta allowed, flotillas of submarines and destroyers also operated from the island, as did RAF bombers by both night and day. On those occasions when the Luftwaffe returned in strength to Sicily, life for these other predators became more difficult, and on occasion they were forced to withdraw. This was never to happen with 830 Squadron, however, which soldiered on regardless.

During the night of 16 July three Swordfish, one of them with a torpedo, found the 6,212- ton tanker *Panuco*, Lieutenant G.M.T. Osborn placing the torpedo directly into the vessel amidships. She was so damaged that she had to return at once to Italy with 6,000 tons of oil still aboard, undelivered. The 6,996-ton tanker *Brarena* was attacked by RAF aircraft during the night of 22/23 July, followed by five of 830 Squadron's Swordfish. Lieutenants Osborn and R.E. Bibby hit her with two torpedoes, and it was thought that a destroyer which was towing the already damaged vessel was also hit by a third torpedo. Following this attack the tanker was abandoned and drifted onto the Kerkenah Bank, where she became a total loss.

This latter attack occurred just as a large convoy was being despatched from Gibraltar, codenamed 'Substance'. Six merchant ships formed this eastbound convoy, while at the same time six empty vessels, plus the fleet auxiliary *Breconshire*, which were all in Valletta's Grand Harbour awaiting escort, sailed west. For this operation *Ark Royal* carried 21 Fulmars and seven Swordfish, the latter to be flown off to Malta to further reinforce 830 Squadron. Two Sea Hurricanes – a type yet to be employed in the Mediterranean – were also embarked. In the event *Ark Royal*'s team were unimpressed: the aircraft proved to have an inferior performance to the Fulmar at low level, which was where most of the shadowers were to be met. Furthermore, the inconvenience of having to maintain the aircraft permanently on deck because they did not feature folding wings as the Fulmar did, and would not fit the carrier's lifts, was not compensated for by the somewhat better performance which they offered at higher altitude.

S.79 torpedo-bombers out from Sardinia on the evening of 22 July failed to find the convoy, but at 0800 hours next day the ships were spotted and were attacked by formations of S.79s at low level, and on this occasion by Z.1007bis bombers at high altitude. Seven Fulmars had been boosted off to join four already on patrol, the new commanding officer of 808 Squadron (Lieutenant E.D.G. Lewin, DSC, of River Plate fame) and his wingman shooting down one Savoia, while a second was claimed by Lieutenant Commander Sholto Douglas and Lieutenant 'Buster' Hallett of 807 Squadron; two more were believed to have been damaged. The Fulmars then pursued the rest of the torpedo-bombers as they headed for the Force 'H' escort, but at low altitude, with little room to manoeuvre, three of them were hit in the engines by return fire and all had to ditch, although all the crews were rescued.

This time the S.79sils were rather more successful than on other occasions. One torpedo struck the light cruiser HMS *Manchester*, which was very badly damaged and had to be withdrawn to Gibraltar, accompanied by the destroyer *Fearless*, which had also sustained substantial damage. The aircraft which had gained the hit on *Manchester* was shot down by the ship's AA, the crew being picked up and made prisoners. Meanwhile, five of the Fulmars had climbed to their maximum altitude after the Z.1007bis formation, but had failed to catch them.

That afternoon, four S.79s – all that remained serviceable in Sardinia – were led to the convoy by a Z.506B. As they approached they were intercepted by a trio of 808 Squadron Fulmars led by Lieutenant R.C. Hay, RM, one being shot down and a second so damaged that it later force-landed in the sea.

That evening Force 'H' turned back westwards, although the Fulmars continued to patrol over the merchant ships until Beaufighters from Malta arrived to take over. Operation 'Substance' delivered 65,000 tons of supplies to the island – the highest delivery to be achieved since the start of the war.

On 31 July 830 Squadron made the first use of ASV (Air to Surface Vessel) radar, with which two of its aircraft were now equipped. The convoy which it had sought was found, one freighter of 6,000 tons being hit and damaged.

With Malta well replenished for the moment, there was a lull in operations throughout August. The only Fleet Air Arm activity of any note centred around 830 Squadron. During the night of 14/15 August six torpedo-carrying Swordfish and two with flares – the formation again guided by the ASV-fitted aircraft – attacked five merchant vessels off Tripoli. Hits were claimed on two of the ships (one by Lieutenant Osborn), with a third hit on a destroyer. Two nights later seven aircraft attacked six merchant ships and an escort of six destroyers west of Lampedusa. This time four hits were claimed, which it was thought struck one vessel of about 8,000 tons and damaged two more. Next day the 5,479-ton *Madalena Odero* was seen beached on Lampedusa, its destruction later being completed by RAF Blenheims. On the last day of the month five Swordfish sank the 861-ton *Egadi*, while during the night of 1/2 September the Fulmars of 800X Squadron gained a success over Sicily when Petty Officer Albert Sabey intercepted and shot down a Fiat BR 20M bomber. During the same night nine Swordfish attacked an escorted convoy of five merchant ships. Various hits were claimed, and the results were highly satisfactory.

The 6,338-ton *Andrea Gritti* blew up and sank while the 6,330-ton *Pietro Barbara* was badly damaged and had to be towed to Messina, where it sank.

The opportunity was taken at this stage to run a further reinforcement of Hurricanes to Malta, most of which were to fly on to North Africa after being refuelled. Consequently on 9 September *Ark Royal* flew off 14 fighters as Operation 'Status', returning four days later, this time accompanied by *Furious*, to launch 46 more as 'Status II'. All but one of these two deliveries of aircraft arrived safely on the island, these unopposed sorties coming to be referred to as 'Club Runs'.

As Force 'H's carriers had been so engaged, on 11 September five of 830 Squadron's Swordfish had followed an ASV-equipped aircraft to the Tunisian coast, where a convoy was being shadowed by another ASV Swordfish. The attack resulted in claims for one ship probably sunk and two damaged. Next day the 6,479-ton *Caffaro* was found damaged but still afloat, and was finished off by Blenheims.

An even bigger Malta convoy was now in preparation, named Operation 'Halberd'. Vessels began gathering at Gibraltar from 19 September, but as they did so a bold Italian attempt to cripple Force 'H' delayed departure. At 0100 hours three *maiale* – small one-man submersibles piloted by frogmen – were launched from the submarine *Scirè*, two being tasked with attaching explosive charges to HMS *Nelson* and one to do the same to *Ark Royal*. In the event they were hindered by patrolling light craft, so attached their charges instead to moored merchant vessels. All exploded, sinking one vessel and damaging two others.

Despite this setback, Force 'H' was able to sail on 24 September, *Ark Royal* now carrying 27 Fulmars of 807 and 808 Squadrons, and accompanied by no less than three battleships – *Nelson*, *Rodney* and *Prince of Wales*, plus five cruisers and 18 destroyers.

The convoy came within range of Sardinian-based units of the *Regia Aeronautica* at dawn on the 27th. Eight Fulmars of 808 Squadron were on patrol, seven more being launched to join them as torpedo-carrying S.79s and S.84s were intercepted ten miles out. The latter aircraft, recently introduced to service, were never to be correctly identified by Allied pilots, and on this occasion, as on others in the future, were thought to be either BR 20s (because of their twin tails) or Z.1007s (because of their three engines). The Fulmar crews were also unaware that an escort of CR.42s was also present. One section of defenders shot down one bomber from the first formation, but six got

LEFT *Staney Orr was one of the two most successful Royal Navy fighter pilots of the Second World War. His six and eight shared victories were all gained whilst flying Fleet Air Arm aircraft from aircraft carriers. His initial successes were claimed over the Mediterranean while flying Fulmars with 806 Squadron during 1940–41, while his final claims were made off Norway in 1944 when he commended 800 Squadron, equipped with Hellcats.*

through to pass over the destroyer screen, whose gunners claimed two more.

One Fulmar failed to return and was thought at first to have fallen to the CR.42s which appeared at this point; but it had in fact been shot down by friendly fire from *Prince of Wales*, the crew being lost. (It is perhaps worth noting here that throughout the war, Royal Navy gunners were notorious for their ignorance of aircraft recognition and their 'shoot first – ask questions later' attitude. In the light of the experience and losses suffered by Royal Navy vessels from air attacks during the early years of the war, this was perhaps understandable.)

As a result of this engagement the Italian crews claimed on their return to have sunk two battleships, the aircraft carrier and one other vessel; in fact all their torpedoes had missed!

A further big raid took place during the afternoon. The attackers were again S.84s, which patrolling Fulmars attempted to deal with but were driven off by CR.42s. The attackers split into two groups, one of which attacked *Nelson*, gaining a hit on her bow which caused considerable damage. In the second group one bomber was hit by AA fire, veered into another, and both crashed. As the group which had torpedoed *Nelson* flew away they were attacked by 807 Squadron Fulmars, which shot down one and claimed damage to another. A CR.42 pilot tried to divert attention from the bombers by flying directly over the ships, but his aircraft was also shot down by AA fire.

Twenty-five minutes later more S.84s approached, Fulmars shooting down one while a second fell to AA. The fighters followed the raiders right through the gun barrage, one pair shooting down another Savoia, but these two got too close to *Rodney* and one was shot down. Sub-Lieutenant Percy Guy and his observer were, however, picked up.

While the attack was under way, a Swordfish which had been undertaking an anti-submarine patrol blundered into seven CR.42s and was badly shot-up, although it escaped full destruction and got back aboard *Ark Royal*.

The Fulmar crews had claimed four victories during this second series of attacks, while AA fire claimed at least two. The Italian 36 *Stormo* had indeed lost six aircraft from the 11 sent out; 38 crewmen failed to return, all but one having lost their lives. Later in the day four 807 Squadron Fulmars intercepted and shot down a Z.506B. Another shadower would be shot down, again by four Fulmars, next morning as Force 'H' headed back west. However, during the preceding night a trio of S.79s from Sicily had managed to torpedo the 12,427-ton freighter *Imperial Star*. She was so damaged that, after the crew had been taken off, she had to be sunk by depth charges next day. 'Halberd' had nonetheless been a great success, with a record 85,000 tons of supplies reaching the island.

Ark Royal was on the way again on 17 October, this time bringing 11 Albacores and two Swordfish of 828 Squadron to Malta. Led by Lieutenant Commander D.E. Langmore, DSC, this unit had previously served aboard HMS *Victorious* and had seen action during an attack on northern Norway (of which more later), during which it had suffered heavy losses. Now it was to reinforce 830 Squadron on the island.

On this first day at sea 808 Squadron Fulmars intercepted and shot down a shadowing Z.506B, while next day, as the TBRs flew off, the squadron claimed another, this time a Fiat BR 20M. The Albacores and Swordfish were flown off successfully, although one of the latter was then lost en route to the island.

Meanwhile, 830 Squadron had enjoyed a further run of successes. During the night of 13/14 October the 7,933-ton *Bainsizza* was sunk, while next night a damaged freighter which had already been torpedoed by an RN submarine was finished off. Just as 828 Squadron arrived, five Swordfish went out on the 18th/19th after four merchant ships and four destroyers which were being shadowed by an ASV aircraft. Wellingtons dropped flares to illuminate the targets on this occasion and two hits with torpedoes were obtained on the 4,786-ton *Caterina*, which blew up violently. Damage to a second vessel was also claimed.

The newly arrived 828 Squadron commenced operations on 8 November when four of its Albacores dive-bombed a submarine depot at Augusta, four more bombing Syracuse harbour by mistake. Three nights later seven of 830's Swordfish went out after a convoy west of Pantelleria, led by the commanding officer, Lieutenant Commander J.G. Hunt. Three crews were forced to turn back due to engine problems, but the other four failed to return. Unable to find the target convoy, they had run low on fuel, forcing them to ditch near Palermo. Two men lost their lives, the others all being taken prisoner, including Hunt and the very successful Lieutenant Osborn.

In North Africa the British were soon to launch a major new offensive which would be codenamed Operation 'Crusader'. With air operations in the Soviet Union becoming restricted by the onset of winter, the Luftwaffe was now returning to Sicily in considerable strength. To be able to continue defending Malta successfully, and allow her strike forces to continue interdicting Axis supply convoys at such a critical period, several more squadrons of Hurricanes were to be brought out to the island (although it was also rumoured that most, if not all, were due to go on to operate in the Caucasus region of South Russia in support of the hard-pressed Soviet forces).

In any event, the elderly but hard-working *Argus* carried the Hurricanes of two RAF squadrons to Gibraltar, where others had been delivered in crates aboard HMS *Athene*. On 12 November both *Ark Royal* and *Argus* set off into the Mediterranean as part of Operation 'Perpetual', carrying 37 of these fighters, 34 of which would reach the island safely after being launched. Next day, as the carriers headed back towards Gibraltar, disaster struck. A salvo of torpedoes fired towards *Ark Royal* by *U-81* gained a single hit on the starboard side, and, although only one fatality resulted, the carrier was doomed. Only 50 miles from Gibraltar when hit, there was an immediate loss of power and heavy flooding. Attempts were made to tow her to harbour, but at dawn on the 14th she sank, despite all efforts. By that time all her crew had been taken off, and the Swordfish in the air at the time of the attack had landed at Gibraltar. The other Swordfish still aboard, and all 807 and 808 Squadrons' Fulmars, went down with her.

There could be no question of the vulnerable old *Argus* continuing deliveries on her own, and consequently the balance of the Hurricanes still at Gibraltar awaiting delivery had to remain there. Force 'H' was now also without a fleet carrier for Mediterranean operations, which – coupled with a new major assault on Malta about to be launched by the Luftwaffe – brought an end to such activities for the time being. The various carriers had undertaken 14 separate deliveries of aircraft to Malta since the first on 2 August 1940; of 361 Hurricanes carried, 333 had arrived safely, as had eight of nine Swordfish and all of 11 Albacores.

The loss of *Ark Royal* did not signal an end to other Fleet Air Arm activities over the Mediterranean and in the Middle East, which continued unabated. During the night of 20/21 November four Albacores of 828 Squadron and three Swordfish of 830, all loaded with torpedoes, were led by an ASV aircraft to the area of Cape Spartivento, where it was believed that an Italian force of two cruisers, four destroyers and four merchant ships were to be found. The Swordfish went in first, but were fired upon by the cruiser *Trieste*. This gave away her position and she was at once torpedoed by the submarine HMS *Utmost*. The Swordfish then attacked the second cruiser, *Duca degli Abruzzi*, and she was badly damaged by their torpedoes and had to be towed into port. The Albacore crews claimed hits on three of the merchant vessels, but these actually suffered no losses.

On Malta, meanwhile, 800X Squadron, which had become known as the Independent Night Fighting Unit, was down to only two Fulmars following a period of useful activity over southern Sicily, and was now stood down. DSCs or DSMs were awarded to four of the unit's personnel.

807 Squadron remained at Gibraltar's North Front airfield for the next six months, as did 812 Squadron. Until this point the RAF units based there had not received any adequate radar equipment to intercept the German U-boats which frequently passed through the Straits into the Mediterranean by night. But 812 Squadron, with a number of ASV-equipped aircraft, was now able to take on this task. Within three weeks five U-boats had been attacked and damaged, forcing them to return to their Atlantic bases for repairs. These efforts culminated during the night of 21/22 December, when *U-451* was sunk off Tangiers with depth charges, the first submarine to be sunk at night by an aircraft.

In Egypt earlier in the year the Fleet Air Arm had enjoyed a small windfall when it was discovered that a consignment of 30 Grumman F4F-3A fighters ordered by the Greek government had only got as far as Port Suez in April, just as Greece fell under German control. These were therefore transferred (or highjacked?) under the provisions of the new Lend-Lease Act, and were subsequently issued to 805 Squadron following the completion of the

unit's withdrawal from Crete during May. Unlike the ex-French aircraft which had been taken over in 1940, and which were powered by the 1,200hp Wright Cyclone single-row radial engine, these featured the Pratt and Whitney Twin Wasp two-row engine of similar power. This resulted in the nose cowling of the aircraft being somewhat deeper, presenting the aircraft with a slightly different visual appearance. At much the same time, 803 and 806 Squadrons were also being re-equipped with ex-RAF Hurricane Is.

As Operation 'Crusader' approached, the RAF, short of fighter aircraft, sought Fleet Air Arm assistance once more, and as a consequence the aircraft and personnel of these three units were temporarily combined to form what was known as the Royal Naval Fighter Squadron (RNFS). A move was made to Landing Ground 109 during November to take part in action over the front as soon as the advance of British Commonwealth forces against the Axis units on the frontier began, with the relief of the besieged port of Tobruk an early priority objective.

The story of the 'Crusader' offensive is not really a Fleet Air Arm one, and has been recounted before. Suffice to say that the RNFS operated throughout, alongside RAF squadrons and forming a part of various fighter wings of that air force until early February 1942. With the offensive at an end, it was then withdrawn to Dekheila to resume defensive duties. During its period at the front at least eight Axis aircraft were claimed shot down, plus a number of probables and damaged. Lieutenant Philip Charlton (known to all as 'Fearless Freddie') achieved some fame on 20 November when he shot down three Ju 87s in a single sortie. He was awarded a DFC by a grateful RAF for achieving this feat. The squadron suffered relatively few losses while involved in these operations.

Throughout these months 826 Squadron with its Albacores remained with RAF 205 Group, its principal duty being the dropping of flares over targets along the Libyan coast in aid of bombing raids by RAF Wellingtons. It was joined by 815 Squadron, which had re-equipped with 12 Albacores and two ASV-equipped Swordfish during August. Subsequently the Albacore crews undertook night bombing attacks on airfields and armoured formations, while the Swordfish were involved in anti-submarine operations in the same general area. At the end of the year these units were joined by 821 Squadron, which had been re-formed in England from a flight of 816 Squadron in July, and had been shipped out to Egypt in November.

CHAPTER 14

THE U-BOAT WAR

The Battle of the Atlantic

As already described, 1940 ended for the Fleet Air Arm with the first success being achieved by the new Grumman Martlets of 804 Squadron, which was also the last occasion on which a Luftwaffe aircraft would be shot down over the United Kingdom by an FAA aircraft.

At the start of 1941 the main Fleet Air Arm involvement in the war had thus moved decisively to the Mediterranean. Nevertheless, a serious situation remained in home waters and in the Atlantic, where the vital merchant shipping upon which Britain relied to continue her involvement in the war was threatened by U-boats, surface raiders and Condors. The last were the four-engined FW 200 long-range patrol bombers of the Luftwaffe, which were proving a deadly threat to ships as they approached the eastern side of the Atlantic Ocean.

While carriers would be called upon to counter the threat of surface raiders when they were known to be at sea, early experience had shown that the use of main force carriers to hunt U-boats was a dangerous and potentially unprofitable exercise. Against the Condors only fighter aviation offered a truly viable alternative. However, fighter aircraft were in short supply, particularly for the Fleet Air Arm, and carriers even more so.

When a scheme was hatched towards the end of 1940 for the mounting of fighter aircraft on catapults fitted to the top decks of ordinary merchant vessels,

LEFT *A German Type VII U-boat surrenders to the Allies.*

the idea was lighted upon by the fertile brain of the Prime Minister, who pressed for its development as rapidly as possible. While the initial thought had been to employ Fulmars in this role, these were required for service on the new armoured carriers as rapidly as they could be produced. Initial tests were indeed undertaken using this type of aircraft, but an alternative solution was then provided by the RAF, which released 50 Hawker Hurricane Is (some of them considerably 'used', it must be said) for this purpose.

Rechristened the Hurricane IA, these fighters then became the chosen weapon with which to equip Catapult Aircraft Merchant Ships – soon to become known as CAM-ships. Thirty-five suitable vessels with displacements of between 2,500 and 12,000 tons were selected, and each was fitted with a standard Royal Navy cordite-powered aircraft catapult which would boost off a Hurricane as soon as an FW 200 appeared.

The problem for the pilot, of course, was that he could not land back on again after an interception, and would either have to ditch alongside the nearest ship or make for land if it was within range. The biggest administrative problem was that stocks of Sea Hurricanes had to be maintained at virtually every port at which a CAM-ship might call

in order that its catapult could be replenished if its defending fighter had been launched during the preceding voyage.

With the intention that one or two CAM-ships should accompany each convoy, the first so fitted, SS *Michael E*, put to sea on 27 May 1941. Unfortunately she was torpedoed before ever having a chance to launch her aircraft. The first aerial victory of an aircraft of this nature was not, in fact, gained by a CAM-ship fighter at all, but by a similarly launched aircraft from HMS *Maplin*, one of four Fighter Catapult Ships converted by the Royal Navy to augment the CAM-ships. The others were *Ariguani*, *Patia* and the old floatplane carrier *Pegasus* (originally *Ark Royal*), all of which were converted during 1941. A fifth such vessel, HMS *Registan*, would follow in 1943.

This first success was gained by Lieutenant R.W.H. Everett on 3 August 1941, and by the end of the year six long-range Luftwaffe aircraft had been shot down by this method. Ultimately, crewing of the CAM-ships was taken over by the RAF, which operated the Merchant Ship Fighter Unit from 9 Group of Fighter Command.

While the advantage of the CAM-ship was that the vessel could still double as a cargo carrier, it was essentially a 'one-shot' weapon, and suffered

BELOW *The first auxiliary carrier, HMS* Audacity *was a conversion of a captured German merchantman. With a deckload of Grumman Martlet fighters of 802 Squadron, she gained several notable successes while escorting Gibraltar-bound convoys late in 1941, until sunk by a torpedo from U-751 on 21 December of that year.*

the logistical difficulties already mentioned. A more appropriate solution, it was realised, would be a small, cheap aircraft carrier. The first attempt to create one utilised the German merchantman *Hannover*, which had been captured in the West Indies during February 1941. She was rapidly converted to become the *Empire Audacity*, with a 475ft deck replacing her superstructure, beneath which was space for fuel storage and a workshop, but no hangar. Displacing 5,600 tons, she could make 15 knots and was armed with a single 4in gun at the stern and six 20mm anti-aircraft cannon. She was the first example of an Escort carrier (CVE). When American-built examples subsequently began arriving in the UK they were soon referred to as 'Woolworth' carriers, while in US service they were referred to as 'Jeep' carriers.

Audacity was ready for service by June 1941, when it was decided that the ideal fighter for operation from her deck – since it had to endure open stowage throughout the voyage – was the Grumman Martlet. At this stage, however, Martlets were in short supply. The Fleet Air Arm had been fortunate to take over the French order for these aircraft, but after taking into account losses at sea during delivery this amounted to only about 100. An additional 100 had been ordered by the British Purchasing Commission, but these would not become available until later in the year.

Consequently those serving in the Orkneys with 804 Squadron were transferred to a newly formed 802 Squadron for service with the new carrier. 804 received instead a number of Fulmars and some of the first Sea Hurricane IAs, which were then beginning to be supplied to the catapult ships. As early as October 1940 investigations had begun regarding the possibility of not only adapting the Hurricane for catapult duties, but also to see if it could be modified for actual carrier use, provided with both carrier spools and an arrester hook. This proved entirely feasible, and with a Vee-framed retractable hook beneath the fuselage it became the Sea Hurricane IB. With quite substantial numbers now becoming available from RAF stocks, conversion to this latter use commenced in 1941. 880 Squadron had formed in January 1941 with three Martlets, but when no more of these fighters were forthcoming three Sea Gladiators were borrowed, followed by nine Sea Hurricane IAs. These were replaced by Mark IBs in July.

Meanwhile, during the spring of 1941 the third of the new armoured carriers, *Victorious*, had become operational, but in May, as already recounted, she was involved in carrying a cargo of Hurricanes to Malta for the RAF. Her own complement of aircraft was therefore limited to six

Fulmars of 800Z Squadron (effectively a detached flight), plus nine Swordfish of 825 Squadron, which were aboard specifically for the defence of the vessel during the delivery operation. Her other unit, 828 Squadron, which was equipped with Albacores and trained for torpedo strike operations, was in the Orkneys, operating under Coastal Command control.

Also in this area was 771 Squadron, a reconnaissance unit which, late in 1940, had been provided with three Martin Maryland bombers, similar to those being employed for such purposes on Malta. During a sortie to Bergen on 22 May, the crew of one of these aircraft noted that the newly commissioned German battleship *Bismarck* had left a fjord where she had been at anchor. This ship was then spotted by RN cruisers in the Denmark Strait on 23 May. Interception of this dangerous vessel immediately became a top priority, and aboard *Victorious* delivery of the Hurricanes had to be put on hold, and the search for the German vessel joined. There was no time for 828 Squadron to join the carrier.

HMS *Hood* and the new *Prince of Wales* had engaged the German ship during the morning of 24 May, but a direct hit on the magazine of the former vessel had caused her to blow up with great loss of life. *Prince of Wales*, before having to break off, had obtained a near miss which had split one of *Bismarck*'s fuel tanks; flooding of one boiler room caused a small drop in her top speed and she began leaving a trail of oil. She parted from her attendant cruiser, *Prinz Eugen*, and sought to head for Brest on the Atlantic coast of France.

As *Victorious* came within range a strike was launched, despite her Swordfish crews not having been fully trained for this role. All nine attacked the battleship at around midnight on 24/25 May, managing to achieve one hit. This, though, struck her armoured belt and inflicted little damage. However, making evasive manoeuvres at high speed widened the split in her fuel tank and more oil began to leak out. To allow all the Swordfish to participate in the attack, 800Z's Fulmars had been employed to shadow *Bismarck*, and in poor weather conditions two of these failed to return; one crew was fortunate enough to be picked up by a passing merchant vessel.

At this stage contact with *Bismarck* was lost. Meanwhile, Force 'H' had put out from Gibraltar to provide cover for a troop convoy which the Home Fleet had been obliged to leave to its own devices while it searched to the north-west of the battleship's last known position. Anticipating that the German vessel would be heading for Brest, *Ark Royal* was moved north to intercept, her

Swordfish spotting *Bismarck* shortly after she had already been seen and reported by an RAF Sunderland just before midday on 26 May. She was shadowed while a strike was prepared, the cruiser HMS *Sheffield* also moving in closer to ensure that contact was maintained. The crews of the 15 Swordfish that were launched were not warned of this, and in poor weather, with low cloud and restricted visibility, 11 of them launched their torpedoes at *Sheffield* – all of which fortunately missed or exploded prematurely. The premature detonations had occurred because the heavy swell had interfered with the magnetically fused firing pistols, and realisation of this allowed the torpedoes carried by the second strike to be reset to a contact-only basis before it took off.

This time *Sheffield* directed the torpedo-bombers to their target, their flight also being assisted by ASV. Night had just fallen by this time, while the weather was too bad to allow a fully co-ordinated attack to be made. The Swordfish therefore went in singly, but managed to obtain two hits. One was again on the armoured belt and was ineffective, but the other hit was right at the rear of the vessel, destroying the steering gear and jamming the rudder. Thus disabled, the great ship could not follow a straight course. Several of the Swordfish had been hit by AA fire during the attack, and three of these crashed as they landed back on *Ark Royal*, while others were damaged beyond repair – one exhibited 175 holes. At this stage the crews were pessimistic, believing that they had not achieved much.

Meanwhile, *Bismarck* was attacked throughout the rest of the night by destroyers, which may have gained a further torpedo hit. At dawn the big ships of both the Home Fleet and Force 'H' were within range and *Bismarck* was soon reduced to a burning wreck, being finished off by a torpedo from the cruiser HMS *Dorsetshire*. A third strike from *Ark Royal* only arrived in time to see the final battle, and the crews were obliged simply to jettison their torpedoes. As had been the case at Cape Matapan, the Fleet Air Arm had fulfilled the role desired by the rest of the Royal Navy – it had slowed the enemy enough to allow the big guns to achieve victory.

Prinz Eugen, meantime, reached Brest on 1 June. Aware that the cruiser was still at large, both *Victorious* and *Ark Royal* had continued to search for her, joined by *Eagle*, newly returned from the Mediterranean Fleet, and by the battleship HMS *Nelson*. On 4 June Swordfish from *Victorious* caught the supply ship *Gonzenheim*, which had been waiting to re-supply *Bismarck* 200 miles north of the Azores; she was scuttled before surface vessels could close with her. Two days later aircraft from *Eagle* sank the blockade-runner *Elbe* with bombs, then captured the tanker *Lothringen* on the 15th. Meanwhile, the other carriers resumed their planned sortie to deliver Hurricanes to Malta, as has already been recounted.

With the Soviet Union now in the war following the German invasion of 22 June 1941, the Fleet Air Arm was given the additional task of aiding their new ally, directly or indirectly. The former method was chosen initially, an attack on communications in northern Norway being deemed achievable and possibly effective. Consequently *Victorious* and *Furious* were despatched northwards late in July to attack the ports of Kirkenes and Petsamo (see sidebar), while a delivery of mines to Archangel was undertaken by the minelayer HMS *Adventure*. During the afternoon of 30 July, therefore, *Victorious* launched 20 Albacores and nine Fulmars towards Kirkenes, while from *Furious* nine Albacores, nine Swordfish and six Fulmars were directed to Petsamo. Unfortunately the carrier force had been spotted by a shadower just prior to the launch of its aircraft and the defences were fully alerted, any chance of surprise being lost.

At Kirkenes the harbour had been cleared of most vessels and the raiders were able to claim only one small freighter sunk and one on fire. Apart from the defences having been alerted, the strike also had the misfortune to arrive just as a force of Ju 87s and their escorting fighters returned from a raid on Russian positions at the front. Both fighters and dive-bombers attacked the British aircraft, 11 Albacores being shot down, as were two Fulmars. The surviving Fulmar crews submitted claims for two Bf 110s and one Bf 109, while the pilot of the only Albacore to return undamaged claimed a Ju 87 with his front gun. Their main opponents had been a somewhat ad hoc Luftwaffe unit called

ORDER OF BATTLE – KIRKENES AND PETSAMO RAID, 30 JULY 1941

HMS *Victorious*

809 Squadron	12 Fulmars
827 Squadron	12 Albacores
828 Squadron	9 Albacores

HMS *Furious*

800 Squadron	9 Fulmars
880A Flight	4 Sea Hurricane IBs
812 Squadron	9 Swordfish
817 Squadron	9 Albacores

Jagdgruppe z.b.V. Petsamo, formed from elements of *Jagdgeschwader* 77. The Bf 110-equipped *Zerstorerstaffel*/JG 77 claimed six Albacores, while 14 *Staffel*/JG 77 pilots in Bf 109Es claimed seven more Albacores, two 'Skuas' and three 'Hurricanes' – from which it seems that Fulmars gave them something of an aircraft recognition headache! Actual German fighter losses appear to have amounted to just one Bf 110.

At Petsamo there was less opposition, but one Albacore and two Fulmars were lost. Although the carriers had been left with just four Sea Hurricanes on *Furious* and three Fulmars on *Victorious*, they were fortunately not attacked. The Sea Hurricane flight had only just become operational on this aircraft. Next day, while returning, the unit's commanding officer Lieutenant Commander F.E.C. 'Butch' Judd claimed one Do 18 shadower shot down – the first claim to be made by pilots operating Sea Hurricanes from a carrier.

During August *Victorious* returned to Arctic waters, this time as part of Force 'M', comprising the carrier, two cruisers and six destroyers, formed to escort HMS *Argus* and seven merchant ships (six

British and one Russian) to Archangel. *Argus* was carrying 24 Hurricanes of the RAF 151 Wing, which was to operate in the Murmansk area to introduce the Hurricane to the Red Naval Air Force, which was subsequently to take over the aircraft. The balance of the Wing's 48 aircraft were being carried in crates by the merchantmen.

Victorious had aboard her fighter squadron, 809, with Fulmars, but following the losses suffered over Kirkenes the TBR units had been replaced by 817 and 832 Squadrons, which between them had 21 Albacores. *Argus* had taken aboard a detachment of two of 802 Squadron's Martlets. While waiting for this carrier and the accompanying freighters to meet the covering force, *Victorious* launched her Albacores just after midnight on 3 September to attack shipping and oil storage tanks at Hammerfest. Little was seen and no attack was actually made, although one Albacore had to be ditched in the sea, her crew being picked up.

This had the effect of awakening the defences to the presence of the convoy, and as a result it was shadowed constantly thereafter. During 3 September Fulmars managed to catch and shoot

ABOVE *HMS* Victorious *moored in Seydisfjord, Iceland, prior to the Petsamo Raid, June 1941. On her deck may be seen some of her recently embarked Albacore torpedo-bombers.*

down one Do 18 flying boat, but this was the only success they were to gain, while one Fulmar crashed on the deck when returning from patrol.

Argus flew off her cargo of Hurricanes on 7 September, also transferring her pair of Martlets to *Victorious* before heading back west for Scapa Flow. Force 'M', meanwhile, returned to the Spitzbergen area to undertake attacks on German shipping along the Norwegian coast. Here, on 12 September, a vessel of about 2,000 tons was claimed sunk; she was the Norwegian passenger steamer *Baro*, which was lost with about 160 casualties, both German and Norwegian. Next morning, as the carrier prepared to launch a second strike, the two Martlets were scrambled after an He 111 shadower, which was shot down into the sea following a long chase by Lieutenant J.W. Sleigh and Sub-Lieutenant H.E. Williams.

Thereafter, *Victorious* and the Home Fleet were much involved in operations to keep the German surface raiders *Tirpitz* and *Lützow* out of the North Atlantic, and to escort convoys to North Russia. Several strikes were flown by Albacores, but without any remarkable result.

Early in September, while *Victorious* was involved in the Arctic, *Empire Audacity* – now HMS *Audacity* – put to sea to undertake her first escort for a convoy heading for Gibraltar, carrying six Martlets of 802 Squadron on her deck. On 15 September one of these engaged a U-boat, which the pilot strafed after spotting it. Next day two of the unit's pilots intercepted and shot down their first Condor, following which the convoy reached Gibraltar safely. Leaving again on 2 October, *Audacity* was back in port on the 27th of that month.

She sailed for a second time two days later, this time with eight Martlets and ten pilots aboard. Due to rough weather, one aircraft crashed while landing, while a second, flown by the commanding officer, Lieutenant Commander J.M. Wintour, was hit by return fire from an FW 200 just as he and another pilot were shooting it down. His aircraft also crashed into the sea, and he was killed.

While *Audacity* was docked at Gibraltar, where the convoy had arrived on 11 November, the news of the loss of *Ark Royal* was received. When *Audacity* sailed again on 14 December, therefore, the convoy of 32 merchant vessels she was to escort contained many of the survivors from the lost carrier. This time the journey was hard-fought as a pack of U-boats sought to inflict heavy losses. This cost the Germans five U-boats and two FW 200s, both shot down by the Martlets. One fighter also exchanged fire with *U-131*, which remained on the surface and was consequently caught and sunk

by the escorts, 802 Squadron therefore sharing in this success. The cost to the defenders was two merchantmen and one destroyer sunk, and three escorts damaged. This was considered a very favourable result for the defenders. However, on 21 December, when *Audacity* broke away from the convoy to increase speed and weave, *U-751* gained a direct torpedo hit on her and she went down with the loss of her remaining aircraft and 75 members of her crew, including her captain.

The effectiveness of the carrier was of considerable concern to the U-boat command, the head of which reported:

'The worst feature was the presence of the aircraft carrier. Small, fast, manoeuvrable aircraft circled the convoy continuously, so that when it was sighted the boats were repeatedly forced to submerge or withdraw. The presence of enemy aircraft also prevented any protracted shadowing or homing procedure by German aircraft. The sinking of the aircraft carrier is therefore of particular importance, not only in this case but also in every future convoy action.'

THE CHANNEL DASH

Following the sinking of *Ark Royal* during November 1941, 825 Squadron passed its remaining aircraft at Gibraltar to 812 Squadron, the crews then returning to the UK to be disbanded. The unit re-formed at Lee-on-Solent on 1 January 1942 with nine Swordfish Is under Lieutenant Commander Eugene Esmonde, who had led the attack on *Bismarck* from *Victorious* during the previous year. At the start of February six Swordfish were detached to Manston in Kent on standby in case the German battlecruisers *Scharnhorst* and *Gneisenau* and their attendant cruiser *Prinz Eugen* should attempt to break out of Brest harbour and make a run for the North German ports.

These vessels did indeed make just such an attempt in the early hours of 12 February. Due to a faulty ASV radar set in a patrolling Coastal Command aircraft they escaped discovery until well into the morning, by which time they were already passing through the narrowest part of the English Channel. Heavy cloud, rain and generally poor visibility aided them considerably, and the ships also enjoyed a well-organised constant fighter patrol overhead.

They were finally sighted, purely by chance and through a gap in the clouds, by a pair of RAF Spitfire pilots who returned to base at once to report what they had seen. By now it was almost too late, but 825 Squadron's Swordfish, loaded with torpedoes and led by their commanding officer, took off to attack. A substantial escort of Spitfires had been planned, but in the panic of this late sighting and the prevailing adverse weather conditions most of the fighters failed to rendezvous with the bombers.

The Swordfish therefore went in low against the formidable anti-aircraft power of the big ships, and under attack by the patrolling Luftwaffe FW 190s. Some of the latter actually had to drop their undercarriages to stay behind the slow biplanes, but the result was a foregone conclusion. Every Swordfish was shot down into the sea without a single hit being achieved. For this gallant attempt, Lieutenant Commander Esmonde was awarded a posthumous Victoria Cross, the Fleet Air Arm's first of the Second World War. Amazingly, five crew members survived and were rescued from the water, every one of them subsequently being decorated.

RAF aircraft continued to attempt to attack the flotilla as it headed north, but in the gloom either failed to find the ships, or, when they did spot them, failed to obtain any hits. They got clean away.

CONVOY PQ18

Following the decision to have the majority of the new escort carriers built in the US under Lend-Lease funding, due to the limited capacity remaining in British shipyards, the first to be completed, HMS *Archer*, was launched in November 1941, followed by *Avenger* in March 1942, and then by *Biter*, *Dasher*, *Battler* and *Attacker* by September of that year; another, *Charger*, was retained by the US Navy for training purposes. On arrival in the UK, however, the vessels constructed for the Royal Navy required extensive modification before use could be made of them. This brought forth an expression of disappointment from the US at the delay in putting them into service. However, when this finally occurred it proved, nonetheless, to be most auspicious.

During June 1942, convoy PQ 17 to Russia had been very badly mauled. Without aircraft carrier escort, 23 of 36 merchant vessels had been lost, ten to U-boat attack and 13 to aircraft. Two more ships were forced to turn back, so that only 11 actually got through. Such a rate of attrition was clearly unsustainable, the slaughter considerably exceeding that experienced on the Malta runs.

A further convoy was planned for August 1942, but *Victorious* was in dockyard for repairs following damage suffered during the 'Pedestal' convoy to Malta earlier that month (see Chapter 16). This left only the new CVE *Avenger* available, with her air group of 12 Sea Hurricanes and three

Swordfish. Nonetheless, she represented part of the first really decent level of support offered to a Polar convoy. PQ 18 comprised 39 supply vessels, but was supported by no less than 46 warships – six cruisers, 20 destroyers, two AA ships, four corvettes, two submarines, three minesweepers and four trawlers – plus, of course, *Avenger*.

Perhaps just as importantly, the Commander of the convoy was Rear Admiral E.K. Boddam-Whetham, who had been the first officer of Commander rank to have qualified as a Fleet Air Arm observer. Commander of the Escort Force was Rear Admiral R.L. Burnett, OBE, flying his flag on the cruiser *Scylla*, while the captain of *Avenger* was Commander A.P. Colthurst, himself a qualified torpedo aircraft pilot. All were men with an appropriate level of understanding of aerial operations.

On the first day within range of Luftwaffe

ABOVE *The Fleet Air Arm's first Victoria Cross of the Second World War was awarded posthumously to Lt Eugene Esmonde following his gallant leadership of 825 Squadron's Swordfish against the German battlecruisers Scharnhorst and Gneisenau in the English Channel on 12 February 1942. He did not return from this disastrous attack during which all the unit's aircraft were shot down.*

ABOVE *Seen from the deck of an aircraft carrier (possibly HMS Avenger), a merchant ship is bombed in the convoy PQ 18. It was the biggest Allied convoy to Russia and fought through a four-day attack by enemy torpedo planes and U-boats to deliver its cargo at an Arctic port.* IWM A12017

attacks from northern Norway – 13 September – the fighters were directed after 'shadowers'; this proved to be a costly mistake, for they missed intercepting a massive attack by 85 bombers. Fifty-five of these were He 111s each carrying two torpedoes, so that 110 of these were launched, eight merchant vessels being sunk. AA gun crews were able to claim only five of the attackers shot down. Less than an hour later came a second assault, during which three more raiders were claimed by the AA.

Thereafter the convoy commander made the very sensible decision to hold back the fighters to concentrate on the bombers when they appeared.

Next morning 20 torpedo-carriers approached, half concentrating on the carrier while the rest sought to hit one of the AA cruisers. Six Sea Hurricanes got off, their pilots and the AA claiming 13 German aircraft shot down; no hits were suffered by any of the ships on this occasion. Twelve dive-bombers then appeared, but all missed. Twenty-five more torpedo aircraft then attacked, half again concentrating on *Avenger*. This time ten fighters had taken off and, with the AA, nine more bombers were claimed. Unfortunately, however, the Sea Hurricanes followed the bombers into the AA screen and three of them were shot down by friendly fire; happily, all three pilots were rescued.

A final attack was made later in the afternoon by 20 more Luftwaffe aircraft, but again no hits were obtained and one more attacker was believed to have been shot down.

The third day proved cloudy and no interceptions were made. However, 50 bombers attempted to attack, and three more were claimed by AA fire.

By this time the convoy had gone beyond the range of aircraft from the German bases in the area, and the escort therefore turned back in order to cover a homeward-bound convoy of 15 empty vessels from earlier operations. Up to this point nine merchant vessels had been lost, but 34 German aircraft had been claimed shot down. Of these, the fighter pilots had claimed five Ju 88s and He 111s, plus some 21 more damaged – many of which were almost certainly then finished off by the guns. Now, on 18 September, the Luftwaffe launched an attack on the returning convoy, sinking one more ship but at a cost of four bombers. Finally the CAM-ship *Empire Morn* launched a Sea Hurricane, the pilot of which shot down two He 115 floatplane shadowers before flying to a Russian airfield to land.

During the heaviest air attack ever to be launched against a Russia-bound convoy, PQ 18 had suffered in total the loss of ten vessels to aircraft and three to U-boats. During the return journey one minesweeper was sunk by a U-boat on 20 September, while another submarine sank a merchant ship.

As the convoy drew out of range of Norwegian-based raiders the RAF was requested to take over escort duties, allowing *Avenger* and her exhausted pilots to return directly to base after ten days of sustained operations in Arctic conditions. Altogether, during a period of 12 days, 17 merchant ships, one destroyer, one minesweeper and one naval oiler had been sunk, while *Avenger* had lost four aircraft and an RAF flying boat had failed to return. The cost to the Germans was very heavy, with three U-boats sunk and five damaged, as well as 39 bombers and two patrol aircraft lost. The Luftwaffe would not be able to attack in such strength again. Thereafter, however, convoys to Russia were suspended until December 1942 due to the need to marshal all available shipping for the forthcoming North-West African landings.

Throughout the few daylight hours of the winter few losses were suffered on future convoys. Not until March 1944 was a CVE involved to any worthwhile extent, when, during a return escort that month, *Chaser*'s fighters damaged a U-boat which was then sunk by a destroyer, her Swordfish subsequently sinking two more submarines.

Later in March an outward-bound convoy was escorted by both *Activity* (a British-converted vessel) and *Tracker*. *Activity* carried seven Wildcats (as they had by then become known) and three Swordfish, while *Tracker* introduced the Avenger to this route, carrying 12 of these aircraft and seven Wildcats. *Tracker* aircraft co-operated with a destroyer in the sinking of one U-boat, while the fighters from the two vessels sank another. The Wildcat pilots also claimed the destruction of no less than six shadowers, including at least two FW 200s, two BV 138s and a Ju 88.

Thereafter the activities of the CVE air groups did much to keep losses on the Russian convoys light, and continued to assist in taking a steady toll of U-boats.

While these Polar convoys represented a considerable success for the Royal Navy, the much busier Atlantic route was still in great need of further aerial escort. Following the conversion of the CAM-ships, therefore, the MAC-ship (Merchant Aircraft Carrier) was instituted in their stead. These had to be based on grain ships or tankers, as a full-length flight deck was constructed on top of each vessel, which could not be achieved where there was a multiplicity of hatches or derricks.

The vessels to be converted had to have a speed of at least 14–15 knots and be capable of providing a flight deck 490ft long by 62ft wide. Later, however, a somewhat lower speed and smaller deck became acceptable. In the event six grain ships and four tankers were completed as MAC-ships, and nine existing tankers were converted to this role. Unlike the tanker conversion, the grain vessels were able to feature a lift and a small hangar, while tanker MAC-ships had to maintain all their aircraft on deck throughout each voyage. Each vessel could, typically, carry four Swordfish. Conversions began in October 1942, the first vessels being ready in May 1943.

The one major advantage of the MAC-ship over the CVE was that it could continue to carry virtually its full merchant cargo, and apart from the aircrews and their essential maintenance personnel the ships were commanded and manned by Merchant Navy seamen.

Throughout 1943–44 the battle with the U-boats in the Atlantic was essentially a CVE affair as the Royal Navy was joined by increasing numbers of US Navy vessels of this type, each carrying an Avenger/Wildcat hunter-killer unit aboard. These, and the surface vessels they worked with, took a steady toll of U-boats, making service in that arm of the Kriegsmarine statistically the most dangerous of any part of any service throughout the war. British CVEs operating in this particular area were *Archer*, *Biter*, *Fencer*, *Pursuer* and *Vindex*.

CHAPTER 15

ENTER THE JAPANESE

Fighting a Fearless Foe

The attack by aircraft from the Imperial Japanese Navy's carrier fleet on the US Fleet at Pearl Harbor in the Hawaiian islands on 7 December 1941 brought the USA fully into the war, which then became of truly global significance. It presented the British with an enormously powerful ally, the war potential of whose industries made victory virtually certain – but only at some time in the future, when it had become fully mobilised.

The opening phase of the new theatre of war, so far as British interests were involved, centred around Malaya and Singapore, where Japanese naval air power was again demonstrated by the sinking of the capital ships *Repulse* and *Prince of Wales* only a few days later. No part was played by the Fleet Air Arm at this stage – fortuitously, it must be said, when one considers the relative strengths and equipment of the two opposing navies. Originally, HMS *Indomitable*, the fourth of the new armoured fleet carriers, had been intended to accompany the two battleships to Singapore, where she too would most probably have been sunk. In the event she had grounded while working-up in the West Indies, and had been delayed in sailing.

When she did arrive, *Indomitable* landed her air group of Fulmars and Albacores at Aden,

LEFT *HMS* Indomitable *in the Indian Ocean with the Eastern Fleet during 1942. A Sea Hurricane may be seen on deck while an Albacore is just about to land on.*

HMS *Indomitable*

800 Squadron	12 Fulmars
880 Squadron	9 Sea Hurricanes
827 Squadron	12 Albacores
831 Squadron	12 Albacores

HMS *Formidable*

888 Squadron	16 Grumman Martlets
820 Squadron	21 Albacores and one Swordfish (target tug)

HMS *Hermes*

No aircraft aboard

RIGHT *Sea Hurricane IB AF966 '7F' of 880 Squadron about to take off from HMS* Indomitable *during 1941, at which time this was the Fleet Air Arm's first unit of these aircraft to become operational.*

BELOW *Airframe mechanics at work on a Sea Hurricane.*

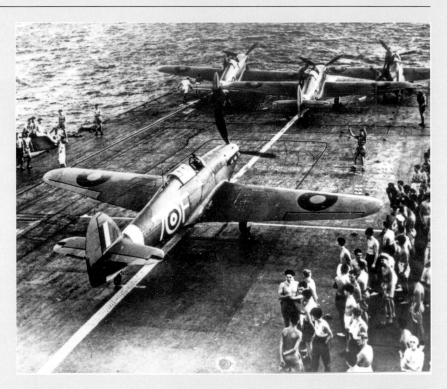

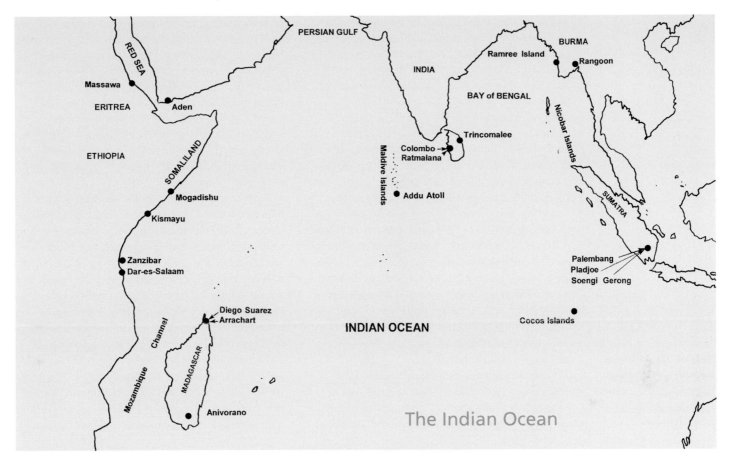

The Indian Ocean

so that she might be employed initially to run deckloads of Hurricanes from East Africa and Aden to Java and Ceylon, together with two squadrons of Fulmars. These were 803 and 806 Squadrons, which had been re-formed in Egypt during March 1942 and re-equipped with a dozen new Fulmars each before being shipped to Ceylon to provide protection for the naval bases at Ratmalana and China Bay.

At this time HMS *Hermes* had also been serving in the Indian Ocean since February 1941, but only with the 12 Swordfish of 814 Squadron. Here she had been involved in commerce protection duties. HMS *Formidable*, with repairs to the damage suffered during the Cretan operations having now been completed, also arrived. Thus the Eastern Fleet, now commanded by Admiral Sir James Somerville, fresh from leading Force 'H', had three carriers with a total strength of 39 fighters and 57 strike aircraft, five battleships – most of them elderly and slow – and a number of modern cruisers, four of which carried Walruses. The main fleet base was at Addu Atoll in the Maldives, with Ceylon as administrative HQ.

During February 1942, 788 Squadron had been formed in Ceylon as a TBR pool with six Swordfish. Colombo was defended by 30 and 258 Squadrons of the RAF with Hurricanes, one of these units

having only recently arrived aboard *Indomitable* while the other had just been re-formed from survivors of the debacle in Singapore and the East Indies. They were joined by the two newly arrived Fulmar units. At Trincomalee were 261 Squadron, with Hurricanes, which had also recently flown off *Indomitable*, and 273 Squadron, a resident unit which had been brought up to strength mainly with Fleet Air Arm crews and a handful of Fulmars; there was also a Station Flight of Fulmars. The island had but one squadron of Blenheims as the only RAF striking force, and two squadrons of Catalina flying boats, both much under strength.

At the start of April, *Indomitable* had aboard 21 fighters and two dozen Albacores, while on *Formidable* were 16 Grumman Martlets and 21 Albacores. *Hermes*, however, had just put ashore her Swordfish, and was temporarily without aircraft.

Towards the end of March the Imperial Japanese Navy sought to destroy the British Eastern Fleet in the Indian Ocean prior to embarking on any further conquests in the Pacific. Admiral Chuichi Nagumo led his First Carrier Striking Force (Nagumo Force) from its base at Staring Bay to commence this sortie on 26 March 1942. This included the aircraft carriers which had devastated Pearl Harbor and Darwin, *Shokaku*, *Zuikaku*, *Akagi*, *Hiryu* and

Soryu, accompanied by four battleships, one light and two heavy cruisers and eight destroyers – a most formidable fleet. The carriers had aboard more than 300 modern aircraft. These included Aichi D3A dive-bombers (later codenamed 'Val' by the Allies), Nakajima B5N torpedo and level bombers (codenamed 'Kate') and the soon to be famous Mitsubishi A6M Zero-Sen fighters – undoubtedly the best carrier fighter in service anywhere in the world at this time. Moreover, all her aircrews were long-serving professionals who enjoyed an extremely high standard of training.

As Nagumo Force sailed, Admiral Sir James Somerville arrived in Ceylon from Force 'H' to take command of the Eastern Fleet. British Intelligence was anticipating the Japanese incursion, although the possibility that it entailed an invasion of Ceylon was considered possible. Arrival was anticipated to be around 1 April, so when nothing had been seen by the evening of the 2nd Somerville ordered his ships to withdraw to Addu Atoll, the fleet's secret base in the Maldive Islands.

On Easter Sunday, 5 April, after some days of searching by Catalinas, the Nagumo Force of carriers was finally spotted. Having failed to find the British ships, Nagumo had ordered a strike to be launched against Colombo. As this intention became clear, the defenders had time to clear most ships from the harbour, there being no major naval vessels there anyway. 788 Squadron's Swordfish were ordered to be flown from Trincomalee to Minneriya as the only available operational land-based anti-shipping force, the RAF Blenheim squadron not having received training for this role. On the way the Swordfish encountered the A6Ms which were escorting the attack force and all six were shot down.

Fighters were scrambled to meet the incoming raid, but many of these were attacked as they were climbing. Six Fulmars, three from each squadron, took off, as well as RAF Hurricanes, but, totally outclassed by the Zero-Sens, lost four of their number, only one of the surviving pilots being able to submit a claim. 30 Squadron lost eight Hurricanes (four pilots killed and one mortally wounded); 258 Squadron lost seven with four more damaged. The final cost to the RAF amounted to 21 Hurricanes, of which two were repairable, and several more damaged. RAF pilots claimed 18 and six probables; additionally, the AA gunners claimed five, to raise total claims to 24, seven probables and nine damaged. Actual casualties inflicted amounted

BELOW *The Japanese aircraft carrier* Akagi, *flagship of Vice-Admiral Chuichi Nagumo.* IWM MH5933

to six D3As plus seven damaged, one A6M plus three damaged; and five B5Ns damaged. IJN fighter pilots claimed 33 and 11 probables, plus eight Swordfish and two probables. D3A crews claimed five more fighters.

In harbour the destroyer *Tenedos* was sunk and the merchant cruiser *Hector* was left on fire, sinking later. Two other vessels were damaged, but the damage to the harbour itself was easily repairable.

Meanwhile, over the Japanese carriers Zero-Sens of the Combat Air Patrol (CAP) intercepted and shot down a Catalina and one of two searching Albacores from the Eastern Fleet. Japanese spotter crews searching for the Eastern Fleet then found the cruisers *Cornwall* and *Dorsetshire* heading to join it after exiting Ceylon. Fifty-three D3As were at once launched, attacking these ships and sinking both in a classic dive-bombing attack.

Aircrews on *Indomitable* impatiently awaited the order to attack the Japanese fleet after cries for help from the cruisers had been picked up on the radio. Vice Admiral Somerville decided, however, that the Albacores were too vulnerable for day attack, and withdrew to keep the Eastern Fleet intact.

Over the next few days Nagumo Force and other IJN vessels disappeared from the British radars as they headed north-east on a hunt through the Bay of Bengal. The date 6 April proved to be the worst day of the war for Allied merchant vessel losses, U-boats notwithstanding. Nineteen ships were sunk, with a total displacement of nearly 100,000 tons. Between the 5th and the 9th another 23 cargo vessels were sunk by the marauding Japanese ships and aircraft. During this period the Eastern Fleet searched without success for the Japanese fleet in the hope of launching a night strike, but having failed to make contact with the raiders Somerville's ships returned to Addu on the 8th.

On 9 April came the second major Japanese strike on Ceylon, Trincomalee being the target. First, another searching Catalina was shot down, following which 91 B5Ns were launched, escorted by 41 A6Ms. The D3As were on this occasion held back in case of a counter-strike by Eastern Fleet aircraft, so that they could then be sent out against any British warships. Sixteen Hurricanes of 261 Squadron were scrambled, or were already up on patrol, joined by four Fulmars of the staff flight. The RAF pilots claimed four bombers and four fighters shot down, one and three as probables, and one fighter plus five bombers damaged. Three A6Ms were actually shot down, but the casualties to the B5Ns amounted to one shot down and one force-landed later due to serious damage, plus

ten more damaged. The cost to the defenders was eight Hurricanes shot down, crash-landed or force-landed, three damaged, and one under repair destroyed on the ground. One Staff Flight Fulmar was also shot down.

IJN total claims included at least 31 fighters and one floatplane shot down. Two Martlets of 888 Squadron which were ashore were not scrambled, and neither were the Fulmars of 273 Squadron. Again, most vessels in the harbour had scattered, but an 8,000-ton freighter, *Sagaing*, had not got out and was beached in flames. She was carrying a Walrus and three disassembled Albacores, all of which were lost.

Two things then happened. Japanese scouts found *Hermes* and three escorting destroyers at sea south of Trincomalee, and 11 Blenheims of 11 Squadron RAF took off to bomb Nagumo Force. Six Fulmars of 273 Squadron were also despatched in the same direction, to patrol independently.

Eighty-five D3As took off, escorted by nine A6Ms, and the first 32 of the dive-bombers to arrive launched an extremely accurate attack on the virtually helpless *Hermes* and HMAS *Vampire*; 40 hits were achieved on the carrier alone in a period of ten minutes and both vessels went down, *Hermes* being the first and only Royal Navy carrier sunk by air action – and the first such victory for the IJN. 273 Squadron's Fulmars then flew into the melee, claiming one D3A shot down, two probables and three damaged.

When the attack began, *Hermes* radioed for help, and eight of 803 and 806 Squadrons' Fulmars got off from the Colombo area. Meanwhile, finding the main target already sunk, the remaining formations of D3As arriving later spotted what they took to be a cargo vessel and two destroyers – actually the RFA *Athelstone* and corvette *Hollyhock*, both of which were sunk. Then the tanker *British Sergeant* and Norwegian freighter *Norviken* were spotted and these vessels were also sunk. Into these later actions flew the Fulmars from Colombo, claiming three D3As shot down for the loss of two of their number. Defending A6M pilots reported attacks by 19 fighters during this series of actions (273, 803 and 806 Squadron Fulmars), claiming five shot down and two probables. Four D3As were actually lost during the attacks, with five more suffering damage.

While all this was going on, the Blenheims approaching the IJN force were met by the CAP A6Ms, which shot down four (claiming six). The survivors turned back but then flew into the returning D3As and their escort, one more being shot down. Another was so badly hit that it crashed on landing, while two more were damaged; only three landed unscathed.

ABOVE *HMS* Hermes *sinks off the coast of Ceylon on 9 April 1942 following an attack by dive-bombers from five Japanese aircraft carriers. Her captain and 18 other officers were lost, together with 288 ratings.*

This brought the raid to an end, as Nagumo Force now turned south-east to head back to the Pacific. The Japanese were elated at having achieved the sinking of a carrier. They also believed that they had destroyed some 120 British aircraft for their own losses of 18 destroyed and 33 damaged. The British authorities, on the other hand, thought that they had stopped an invasion of Ceylon and inflicted severe damage on the air groups – they had claimed a total of 56 shot down and 26 probables by all the defences, at a cost of 48 aircraft in the air plus others on the ground.

This had not, in fact, been an invasion – it had been a raid in support of the advance into Burma, to secure safety from any attacks on their main supply port of Rangoon. Although undoubtedly successful, it had nonetheless failed in its main purpose, which had been to destroy the Eastern Fleet. Nagumo Force had returned to its base to refuel and replace

losses in time for its next major foray, which was to be to the Pacific island of Midway. In the event the totally unexpected defeat which the IJN suffered at the hands of the US Navy ensured that it would never again be in a position to launch a major foray into the Indian Ocean. During the rest of the Far Eastern war no Japanese warship larger than a cruiser would venture into the area.

OPERATION 'IRONCLAD'

The Indian Ocean now mainly became the scene of a submarine war for the Axis. The Japanese suggested to their German allies that a joint occupation of Madagascar would be propitious to provide bases for the two nations' submarine flotillas; however, the Germans refused to consider such a plan. Nevertheless, the British were indeed alarmed about such a possibility due to the increasingly pro-Axis stance of Vichy France. The

Indomitable, with two squadrons of Fulmars (12 aircraft, eight of 800 Squadron and four of 806 Squadron), nine Sea Hurricanes of 880 Squadron and 24 Albacores of 827 and 831 Squadrons, would target the French airfields.

Landings and strikes began on 5 May; 18 Swordfish sought vessels in Diego Suarez Bay, sinking the submarine *Beveziers* with torpedoes, bombs and depth charges. Albacores bombed Arrachart airfield, destroying five Moranes and two Potez on the ground there. This attack caused the French to evacuate the surviving aircraft to Anivorano. One Potez and one Morane were also reported missing on this date, although no British claims have been found.

Next day Swordfish from 829 Squadron were again successful, sinking the submarine *Le Heros*, while Albacores and fighters strafed the airfield again. The day also brought aerial combat for the first time when 881 Squadron Martlets on patrol encountered three Potez early in the day and shot down two. The same squadron enjoyed further success on 7 May, this time becoming engaged with Moranes. Initially one Martlet was hit and force-landed in the sea, but the others turned on their attackers, claiming four of the French fighters shot down; three were actually destroyed.

With the landings successfully accomplished for a loss of only four Fleet Air Arm aircraft to all causes, this had proved to be a very satisfactory venture. The landings had coincided with the Coral Sea battle – the first major aircraft carrier engagement of the war. The rest of the island would be occupied later, but while aircraft carrier support for further landings would follow, no opposition would be encountered in the air.

In July *Indomitable* departed for Gibraltar for the Operation 'Pedestal' Malta convoy. By arrangement with the US Navy on 28 July *Illustrious* and *Formidable* sortied into the Bay of Bengal as a diversion for the US landings on Guadalcanal in the Solomons. During this operation Martlets of 888 Squadron intercepted and shot down an IJN H6K flying boat from the Andamans on 2 August – the only encounter between Fleet Air Arm Martlets and Japanese aircraft that would ever occur.

Immediately following this sortie, *Formidable* departed for the Mediterranean on 24 August due to *Indomitable* having suffered severe damage during the 'Pedestal' convoy. *Illustrious* remained with the Eastern Fleet for the rest of the year, but in January 1943 departed for a refit. With no major threat now apparent, the Eastern Fleet would have no carriers with it for the next nine months.

decision had therefore been taken to occupy Diego Suarez at the north tip of the island – one of the biggest natural harbours in the world – even before the attack on Ceylon had occurred.

To implement this project, Force 'F' was formed and sailed from Gibraltar to South Africa on 1 April with the newly repaired *Illustrious* in support. On arrival, Force 'F' was supposed to have been joined by *Hermes*, but following the loss of that carrier *Indomitable* was substituted; *Formidable* remained with the Eastern Fleet to provide a covering force in case of Japanese interference. The French, meanwhile, had reinforced the island during 1941 with Potez 63s and Morane 406s, forming the *Groupe Aerienne Mixte*. Force 'F' sailed in late April. *Illustrious* now carried two squadrons of Martlets (881 and 882 Squadrons), a single nightfighter Fulmar and 20 Swordfish of 810 and 829 Squadrons. She would provide air cover.

CHAPTER 16

BACK TO THE MED

Operations 'Pedestal' and 'Torch'

Following the departure of 803 and 806 Squadrons to Ceylon, 805 Squadron remained in the Western Desert with its Martlets until June 1942, when it moved back to the Canal Zone to provide protection for the naval base area. It then moved to Kenya in August, where an increasingly substantial Fleet Air Arm training centre had been established. Here, however, it was disbanded in January 1943.

Prior to 805 Squadron's departure from Egypt it had been joined by an RN Fighter Flight, which had been formed on the departure of 803 and 806 Squadrons. Equipped with Fulmars, and later with a few RAF Hurricanes, this unit became 889 Squadron in March 1942, remaining in existence in the area until disbanded in February 1943.

At the start of 1942 *Furious* was undergoing a refit in the US and the only carrier which could be made available to replace *Ark Royal* was *Eagle*. This elderly vessel made three reinforcement trips during March, joined on one occasion by *Argus*. In April the large US carrier *Wasp* was loaned to the British to deliver 47 Spitfires, but co-ordination of events on their arrival in Malta was not what it should have been, and few were still serviceable within a few days. Pressed by

LEFT *These Royal Navy sub-lieutenant pilots are pictured on the flight deck of a carrier, possibly HMS* Formidable. *The two men on the left wear the insignia of the Royal Naval Volunteer Reserve; the pilot on the right is in the Royal Naval Reserve. Behind them is a Seafire IIc.* IWM TR1121

Churchill, President Franklin D. Roosevelt agreed to *Wasp* making a second delivery in May, this time accompanied by *Eagle*, and the 64 Spitfires flown off on this occasion, to a much better organised reception, were to make all the difference to the defenders.

Three more deliveries of fighters were made by the two British carriers up to early June, but a desperate shortage of supplies now made the running of a full convoy to the island vital. Consequently convoys were launched from each end of the Mediterranean in mid-June, that from the west codenamed 'Harpoon', and that from the east 'Vigorous'. Of course, as the Mediterranean Fleet now had no carriers only the former could be provided with protection from such vessels serving with Force 'H', consisting of *Eagle* and *Argus*. *Eagle* provided the bulk of the fighter defence, carrying four Sea Hurricanes of 813F Squadron, 12 more of 801 Squadron and four Fulmars of 807 Squadron (based on Gibraltar since the loss of *Ark Royal*). *Argus* carried two more of 807's Fulmars, plus 13 Swordfish of 813 and 824 Squadrons for anti-submarine work. Five merchant vessels made up the transport element of the convoy.

In the event the 'Vigorous' convoy was forced to turn back when its escorts ran low on AA ammunition after sustained air attack, but 'Harpoon' fought through in the face of constant and determined attack, mainly by Italian aircraft from Sardinia and Sicily. Eleven victories were claimed by the FAA fighters, and when defence of the convoy was handed over to Malta only one freighter and one destroyer had been lost. However, three more merchant vessels were sunk next day as they neared the island, all by air attack. The defence had cost the FAA three Sea Hurricanes and four Fulmars.

Eagle made two more deliveries of Spitfires in July, but the small number of ships to get through to the island during 'Harpoon' meant that another supreme effort was required. Consequently Operation 'Pedestal' was organised, representing the greatest FAA operation of the war so far. Six fast MVs and a tanker (*Ohio*) were to be escorted by *Eagle*, by *Victorious* from the Home Fleet, and by *Indomitable* – returned from the Indian Ocean, where it had been based since becoming operational, specifically for this venture. *Furious* was also to deliver yet a further 38 Spitfires. Gun support was provided by two battleships, seven light cruisers and 26 destroyers.

As this vast collection of ships sailed into the Mediterranean on 11 August 1942 it was spotted by *U-73*, which hit *Eagle* with four torpedoes just as *Furious* was flying off the Spitfires. *Eagle* went down quickly – the last fleet carrier to be lost by the RN during the war. Her patrolling fighters were able to land on other carriers in the group, however, and were available for action on the 12th, when the air attacks really began. In two days of fighting the FAA fighter pilots claimed 39 Axis aircraft shot down plus several more probables. The cost was seven Sea Hurricanes, including one by ships' gunfire, with four pilots killed; three Fulmars with the loss of all their crews; and one Martlet together with its pilot, the commanding officer, Lieutenant R.L. 'Sloppy' Johnston. A further Martlet and a Fulmar had ditched and four badly damaged aircraft had to be pushed over the side. Lieutenant R.J. Cork, one of the Battle of Britain 'stars', had claimed four victories and one shared while flying the only cannon-armed Sea Hurricane IC available. *Victorious* was hit by a heavy bomb which broke up on her deck, fortunately without causing serious damage. *Indomitable*, however, suffered two damaging hits which would require her departure to the US for some four months of repairs. During the fighting 800 Squadron's commanding officer, Lieutenant Commander J.M. Bruen, claimed two bombers shot down and a third shared, while a young Scot in that unit named Blyth Ritchie made similar claims, but against Ju 87 dive-bombers.

FLEET AIR ARM ORDER OF BATTLE – OPERATION 'PEDESTAL', AUGUST 1942

HMS *Victorious*

809 Squadron	12 Fulmars
884 Squadron	6 Fulmars
885 Squadron	6 Sea Hurricanes
817 Squadron	2 Albacores (9 detached)
832 Squadron	12 Albacores

HMS *Indomitable*

800 Squadron	12 Sea Hurricanes
806 Squadron	6 Martlets
880 Squadron	12 Sea Hurricanes
827 Squadron	12 Albacores
831 Squadron	12 Albacores

HMS *Eagle*

801 Squadron	12 Sea Hurricanes (plus four in reserve)
813 Squadron	4 Sea Hurricanes

HMS *Furious*

822 Squadron	4 Albacores
	38 Spitfires for delivery by flying off to Malta

Furious meantime returned with another 32 Spitfires, and would bring in a final cargo of 31 more on 29 October, bringing the number of such operations to 25, during which 764 aircraft had been carried; 718 of these arrived safely, 34 were lost, and 12 which did not fly off were returned to Gibraltar for later delivery.

However, by the date of that last delivery the siege of Malta was virtually at an end, while in North Africa the Battle of El Alamein was at its height. The next Fleet Air Arm operations in the area would be of a very different nature, despite taking place only a few days later.

On 8 November 1942 Operation 'Torch' saw Anglo-American forces landing in French North-West Africa, at Algiers, Oran, and on the Moroccan Atlantic coast. The last was a wholly US operation, supported by USN aircraft carriers and their air groups, all of which had sailed directly from the USA. Support for the landings on the Mediterranean coast was entirely a British affair, involving not only the experienced fleet carriers, but also three of the new US-built escort vessels (CVEs). Also appearing in strength for the first time were examples of the Fleet Air Arm's new Seafire fighter.

The Oran group included *Furious*, the old *Argus*, and the CVEs *Biter*, *Dasher* and *Avenger*, while Force 'H' provided a covering force standing offshore, including two fleet carriers, *Victorious* and *Formidable*. For this operation, in an effort to persuade the Vichy French that it was essentially an entirely US effort, all the Fleet Air Arm aircraft were painted with US white star markings in place of their normal British roundels.

Furious's aircraft claimed 47 French aircraft destroyed on the ground at La Senia in a single strafing attack. However, eight 822 Squadron Albacores dive-bombing here were intercepted by Vichy D.520s, three being shot down and three damaged, while a seventh fell to AA fire. Escorting Sea Hurricanes fell on the attackers, claiming five shot down. Over the same area another D.520 was shot down by Lieutenant G.C. Baldwin in a Seafire of 807 Squadron, the first victory to be claimed for this type. There were several more engagements during the day between Seafires, Sea Hurricanes and D.520s, with claims made by both sides.

There was less action in the Algiers area, Seafires shooting down a single Douglas DB 7, while 882 Squadron Martlets strafed two French aircraft on the ground at Blida airfield. Later in the morning other pilots from this unit saw nothing while patrolling overhead, so Lieutenant B.H.C. Nation landed and took possession of the base on behalf of the Allied forces.

Next day, as RAF fighters began flying in, Luftwaffe bombers launched attacks during which patrolling Martlets were able to claim at least two shot down. Fleet Air Arm losses during 'Torch' totalled 15 Sea Hurricanes, at least 12 Seafires, eight Martlets, eight Albacores and two Fulmars, though most were described as being due to 'insufficient time in type'. The accuracy of the pilots' firing was described as being generally of a very low order, but as many of the units were newly formed and their personnel very inexperienced the overall results were not entirely unsatisfactory, despite the high level of accidental losses during operational flying. 800 Squadron aboard *Biter* were a more experienced group, however, and several of this unit's pilots had done

FLEET AIR ARM ORDER OF BATTLE – OPERATION 'TORCH', NOVEMBER 1942

HMS *Formidable*
885 Squadron	6 Seafire IICs
888 Squadron	12 Martlet IIs
893 Squadron	12 Martlet IVs
820 Squadron	12 Albacores

HMS *Victorious*
809 Squadron	6 Fulmar IIs
882 Squadron	12 Martlet IVs
884 Squadron	6 Seafire IICs
817 Squadron	9 Albacores
832 Squadron	9 Albacores

HMS *Furious*
801 Squadron	12 Seafire IBs
807 Squadron	12 Seafire IICs
822 Squadron	8 Albacores, 1 Fulmar FR II

HMS *Biter*
800 Squadron	15 Sea Hurricane IIBs and IICs
833A Flight	3 Swordfish

HMS *Dasher*
804 Squadron	6 Sea Hurricane IICs
891 Squadron	6 Sea Hurricane IIBs

HMS *Argus*
880 Squadron	18 Seafire IICs

HMS *Avenger*
802 Squadron	9 Sea Hurricane IICs
883 Squadron	6 Sea Hurricane IICs
833B Flight	3 Swordfish

well. That old hand Lieutenant Commander J.M. 'Bill' Bruen had claimed one D.520, as had the rising 'star', Blyth Ritchie. Also now serving with this unit was Sub-Lieutenant R.M. Crosley, who had already claimed one and one shared, plus a probable while flying with 813 Squadron during the 'Harpoon' convoy, who now added claims for two of the French fighters.

Argus took on four Sea Hurricanes from *Avenger*, which had gone into harbour at Algiers with engine trouble, and on 11 November provided fighter cover for landings at the small port of Bougie, further east near the Tunisian border. On 15 November, while escorting a convoy of empty vessels back towards the UK, *Avenger* was torpedoed by *U-155* and blew up with heavy losses, only 17 members of the crew surviving. Aboard her, 802 Squadron was lost in its entirety for the second time.

Even at the end of 1942 the Royal Navy was still very short of the aircraft carriers and other ships which the Admiralty desired. Of the six armoured carriers ordered during 1937–39, four had now been delivered – and were in service or repair. These were *Illustrious*, *Formidable*, *Victorious* and *Indomitable*. Work was progressing on *Implacable*, but not on *Indefatigable*. Since the spring of 1940 most work on big vessels in British shipyards had been halted so that anti-invasion and anti-submarine requirements could be concentrated on. This had also affected the construction of two battleships and a number of cruisers and destroyers. The only exception had been the fast

battleship *Vanguard*, for which the guns were already available.

When the Admiralty sought to get construction resumed, Churchill's reply was: 'We cannot at the present time contemplate any construction of heavy ships that cannot be completed in 1942.' During 1941 the Admiralty wished to give priority to battleships, since these could provide striking power in all weathers and by night as well as day. At this stage the effectiveness of aircraft had still not convinced the doubters that they could sink battleships at sea. The experience of the Pacific War, however, swiftly changed that perception during 1942.

By the middle of that year the Admiralty had issued orders for four new large fleet carriers termed the *Audacious* class. These new leviathans would have a displacement of circa 36,800 tons. Also ordered were ten light fleet carriers of the *Colossus* class (13,190 tons) and six of the *Majestic* class (14,000 tons). They also wanted 32 escort carriers for convoy work, but these were all to be constructed in the USA, where dockyards were now introducing assembly line mass-production techniques. The first fruits of this arrangement had already been employed during the recent 'Torch' operations. In the meantime, however, four unfinished merchant ship hulls in the 12–14,000-ton category were taken over in British shipyards for completion as escort carriers named *Activity*, *Campania*, *Nairana* and *Vindex* – the names that had been applied to the First World War floatplane carriers.

CHAPTER 17

EAST OF MALTA

Operations in the Med and the Far East

Following the loss of four of its six large fleet carriers during 1942, and with a fifth having suffered heavy damage, the US Navy was very short of such vessels as 1943 approached, pending delivery of the new *Essex*-class ships with which that service would come to dominate the Pacific Ocean.

During this hiatus help was requested from the Royal Navy. Consequently, following the conclusion of the 'Torch' operations in North-West Africa, *Victorious* was loaned to the Americans from the Home Fleet, her place being taken by *Furious*, which transferred from the Mediterranean. *Victorious* sailed for the US at the end of December 1942, initially refitting at the Norfolk Navy Yard before passing through the Panama Canal for the Hawaiian Islands. Aboard she carried three squadrons of Martlet IVs (882, 896 and 898) and one of newly arrived Grumman Tarpons (832). This air group would therefore appear to match closely the F4F-4 Wildcats and TBF Avengers likely to be employed by US vessels. However, the 'fit' was not perfect, since the Martlet IVs were essentially an export version of the Grumman fighter, and were fitted with the single-row Wright Cyclone engine

LEFT *HMS* Victorious *is seen here during her attachment to the US Navy in the South West Pacific during mid-1943. On her deck are a number of Wildcat fighters (newly renamed from Martlet); some of these may be seen to be bearing US markings. Running short of aircraft, the carrier air group had borrowed a number of US Navy F4Fs from USS* Saratoga.

rather than the double-row Pratt & Whitney Twin Wasp of the F4F-4.

Victorious left Hawaii on 8 May 1943, just a year after the 'Ironclad' operation in the Indian Ocean. While there she had represented the sole carrier defence of the Hawaii–Midway island chain. Joining USS Saratoga at Noumea, New Caledonia, on 17 May – the only available US Navy fleet carrier at this time – the two vessels and their consorts formed Task Force 14. Their initial voyage was an exercise in methodology and co-operation in the Coral Sea, as a result of which it was agreed that Victorious would operate as a fighter carrier, for which her air defence equipment and size suited her well. All Avengers/ Tarpons and SBD Dauntless dive-bombers were embarked on the US carrier with a small group of F4F-4s for her immediate defence.

From 27 June to 25 July the carriers were involved in covering the landings on New Georgia – Operation 'Toenail' – but no aerial opposition was encountered. At this stage of the war the Imperial Japanese Navy was little better placed than the Allies following their own carrier losses during the previous year. No attempt was made to interfere with the landings.

With land-based US aircraft available on Guadalcanal and in the Russell Islands, and with three USN escort carriers also to hand for close-in support, there was little for the big carriers to do. Once New Georgia was secure there was no longer a vital need to retain Victorious in the area, and on 31 July she departed for home, arriving back during September 1943.

Meanwhile, following the 'Torch' landings there had been little call for carrier involvement in the Mediterranean during the next eight months either. Force 'H' had remained ready in case the Italian Fleet, or any elements of the French Fleet in Toulon, should sortie. Meanwhile, 820 Squadron's Albacores went ashore to Bone, where they were joined by 813 Squadron Swordfish, to join RAF Wellingtons in night attacks on Axis shipping seeking to resupply, and then to evacuate, the forces retreating into northern Tunisia. Such attacks continued to be made by the bomber units on Malta, now joined by 821 Squadron from Egypt.

With the fall of Tunisia early in May 1943 the whole North African seaboard was in Allied hands, and plans were prepared for the invasion of Sicily – the first thrust into what Churchill had called 'the soft underbelly of Europe'. This commenced on 10 July 1943, but as southern Sicily was in range of land-based fighters on Malta, Gozo and Pantelleria, and of bomber aircraft in Tunisia, there was no necessity for aircraft carrier involvement. Their next operation was participation in the providing of air cover for the landings on Sicily in July. Indomitable and Formidable with Force 'H' remained available, again in case of any action by the Italian Fleet. The former carrier now had an air group comprising 40 Seafires of 807, 880 and 899 Squadrons, and 15 Albacores of 817 Squadron, while the latter had five Seafires of 885 Squadron, 28 Martlet IVs of 888 and 893 Squadrons, and a dozen Albacores of 820 Squadron.

So beaten down were the Luftwaffe and Regia Aeronautica by now that there was little for the carriers to do. No Italian warships made any attempt to intervene. However, at evening on 16 July, six days after the initial landings, a single

RIGHT *Following action during the invasion of Southern France and a sweep through the Aegean, HMS* Attacker *became involved in carrying supplies of aircraft to Ceylon. She is seen here loaded with Seafires, which appear to have been painted with East Indies Fleet recognition bands around the wings. A resupply barge is moored alongside.*

Ju 88 put an air-launched torpedo into *Indomitable*'s side, damaging a boiler room seriously. On her first operation since 'Pedestal' nearly a year earlier, she was again out of action for almost a further year. Her place was taken by *Illustrious*.

On 9 September 1943 came the landings at Salerno on the south-east coast of Italy (Operation 'Husky'). At maximum range for the RAF and USAAF fighters now based in Sicily, this appeared to offer the Royal Navy's carriers a great opportunity to distinguish themselves while covering the initial days of the landings, until air strips were made available on shore. Force 'V' was formed with four CVEs – *Attacker*, *Battler*, *Hunter* and *Stalker* – and a new repair carrier, *Unicorn*, for the provision of fighter cover and close support to the forces ashore. These ships were under the command of Rear Admiral Sir Philip Vian, whose name would soon become familiar throughout the Fleet Air Arm. As before, Force 'H' provided the heavy support, and included the fleet carriers *Formidable* and *Illustrious*, which were guarding, once again, against the possibility of an Italian Fleet sortie. As it transpired this was the last time that this was necessary, since the Italian armistice occurred as the landings were going ahead. Their fleet subsequently sailed to Malta to surrender.

The Seafires – equivalent by now only to obsolescent models of the Spitfire – were unable to catch raiding Bf 109s and FW 190s, which attempted to make many fighter-bomber attacks. However, they did prove effective in breaking up these attacks and forcing them to turn back. Only once did the Germans stay and fight, when two Bf 109s were claimed shot down. Martlets of the covering force claimed one Italian aircraft shot down and one 'captured'.

Within two and a half days Force 'V' was almost out of serviceable aircraft, but was reinforced on 11 September with *Formidable*'s and *Illustrious*'s Seafires, these two carriers then withdrawing to Malta since the threat of the Italian Fleet was ended. Next day 26 Seafires were flown ashore to the first landing ground to be prepared at Paestum. Here they operated until 15 September, when the surviving aircraft returned to their carriers, the crisis over. RAF and USAAF fighters then flew in to take over. No Seafires were lost in combat, but four were written off due to engine failures and 32 in deck landing accidents, principally due to their narrow, weak undercarriages. This high level of damage was subsequently considered to have been exacerbated by Admiral Vian's decision to position his carriers too close inshore, causing them to run out of searoom when manoeuvring to allow the fighters to land.

However, the Seafires' role had been important.

FLEET AIR ARM ORDER OF BATTLE – OPERATION 'HUSKY', 9 SEPTEMBER 1943

HMS *Illustrious*

878 Squadron	14 Martlet IVs
890 Squadron	14 Martlet IVs
894 Squadron	10 Seafire IICs

HMS *Formidable*

885 Squadron	5 Seafire IICs
888 Squadron	16 Martlet IVs
803 Squadron	16 Martlet IVs
820 Squadron	12 Albacores

HMS *Attacker*

879 Squadron	10 Seafire IICs
886 Squadron	9 Seafire IICs

HMS *Battler*

807 Squadron	9 Seafire IICs
808 Squadron	9 Seafire IICs

HMS *Hunter*

834 Fighter Flight	6 Seafire IICs
899 Squadron	14 Seafire IICs

HMS *Stalker*

833 Fighter Flight	6 Seafire IICs
880 Squadron	13 Seafire IICs

HMS *Unicorn*

809 Squadron	10 Seafire IICs
887 Squadron	10 Seafire IICs
897 Squadron	10 Seafire IICs
818 Flight	3 Swordfish
885 Squadron	2 Seafire IICs (ex-*Formidable*)
888/893 Squadron	17 Martlet IVs (ex-*Formidable*)
894 Squadron	6 Seafire IICs (ex-*Illustrious*)

Some 713 sorties had been flown during 42 daylight hours, and while this represented only 20 per cent of the total number of sorties flown by Allied fighters over the beachhead, it did represent over 50 per cent of the hours spent over the area because of the great range at which those from Sicily had to operate. Force 'V' was disbanded on 20 September, the CVEs then returning to the UK to refit and rearm their squadrons.

No carriers were called upon to support the landings at Anzio the following January, and indeed the next Royal Navy carrier involvement would not occur until the invasion of Southern France in August 1944, of which more later.

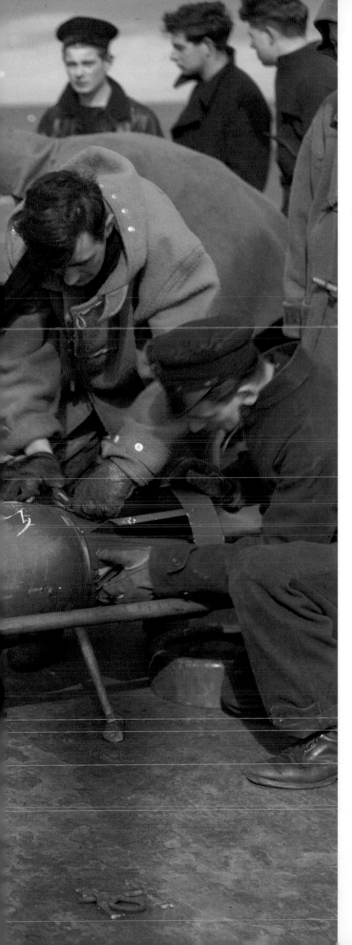

CHAPTER 18

TURNING THE CORNER

Gaining the Upper Hand in Atlantic Waters

At the start of 1943, following the replacement of *Victorious* by *Furious*, the only other air component available to the Home Fleet was the CVE *Dasher*. However, as this carrier prepared for a planned night strike with torpedoes against the German capital ship *Tirpitz* in Altenfjord, she was destroyed by an explosion of aviation fuel while in the Firth of Clyde on 27 March 1943. In July *Illustrious* joined the fleet, as did *Unicorn* – although her stay was brief, as she then headed for the Mediterranean to take part in the Salerno landings in September.

In the autumn *Illustrious* too headed for the Med, leaving such action as there was to be undertaken by USS *Ranger*, which served with the Home Fleet during September/October.

By the spring of 1944 *Tirpitz* had been damaged by midget submarines and *Scharnhorst* had been sunk by *Duke of York* during the last capital ship encounter in the West. This greatly reduced the threat posed by German surface raiders to the North Atlantic and Arctic convoys, while attacks on the damaged *Tirpitz* in Kaalfjord offered much scope for the training of new FAA crews in the use of new equipment.

The FAA was now receiving growing numbers of well-trained aircrews, and new, more modern

LEFT *Fleet Air Arm personnel fusing bombs on the flight deck of an aircraft carrier. The bombs were then loaded onto Barracuda aircraft which attacked the German battleship* Tirpitz *in Alten Fjord, Norway, 3 April 1944.* IWM TR1812

and effective aircraft from US production. Indeed, from this time more and more new squadrons were forming in the US, rather than in the UK. Substantial numbers of the latest models of the well-proven Martlet were now becoming available as the Mark V – the name now being changed to its US title of Wildcat. The improved Grumman Hellcat (initially known to the Fleet Air Arm as the Gannet) and Vought Corsair fighters were also beginning to arrive, as were the first of a new dive/torpedo-bomber from Fairey, the Barracuda. The latter were joined by another Grumman aircraft for similar purposes, which was initially named the Tarpon but soon reverted to its US name of Avenger.

On 3 April 1944 Operation 'Tungsten' was launched against *Tirpitz*. This involved the carriers *Victorious* (1834 and 1836 Squadrons forming 47 Naval Fighter Wing, with 14 Corsairs each, and 827 and 829 Squadrons with 21 Barracudas); *Furious* (801 and 880 Squadrons with 14 Seafires, and 830 and 831 Squadrons with 18 Barracudas); *Emperor* (800 and 804 Squadrons with 20 Hellcats);

OPPOSITE *Built in larger numbers than any other aircraft ever to serve with the Fleet Air Arm, the Fairey Barracuda was developed as a torpedo and dive-bomber. Entering service at the start of 1943, the aircraft commenced with strikes on the German bases and harbours in Norway. Although despatched to the Indian Ocean in considerable numbers, the aircraft was quickly replaced by the Grumman Avenger for service with the British Pacific Fleet due to the latter's greater range.*

Pursuer (881 and 896 Squadrons with 20 Wildcat Vs); *Searcher* (882 and 898 Squadrons with 20 Wildcat Vs); and *Fencer* serving as anti-submarine CVE with 842 Squadron, equipped with 12 Swordfish and eight Wildcat IVs. *Tirpitz* was damaged again, putting her out of action for three more months.

Little need existed for the Royal Navy carrier force to take any part in the D-Day landings, although a number of Seafire squadrons were attached to the RAF's 2nd Tactical Air Force to spot gunfire for

BELOW *Fleet Air Arm Seafires of the 3rd Naval Fighter Wing at Lee-on-Solent formed part of the Air Spotting Pool, spotting for the guns of warships supporting the Normandy landings in June 1944. One of the units so involved was 885 Squadron, a Seafire IIC from which is seen here over Northern Ireland a few weeks later.*

ABOVE *HMS Emperor was a US-built escort carrier, commissioned by the US Navy in May 1943 as ACV-34 (USS Rhybus). Three months later she was transferred to the Royal Navy, then seeing service in both the North Atlantic and the Indian Ocean. Typical of her class of vessel, she is seen here in 1944 in the former location, her decks loaded with Grumman Hellcats.*

RIGHT *Sub Lt H.H. Salisbury, RNVR, of the Fleet Air Arm, a former station inspector at Bow Street Station, adjusts his helmet before a flight. He is standing in front of Supermarine Seafire NX942 at RNAS Yeovilton, with others in the background, 2 September 1943.*
IWM TR1276

cruisers and destroyers operating off the Normandy coast in support of the troops ashore. Operations along the Norwegian coast were to continue for the rest of the war, penning in *Tirpitz* and providing an ongoing illusion to the Germans that a landing there might take place at any time.

A second major strike on *Tirpitz* took place on 17 July as Operation 'Mascot'. This time it included *Formidable* (18 Corsairs of 1841 Squadron, and 24 Barracudas of 827 and 830 Squadrons); *Furious* (20 Hellcats of 1840 Squadron, plus three Seafires of 880 Squadron and three Swordfish); and a fifth new Fleet carrier, *Indefatigable* (12 Seafire IIIs – the improved, fully navalised aircraft with folding wings – of 894 Squadron, 12 Fireflies of 1770 Squadron, and 24 Barracudas of 820 and 826 Squadrons). The Firefly was another aircraft from the Fairey stable; it was a modern version of the Fulmar, to all intents and purposes, powered by a Griffon engine and armed with four 20mm cannon, but once again a two-seater.

A series of further attacks codenamed Operation 'Goodwood' followed during three days in August. Again it was *Formidable*, *Furious* and

Indefatigable which took part, with a slightly different mix of Corsairs, Hellcats, Seafires, Fireflies and Barracudas. Anti-submarine duties were undertaken by the small carriers *Nabob* and *Trumpeter*, each of which carried four Wildcats and a batch of Grumman Avengers – newly acquired torpedo and level bombers. One Barracuda and ten fighters were lost in the 242 sorties flown against *Tirpitz*, which escaped serious damage for the second time due to an effective smokescreen. However, 887 Squadron's Seafires sank seven floatplanes at Banak base. The Canadian-crewed *Nabob* was hit by an acoustic torpedo fired by *U-354*, and while she managed to get back to Scapa Flow in a desperate condition she was found to be beyond economic repair and was later scrapped.

Tirpitz was finally sunk on 12 November 1944 by RAF Lancasters of 617 Squadron using 12,000lb 'Tallboy' bombs. By this time the vast majority of Royal Navy carriers, including all the fleet vessels, had departed to pastures new. Escort carriers continued to operate along the Norwegian coast until the closing days of the war. The final 'big ship'

BELOW *Wildcat Vs and Avengers of 846 Squadron believed to be aboard HMS* Trumpeter *off the Norwegian coast in summer 1944 (note invasion stripes, indicating that the photograph was taken in mid-summer 1944, after the commencement of the Normandy landings).*

operations were undertaken by *Implacable* – the last new fleet carrier to be delivered before the war ended – during October and December 1944. Several combats were fought during this period. In one fight with the Luftwaffe's *Jagdgeschwader* 5, the only FW 190 to be shot down by a Hellcat was claimed by Lieutenant Blyth Ritchie from *Emperor*'s 800 Squadron on 8 May 1944. Six days later this unit's aircraft also despatched a number of He 115 floatplanes. The successful pilots included Lieutenant Ritchie and Lieutenant Commander Stanley Orr, who was now commanding the unit. In defending anti-submarine Avengers from attack by Bf 109Gs, Wildcats claimed five destroyed or damaged without loss.

CVEs carrying mixed complements of aircraft – initially Sea Hurricanes and Swordfish, but subsequently Avengers and Wildcats – spent a good deal of time escorting convoys across the North Atlantic and to North Russia. By the end of the war FAA aircraft had destroyed 16 submarines (15 U-boats and one Italian) and shared in the destruction of 16 more (14 U-boats, one Italian and one Vichy French), and the vast majority of these sinkings were achieved by aircraft operating from CVEs. Of those achieved by FAA aircraft alone, 12 were the victims of Swordfish, one of Albacores, one of Avengers and one shared by an Avenger and a Swordfish.

THE MEDITERRANEAN AND AEGEAN, 1944
In mid-August 1944 US, French and British forces landed in Southern France in Operation 'Dragoon'. Royal Navy support included seven CVEs – *Attacker*, *Emperor*, *Hunter*, *Khedive*, *Pursuer*, *Searcher* and *Stalker* – which between them carried seven squadrons of fighters, four with Seafire IIIs, two with Wildcat Vs and VIs, and one with Hellcats. Prior to this, 28 Seafires drawn from 807, 809 and 879 Squadrons had formed 'D' Naval Fighter Wing, and had operated in Italy with the Desert Air Force until mid-July.

BELOW *Avenger IIs of 853 Squadron from HMS* Tracker *on their way to bomb targets in Aaransund, Norway, on 12 September 1944.*

During and immediately after the landings the Royal Navy ships operated alongside two US Navy carriers between 15 and 27 August, and were involved in patrols and fighter-bomber operations. Twenty-one aircraft were lost to flak, and 60 more in operational and deck-landing accidents.

Following these actions, the British carriers swept through the Aegean from 9 September to 29 October, attacking German island garrisons. Throughout this period only two German aircraft were seen and shot down. *Khedive*, *Searcher* and *Pursuer* returned to the UK at the end of September. This effectively ended FAA operations in the Mediterranean and Middle East.

LEFT *Lt Blyth Ritchie DSC & Bar, a Scot, saw action as a fighter pilot with 800 Squadron during the Operation 'Pedestal' convoy to Malta, and during the 'Torch' landings in North-West Africa, on both occasions flying Sea Hurricanes. He subsequently flew Hellcats over the Norwegian coast, achieving the only Fleet Air Arm victory over a Luftwaffe FW 190. He was killed soon afterwards in a mid-air collision while acting as an instructor.*

BELOW *A pair of almost all-white Sea Hurricane IICs of 835 Squadron aboard HMS* Nairana *for North Atlantic convoy escort work during the opening months of 1944.*

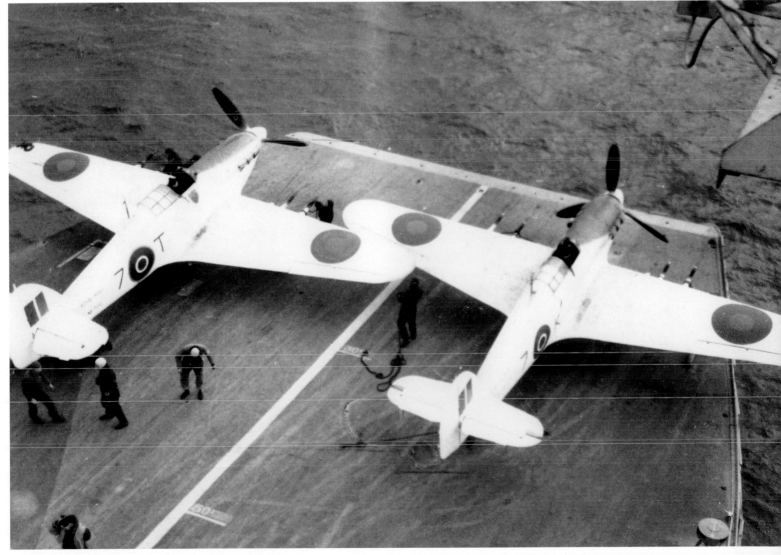

CHAPTER 19

UNFINISHED BUSINESS

War of Attrition in the Far East

The anti-submarine war in the Indian Ocean had been handled mainly by the RAF's Catalinas and Wellington patrol bombers (which would have been Navy aircraft in the US and Japanese forces). The first aircraft carrier support that could be spared arrived in the shape of CVE *Battler* in October 1943, immediately after the Salerno operations in the Mediterranean; she carried a composite air group operating Swordfish and Seafires. From spring 1944 four more CVEs began arriving (*Atheling*, *Shah*, *Begum* and *Ameer*), while in January 1944 *Illustrious* returned from the USA, accompanied by three capital ships. She brought with her the first Corsairs and Barracudas.

Following USN raids on Truk, the main Japanese battlefleet (five battleships and three large aircraft carriers) moved to Singapore in March 1944. Initially this was of concern, for it represented a much stronger force than the Eastern Fleet. However, with fuel short and many more vital responsibilities to consider, no attempt was made by the Japanese to mount any major sorties into the Indian Ocean. The only incident to occur was when three heavy cruisers sortied into the

RIGHT *Later models of the Grumman Martlet regained their original American name of Wildcat from 1943. These FM-2 Wildcat VIs served with a fighter flight attached to 853 Squadron in May 1944 aboard HMS* Tracker. *Note the tail wheel outriggers which allow the aircraft to be stowed almost fully clear of the main flight deck.*

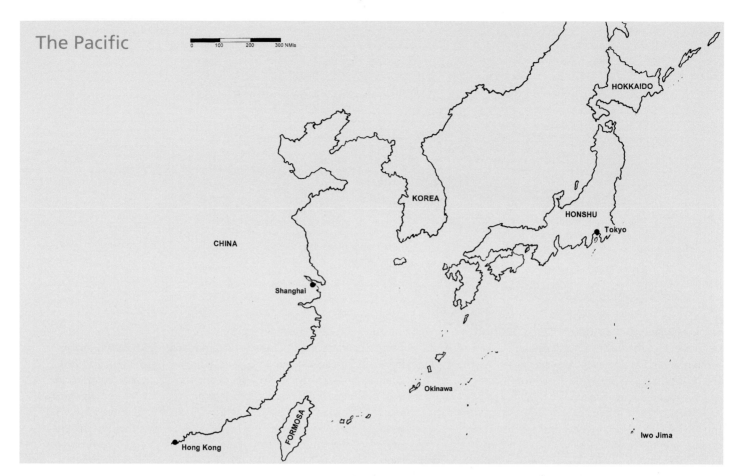

0   100   200   300 NMls

HOKKAIDO

KOREA

CHINA

HONSHU

Tokyo

Shanghai

Okinawa

FORMOSA

Iwo Jima

Hong Kong

RIGHT *The Chance-Vought Corsair became the most important Fleet Air Arm carrier fighter during the closing months of the war. First received under Lend-Lease in mid-1943, the aircraft was to serve with 19 squadrons. In action off the coast of Norway in April 1944, the aircraft then equipped most of the fleet carriers with the Eastern Fleet, subsequently joining the British Pacific Fleet where it remained the predominant type until the end of the war. Here, aircraft of 1830 Squadron prepare to take off from HMS* Illustrious *during 1945.*

southern area to sink two merchant vessels off the Cocos Islands. *Illustrious* and USS *Saratoga* – now on a short loan to the Royal Navy to allow powerful strikes to be launched against Japanese-occupied areas – put to sea, but saw nothing.

Ceylon had by now been developed into a major Royal Navy base, together with areas of South India, and here a steady build-up was under way. On 16 April 1944, 27 warships of six Allied nations sailed from Ceylon to attack Sabang Island. *Illustrious* carried 17 Barracudas and 13 Corsairs, while *Saratoga* had 11 TBFs (Avengers), 18 SBDs (Dauntlesses) and 24 F6Fs (Hellcats). Few ships were found, but the fighters claimed 24 aircraft on the ground. Three land-based Mitsubishi G4M bombers (Allied codename 'Betty') tried to attack, but were shot down by *Saratoga*'s CAP.

Saratoga then departed for a refit in the US. *Illustrious* accompanied her as far as Java, where the two vessels launched a strike on 17 May. Because of the distances to be flown, *Illustrious* had exchanged her Barracudas for Avengers. Arriving at their target, the 45 Avengers and SBDs and 40 fighters achieved surprise, but did little damage.

Between 10 and 13 June 1944 *Illustrious* swept through the Bay of Bengal as a diversion to US invasions in the Marianas, accompanied on this occasion by *Atheling* with Seafires and Wildcats (ex-Martlets). On 19 June *Illustrious* struck at targets in the Andamans on the same day on which the US Navy's famous 'Marianas Turkey Shoot' was taking place. Although the ship now had 57 Corsairs and Barracudas aboard, once more the damage inflicted was slight.

At the start of July *Victorious* and *Indomitable* arrived. The latter carried a Wing of Hellcats, while the former had aboard more Corsairs. On 25 July cover was provided for a bombardment of Sabang, but no air strikes were included. During the fleet's withdrawal Imperial Japanese Army Air Force aircraft appeared, allowing Corsair pilots to claim four Nakajima Ki 43 ('Oscar') fighters and a Mitsubishi Ki 21 ('Sally') bomber shot down for no loss. These proved to be the first aerial victories achieved by carrier-borne Corsairs. Following this operation, *Illustrious* departed to South Africa for a refit.

Indomitable and *Victorious* launched strikes on Sumatra at the end of August and again on 18 September, but Admirals C. Moody (Rear Admiral, Aircraft Carrier Squadrons) and Sir Bruce Fraser (the new Commander-in-Chief, Eastern Fleet) were not impressed by the performance of their air groups, and a period of intensive training followed.

The date 12 October brought another diversionary operation as the two carriers raided the Nicobar Islands in support of US landings in

BELOW *Corsairs of 1834 and 1836 Squadrons forming 47 Naval Fighter Wing, operating from HMS* Victorious, *set out in full Wing formation over the Pacific.*

the Philippines. A repeat attack was made on 19 October and both air groups met enemy aircraft, Fleet Air Arm fighter pilots claiming seven Ki 43s for the loss of two Corsairs and a Hellcat.

Two more months of training followed as *Illustrious* returned from her refit and *Indefatigable* – another of the armoured fleet carriers ordered before the war – arrived. She carried with her two squadrons of the latest Seafire IIIs and one of the new Fireflies, plus one of Avengers. With her came the very experienced Rear Admiral Sir Philip Vian to command the 1st Aircraft Carrier Squadron.

The first major raid by this strengthened force was launched on 20 December when a raid was mounted against the Pangkalan Brandan oil refinery in Sumatra, but bad weather prevented a successful attack being made. A repeat attempt in good weather on 4 January 1945 was entirely more successful. Considerable damage was inflicted on the refinery, the attack force including rocket-firing Fireflies for the first time. Escorting fighters claimed a dozen victories plus some 20 more aircraft on the ground, all for the loss of a single Avenger.

On 16 January the Eastern Fleet became the British Pacific Fleet (BPF) and began preparing to depart for the Pacific Ocean to operate with the US Navy. On the way, more attacks were to be made on Sumatra. The BPF initially comprised four fleet carriers, the battleship *King George V*, three cruisers and ten destroyers.

Meanwhile, the CVEs remaining in the Indian Ocean became the nucleus of the East Indies Fleet. Their main operations were to be along the coast of Burma and over the Japanese-held islands, in support of the advance of 14th Army towards Rangoon. Wildcats were now withdrawn from operational squadrons to allow a fighter pilot reserve to be built up in Ceylon for the BPF, but *Ameer* and *Empress* embarked Hellcats instead. The first major action for the new fleet was in support of landings on Ramree Island.

Reconnaissances were flown southwards along the coast of Malaya, where the first opposition was encountered on 1 March 1945, when Hellcats of 804 Squadron claimed three JAAF fighters shot down. The strength of this fleet was rapidly enhanced following the end of the European war, and for the Rangoon landings at the start of May four CVEs with about 100 Hellcats and Seafires were on hand to provide support. None was in fact required – the Japanese had gone.

Raids were then made on Car Nicobar, where considerable numbers of aircraft were claimed destroyed on the ground. By VJ Day there were nine Assault CVEs and four Strike CVEs in the Indian Ocean with 220 fighters and 40 strike aircraft. However, five of these carriers had arrived too late to see any action.

THE BRITISH PACIFIC FLEET

As the BPF sailed for the Pacific a series of strikes were launched against the Sumatran oil refineries under the codename Operation 'Meridian'. The first of these, on 24 January 1945, was made by 43 Avengers, 12 Fireflies and 50 escorting Corsairs and Hellcats, the latter also attacking the airfields. Despite the presence of barrage balloons, defending fighters and flak, the output of the Pladjoe refinery was halved for the next three months, while most of the oil in storage tanks awaiting shipment was burnt. The Fleet Air Arm fighters claimed 34 aircraft on the ground and 14 more shot down. Seven FAA aircraft were lost to all causes.

Five days later the Soengi Gerong refinery in the Palembang area was also attacked: all production was halted for two months, and it was only ever able to attain a fraction of its former output for the rest of the war – all at a time when the Japanese were desperately short of aviation fuel. Thirty-eight more JAAF aircraft were claimed destroyed on the ground and more than 30 others were believed to have been shot down in aerial combat. Sixteen British aircraft were lost over the target area.

Meanwhile, JAAF reconnaissance had found the carriers, and although three 'snoopers' were shot down by the CAP a low-level raid by seven twin-engined bombers of a special unit were able to make an attack. The CAP, consisting mainly of Seafires, joined by the first of the returning fighters from the raid on the refinery, were able to shoot down all of them. During one of the Palembang strikes one of the last surviving Japanese tankers had also been damaged beyond repair. The cost of the two raids had been 25 Royal Navy aircraft, but the output of aviation fuel had been reduced to 35 per cent of its normal level, while about 140 Japanese aircraft of all types had been destroyed or damaged.

There is a sad ending to this story, however. A number of aircrew shot down during the attacks were captured, interrogated briefly by the Kempei

Tai – the Japanese equivalent of the Gestapo – and swiftly executed. Nine other airmen initially evaded capture, but were subsequently arrested by the Palembang gendarmerie and handed over to the Japanese. Apparently the Kempei Tai had been criticised in the meantime for the lack of worthwhile intelligence obtained from the earlier captives, and consequently the survivors were later shipped to Singapore and held in the notorious Outram Road jail. Several of them were also subsequently executed.

The Sumatran raids were probably the Fleet Air Arm's greatest single contribution to the Allied war effort, and were certainly the biggest single operation undertaken to date. However, the losses suffered did mean that, before being able to undertake any further effective action, the BPF had to make first for Sydney, Australia, for replacements and supplies. This port was reached on 10 February 1945.

The next Allied area of operations was still in doubt. General Douglas McArthur wanted the BPF to support landings in Borneo and Mindaneo in the Philippines, while Admiral Chester W. Nimitz (US Commander-in-Chief, Pacific Fleet) wanted the fleet as his strategic reserve for the upcoming invasion of Okinawa. The latter plan prevailed.

During the Sumatran operations, shellfire had

FLEET AIR ARM ORDER OF BATTLE – OPERATION 'MERIDIAN', JANUARY 1945

HMS Indomitable

1839 Squadron	15 Hellcat Is
1844 Squadron	14 Hellcat Is
857 Squadron	21 Avenger IIs

HMS Illustrious

1830 Squadron	16 Corsair IIs
1833 Squadron	16 Corsair IIs
854 Squadron	21 Avenger Is and IIs

HMS Victorious

1834 Squadron	18 Corsair IIs
1836 Squadron	16 Corsair IIs
849 Squadron	21 Avenger IIs
Ship's Flight	2 Walruses

HMS Indefatigable

887 Squadron	24 Seafire IIIs
894 Squadron	16 Seafire IIIs
1770 Squadron	12 Firefly Is
820 Squadron	21 Avenger IIs

RIGHT *Air Group Leader on HMS Victorious with the British Pacific Fleet was Major R.C. Hay, DSO, DSC & Bar, one of the Fleet Air Arm's few Royal Marine pilots. Having flown Skuas during the Norwegian operations and Fulmars over the Mediterranean, Ronnie Hay then achieved considerable success piloting Corsairs – particularly during the January 1945 raids on the Palembang oil refineries. He is seen here (right) with his Corsair and one of the pilots of his Wing.*

damaged the central propeller shaft of *Illustrious*, and even after repairs she was able only to sail at a maximum 25 knots, which slowed the rest of the Fleet. *Formidable* was on her way from the UK but was not due to arrive until mid-April, so it was necessary to retain *Illustrious* until then.

Becoming TF (Task Force) 57 of the US 5th Fleet, the BPF sailed for the Carolines on 19 March. During a series of big raids on the Bonins by TF 58, during which many Japanese aircraft had been destroyed, three of the US attack carriers

(equivalent to fleet carriers) had been damaged off Kyushu, and the BPF was now to take their place.

There had been considerable US opposition to the BPF operating in the Pacific. This was seen as essentially a US area of interest, where the USN was now operating like a very polished and efficient machine. Criticisms included the fact that, due to their armoured decks, the British vessels carried only about half as many aircraft as comparable US carriers, while the multiplicity of aircraft types used by the RN would give rise to resupply problems;

RIGHT *HMS* Illustrious, *Indian Ocean. Lamps and reflectors replace fabric bats for this Deck Landing Control Officer.*

but above all, the RN simply lacked the modern supporting Fleet Train of oilers, supply ships, etc. which the USN now had. Consequently the BPF could be expected to be delayed by the late arrival of these vessels, and then further by the slowness of the refuelling operations.

Since the beginning of the Philippine landings the Japanese had made increasing use of suicide attacks – known as *Kamikaze* ('Divine Wind'). At first these had been undertaken by standard units in which the aircrews had volunteered for such duty. So effective had these attacks proved to be, compared with the poor results now being achieved in conventional attacks, that very rapidly special units began to be formed specifically for such operations. To attack accurately in the face of sustained AA fire required both training and experience, attributes which few remaining Japanese aircrew now possessed. Simply to dive your aircraft directly into a target proved to be considerably easier once the determination to do so existed. The Japanese authorities quickly realised that it was not a good idea to allow what remained of their best and most fully trained pilots to immolate themselves in this way, and they sought instead to use newly trained pilots and – increasingly – old or training aircraft.

The results achieved had become of growing concern to the Allies. The USN was now experiencing considerably increased shipping casualties as a result of such attacks, which were proving particularly devastating against the wooden decks of their aircraft carriers. The armoured deck

was about to prove its undoubted advantage in such circumstances.

The Sakishima Gunto Islands lie between Formosa (Taiwan) and Okinawa, and were ideally placed as refuelling bases for aircraft ferrying between the two – or indeed, as operational bases for aircraft seeking to operate off Okinawa. The BPF was therefore directed to neutralise these islands during the period of the US landings on Okinawa. The carrier air groups were to undertake a rotating two-day series of strikes with US CVEs. The first commenced on 26 March. The target was a difficult one, being heavily defended by flak, while the crushed coral runways were very easily repaired, and required constant re-cratering to render them inoperable. The airfields were also crowded with dummies to form 'flak-traps' for strafing aircraft, and indeed 14 of the aircraft claimed on the ground in the first round of attacks were probably fakes of this kind.

It was here that the first Kamikaze attacks on the BPF hit *Indefatigable* – but she was quickly repaired and back in action, thanks entirely to her armoured deck.

It was then thought that many of the aircraft attacking the ships off Okinawa were coming from Formosa and the BPF was directed to strike here. Forty-eight Avengers and 40 Corsairs went in on 11 April, but bad weather adversely affected their efforts. No strikes were attempted next day, but two Firefly pilots spotted five aircraft heading for Okinawa and despatched four of them. A Japanese attack on the BPF that evening was thwarted by

RIGHT *An Avenger from 857 Squadron passing over HMS* Indomitable *following a raid on the Sakishima Gunto Islands during 1945.*

Hellcats and Corsairs, the pilots of which claimed four shot down and others damaged.

Two more days of strikes followed during which 16 aircraft were claimed shot down for the loss of one Avenger and one Corsair to flak, and one Hellcat in combat.

A return to the Sakishima Gunto Islands followed, from where enemy aircraft were again operating, making the area very dangerous for the US CVEs. Here at last *Illustrious* was replaced by *Formidable*, whose air group was an important reinforcement for the rather depleted and tired groups on the other carriers. Strikes on 16, 17 and 20 April allowed 50,000lb of bombs to be dropped on these targets before the BPF withdrew to refuel.

A return to the Sakishima Gunto group for further strikes followed early in May. On the 4th 20 Japanese aircraft attacked the fleet, eight being shot down – seven of them by the CAP. A few got through, however, Kamikazes hitting both *Indomitable* and *Formidable* – but both survived and were soon operating again, although 11 aircraft had been destroyed on their decks.

On 9 May further Kamikaze raids were made and *Formidable* was hit again. This time she had just recovered a strike, so 18 Avengers and Corsairs were destroyed. Nonetheless, she was serviceable again in 50 minutes, although down to only 15 usable aircraft. *Victorious* was also hit twice and four Corsairs destroyed on her deck, but she too was almost immediately back in action. These were to be the last Kamikaze attacks on the BPF.

During the period 1 April–15 May seven US attack and escort carriers had been hit by Kamikazes and all rendered unfit for further service during the Okinawa campaign. Four RN carriers had been hit, two of them twice, but were all operational again in a few hours. Typically, even a hit where armoured plates joined did little more than make a dent perhaps one or two feet deep. Quick-setting concrete would be poured in, and as soon as it set aircraft began flying off again.

During 62 days at sea the BPF had launched over 5,000 sorties, claiming 42 aerial victories and over 100 aircraft destroyed or damaged on the ground. Some 186 small vessels had also been sunk or damaged. During these operations 160 aircraft had been written off and 29 more damaged. Of these, however, only 26 had been lost in action and 43 in Kamikaze attacks.

Following a well-deserved rest, the fleet headed back to the Japanese coast during July 1945, now joined by another new carrier, *Implacable*. Like *Indefatigable*, this vessel carried a Wing of Seafire IIIs plus single squadrons of Fireflies and Avengers. Provision of external fuel tanks for the Seafires now extended their range to that of a bomb-carrying Corsair, thus no longer restricting them to CAP duty.

Victorious, *Formidable*, *Implacable* and *King George V* commenced operations on 17 July; they would be reinforced by *Indefatigable* a few days later. On 24 July attacks were made on the escort carrier *Kaijo*, the only aircraft carrier ever to be attacked by Fleet Air Arm aircraft. She was left on

LEFT *Avengers of 857 Squadron from HMS* Indomitable *pass over Task Force 57 on return from a raid on Sakishima Gunto in the Pacific.*

BELOW *HMS* Formidable *is seen here while serving with the British Pacific Fleet during 1945. She had just been hit by a 'Kamikaze' suicide attack during May. Despite many aircraft being destroyed on her deck, the armour saved her from really serious damage and she was serviceable again in less than an hour.*

ABOVE *Seafire IIIs of 801 and 880 Squadron aboard HMS* Implacable *with Avengers ranged on deck behind them. These fighters have been fitted with 89 gallon drop-tanks which had been designed for use by USAAF Curtiss P-40s. The extension in range thereby achieved greatly increased the effectiveness of these aircraft for the British Pacific Fleet.*

fire with her back broken, to be finished off by US aircraft later. At evening that day Hellcats from *Formidable* intercepted incoming IJN torpedo-bombers (the new B7A 'Grace') and claimed three shot down.

The date 9 August saw an attack on shipping in the harbour of Onagawa Wan, south of Tokyo. Here Lieutenant R. Hampton Gray, DSC, RCNVR, led Corsairs of 1841 Squadron from *Formidable* to sink the escort sloop *Amakusa*. With his aircraft hit by flak and on fire, he pressed home his attack but was shot down and killed. He was awarded the Fleet Air Arm's fourth VC – only the second of the war, and, like the first, posthumous.

Sweeping over Japanese airfields, Fleet Air Arm pilots claimed more than 50 aircraft destroyed on the ground for the loss of seven aircraft and five pilots; the two-day series of attacks had cost altogether 13 aircraft and nine crews.

The date 13 August brought large-scale attacks on the Allied carriers by Japanese aircraft for the last time, but these were dealt with in the main by the USN CAPs. Two days later, on the last day of hostilities, Avengers from *Indefatigable*'s 820 Squadron were intercepted by A6M Zero-Sens. Ten Seafires from the carrier's 24 Naval Fighter Wing (887 and 894

Squadrons) intervened and claimed eight shot down for one loss; one Avenger was damaged and ditched on return. However, the Seafire pilot, Sub-Lieutenant Freddy Hockley, fell into Japanese hands and during the last few hours of the war he was executed and cremated, the last of at least 30 FAA aircrew to be executed while in captivity. Then the war was over.

Had the Seafires claimed the final victories of the Pacific War? The US Navy had made claims for 35 aircraft shot down during an early series of sweeps, two more around midday, and then a final three between 1300 and 1400 hours. Fighting Squadron VF-31, which recorded the last of these, would claim to have achieved that honour – but the Fleet Air Arm ran them close!

This final operational period had brought a considerably lower percentage of operational deck-landing accidents than had been the case in earlier periods. Nearly 3,000 more sorties had been flown; 14 aerial victories claimed, together with 442 aircraft destroyed or damaged on the ground and over a third of a million tons of shipping sunk or damaged. Forty Royal Navy aircraft had been shot down by flak and just two by fighters, aircrew losses amounting to 35. But only 52 aircraft had been written off in accidents.

The BPF remained with the US 3rd Fleet until the signing of the surrender in Tokyo Bay on 2 September. During this period, on 26 August a typhoon hit Task Group Three (TG38-3), in which *Indefatigable* was serving with four *Essex*-class carriers. Two of these were badly damaged by the violent weather, but the British vessels rode it out without adverse effect. This occasioned Captain Q.D. Graham to respond, to an enquiry from his allies as to the level of damage suffered: 'What typhoon?'

Meanwhile, on VJ-Day four new light fleet carriers – *Venerable*, *Glory*, *Colossus* and *Vengeance*, forming the 11th Aircraft Carrier Squadron – had arrived in Sydney, loaded with Corsairs and Barracudas. They were too late, and would be used only for the reoccupation of British colonial territories – although later some were to see action off the coast of Korea. *Glory* at least enjoyed the honour of taking the surrender of the Japanese forces at Hong Kong. The BPF was all too soon disbanded, and its Lend-Lease aircraft disposed of as required by that agreement – most of them by the sad means of simply pushing them over the side to fall to the bottom of the sea. Only a small handful were preserved for posterity.

ABOVE *The wings on a Seafire III of 801 Squadron are folded aboard HMS* Implacable *shortly before the conclusion of the Pacific War.*

LEFT *The Fleet Air Arm's second Victoria Cross of the Second World War – again awarded posthumously – went to Canadian Lt R. Hampton Gray, DSC, of 1841 Squadron. 'Hammy' Gray pressed home an attack on the Japanese sloop* Amakusa *which resulted in the destruction of this vessel, but while doing so his Corsair was shot down by AA fire and he was killed.*

CHAPTER 20

FLYING NUMBERS

Aircraft for the Fleet

The sheer number of aircraft required in a war such as had just occurred almost beggars belief. Wastage was always very high – mostly, it must be said, in consequence of accidents, operational or otherwise – particularly in a service where deck landings, always a particularly risky venture, were the daily norm. Couple that with the large number of rapidly trained young volunteers and the degree of risk becomes quite obvious.

By comparison with the major 'players' – the RAF, USAAF, USN, Red Air Force, Luftwaffe, etc. – the Fleet Air Arm was an air force of relatively modest size. Growth, for the reasons we have seen, remained likewise fairly modest during the initial two to three years of the war. From 1942 onwards a very rapid expansion began, fuelled in no small part by the introduction during 1941 of the Lend-Lease Act by the US government. David Brown, in his *Carrier Operations in the Second World War*, makes the point that in May 1940 the operational strength of aircraft on the five carriers available to the Royal Navy amounted to about 80

LEFT *This Fleet Air Arm Supermarine Spitfire X4652 is being refuelled by petrol bowser at RNAS Yeovilton, Somerset, on 2 September 1943. The rather elderly Mark I had seen first-line service with five RAF squadrons and had then been posted to an Operational Training Unit before being transferred to the Navy in August 1943. X4652 then served with 761 Squadron at Henstridge but was ground-looped when landing on 5 March 1944, bringing its long career to an end. IWM TR1275*

aircraft. Five years later 16 fleet and escort carriers were operational, carrying between them over 500 aircraft, while 12 more were on the way, with almost a further 400 aircraft.

The point has also been made that until 1943 the Fleet Air Arm had been somewhat ill-served by the British aircraft industry. This was for a variety of reasons, some of which were undoubtedly due to the Admiralty's own misjudgement and lack of foresight in the machines they were having developed and were acquiring. Indeed, throughout the war no aircraft designed and built to naval requirements in the United Kingdom can properly be termed 'world class'.

Prior to and at the outbreak of war, total numbers of aircraft acquired for the Fleet Air Arm included 114 Sea Gladiators, 192 Skuas and 136 examples of the benighted Roc. Once the Fulmar and Albacore got properly into production, quantities rose sharply under the pressures of war, but totals still only reached 600 Fulmars and 900 Albacores. Of course, the much-loved but definitely obsolescent Swordfish was ordered in larger numbers for its much greater number of units, and was kept in production for longer. Its service life was also considerably extended by the need to use it on the small carriers and MAC-ships, for which its performance rendered it more suitable than the more powerful monoplanes. The total ordered rose to almost 3,000 examples, although the final 400 were cancelled.

Surprisingly, the second most numerous of the pre-war operational types to be ordered was the faithful Walrus, with nearly 750 examples delivered.

The arrival, almost by default, of the first US aircraft, the Martlet, had been fortuitous. But the initial quantities available prevented this tough, well-designed little fighter, built specifically for carrier operations, from being employed to re-equip the Fleet Air Arm's fighter squadrons, as would undoubtedly have been desirable.

The experience gained with the landing on of 46 Squadron RAF's Hurricanes on HMS *Glorious*, coupled with the release of large numbers of RAF aircraft of this type, made it virtually inevitable that the initial standard single-seat day fighter for the Fleet Air Arm squadrons would become the Sea Hurricane. It should not be forgotten, however, that the reason the RAF was willing and able to release these aircraft was that the Mark I Hurricane, which had enjoyed a performance barely adequate to allow its employment during 1940, had been superseded by the considerably improved Mark II. Even this more powerful model still fell short of the performances of the Mark I Spitfire and the E model of the Messerschmitt Bf 109. By early

1941 the Spitfire II and V and the Bf 109F were appearing in increasing numbers. As a result, the Hurricane II swiftly found itself as outclassed in fighter-versus-fighter engagements as had the Mark I some months earlier.

Of course, the preconception that carrier fighters would in the main be engaged with the opposition's reconnaissance and bomber aircraft, rather than fighters, rendered the Sea Hurricane at least acceptable, even if of questionable value on those occasions when it might meet serious opposition. At least it was a tough, versatile machine which adapted quite well to the hurly-burly of carrier life, and – to be fair – remained an important element of the RAF's own first-line inventory in both the Middle East and Far East until much later than had been the case at home. The vast majority of the 600-plus Sea Hurricanes which served with the Fleet Air Arm were ex-RAF machines which had undergone conversion. No more than ten per cent were ordered directly from Hawker by the Admiralty.

It is not, perhaps, surprising that the next acquisition should be the Spitfire. This charismatic aircraft was carefully husbanded for home defence for as long as possible. It was only in March 1942 that the first had been grudgingly released to take part in the critical defence of Malta. Even at the time of the start of the Alamein battle in North Africa in October 1942, the Western Desert Air Force still had no more than three operational squadrons of these aircraft. Not until the launch of Operation 'Torch' the following month did RAF Spitfires begin to appear overseas in appreciable numbers – and then only in the Mark V version, which was fast approaching obsolescence itself.

The Admiralty must therefore be judged to have been fortunate to acquire navalised versions of this aircraft sufficiently early to be operational on some of its carriers for that same operation. During 1942 the RAF had commenced the release of some 280 Spitfires to the Navy, some of them Mark VBs, but many being Mark IAs of Battle of Britain vintage. Some of the former were fitted with arrester hooks, and were issued to Fleet Air Arm fighter squadrons in the UK, although all the Spitfires received (apart from a small number of PR XIII unarmed photographic reconnaissance versions) appear to have been employed either for operational training purposes, or for 'working-up' squadrons prior to receipt of the 'built-for-purpose' Seafire variants.

However, the Seafire was in no way entirely suitable for carrier use. Although a delight to fly, its narrow undercarriage proved to be weak and ill-suited to shipboard landings, resulting in a very high percentage of accidents at this point throughout its service life. The range achievable with its decidedly limited fuel capacity was also a problem. Neither of the initial versions, the Marks IB and IIC, had a performance even equal to that of the Spitfire VB of which they were essentially navalised versions. Even the Mark III, built from the start as an aircraft for naval use and featuring folding-wing mechanisms, and built in greater numbers than any other mark of Seafire, did not have an enhanced performance.

Late in the war – too late to see operational service – there came a version with the more powerful Rolls-Royce Griffon engine, which was equivalent to the RAF's Spitfire XII. Ordered as the Marks XV and XVII, this version had a considerably better performance. However, its 'navalisation' rendered its top speed still some 15mph below that of the RAF's superlative Merlin-engined Spitfire IX, which had entered service during 1942! Despite these faults, no other fighter aircraft would match the numbers of Seafires delivered, which would approach 3,000 by the end of the war.

The only new aircraft designed and built specifically to Admiralty requirements during the war both emanated from the Fairey company, manufacturers already of the Swordfish, Albacore, Fulmar and Sea Fox. The Firefly was designed to a similar specification to that of the Fulmar, but featured the Griffon engine. It proved to be a versatile and reliable aircraft, but with a performance – due to its two-seater configuration – little different to that of a Hurricane I. It only entered service during 1944, and then only on a relatively limited basis since much of its role was by then being adequately performed by aircraft of US manufacture, but with substantially better performance. Some 800 were built during the war.

Fairey also produced the only aircraft designed in the UK to take over the role of the TBR biplanes. This was the Barracuda, a Merlin-engined attempt to include in one aircraft the roles of level and dive-bombing, plus torpedo-launching. A decidedly odd-looking aircraft, like the Seafire it lacked range. Reputedly, when one was landed on the deck of a US Navy carrier by a pilot visiting that vessel, the American Air Group Commander commented: 'Gee, is that what you Limeys are using instead of aircraft these days?' Despite its faults, the Barracuda had so many TBR aircraft to replace in the first instance, that it became the subject of the largest procurement by the Admiralty, ordered in greater quantities even than the Seafire. More than 3,500 were sought, although the final 300 of these were cancelled. Between January 1943 and the end of the war some 23 squadrons would fly Barracudas.

British production also provided 250

Supermarine Sea Otters during 1943; this development of the Walrus had first appeared in 1938, but orders were not placed for some time. A further 100 were ordered, but only 41 of these were to be completed. Not to be overlooked, however, were large numbers of non-operational aircraft acquired for the Fleet Requirements and training squadrons. A variety were also obtained for testing, but were then found to be wanting as operational types.

As already noted, the true salvation of the Fleet Air Arm during the war proved to be the US aviation industry. In the United States aircraft had long been developed and built specifically for the US Navy, the air force of which had remained a service wholly controlled by that parent organisation throughout its existence. In consequence the aircraft constructed had been designed from the start for carrier operation with the benefit of advice from experienced career naval aviators.

The Fleet Air Arm had early found the Grumman Martlet to be an excellent carrier fighter aircraft and was anxious to obtain more. The versions already obtained equated to the US Navy's F4F-3, and the initial 30 of this Twin Wasp-powered version were delivered as the Mark III. These were followed by 220 Mark IVs, which equated to the Cyclone-powered F4F-4B, featuring folding wings and armament enhanced to six .50in machine guns.

In the meantime the aircraft had become somewhat obsolescent, and following stalwart service in the Pacific – where it had proved to be outclassed by the Japanese A6M Zero-Sen – it had been superseded in the US Navy by the F6F Hellcat from the same stable. It remained an excellent aircraft for use on the smaller escort carriers, and was therefore maintained in production, but by Goodyear (under licence) rather than by the parent company. Some 312

ABOVE *Very similar in general appearance to its predecessor, the Walrus, the Supermarine Sea Otter entered service in 1944 to undertake similar functions. An amphibian, it could operate from carrier decks or from catapults. The aircraft was employed in the air-sea rescue role at the start of the Korean War, but was swiftly replaced by the new helicopter.*

Goodyear FM-1s and 370 FM-2s, with redesigned tail units, were supplied to the Fleet Air Arm for use in a similar capacity, where they were known as the Marks V and VI. A decision had also been taken that the US names for aircraft in use by the Fleet Air Arm should be adopted from 1 January 1944, at which point all Martlets became Wildcats, while the intention to name the Hellcat and the Avenger as Gannet and Tarpon respectively was dropped.

The first of the new generation of US aircraft to become available to the Fleet Air Arm was the Grumman Avenger – essentially a TBR aircraft which had first appeared in small numbers during the Midway battle in 1942. The first British squadron was formed with these aircraft in January 1943, and by the end of the year nine units were flying them. Several of these were squadrons which operated from escort carriers and also included Wildcats in their inventory. When war in the Far East began to require aircraft with a longer range than that achieved with the Barracuda, more squadrons converted to the Avenger, bringing the total number of units with Avengers on hand as at least a part of their establishment to 14. In all, more than 950 Avengers reached the Royal Navy prior to the end of the war.

The US Navy had concluded that its high-performance Vought F4U Corsair was basically unsuitable for carrier operations due to a propensity to bounce on landing. Consequently these superb fighter aircraft were passed in the main to the US Marine Corps for use from Pacific island bases. Supplies began to reach the Royal Navy early in 1943, where the recipients begged to differ. With certain modifications to the undercarriage oleo legs, and other modifications which included clipping off the ends of the wingtips in order that when its wings were folded the aircraft would still fit within the hangars of the Royal Navy's armoured-deck aircraft carriers, the Corsair became the Fleet Air Arm's predominant

fighter aircraft for the later years of the conflict.

Increasingly, as US aircraft were delivered to the US Navy, formation and initial work-up of squadrons took place in the USA in the first instance. Eight squadrons of Corsairs were formed between June and October 1943, and it was these units which were subsequently to bear the brunt of the war in the Pacific with the BPF. Eleven more squadrons would be formed between March 1944 and April 1945, but two of these would be re-equipped, while two more were disbanded late in 1944. Of the remainder, not all would enter action before the war ended. More than 2,000 Corsairs reached the Fleet Air Arm, many of them of the later Mark IV version.

Although the Corsair had been chosen as the Fleet Air Arm's main fighter, supplies of the Grumman F6F Hellcat also became available during 1943, at much the same time as the Corsair was entering service. Two existing long-serving fighter squadrons, 800 and 804, were re-equipped with these aircraft. Two more, 1839 and 1844, were formed later in the year and were to see extended service with the BPF. Eight more squadrons of the East Indies Fleet in the Indian Ocean were to receive these aircraft to replace Seafires during 1944–45, the Hellcat being a much more suitable aircraft for operations from that force's CVEs than was the Corsair. Only two further new squadrons of Hellcats were formed, one of which was then disbanded to provide sufficient aircraft for the other. Although of less significance to the Fleet Air Arm than the Corsair, more than 1,175 examples had been received by the war's end.

Of other types supplied under Lend-Lease funds, perhaps the most important in operational terms were 100 Vought O2U Kingfisher floatplanes. These little aircraft saw service administered by 703 Squadron, which maintained them on the catapults of a number of Armed Merchant Cruisers. Notably, they served with HMS *Canton* in the

RIGHT *Delivered to the Fleet Air Arm under Lend-Lease at much the same time as the Corsair, the Grumman Hellcat was initially involved in strikes on the battleship* Tirpitz *and other targets along the Norwegian coast from mid-1943 onwards. Subsequently it was to equip some dozen British squadrons, most seeing service over the Indian Ocean during 1944–45. Just two squadrons accompanied the British Pacific Fleet aboard HMS* Indomitable, *but these units achieved considerable success during the final seven months of the war.*

Indian Ocean, hunting for German and Japanese submarines during the opening months of 1944.

It is probably as well to include here a brief synopsis of the allocation of squadron numbers as the size of the service increased. The initial series 700–749 had originally been retained for catapult squadrons, and later for amphibian and floatplane units. Subsequently a number of training units and aircrew pool squadrons were to be numbered in this sequence. The 750–799 numbers were retained for training and ancillary squadrons, including target towing, communications and all sorts of operational training units. Virtually every number in this sequence of generically termed Fleet Requirements Squadrons would be in use by 1945.

As has already been described, the sequence 800–809 had been allocated to fighter units. However, these had been used up by the start of 1941, and subsequently 880–899 were also allocated for this use; 870–879 numbers were later added to this range, but only two units, 878 and 879, were to operate under these numbers during the war. The torpedo-bomber and spotter reconnaissance categories had been merged by the time war broke out, and consequently 810–869 Squadrons were so allocated. This was to be the only other range which did not employ all the numbers available, 14 remaining unallocated at the end of the conflict.

One anomaly related to squadrons with the numbers 1700–1703. These were all allocated late in the war as amphibian bomber-reconnaissance units, all equipped with Sea Otters.

With 899 Squadron having come into existence at the end of 1942, new numbers were required for further fighter units which were definitely to follow within the next six months. Thus numbers in the 1800 range were allocated almost entirely for units formed in the USA with Lend-Lease aircraft. The first of these, 1820 Squadron, was formed with Curtiss SB2C Helldiver dive-bombers, but training showed these aircraft to be unsuitable for operational duties, and the unit was disbanded the following January. Meanwhile, 1830–1838 had been allocated for the initial Corsair units, followed by 1839, 1840 and 1844 for Hellcats. During 1944, 1841–1843, 1845–1846 and 1848–1853 were all to become Corsair units. While all of these were disbanded when the Pacific War ended, 1830–1834 Squadrons were reborn during the late 1940s/early 1950s as units of the RN Volunteer Reserve; all but 1831 would be disbanded again in 1957.

Finally, another series had come into use in the upper 1700 range with the introduction to service of the Firefly in 1944. The first three squadrons of these aircraft were given the numbers 1770–1773, while three more units formed with Firefly night fighters during early 1945 became 1790–1792 Squadrons.

One further point which needs to be made is that the Fleet Air Arm tended not to follow the RAF practice of maintaining a squadron number through changes of equipment, role, etc. It was much more frequent practice at the end of a tour on board a carrier, or at the time of withdrawal of particular equipment, for the unit to be disbanded, followed possibly – but not always – by its re-formation some time later. The gap between disbandment and re-formation could sometimes run into years, particularly during the years subsequent to 1945.

ABOVE *The Vought-Sikorsky Kingfisher was supplied to the Fleet Air Arm in limited numbers under Lend-Lease to operate as a catapult-launched spotter from Royal Navy cruisers. In this role it saw service in the South Atlantic and Indian Ocean.*

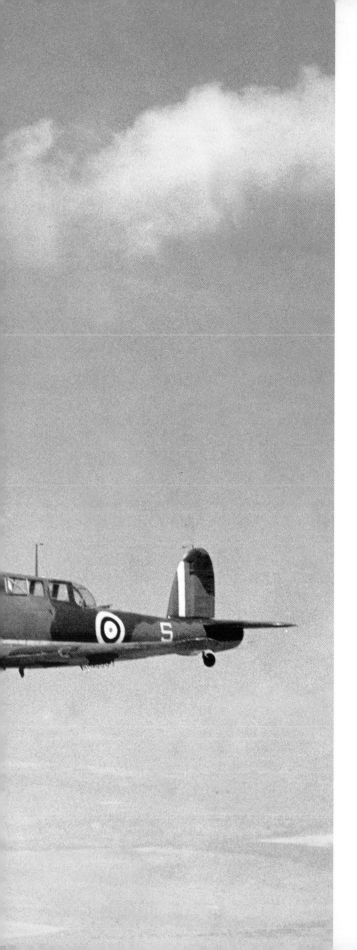

CHAPTER 21

DIVE-BOMBING

An Afterthought

O n concluding the section of this book
detailing the events of the Second World
War, one matter occurs to this author
as worthy of further consideration. The Fleet Air
Arm's first notable action of the war was the sinking
by dive-bombing of the German cruiser *Königsberg*
in Bergen harbour during April 1940. Thereafter,
of the Royal Navy's aircraft carriers lost in action
during the war three fell victim to U-boats and one
to surface-vessel gunfire. Only one, *Hermes*, was
sunk by air attack, and that was by dive-bombing.
Three of the newer generation of armoured fleet
carriers – *Illustrious*, *Formidable* and *Indomitable*
– were also substantially damaged and put out of
action for considerable periods of time by dive-
bomber attacks.

During the Pacific War the main weapon of
attack of both the US Navy and the Imperial
Japanese Navy was the dive-bomber. These aircraft
were not only responsible for most of the carrier
losses on both sides during the critical Battle of
Midway, but also played a major part in the attack
on the US battleships at Pearl Harbor, and in several
of the other major Pacific engagements.

Yet although the Fleet Air Arm tested the
American Douglas SBD Dauntless dive-bomber,
and even acquired Curtiss SB2C Helldivers –
which were subsequently discarded without ever
seeing active service – the Royal Navy never took
a dedicated dive-bombing aircraft to sea again
following the departure from service of the Skua.

LEFT *Skuas of 801 Squadron.*

ABOVE *Junkers Ju 87 Stuka of I/St.G1, Sicily, May 1941.* Bundesarchiv

Clearly, the dreadful losses of Skuas over Trondheim in June 1940, perhaps coupled with the RAF's own experience in demonstrating the vulnerability of such aircraft as the Luftwaffe's Ju 87 'Stuka' to fighter attack during the 1940 operations over France and England, and later over Malta and North Africa, militated against a desire to acquire such aircraft for the British Services. However, given the experiences of the Royal Navy's own vessels when subjected to attack by aircraft of this nature, one is bound to ask 'Did the Navy miss a trick in eschewing them?' While the initial answer may well be in the affirmative, a consideration of the differences between the Royal Navy's experience with aircraft carriers and that of the other nations would seem perhaps to alter this view.

Unlike the Japanese and Americans, the Royal Navy's carriers never became involved in fleet-versus-fleet engagements, far from land bases. In such circumstances the relatively small numbers of fighters available to each side allowed their dive-bomber units to operate with a better chance of survival. For the Japanese, this would become less

so as the war progressed and the targets of their dive-bomber crews became on increasingly more occasions relatively well-defended targets on land, rather than warships at sea.

In all the cases where British carriers were sunk or damaged by air attack, the vessels were operating with relatively inadequate fighter cover, or at sea, away from the possibility of support from land-based fighters. Similarly, when the Fleet Air Arm's operations involved attacks on targets ashore, any actions by dive-bombers might have been likely to encounter sustained opposition from superior land-based fighters. Alternatively, on the frequent occasions when these operations were essentially defensive, the role of the fighter was predominant, such as on the Malta convoys, and the presence aboard of dive-bombers would have done little to improve the situation.

The conclusion therefore drawn by this author is that, given the specific nature of the operations undertaken by the Royal Navy's carriers, the absence after 1940 of dedicated dive-bomber aircraft probably had little effect upon what was achieved.

ABOVE *An SB2-C Helldiver onboard a US Navy escort carrier.* US National Archives

LEFT *Douglas SDB Dauntless two-seat dive-bomber.* US National Archives

CHAPTER 22

PEACE DAWNS

But Storm Clouds Gather

As the war in Europe drew to a close and the prospect of a prolonged Far Eastern conflict was replaced by the hope and expectation of a fairly early victory, it became time to reconsider the Royal Navy's aircraft carrier requirements for the foreseeable future. At that stage the RN's establishment had risen to 52 carriers already in service and 18 more under construction – totals which at the centenary of British Naval Aviation seem almost inconceivable in the circumstances of the early 21st century.

At the heart of this mighty force were the six fleet carriers (CV) of the *Illustrious* class. Two more such large vessels, known at the time as the *Audacious* class, were under construction. Of the new class of light fleet carrier (CVL), *Unicorn* and three *Colossus*-class vessels were already in service, while seven more of the latter class and six *Majestic*-class carriers were under construction, as were three *Hermes*-class vessels, with a fourth on order.

Of the escort vessels (CVE), eight of the *Attacker* class were on hand, together with 26 *Ruler*-class (US-built) ships. Finally, there remained eight miscellaneous carriers which included the venerable *Argus* and *Furious*. Both these now-obsolete ships would be scrapped before the end of the decade. Apart from this conglomeration of vessels, there

LEFT *Seafire XVs arrived in the Pacific just as the war ended. A pair of these Griffon-engined fighters are seen here over Hong Kong in 1946. They were serving with 802 Squadron aboard HMS* Venerable.

remained 19 merchant aircraft carriers, converted from merchant vessels to operate four aircraft each on convoy anti-submarine duties. The latter had no further use once Germany was out of the war and were swiftly converted back to their original uses. During January 1945 one CVE – *Biter* – was transferred to the French Navy to provide the resurrected *Aeronavale* with its sole operational carrier at the time.

When Japan surrendered earlier than anticipated in August 1945, largely as a consequence of the dropping on that country by the USAAF of the first of two thermo-nuclear devices, further reappraisal rapidly became necessary.

It needs to be recalled that by 1945 the United Kingdom was virtually bankrupt as a result of two major wars in a period of little more than 30 years. The populace, desperately weary of war, had just elected a socialist government with a sweeping majority. The latter, set upon the creation of a welfare state, the nationalisation of major industries, and a crash programme of building to make good the ravages of wartime bombing, was anxious to dismantle as much as possible of the armaments programme to allow these peacetime aims to be met.

Against this scenario the country entered a period of sustained austerity. High taxation and continued rationing – particularly of foodstuffs – coupled with little amelioration of the State control of many aspects of life, meant that peace brought but little respite, at least insofar as living standards were concerned.

The potential for an early massive reduction in military expenditure and the return to civilian life of the majority of the personnel of the armed forces offered a major opportunity to begin to alter the balance. Hopes of an early rapport with the Soviet Union were swiftly disabused, however, and by 1948 the crisis which occurred when the Russians virtually closed off Berlin to the West had brought a realisation that a new military threat must now be perceived to exist from the East. Clearly the run-down of forces could no longer be achieved as precipitately as might have been hoped. Indeed, a new arms race was beginning.

Thus, with Japan forced to capitulate and the United States Navy predominant in the world at sea, the role of the Royal Navy returned very much to its traditional one of defending the home country from seaborne threat, and protecting the trade routes to what remained of the Empire – or Commonwealth, as it now increasingly became known and accepted, both in fact and perception.

The end of the war and the terms of the Lend-Lease Act required that all the US-built CVEs should be handed back to their effective owner. Some 35 such vessels, either in service or under construction, were indeed returned, virtually all of them then being converted to merchant ship configurations and disposed of accordingly. Amongst the RN's home-built CVEs, similar conversion and disposal took place with *Pretoria Castle*, *Activity* and *Vindex*, while *Nairana* was sold to the Netherlands during 1946. Of this class of vessel, only *Campania* was retained, and she would be scrapped in 1955.

Perhaps the biggest saving had already been achieved by the cancellation during 1945 of nine carriers which had been ordered, but of which construction had not yet commenced. Three very large 45,000-ton vessels of a new designation – CVB – to be named *Gibraltar*, *Malta* and *New Zealand*, were all cancelled. Two 36,000-ton CVs, *Africa* and *Eagle*, were also cancelled, although two more which were under construction as the new *Audacious* class (see above and below) would ultimately continue to be built.

The remaining four cancellations related to *Hermes*-class CVLs – *Arrogant*, *Monmouth*, *Polyphemus*, and *Hermes* herself. Of the three other vessels of this class under construction and not cancelled, *Elephant* was renamed *Hermes* in order to maintain the vessel-class nomenclature. Meanwhile, the first of the new CVs, *Audacious*, was renamed *Eagle* when the planned vessel of that name was cancelled, while the second, still under construction initially as *Irresistible*, became *Ark Royal*. The only projected but unstarted vessel to remain in the programme was the 18,300-ton CVL *Bulwark*.

Even more than the reduction of the carrier force, the loss of the American-built aircraft occasioned by the need to hand them back to the United States following the close of hostilities left the Fleet Air Arm hugely constrained. The pity was that so many of those splendid Corsairs, Hellcats and Avengers were simply pushed over the side of their parent carriers into the depths of the Pacific Ocean, since the British Government was unable – or unwilling – to pay for their purchase. Certainly, by this time the US Navy had insufficient facilities (or, indeed, need) for large numbers of these aircraft to add to their own bulging arsenals.

The overall effect was that, although the war's end had found the Royal Navy with six *Illustrious*-class CVs and eight CVLs available for peacetime operations, supplemented by three maintenance carriers, by 1947 most of these had been placed in reserve, only three vessels remaining in active service – *Implacable* as a training vessel in UK waters, and the CVLs *Ocean* and *Triumph*. During that year CVL *Warrior*, newly completed and fitted out, was loaned to the Royal Canadian Navy for a period of two years until *Majestic*, which had been laid down in 1943, was completed for that Dominion. The following year (1948) *Venerable* followed *Nairana* into the Dutch Navy, while in 1951 *Colossus* went to the French.

Denuded of Corsairs, Hellcats, Wildcats and Avengers, little more remained than Seafires and Fireflies, together with the ubiquitous Sea Otters and Walruses. Seafires of a more modern ilk were coming to hand, the Griffon-engined Marks XV, XVII being followed by the Marks 45, 46 and 47. While Marks XV and XVII had incorporated a wing-folding mechanism similar to that employed in the Mark III, Marks 45 and 46 did not. In its later versions the Spitfire had undergone quite radical redesign, becoming almost an entirely new aircraft, with a redesigned wing planform incorporating four 20mm cannon, and a redesigned and considerably larger fin and rudder. Seafires 45 and 46 were equivalent to Spitfires 21 and 22, and for the Fleet Air Arm were seen as interim aircraft only. The numbers on order were substantially reduced by cancellations at the end of the war, and although issued to the Service Trials Unit, 778 Squadron, neither model was to be employed by any first-line squadrons.

The Seafire 47 was a different matter altogether. The equivalent of the last Spitfire to be produced, the Mark 24, it featured a new hydraulic wing-folding mechanism and extremely good performance. It was capable of 451mph at 20,000ft, had a service ceiling of 43,100ft and an initial climb rate of 4,800ft per minute. As such it was reaching the latest modern standards as far as piston-engined aircraft were concerned, although it continued to display the disconcerting predilection for its undercarriage to collapse during landings. However, the more robust Hawker Sea Fury which had a marginally even better performance was on order, representing the ultimate in fighter design prior to the arrival of the first jet engine-powered aircraft. These, though, were still some way in the future.

With the Avenger gone, the Barracuda almost forgotten and the faithful Swordfish now totally obsolete, the biggest problem was in dealing with anti-submarine duties. Although designed for, built and operated in the fighter-bomber and fighter-reconnaissance role, the Fairey Firefly now offered itself as a candidate for development, its two-seat configuration finally proving of some positive advantage. Thus while the complement of most carrier air groups during the late 1940s and early 1950s appeared to represent an entirely fighter-equipped establishment, in fact many of the Fireflies were of the AS (anti-submarine) variety. Obviously, they were also able to undertake the fighter ground-attack role when so required, particularly as they retained their basic fixed armament of four 20mm Hispano cannon as well as their ability to carry an offensive load of rockets or bombs beneath their wings.

BELOW *SX345 was a Seafire XVII of 800 Squadron, serving with this unit from 1947 to 1949 aboard* HMS *Triumph.*

CHAPTER 23

THE 38th PARALLEL

War in Korea

During 1949 *Triumph* sailed for Singapore with an air group of 12 Seafire 47s and 12 elderly Firefly FR 1s. While the Malayan Emergency was mainly an RAF responsibility, the naval aircraft undertook some strikes against Communist insurgent targets from bases ashore for a limited period.

On 25 June 1950 North Korean forces swept across the 38th Parallel, which since the conclusion of the Second World War had divided inhospitable and poverty-stricken Korea between a Communist-ruled North and a capitalist-inspired South. US forces at once responded. This was followed by a more general United Nations condemnation of the North's aggression, and a wider response to a call for the provision of armed forces to restore the situation.

While the Korean War which rapidly developed was to be fought on behalf of South Korea mainly by US forces, and by those of the young republic itself, large numbers of other countries were soon providing support of one kind or another. These were ultimately to include nations such as Turkey and Greece, and a fairly major contribution from the British Commonwealth. Notable amongst the latter, of course, was the parent nation, joined by Australia, Canada, New Zealand and South Africa.

Apart from the despatch of a substantial element of ground forces, the United Kingdom and the

RIGHT *The Fleet Air Arm's first operational helicopter was the Dragonfly. This is a Westland-built HR Mark 3, seen here serving with 705 Squadron at Lee-on-Solent.*

ABOVE *Commissioned in April 1946, HMS Triumph was the first Royal Navy carrier to see service off the coast of Korea immediately after the outbreak of war there in 1950.*

RIGHT *Sea Furies and Fireflies on HMS Theseus off Korea during the winter of 1952–53.*

100 YEARS OF BRITISH NAVAL AVIATION

Dominions mentioned above all committed naval vessels and/or air force units to the UN force.

After the initial North Korean invasion had been halted by an initially inadequate UN force, just prior to the whole of the South being overrun, US reinforcements were employed by the Commander-in-Chief, Douglas McArthur, to stage an amphibious landing on the east coast of the Korean peninsula at Pusan, well in the invaders' rear. This bold move changed the situation rapidly, and soon the North Korean army was in full retreat.

Unfortunately, McArthur's decision to pursue his opponents right up to their northern frontier with (newly) Communist China rebounded on him, when a massive Chinese army crossed the border and sent the UN forces reeling back. Eventually a line was stabilised close to the 38th Parallel and a static situation of trench warfare ensued which was to continue for the rest of the conflict until a ceasefire was eventually agreed in 1953.

Against this backdrop, the Royal Navy was to maintain an almost permanent aircraft carrier presence in the China Sea, off the west coast of Korea. When fighting broke out, *Triumph* was nearest to the scene of action, and sailed at once for the area. Here her air group joined that of the only USN carrier then available, USS *Valley Forge*, in the Yellow Sea during the night of 1/2 July, to form Task Group 77.3 of Task Force 77, the Allied Striking Force. These two ships would launch the first strike of the war by carrier aircraft on the 3rd.

At 0500 hours US Navy F9F Panther jet fighters took off to provide CAP over the carriers, while at 0545 12 Fireflies and nine Seafires, armed with rocket projectiles, left Triumph to attack an airfield and rail bridge at Haeju. They were followed 15 minutes later by 16 F4U Corsairs and 12 AD Skyraiders from *Valley Forge* which were to strike the main North Korean airbase at Pyongyang. Eight more F9Fs were last off, due to their higher speed, to provide cover and strafe if appropriate. The Panthers arrived over Pyongyang first and shot down two Yak fighters found in the air there. The airfield was comprehensively strafed and bombed by the US aircraft, and nine more aircraft were claimed to have been destroyed on the ground. The Fleet Air Arm's attack was also completed satisfactorily, both strikes gaining complete surprise, allowing the whole Allied force to return without suffering damage. Another series of strikes were made during the afternoon.

Triumph had carried aboard one of the faithful Sea Otter amphibians for air-sea rescue work. Early experience soon indicated that the new Sikorsky S-51 Dragonfly helicopters of the US Navy were much better-suited for this role, particularly in

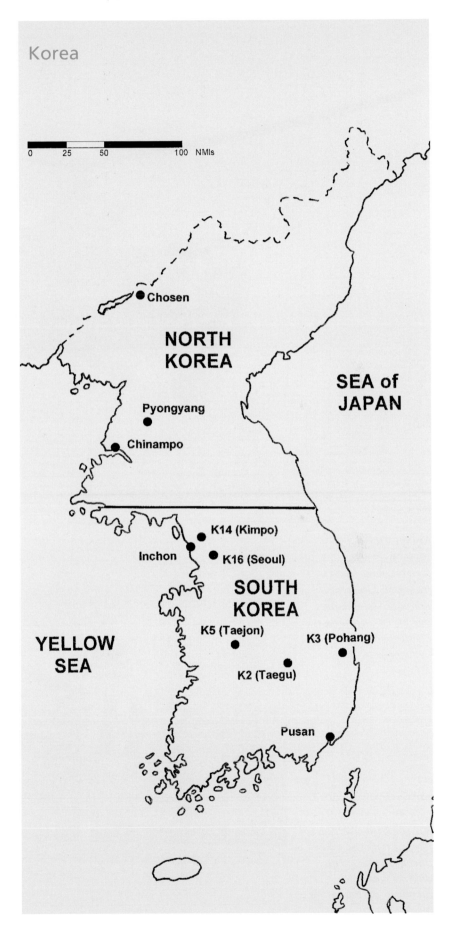

Korea

ABOVE *Dragonfly 'Stella By Starlight' is seen on planeguard from HMS* Ocean *over Korean coastal waters during 1952 – the first operational use of helicopters by the Fleet Air Arm.*

RIGHT *Hawker Sea Fury FB 11, TF958 of 807 Squadron, served aboard HMS* Theseus *during 1950–51. This aircraft was twice damaged during sorties over Korea.*

rough weather. Consequently, one of the US aircraft and its crew was loaned to the British until the Navy's own Dragonflies could be shipped out from the UK (of which more later).

The air war over Korea subsequently broke down into two distinct parts. The arrival on the Chinese side of the border of MiG-15 jet fighters quite early in the conflict rapidly rendered day raids on the North by formations of USAF B-29 Superfortresses too expensive to maintain. This required their relegation to less-accurate night bombing. The very latest US F-86 Sabre swept-wing jet fighters were introduced to the area in gradually increasing numbers, and these commenced an air superiority struggle with their Russian-built counterparts which was to continue throughout the war. This, however, was all fought well over the northern part of the war zone, over what became known as 'MiG Alley'.

Above the front line, and the supply routes leading to it, the predominant power of the UN air forces, both ground-based and carrier-borne, was concentrated on the ground-attack and interdiction role. The short range of the MiGs, initially flown entirely by Russian personnel, but subsequently increasingly by Chinese and North Korean pilots, rendered it difficult for them to operate effectively above this area.

Consequently, with high-performance jet aircraft only rarely appearing as a threat to UN fighter-bombers, it proved practicable to continue to employ piston-engine aircraft here with the advantage offered by their greater range and loiter capability when compared with jet aircraft of the period. This was common to all those taking part, the US Navy maintaining in service large numbers of Corsairs and Skyraiders, while initially at least the USAF, ROK (South Korean) air force and the Australian and South African squadrons sent to the area employed the North American P-51 Mustang of similar vintage.

Against this background the continued use by the Royal Navy of the Seafire and Firefly, soon joined by the newer Sea Fury, may be seen to be entirely logical and practical. These three aircraft types were thus employed throughout the conflict with considerable effect.

The opportunity was also taken to rotate to the area most of the British light carriers in order that the widest possible experience might be gained. *Triumph* remained with TG 77 until 8 October 1950, when she was relieved by *Theseus*, which brought a slightly more appropriately equipped air group with Sea Furies (of 807 Squadron) and later model Fireflies. In April 1951 *Glory* replaced *Theseus*, while in September of that year it was the turn of HMAS *Sydney*, which operated two squadrons of Sea Fury FB 11s and one of Firefly AS 4s of the Royal Australian Navy's Fleet Air Arm. This carrier soon set a record by launching 89 sorties in one day.

Glory returned in February 1952, serving until May when *Ocean* took over. This vessel's Sea Furies

BELOW HMS Glory *was one of the light carriers ready at Sydney when the Second World War ended before they could enter action. She was the only British aircraft carrier to undertake two tours of duty off Korea during 1951–53. She remained in service for a further ten years before being sold for scrap. Here her deck-load of Sea Furies and Fireflies all carry the tactical stripe markings around the wings and fuselages applied to Fleet Air Arm aircraft throughout the conflict.*

Lt Peter 'Hoagy' Carmichael, 802 Squadron, HMS *Ocean*, describes shooting down a MiG-15 on 9 August 1952.

'My No 2, a fellow called Carl Davis, said "MiGs 12 o'clock !" So 12 o'clock is, you know, directly above and in front. There were eight MiGs – I think they were inexperienced pilots. They were about 250mph faster than we were and what they were doing was making an attack on us and just pulling straight up and disappearing, and coming back. Well, then they got fed up with this, and the four that I had, one of them anyway, he made an attack at me. Of course that was his fatal mistake as he tried to follow me because I could turn inside him so much quicker than he could and at low level he reduced his speed to get near me. And so, in no time at all I had got behind him and I fired until he went down and hit the ground to the left of where I was flying. Which was a great crash for us all to see.'

ABOVE *A Firefly is rearmed with 20mm cannon shells and 60lb rocket projectiles ready for another sortie over Korea.*

and Firefly AS 5s now exceeded the Australian record, undertaking 123 sorties in a single day on one occasion. This ship was also to gain another notable success. For the reasons already explained, MiGs only rarely became a serious danger to RN aircraft, However, on 9 August 1952 a section of four Sea Furies from 802 Squadron were attacked by eight MiGs north of Chinampo. The formation leader, Lieutenant Peter 'Hoagy' Carmichael, gained hits on one of the attackers which was seen to fall to earth and blow up.

Glory undertook a third tour from November 1952 to May 1953, when *Ocean* returned, remaining until hostilities came to a halt at the end of June 1953. During this period *Unicorn* had also arrived in the area to undertake her specialist aircraft replacement function, ferrying up aircraft and supplies from Singapore to make good attrition.

During the Korean operations the Royal Navy's carriers launched some 23,000 sorties, almost all of a ground-attack nature. In human terms these cost the lives in action of 22 aircrew, while 11 more were killed in accidents.

BRITISH AIRCRAFT CARRIERS AND THEIR AIR GROUPS OPERATING OVER KOREA

HMS *Triumph* — 23 June–29 September 1950
13th Carrier Air Group — Lt Cdr P.B. Jackson
800 Squadron — Seafire F 47 — Lt Cdr I.M. MacLachlan/
Lt Cdr T.D. Jandley
827 Squadron — Firefly FR 1 — Lt Cdr B.C. Lyons

HMS *Theseus* — 29 September 1950–23 April 1951
17th Carrier Air Group — Lt Cdr F. Stovin-Bradford, DSC/
Lt Cdr G.A. Thompson
807 Squadron — Sea Fury FB 11 — Lt Cdr M.P. Gordon-Smith, DSC/
Lt Cdr A.J. Thomson, DSC
810 Squadron — Firefly AS 5 — Lt Cdr K.S. Pattisson, DSC

HMS *Glory* — 23 April–30 September 1950
14th Carrier Air Group — Lt Cdr S.J. Hall, DSC
804 Squadron — Sea Fury FB 11 — Lt Cdr J.S. Bailey, OBE
812 Squadron — Firefly 5 — Lt Cdr F.A. Swanton, DSC*

HMAS *Sydney* — 30 September 1951–27 January 1952
21st Carrier Air Group — Lt Cdr M.F. Fell, DSO, DSC
805 Squadron — Sea Fury FB 11 — Lt Cdr W.G. Bowles
808 Squadron — Sea Fury FB 11 — Lt Cdr J.L. Appleby
817 Squadron — Firefly FB(AS) 5 — Lt Cdr R.B. Lunberg

HMS *Glory* — 27 January–5 May 1952
14th Carrier Air Group — Lt Cdr F.A. Swanton, DSC
804 Squadron — Sea Fury FB 11 — Lt Cdr J.S. Bailey, OBE
812 Squadron — Firefly AS 6 — Lt Cdr J.M. Cuthbertson

HMS *Ocean* — 5 May–8 November 1952
(No CAG)
Commander Flying — Lt Cdr A.F. Black, DSC/
Lt Cdr S.G. Orr, DSC**, AFC
802 Squadron — Sea Fury FB 11 — Lt Cdr S.F. Shotton, DSC/
Lt Cdr P.H. London, DSC
825 Squadron — Firefly FR(AS) 5 — Lt Cdr C.K. Roberts

HMS *Glory* — 8 November 1952–19 May 1953
(No CAG)
Commander Flying — Cdr J.W. Sleigh, DSO, DSC
801 Squadron — Sea Fury FB 11 — Cdr B.C.G. Place, VC, DSC/
Lt Cdr P.B. Stuart
821 Squadron — Firefly RF 5 — Lt Cdr J.R.N. Gardner

HMS *Ocean* — 19 May–31 November 1953
(No CAG)
Commander Flying — Lt Cdr W.C. Simpson, DSC
807 Squadron — Sea Fury FB 11 — Lt Cdr T.L.M. Brander, DSC
810 Squadron — Firefly FR 5 — Lt Cdr A.W. Bloomer

CHAPTER 24

FASTER AND FASTER

The Coming of the Jets

The ending of the Second World War had led swiftly to the Fleet Air Arm becoming equipped, as we have seen, with the residue of its British-built aircraft – Seafire XVs and XVIIs and the Firefly, the latter initially in its Mark I version. This latter aircraft was still being developed, the night fighter NF I and NF II of the war years being converted to the NF 1 version by the addition of a radar pod beneath the nose of the standard fighter. It was followed by the FR Mark I which incorporated ASH shipping detection radar. Some 376 of this version of the aircraft had been produced by the latter part of 1945.

However, the availability of the two-stage Griffon 74 engine which increased horsepower from 1,765 to 2,245 brought a commensurate very considerable improvement in performance. After testing, the production variant became the Firefly FR IV, with a revised wing planform and completely redesigned fin and rudder, this version entering first-line service with 810 and 825 Squadrons during 1947.

The Seafire XV/XVII series had re-equipped 802, 803, 805 and 806 Squadrons by the end of 1945, and were to be replaced by the Seafire 47, which has already been described. However, two new fighters had also appeared, both of which

LEFT *The first deck landing by a jet aircraft was undertaken on 3 December 1945 by Lt Cdr E.M. 'Winkle' Brown in De Havilland Sea Vampire LZ551, seen here about to touch down on HMS Ocean to complete this epoch-marking event.*

offered enhanced performance. As ever, however, these had begun life as fighters for the RAF. The Supermarine Spiteful was essentially a late-model Griffon-powered Spitfire with straight-edged laminar flow wings in place of the well-known elliptical lifting surfaces. The resultant aircraft could achieve 483mph at 26,000ft. A navalised version had been developed as the Seafang 32, which featured both an arrester hook and folding wings, the navalisation reducing that impressive top speed to a still very respectable 475mph. Some 150 were ordered before the end of the war, but after ten Seafang 31s (without folding wings) and eight Mark 32s had been delivered the order was cancelled during 1946. In practice, while the Seafire 47's top speed was marginally below that of the Seafang, its climb rate and service ceiling were better. As a known and proven aircraft, despite the failings resulting from its undercarriage, the Admiralty preferred it for peacetime service to the as-yet unproven Seafang.

The second new aircraft derived from the Hawker Fury, a lightweight development of the successful Tempest fighter, and was powered by a Bristol Centaurus radial engine. Though offering great promise, the Fury was not proceeded with by the RAF due to its intention to concentrate on jet aircraft. The Admiralty, however, continued its interest in the navalised Sea Fury, which was a tough, rugged aircraft offering even better performance than the Seafang. Although orders were cut back to 100 in January 1945, production was to continue, and while it would be 1948 before the first examples began to replace the Seafire XVs and XVIIs it would ultimately become the Service's standard shipboard fighter for some years.

One aircraft which had been specifically designed and built for the Royal Navy during this period was the unusual Blackburn Firebrand. Envisaged originally as a single-seat interceptor fighter, the Firebrand subsequently became a torpedo-strike fighter. Following development and testing during the war it subsequently went into production as the Mark III, powered by a 2,520hp Centaurus engine which gave it the very respectable top speed of 350mph at 13,000ft; even when carrying a 1,850lb torpedo, it could still reach 342mph. Twenty-four were produced in 1944, followed by the Firebrand IV of which 102 were built. The type went into service with 813 Squadron in September 1945, later serving aboard HMS *Implacable*. Many teething troubles were experienced, however, and the only other unit to receive these aircraft was 827 Squadron in October 1950.

During the closing stages of the Second World War the Fleet Air Arm had also been seeking a long-range fighter to accompany strike aircraft on the longer sorties which were likely to occur in the Pacific. The selected aircraft was again a navalised version of an RAF aircraft, in this case the single-seat, twin-engined De Havilland Hornet F.20. The aircraft entered service during 1947, joining 801 Squadron in July of that year. It served briefly aboard HMS *Implacable*, then undertook a full tour on *Indomitable* until re-equipment with Sea Furies took place in March 1951.

Meanwhile, three aircraft joined the re-formed 806 Squadron, together with two Sea Furies and a lone Sea Vampire to form a unique RN Aerobatic Flight. Transported across the Atlantic on the light carrier HMCS *Magnificent* in May 1951, the flight

RIGHT, TOP *The big Blackburn Firebrand torpedo-fighters served first with 813 Squadron. Here EK625 is seen passing over a carrier, believed to be HMS* Implacable.

RIGHT, MIDDLE *The De Havilland Sea Hornet F.20 was the first twin-engine fighter to serve with the Fleet Air Arm. These three Hornets are believed to have formed part of a flight serving with 728 Squadron. This was a Fleet Requirements unit based on Malta.*

RIGHT, BOTTOM *Sea Hornet NF 21 of 809 Squadron in flight. This aircraft was flown by the commanding officer, Lt Cdr J.O. Armour, who had served as a night fighter pilot attached to the RAF during 1944 when still a Royal Marine. His radar operator in this aircraft was Lt W.S. Carter.*

spent eight weeks display-flying throughout the USA before returning to the UK for disbandment in September.

Meanwhile, a night fighter version of the Hornet had been developed specially for the Navy. The NF.21 featured a separate radar operator's cockpit in the fuselage and enlarged tail surfaces. Following protracted trials at the Naval Air Fighting Development and Service Trials Unit at Ford, it entered service in January 1949, 809 Squadron being re-formed for this purpose under the command of Lieutenant Commander J.O. Armour, an ex-Royal Marine who had flown Mosquito night fighters on attachment to the RAF during 1944.

After brief work-up service aboard *Illustrious*, the unit joined the Royal Navy's only All-Weather Air Group on HMS *Vengeance* in May 1951. The NF.21 remained in service with this unit until replaced by Sea Venoms in May 1954.

Meanwhile, the development of jet-propelled aircraft proceeded apace. Before the war had ended the RAF had ordered the De Havilland Vampire F.1. This was a small, fairly lightweight aircraft with a tricycle undercarriage. Pleasant and relatively easy to fly, it also offered the then very high top speed of 532mph at 17,500ft. The third prototype was adapted for deck-landing trials, and on 3 December 1945 became the first jet aircraft ever to be landed on an aircraft carrier, a feat accomplished by Lieutenant Commander E.M. 'Winkle' Brown, previously a Martlet pilot aboard HMS *Audacity* during 1941. He had also undertaken the Empire Test Pilots' School course, and had visited Germany where he inspected and flew many types of German aircraft. The results proved satisfactory and the aircraft was ordered

into production for the Fleet Air Arm as the Sea Vampire F.20.

Subsequently a strengthened version, the F.Mark 21, was used for trial landings on a rubberised deck with the undercarriage retracted. Again the tests were mainly in the hands of Lieutenant Commander Brown, but in the event, although quite successful, came to nothing in the first instance. They did, however, lead indirectly to the angled deck, designed initially to allow room for wheeless aircraft to be parked on a carrier. The Sea Vampire served with 792 Squadron – the Naval Jet Evaluation and Training Unit, with 778 Service Trials Squadron – but was not to enter service with an operational unit.

The first jet to see such service was effectively another RAF 'cast-off', the Supermarine Attacker. This was very much an interim aircraft, featuring the laminar flow wings of the Spiteful/Seafang aircraft, now married to a rather rotund fuselage housing a Rolls-Royce Nene turbojet engine. It was almost unique in being a 'tail-dragger', featuring a tail wheel instead of the more usual tricycle arrangement favoured for jet aircraft, which tended

ABOVE *A pair of Sea Vampires of Air Handling Unit, Malta, are seen parked on HMS Theseus in about 1950, flanked by the carrier's resident Sea Furies.*

BELOW *The Fleet Air Arm's first fully operational jet fighter was the Supermarine Attacker. WA494 of 800 Squadron is seen here in flight while serving on HMS Eagle.*

to offer a better view forward over the nose, there being no engine or propeller in front of the pilot. Originally the Supermarine E.10/44, it had lost RAF interest early in its development, but was brought forward for carrier employment. Various problems delayed production and the type did not enter service as the Fleet Air Arm's first turbojet fighter until August 1951.

Thereafter it was to equip only three regular squadrons, 800, 803 and 890. Its service was also quite short, all of them having been replaced before the end of 1954. However, the aircraft then went to equip three RN Volunteer Reserve squadrons, 1831, 1832 and 1833; 1832 Squadron would receive Sea Hawks to replace their Attackers in November 1956, but during spring 1957 all these units were disbanded during a period of defence cuts.

By the time the first Attackers entered service the Korean War was under way and the US Navy had settled on two main designs, the McDonnell F2H Banshee and the Grumman F9F Panther. The performances of both were not greatly dissimilar to that of the Attacker, but both were already fully in service by 1950, the Panther remaining the predominant US Navy jet fighter type throughout the Korean operations. At this time it was already considerably outclassed by the MiG-15 swept-wing fighters of the air forces supporting the North Koreans.

It is, perhaps, worth noting that the Rolls-Royce Nene engine which powered both the Attacker and its replacement, the Sea Hawk, was also essentially the same powerplant as that which powered the Panther, Sabre *and* MiG-15 over Korea!

A number of other aircraft had been ordered during this period, although in several cases development was protracted. During 1945 a replacement for the Firebrand torpedo-strike fighter had been sought. The chosen aircraft was the Westland Wyvern, designed initially to be

LEFT *Attackers of 800 and 803 Squadrons lined up on the foredeck of HMS Eagle. Aircraft of the former unit carry the identification numbers 101–109, while those of the latter carry 111–119.*

LEFT *A Sea Vampire F.20 from Culdrose is taken down on HMS Theseus's lift during the early summer of 1950. A second such aircraft is parked nearby, together with several Seafires.*

BELOW *Although the Sea Vampire F.20 did not see widespread use by the Fleet Air Arm, the two-seat trainer version was employed considerably, particularly for training Sea Venom crews. A T.22, XA112 of 738 Squadron at Lossiemouth, is seen here.*

RIGHT *Sea Hawks of 898 Squadron on HMS* Albion *in January 1955, leaving Toulon, Southern France, following a visit.*

BELOW *Formation of Wyvern S.4s of 830 and 831 Squadrons from HMS* Eagle *during 1955.*

powered by the massive Rolls-Royce Eagle piston engine; five test examples were ordered. The availability of turbo-propeller engines caused this to be selected as the engine type for the production aircraft, but tests were initially undertaken to decide which of two engines should be employed. The Armstrong Siddeley Python was finally chosen, but the delays associated with these changes, and with the teething troubles of such a radical new powerplant, meant that six and a half years had elapsed before the aircraft finally entered service to replace the Firebrands of 813 Squadron in March 1953. The second such unit, 827, did not receive its Wyverns for a further 18 months, but a year later in November 1955 two more units, 830 and 831 Squadrons, also took Wyverns on strength,

although 827 Squadron was disbanded a month later. By now, of course, the Wyvern was quite obsolescent, and its service life was brief, all having departed by the spring of 1958.

Non-availability of suitable British aircraft led to the acquisition of US products during the early 1950s. With no suitable Airborne Early Warning aircraft to hand, the UK became the first foreign purchaser of the Douglas Skyraider, acquiring 36 AD-4W aircraft as the Skyraider AEW 1. Worked up by 778 Squadron during 1951, 849 Squadron was then re-formed in July 1952 as parent unit, the aircraft then being parcelled out to the various aircraft carriers in detachments of four. They continued to serve in this role until 1962, when the 12 remaining serviceable examples were sold to Sweden.

ABOVE *Sea Hawks of 897 Squadron sit on the flight deck of HMS Eagle with Sea Venoms and a Skyraider. All aircraft carry the special black/yellow recognition stripes applied during the brief Suez operation in 1956.*

BELOW *De Havilland Sea Venom FAW 21s on HMS Ark Royal.*

For similar reasons the Grumman Avenger re-entered Fleet Air Arm service in an anti-submarine role to replace some of the ageing Fireflies. Some 100 TBM-3E and 3S aircraft were acquired with MDAP funds as the Avenger AS Mark 4; these were funds provided by the USA to assist in the rearming of member states of the new North Atlantic Treaty Organisation (NATO). The first went to 815 Squadron, which had become the Naval Joint Anti-Submarine School in May 1953, replacing the last Barracuda 3s still in service. Shortly thereafter, 814, 820 and 824 Squadrons all had their Firefly AS 6s replaced by the Avengers, which continued to serve until the Fairey Gannet became available. The final Fleet Air Arm use of the Avenger was made by 831 Squadron, one of the

ex-Wyvern units, which was re-formed in May 1958 as an Electronic Warfare squadron equipped with Avengers and four Sea Venoms.

During the early 1950s the three most eagerly awaited aircraft were the Hawker Sea Hawk, De Havilland Sea Venom and Fairey Gannet. Anxious to develop a jet fighter to follow its successful Tempest and Sea Fury series of piston-engined fighters, Hawker now produced its first such aircraft, the P.1040. With enough aircraft remaining after the war, and with other types still on order, no great initial enthusiasm was expressed by either the RAF or the Fleet Air Arm. However, the Admiralty on this occasion foresaw the need for a better-performing jet fighter than the Attacker, and ordered a prototype in May 1946. Hawker went on to build swept-wing developments as the P.1052 and the P.1081, which ultimately led to the RAF's iconic Hunter.

In the meantime the navalised P.1040 was delivered in 1948, and following tests 151 were ordered in November 1949 to be called the Sea Hawk F.1. With the outbreak of the Korean War, the urgent need to supply the British Services with modern aircraft was seen as critical. The run-down of the military industry following the end of the Second World War caused considerable delays in resuming production schedules, but Sir Winston Churchill's new government which came to power in 1951 sought to address this by allocating to certain aircraft a 'Super Priority' status; the Sea Hawk was one of those selected.

As a result of these delays, and despite the Government's efforts, the first squadron of Sea Hawks, 806 'Ace of Spades', did not become available until March 1953. The unit was therefore able to take part in a flypast of 300 naval aircraft during

the Queen's Coronation Review of the fleet on 15 June that year. Aesthetically a very attractive aircraft, the Sea Hawk was ultimately to equip 14 squadrons by September 1957, and also to go to one unit of the Volunteer Reserve. Improved versions soon appeared as the Marks 2 and 3, which were able to carry bombs or rocket projectiles, the FB 3 becoming the most widely used. Orders for 97 FGA Mark 4s followed, while 50 FB 3s were up-engined to become FB 5s. Ultimately, in 1956 86 FB 6s were ordered, allowing the Sea Hawk to soldier on to the end of the decade.

The Sea Hawk was undoubtedly a reliable and popular aircraft. Sadly, however, it was already outclassed internationally before it even entered service, and by the time it did so the Royal Navy had become the only major air force in the world re-equipping with a fighter which did not feature swept-back wings. It was just as well, perhaps, that the Fleet Air Arm was never called upon to engage an opponent so equipped during the period when the Sea Hawk remained its predominant fighter type.

At the start of the 1950s the RAF had purchased the De Havilland Venom as a fighter-bomber to replace the Vampire. From this had been developed the two-seat Venom NF 2 night and all-weather fighter. This version was of considerable interest to the Admiralty, and navalised versions were produced and tested as the Sea Venom NF 20 and NF 21, and ultimately as the improved FAW 22.

Of very similar performance envelope to the Sea Hawk, this fighter became operational soon after the Hawker aircraft, 890 Squadron taking it into service in March 1954. 809, 891, 892 and 894 Squadrons were all subsequently equipped with Sea Venoms during 1954–57, while 831 Squadron received a number of Mark 21 and 22 ECM versions in 1958.

The Gannet, as with other Fairey aircraft, was designed and constructed specifically for an Admiralty requirement. A large, portly aircraft, it was powered by a Double Mamba turboprop engine with contra-rotating propellers. This was in fact two linked engines, both of which would be employed for take-off or landing, but when in the air one of them could be shut down, allowing economic long-range cruising. Supplied initially as an anti-submarine aircraft, the Gannet would later be developed for AEW service. In this latter role the large ASV and sonar operators' cockpit mid-fuselage was removed, and despite the installation of a huge 'guppy' radome beneath the fuselage the aircraft assumed a decidedly slimmer appearance.

ABOVE *A formation of Gannet AS 1s from 820 Squadron aboard HMS* Bulwark.

BELOW *Fairey Gannet AS 1 on HMS* Ark Royal.

The first Gannet AS 1s replaced 826 Squadron's Fireflies in January 1955, and took over from the Avengers of 824 Squadron the following month. Thereafter, in rapid succession, three more Firefly squadrons and two Avenger squadrons all received the new aircraft, as did 847 Squadron. Thus eight units had become operational with Gannets in little more than a year. One more Avenger unit followed in January 1957, and 810 Squadron also re-formed with Gannets in April 1959.

Yet the service life of this purpose-built aircraft proved to be almost incredibly brief. By the end of the 1950s only one Gannet AS unit – the most recently formed, 810 Squadron – remained so equipped, which retained it only until mid-1960. So what had happened to cause this? The answer is the arrival of the multi-role helicopter. Gannets did continue to serve with two squadrons, but not in their designed anti-submarine role. In May 1958 the specialist Countermeasures unit, 831 Squadron,

ABOVE *An 849 Squadron Gannet AEW 3 in flight.*

had received some AS 1 Gannets for a very brief period, but these were swiftly followed by the ECM Mark 4 and Mark 6 aircraft, which stayed with the unit until its disbandment in 1966. From 1960 the equally specialist AEW unit, 849 Squadron, began receiving Gannet AEW 3s to replace the surviving Skyraiders, this remaining the sole Gannet-equipped unit until the mid-1970s. As with the Skyraider, however, only small detachments of aircraft needed to be retained on each operational carrier, and this required only a single squadron as parent unit.

The helicopter was already well known to the FAA, but the limited capacity and performance of the early versions of these aircraft had restricted their use to relatively modest tasks. Sikorsky, a US manufacturer, had produced the first service helicopter, the R-4 Hoverfly, during the latter stages of the Second World War. The RN had been involved in a joint helicopter development unit at New York as early as 1944, while 52 of these aircraft were delivered to the UK by way of Lend-Lease early in 1945; most of them served initially with a flight of 771 Squadron at Twatt.

Even before the loan of US Navy Dragonflies during the opening months of the Korean War (as has already been mentioned), the British Westland aircraft company had obtained a licence during 1947 to build this aircraft in the UK; 72 would be constructed for the Royal Navy. Consequently, in May 1947 705 Squadron was formed as a Helicopter Fleet Requirements Unit, taking over the existing helicopters from the 771 Squadron flight and becoming responsible for all FAA helicopter operations, crew training, evaluation and development work. Dragonflies began reaching the unit during 1950, and were to serve with it for the next 12 years, alongside a small number of Hiller HT1 and HT2 machines.

The use of helicopters by the US armed services in Korea had brought home just how useful this new form of aircraft could be, now that it had been developed to a level where it had become reliable, maintainable, and capable of carrying a useful load. Initially its use had been perceived principally as the lifting of troops and vital equipment into locations where landing strips were not available. Its suitability for picking up downed aircrew from behind enemy lines or from the sea had also adequately been demonstrated.

However, it was soon realised that it possessed a number of enormous advantages as a form of anti-submarine weapon. It did not require a flight deck to take off or land upon; it took far less space within the hangars of aircraft carriers; and above all it could hover directly above a sonar contact, using a 'dunking' sonar to pinpoint the location precisely rather than having to circle at a distance. Further,

as a relatively light and basically simple piece of machinery it offered substantial cost savings to any cash-strapped government!

Finally, there was a suitable helicopter immediately available. The Sikorsky S.55 was already in service with all three US services, and initially 25 of these were supplied for the Fleet Air Arm in 1952 under MDAP arrangements, as the Whirlwind HAR 21 transport version and the HAS 22 for anti-submarine work. Licensed production in the UK then followed at Westland Aircraft, the first home-built HAR 1s appearing towards the end of 1953, followed by the HAS 7 in 1956. In October 1952 848 Squadron was formed with ten of the US-built HAR 21s and was at once shipped to the Far East aboard the ferry carrier *Perseus*. Following arrival in Singapore in January 1953, the unit undertook anti-terrorist operations in Malaya. Five Westland-built HAR 1s were added in 1954 for search and rescue duties, but at the end of 1956 the unit was disbanded.

Initially two new squadrons were formed with Whirlwinds during 1954, these being 845 and 848, but between 1958 and 1960, four Gannet anti-submarine squadrons were converted to the helicopter. By 1964 another Gannet unit had gone, while two further new Whirlwind squadrons were formed. The Fleet Air Arm had begun to take on a new shape.

LEFT TOP *Westland Whirlwind HAS 7s of 820 Squadron from HMS* Albion *during 1958.*

LEFT BOTTOM *Whirlwind HAR 3, XG581, 982/B, of 'D' Flight, 701 Squadron, seen during 1957 while engaged in transporting the equipment of 898 Squadron from HMS* Ark Royal *to HMS* Bulwark.

OPPOSITE TOP *The 21ft sailing dinghy* Avocet *ran aground off Portsmouth in June 1976. A Whirlwind Mk 9 from HMS* Daedlus, *Lee-on-Solent, flown by Lt Colin Rose, tows the stranded dinghy to deeper water. Note the Navy diver in the sea below the helicopter.*

OPPOSITE BOTTOM LEFT *Wessex HU5 from 771 Squadron, HMS* Osprey, *Portland, on a SAR exercise in 1973.*

OPPOSITE BOTTOM RIGHT *Rescue teams in five Sea King helicopters from RNAS Culdrose snatched seven survivors from mountainous seas after the storm-battered Danish coaster* Merc Enterprise *capsized off the Devon coast in January 1974.*

CHAPTER 25

BIGGER AND BETTER

The New Carriers

As has already been mentioned, construction of two carriers of the proposed *Audacious* class continued despite the general reduction put in hand at the end of the Second World War. The first of these was *Eagle*, which was launched in 1946, although work on preparing her for commissioning was then halted until the intensification of the 'Cold War' required her completion to be resumed. She was eventually commissioned in October 1951, providing the Royal Navy with a 36,800-ton vessel, more than 800ft long. She also carried the heaviest AA defences yet fitted to a British carrier, and could operate 80–100 aircraft, dependent upon type. Her sister ship, *Ark Royal* (originally to have been *Irresistible*), was also taken in hand at this time, and was launched on 3 May 1950. These were to be the two largest aircraft carriers ever to serve with the Royal Navy.

Before *Ark Royal* was completed, however, a number of very significant changes were made. As a result of studies being undertaken jointly by the Royal Navy and the Royal Aircraft Establishment in regard to the problems associated with the operation of jet aircraft of increasing speed and weight, a radical new concept had been discussed. The Chairman of a conference held to consider this matter was Captain Dennis Campbell, RN, at the

LEFT *Two of 809 Squadron's Sea Hornet NF 21s are seen here on deck, probably aboard HMS* Eagle, *with a line of Supermarine Attackers behind.*

time Assistant Chief Naval Representative to the Ministry of Aviation.

With the angled deck considered at the time of the 'rubber-deck' landings in mind, Captain Campbell – an experienced naval aviator himself – proposed that the landing deck should be offset (or skewed) at an angle to the ship's hull, to allow any aircraft which missed the arrester wires on landing to accelerate back into the air and go round again, rather than being faced with a crash into the barrier and aircraft park at the front of the ship. Campbell's initial suggestion was for a 10° angle to be employed, but in the event this was to prove sharper than was actually necessary.

This suggestion having been laid before the committee in August 1951, six months later the outline of an angled deck was painted on the existing flight deck of the CVL *Triumph*, various obstructions being removed to allow a touch-and-go landing of the nature proposed to be tested.

Shortly after this, similar tests were made by the US Navy on USS *Midway*, which had an angled deck painted on in a similar manner to that on *Triumph*. In both cases the results were entirely satisfactory, although emergency barriers for any normal 'axial' landings were left in place during the tests. Following this, the USS *Antietam* was converted to become the first true angled-deck carrier during the latter part of 1952, featuring an 8° angle, with arrester gear orientated towards the new deck direction.

With the new methodology thereby firmly

BELOW *HMS* Centaur *with Sea Hawks, Sea Venoms and Gannets embarked.*

proven and established, *Ark Royal*'s commissioning was delayed to allow a 5½° angled deck to be incorporated. She was also fitted with two more British innovations. The first of these was the inclusion of two steam-powered catapults, which were able to provide more powerful acceleration than the existing hydraulic system. Development of these new catapults was undertaken under the leadership of Commander C.C. Mitchell, who was initially influenced by German V-1 'flying bomb' technology discovered following the end of the Second World War. The second innovation was the mirror landing aid, which replaced the traditional 'batsman'. A large fixed mirror at the stern of the carrier allowed the pilot to line himself up visually more quickly and accurately than was possible while watching the signals of a deck-landing officer. Captain Campbell had again been involved in formulating this idea, he and Commander Nick Goodhart having undertaken initial experiments with a secretary's powder compact and a pocket torch!

Ark Royal was also fitted with a deck-edge lift, the first to be incorporated in a British carrier. With the normal pair of centre-line lifts, this speeded up the handling of the large number of aircraft the vessel could carry. However, this lift was apparently not considered too great an asset, for it was removed when the carrier underwent a refit in 1959. When commissioned in February 1955, almost 12 years since her keel had been laid down, her first commanding officer was none other than Captain Dennis Campbell. Like *Eagle*, she was fitted with a substantial battery of 4.5in and 40mm anti-aircraft guns.

Even as the older *Illustrious*-class carriers were being taken out of service or scrapped, one of their number, *Victorious*, which had been in use for training purposes, was retained for complete rebuilding between 1950 and 1958. With her overall length increased to 781ft and her displacement to 30,000 tons, she was fitted with an angled flight deck, steam catapults and new electronics, plus a dozen 3in and six 40mm AA weapons.

Three light carriers (CVLs) were also completed during the 1950s. The first of these was *Centaur*, commissioned in September 1953. She was followed by *Albion* in May 1954 and *Bulwark* in November of that year. These vessels were all of the *Hermes* class, although the ship of that name was in fact the last to be completed, not being ready until November 1959. These vessels all featured angled decks and were just under 740ft long. Each could operate about 45 aircraft, and was armed with 26 40mm AA guns. Displacement in each case was 22,000 tons.

CHAPTER 26

END OF EMPIRE

Operation 'Musketeer' and the Suez Debacle

The summer of 1956 found the Royal Navy with three fleet carriers and eight light fleet carriers on hand – at least, theoretically. However, following the successful trials with an angled deck the decision had been made not to operate jet aircraft from 'axial' carriers. As a result most ships were in dockyards to have angled decks installed, together with the new steam catapults. The opportunity was taken to undertake general overhauls at the same time.

The British Government had also recently changed its defence policy to one relying upon nuclear weapons rather than conventional forces. Troop reductions were consequently being made all around the world, and National Service was planned to be brought to an end soon. Even the Canal Zone in Egypt was evacuated.

Then late in July 1956 the Egyptian President, Gamel Abdel Nasser, announced his intention to nationalise the Suez Canal, a move which appeared to be a considerable threat to the strategic and economic interests of both Britain and France. This was more than suspicion, as the Egyptians had already been using their relatively limited control of the Canal to prevent shipping of any nationality from using the waterway if their destination or

LEFT *The only* Illustrious-*class carrier not to be seriously damaged during the Second World War, HMS* Victorious *was comprehensively rebuilt to modern standards in 1957. After re-commissioning she continued to serve until 1968. On deck are Sea Vixens and Whirlwind helicopters.*

port of departure was in Israel. With Britain and France still having substantial colonial interests in the Far East the Canal's nationalisation was a most alarming development, and consideration of what action should be taken began forthwith.

At this point the Royal Navy had only *Eagle* in the Mediterranean. *Ark Royal*, *Albion* and *Centaur* were all undergoing refits, while *Victorious* was being modernised more comprehensively. *Bulwark* was being used for flight trials and training, *Ocean* and *Theseus* were both in use as officer-recruit training ships, and *Triumph* was in reserve awaiting conversion to the same role. *Glory* and *Perseus* were also in reserve with plans for their future as yet unresolved.

Bulwark, which had been kept in readiness in case of emergencies during the modernisation programme, immediately took aboard an air group and sailed for the Mediterranean on 6 August. Her sister vessel, *Albion*, was made ready despite the unfinished state of her dockyard work, while the two old officers' training ships were rapidly fitted as emergency troop transports. These latter works were completed by 26 September, but were then ordered to be modified to allow for a reversion to carrier use; they were ready by the end of the month. *Ocean* then took aboard 845 Squadron with Whirlwinds, while *Theseus* prepared to carry the Joint Army/RAF Experimental Helicopter Unit, which was equipped with Whirlwinds and Bristol Sycamores. In the circumstances there was no opportunity to practise working the still very new helicopters together with the Royal Marines whom it was planned they would carry should the need arise.

RAF and French *Armée de l'Air* units flew out to Cyprus, but the range for fighters and fighter-bombers to operate from here over the Canal Zone was extreme, so an aircraft carrier presence was extremely desirable if any action was to take place. Unbeknown to the British, the French had clandestinely agreed to support Israeli action, and had even moved some of their fighter units to airfields in Israel to provide air defence while Israeli aircraft struck at Egyptian targets. Therefore, seizing this opportunity to neutralise Egypt before it was able to deploy and use aircraft and other weapons and munitions recently received from Eastern Bloc states, Israeli paratroops dropped in the Sinai on 29 October 1956 and advanced on the Canal. It seems that the Egyptians were as surprised as the British at this intercession, as their forces fell back rapidly.

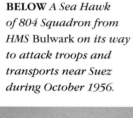

BELOW *A Sea Hawk of 804 Squadron from* HMS Bulwark *on its way to attack troops and transports near Suez during October 1956.*

Using this situation as a convenient excuse for intervention, the British and French governments issued an ultimatum next day, calling on both sides to withdraw their troops ten miles back from the banks of the Canal, and stating that 'in order to guarantee the freedom of transit through the Canal by the ships of all nations and in order to separate the belligerents, the Egyptian government must accept the temporary occupation by Anglo-French forces of key positions at Port Said, Ismailia and Suez'. The Israeli forces were still not yet within ten miles of the Canal, and obligingly agreed to abide by the ultimatum almost at once. The Egyptians, however, did not, and a poorly organised Anglo-French invasion was put in hand. This began with some air strikes from Cyprus that evening, followed next morning by attacks by carrier-borne aircraft.

Normally each Royal Navy carrier air group included a squadron of eight AS Gannets, but as no submarine involvement was anticipated these had been left behind, allowing additional fighter aircraft to be carried instead. The ships involved did, however, retain their flights of Skyraiders (or in one case, Avengers), and this was to prove the last occasion on which piston-engined fixed-wing aircraft would operate from British carriers.

Although the expedition, codenamed Operation 'Musketeer', occurred little more than three years after the end of the Korean War, the whole Fleet Air Arm inventory now consisted of the new jet

or prop-jet aircraft which had recently come into service. This was in distinct contrast to the French contingent, whose two carriers, *Arromanches* and *La Fayette*, both employed Vought Corsairs for their strike units.

Thus it was that on 1 November 40 Sea Hawks and escorting Sea Venoms strafed Egyptian airfields in the Nile Delta, claiming to have destroyed MiG-15 fighters and Ilyushin Il-28 jet bombers. Other Sea Hawks meanwhile provided CAP over the carriers, while Skyraiders and Avengers sought to identify any incoming counter-strikes by the Egyptians; in the event this threat did not materialise. While there was still a possibility of Egyptian fighter involvement, the Wyverns and Corsairs were held back to operate along the coast, looking for potential Egyptian naval reaction.

Due to the lack of any Egyptian fighter defence during the first day's raids, the FAA's propeller-driven aircraft joined the general assault on the second day. By evening little resistance was to be found and it would have been possible to undertake a landing forthwith. However, the surface-borne elements of the landing force were not due to arrive until 5 November, and a paratroop drop was held back until that date. On the 2nd one Sea Venom had been hit by AA fire and the observer seriously wounded, the pilot therefore landing the damaged aircraft back on *Eagle* on its belly. A single Sea Hawk had crashed while landing on *Bulwark*, the pilot being killed.

A proposal to land 600 Royal Marines from *Ocean* and *Theseus* to support an earlier paratroop drop was turned down, and the paratroops went in as planned, supported by all the naval strike aircraft. Helicopters flew in supplies and brought out wounded successfully. Finally, on the 6th, the surface assault got under way and the helicopters then began ferrying in about half of the Marines, the rest going in by sea. The naval Whirlwinds each carried seven fully equipped Marines, the Army ones carried five men, and the Sycamores three each. All together 415 men and 23 tons of ammunition and other supplies were carried ashore in just 89 minutes. Only one helicopter was lost when it ran out of fuel and crashed into the sea.

Once ashore the troops advanced swiftly until halted by a United Nations ceasefire call as at midnight on 6/7 November, since by this time world opinion had turned against the action being taken. The British and French governments found that even their US ally had turned on them, joining the Soviet Union in condemning the invasion. It was subsequently felt that the operation had been considerably marred by the long delay in following up the first two days of successful air strikes, which

would have enabled the actual landings to go in on the 3rd or 4th before world opinion had a chance to take shape.

Losses to the invaders were relatively light. Apart from the two crashes already mentioned, two Sea Hawks and two Wyverns were shot down by AA, all the pilots being rescued. One Corsair and two RAF aircraft were also lost.

While the results of the Suez adventure considerably diminished the international standing of Britain and France and led directly to the fall of the British Prime Minister, Sir Anthony Eden, its effects on defence planning thereafter seem generally to have been beneficial. The effectiveness of aircraft carriers in 'limited war' scenarios was fully proven, as were the benefits arising both from the angled deck and from the use of helicopters. Britain now commenced establishing 'rapid reaction' forces for unexpected or distant calls upon the nation's resources.

FLEET AIR ARM ORDER OF BATTLE – OPERATION 'MUSKETEER', 1 NOVEMBER 1956

HMS *Eagle*

892 Squadron }	17 Sea Venoms	Lt Cdr M.H.J. Petrie
893 Squadron }		Lt Cdr M.W. Healey
897 Squadron }	24 Sea Hawks	Lt Cdr A.R. Rawbone
899 Squadron }		Lt Cdr A.B.B. Clark
849A Flight	4 Skyraiders	
SAR Flight	2 Dragonflies	

HMS *Albion*

809 Squadron	8 Sea Venoms	Lt Cdr R.A. Shilcock
800 Squadron	10 Sea Hawks	Lt Cdr J.D. Russell
849C Flight	2 Skyraiders	
SAR Flight	2 Dragonflies	

HMS *Bulwark*

802 Squadron }		Lt Cdr R.L. Eveleigh
804 Squadron }	30 Sea Hawks	Lt Cdr R. von T.B. Kettle
810 Squadron }		Lt Cdr P.M. Lamb
895 Squadron }		Lt Cdr J.M. James
Ship's Flight	2 Avengers	
SAR Flight	2 Dragonflies	

HMS *Theseus*

845 Squadron	10 Whirlwinds	Lt Cdr J.C. Jacob

HMS *Ocean*

Joint Army/RAF Helicopter Unit	Whirlwinds & Sycamores	

CHAPTER 27

AFTER SUEZ

The World's Policeman

Although the Defence White Paper produced after the Suez debacle identified the need for enhanced conventional forces, particularly east of Suez where the United Kingdom had many treaty obligations and a considerable part still to play, it continued to lay stress upon the development of a nuclear force as a deterrent to possible Soviet aggression.

After Suez the Royal Navy usually managed to ensure that four strike carriers (as fleet carriers had come to be known) would be available at any one time. *Ark Royal* had, of course, not been available at the time of Suez, but had now completed her refit. *Victorious*, the last of the wartime *Illustrious*-class vessels, had been almost entirely rebuilt to modern standards and would be available in 1958. *Eagle* was due to commence a five-year modernisation programme, while *Centaur*, completed in 1953, would stand in for *Eagle* during this period. Although of only half the displacement of *Eagle*, *Centaur* had been redesigned while under construction to incorporate large carrier features.

Hermes, of similar displacement, would be commissioned during 1959. She had been redesigned to incorporate an angled deck, a deck-edge lift on the port side, two steam catapults, and a set of very advanced electronics. The ship had one problem, however: she could only carry about two-dozen aircraft, which was a distinct disadvantage.

RIGHT *Phantom of 892 Squadron taking off from* HMS Ark Royal.

Amongst the smaller carriers, the new commando/helicopter requirement began to be fully catered for. *Bulwark* undertook her final cruise as a fixed-wing carrier during 1958, then entered dockyard for conversion to this role. She was soon followed by her sister ship, *Albion*, so that at least one of these vessels would always be available east of Suez in the foreseeable future.

A wholesale cull of what remained then followed. Between 1958 and 1962 *Perseus*, *Glory*, *Ocean* and *Theseus* were all scrapped, while *Triumph* was converted to become a repair vessel. In 1963 *Majestic*, which had been returned from its loan to the Canadian Navy during 1957, was also scrapped, and the unfinished *Leviathan* was broken up in 1968.

Bulwark resumed service on 19 January 1960 as the first commando carrier. As such she was able to carry 600 Royal Marines and their equipment, plus 16 Whirlwind HAR helicopters with five more available as spares. During the 1960s much of the action to be seen by the Fleet Air Arm centred around the helicopter crews on this and other ships of this class, as will be recounted later.

It was to be the new commando ships – soon no longer referred to as carriers, in order to avoid confusion with vessels carrying fixed-wing aircraft – which saw action next. Late in June 1961 Abdul Karim Kassem, at that time dictator of Iraq, laid claim to the oil-rich Sheikdom of Kuwait. This very small state had just one battalion of 1,500 men for its defence, but was at once offered support by the UK and various Arab states. Wary of precipitating Iraqi action before help could arrive, the Sheik was reluctant to acquiesce. Only sea power could overcome this situation swiftly, but it was known that apart from other recently acquired Soviet weaponry, the Iraqi air force possessed a number of high-performance MiG-19 fighters. However, much of the Iraqi army was tied up in the north of the country, seeking to pacify dissident Kurds. In the south was just one armoured brigade near Basra, but this was only about 50 miles by road from Kuwait.

Because amphibious landing ships enjoyed only slow speeds, and well aware after Suez of the need for speed, the British were maintaining an LST (Landing Ship-Tank) loaded with armoured vehicles in the Persian Gulf, based on Aden. As it happened, during June a second, civilian-manned LST had arrived with a replacement load of tanks and their crews to relieve the existing force.

Aware that a takeover of Kuwait by Kassem could have severe political and financial implications for the West, action was considered urgently necessary. *Bulwark* was at Karachi and sailed on 29 June for the Gulf. *Victorious* was in the South China Sea at this time – about as far away from the theatre as it was possible to be – but was at once ordered to make all speed for the Gulf.

Until the 29th Kassem's threats had been expressed merely in words, but now the news came that some of his forces were moving south towards Kuwait. Next day the Sheik finally asked his allies for their help in resisting Kassem's aggression, just as *Bulwark* steamed into the Gulf. Arriving off Kuwait the next day she immediately began landing commandos ashore. An HQ ship, one of the LSTs and a frigate soon joined her.

Concern that the ships might be attacked by high-performance Iraqi jets was relieved when a sandstorm blew up. This also brought cooler temperatures, which allowed more helicopter flights to be made to fly troops ashore. Royal Marines swiftly occupied the airport, allowing a squadron of RAF Hunter fighters to fly in from Bahrain, while landing craft from *Bulwark* began carrying ashore the Marines' trucks and trailers. Transport aircraft then started flying in more British troops, who were soon joined by two squadrons of Canberra bombers and a further unit of Hunters. On 9 July *Victorious* arrived offshore to provide an organised air defence capability.

Meanwhile, the strike carrier *Centaur* was also on her way through the Suez Canal, and by 5/6 July was standing off Aden. By 8 July it was very clear that the British would defend Kuwait, at which juncture Kassem explained that he had only sought to establish his claim, and had no intention of using any force.

Bulwark then re-embarked her complement, but a British contingent remained in Kuwait until an Arab League force of 2,500 arrived to ensure the independence of the Sheikdom. Captain R.D. Franks, commander of *Bulwark*, announced:

'I could not be more grateful to General Kassem; the operation was tailor-made to our requirements. The whole concept of the commando ship and our 18 months of extensive training was proved to be exactly what was required. We were able to put a small but efficient unit down in the right place at the right time and support it with all its requirements, which undoubtedly helped to douse this particular "bush-fire".'

Shortly after this event, in August 1962 *Albion* was commissioned as the second commando ship. While *Bulwark*'s contingent of Royal Marines had included their own artillery, in *Albion*'s case four 105mm howitzers and crews of the Royal Artillery formed a part of the ship's complement. Initially eight Whirlwinds and 12 Wessex were also carried, the latter helicopter capable of carrying 12 men and being fitted with machine guns, pods of 2in rockets, or Nord SS 11 wire-guided anti-tank missiles.

Sailing for the east of Suez station in November, the ship received orders to speed up when en route to Singapore as trouble in Borneo had broken out during December. A rebellion in the Sultanate of Brunei, a British protectorate within the colony of Sarawak, was quickly put down by British troops. Its leader fled to the Philippines, but many of the rebels crossed into adjoining Indonesian territory, where they were rearmed and trained by their hosts and commenced guerrilla infiltration back into Brunei.

On arrival at Singapore, *Albion* took on troops to reinforce those already in Borneo, 18 helicopters at once starting to ferry them and to support the troops ashore. Here the Whirlwinds also went ashore to operate from land bases while the longer-ranging Wessex helicopters flew from the ship.

These operations subsequently developed into the single longest overseas deployment for the Fleet Air Arm up to that time. It also led to the commando helicopters and their crews being nicknamed 'Junglies' – a term still in use to this day. The amount of experience gained here in flying into airstrips which were usually no more than tiny clearings in the jungle, and sometimes in the face of hostile fire, was to prove of enormous value to the Service's rotary wing units thereafter. Operations were to continue here for the next three years, during which time the Royal Navy's

main duty became the guarding of the Malaysian coastline against any hostile landings.

At much the same time civil war broke out in the Yemen, and while the British involvement was mainly by land forces, seaborne logistical support was provided.

In January 1964 a revolution occurred in Zanzibar, followed by mutinies in several army units in Tanganyika (now Tanzania). Trouble was also believed to be brewing in nearby Kenya and Uganda, all these nations being members of the British Commonwealth. In the latter two countries the government maintained control of the main airfields, allowing British troops to be flown in from the UK and Aden. In Tanganyika the rebels held the airfields, the capital city of Dar-es-Salaam, and its docks.

At the time the only readily available vessel was the strike carrier *Centaur*, which had just arrived at Aden. Here she embarked 600 Marine commandos with their trucks and other equipment, plus two large RAF Belvedere passenger-carrying helicopters. With her own six Wessex HAS 1s stripped out, the ship sailed down to the Tanganyikan coast, where on arrival an accompanying destroyer opened fire with airburst 4.5in shells as a demonstration of force. *Centaur*'s helicopters landed the whole force of Marines in just 70 minutes, allowing them to undertake demonstration fire with their anti-tank rocket launchers. This rapidly ended any further hostilities by the mutineers in the docks area. In the vehicles flown in by the Belvederes, the Marines then moved on to the airport and

BELOW *Westland Wessex HAS 1 of 814 Squadron in Borneo during 1964.*

Dar-es-Salaam, where they met with no opposition. By the end of the month the situation had been satisfactorily resolved.

Meanwhile, this period was also marked by the arrival of a whole new generation of considerably more potent aircraft. First of these was the Supermarine Scimitar, which began to replace the Sea Hawk as the Navy's primary fighter-bomber at the start of 1958. By early 1960 four squadrons of these big twin-engined swept-wing aircraft were available. Able to exceed Mach 1 in a shallow dive, the Scimitar could carry a very substantial load of weapons, featuring up to 3,000lb of ordnance on each of four underwing racks. A typical load might incorporate four 1,000lb bombs and 24 3in rocket projectiles, or four Bullpup missiles. The

ABOVE *Showing well the squadron's 'scimitar' emblem on the tailfin is this 807 Squadron Scimitar.*

RIGHT *Scimitar F 1s of the 800 Squadron aerobatic team from HMS* Ark Royal *in 1961.*

BELOW *Scimitar F 1 XD241 of 803 Squadron taking off from HMS* Hermes.

aircraft was also fitted internally with a permanent armament of four 30mm Avon cannons, although on some aircraft these were removed to allow a pair of Sidewinder air-to-air radar-guided missiles to be carried. In this aircraft the Fleet Air Arm also had, for the first time, the capacity to carry a tactical nuclear weapon.

800, 803, 804, and 807 Squadrons were all to fly the Scimitar, but the arrival of this aircraft and the diminishing number of strike carriers available caused the disbandment of nine other Sea Hawk units by the end of the decade.

To replace the well-liked Sea Venom came the De Havilland Sea Vixen, a twin-engined all-weather fighter which like its predecessor featured the familiar De Havilland twin-boom layout. The Sea Vixen carried a pair of retractable rocket pods each containing 14 unguided 2in rockets, plus four Firestreak infrared homing missiles. It could double as a ground-attack aircraft, although only carrying about half the offensive load which the Scimitar could cope with.

The first squadron to introduce the Sea Vixen, 892, received these aircraft in August 1959, followed by 890, 893, and 899 Squadrons; three other Sea Venom units were then disbanded. Thus by the start of the 1960s the Fleet Air Arm had available four squadrons of Scimitars and four of Sea Vixens. Either aircraft could also act as an aerial tanker, allowing refuelling in flight to take place.

Close behind these powerful new fixed-wing aircraft came a new generation of helicopters. Westland obtained the necessary licences to build

TOP *Sea Vixen FAW 1 XJ488 of 892 Squadron.*

ABOVE *Four Sea Vixen FAW 2s of 899 Squadron from HMS* Eagle. *Note how the tail booms are extended forward to the leading edge of the wing on this mark of aircraft.*

LEFT *Sea Vixen FAW 1 with submarine HMS* Turpin.

ABOVE *Sea Vixen FAW 1s of 890 Squadron on HMS* Hermes, *June 1961.*

RIGHT *Sea Vixen FAW 2 of 899 Squadron from HMS* Eagle *firing rockets during 1969.*

the latest Sikorsky product, the S.58, as the Wessex. The British version differed from its US counterpart in substituting a gas turbine engine rather than a piston powerplant. Although of slightly less power than the latter, the turbine was also considerably lighter, which endowed the Wessex with a somewhat better overall performance. At least ten Fleet Air Arm squadrons would operate the Wessex in either its anti-submarine or its transport and rescue versions during the 1960s.

The year 1960 also saw the introduction into service of a smaller helicopter, the Westland Wasp, designed to operate from a platform on the stern of the Royal Navy's cruisers, destroyers and frigates. Three squadrons of these little aircraft were to be formed during the decade, operating on a detached basis from their parent units.

Even as the Sea Vixen and Scimitar were coming fully into service, a new strike aircraft was under development which in the early 1960s was one of the most advanced of its kind in the world. Capable of about 720mph (Mach 0.95), the Blackburn (subsequently Hawker Siddeley) Buccaneer was in fact the first aircraft to be designed for high-speed, low-level attack at sea level, allowing it to come in below radar and missile defence levels. It also enjoyed a remarkable range, of considerable advantage to a carrier-based type. Not only did its wings fold, but so too did both its nose and tail

ABOVE *Wasp HAS 1 XS544 of 829/703 Squadron on board HMS* Aurora.

LEFT *Westland Wessex HU 5 of 707 Squadron at Yeovilton.*

ABOVE *Wessex HU 5 of 771 Squadron at Culdrose. This is XT474 920/CU.*

OPPOSITE *A pair of 800 Squadron Buccaneer S.1s are seen flying over HMS Eagle. These are XN968 and XN970.*

RIGHT *Wasp HAS 1 XT790 of 829 Squadron fires a wire-guided Nord SS10 anti-tank missile.*

ABOVE *NA39 Buccaneer pre-production aircraft XK531, 680/LM, of 700Z Squadron, Intensive Flight Trials Unit, RNAS Lossiemouth, August 1961.*

cones, allowing for very economical use of space in ships' hangars.

At the time of its introduction into service it was fitted with much electronic guidance equipment, and it could carry both conventional and nuclear weaponry of up to 4,000lb weight in its internal revolving bomb-bay, plus a further 4,000lb (or Bullpup missiles) on underwing points.

The first Buccaneer squadron was 801, re-formed in July 1962, while the second, also a re-formation, was 809 Squadron in January 1963. Thereafter 800 and 803 Squadrons exchanged their Scimitars for these aircraft in 1964 and 1967 respectively. With the introduction of the Buccaneer, the role of the Scimitar increasingly became that of aerial tanker for its replacement and for Sea Vixens. The Supermarine aircraft was finally phased out of service around the end of 1966.

Aboard the strike carriers throughout this period, the main aircraft were, of course, supported by detachments of Gannet AEW 3 aircraft, while Whirlwinds or Wessex helicopters stood ready to rescue any aircrew who were unfortunate enough to come down in the sea.

Meanwhile, no sooner was the Tanganyikan situation described above resolved than the government of Ian Smith in Southern Rhodesia (now Zimbabwe) made a Unilateral Declaration of Independence from the UK on 11 November 1965. The British Prime Minister, Harold Wilson, described this as 'illegal' and 'treasonable'. An economic blockade was instituted, particularly aimed at preventing the delivery of stocks of oil to the country, and this action was approved by the United Nations.

HMS *Eagle* sailed from Singapore to undertake what became known as the 'Beira Patrol'. During the next two months 20 sorties a day were flown by Sea Vixens, Scimitars, Buccaneers, Gannets and helicopters over the Mozambique Channel. To achieve this the carrier remained at sea for a record 72 days before being relieved by *Ark Royal*. By this time *Eagle* had steamed some 30,000 miles since leaving Singapore, her air group flying over 1,000 sorties by fixed-wing aircraft and 800 planeguard and close search flights by helicopters. More than 750 ships had been checked.

Ark Royal was to undertake similar patrols, the two vessels maintaining these in turn for over two years. While these patrols were in themselves successful, they failed in their purpose of bringing down Smith's illegal regime.

There would be one more entry into service before this decade was through, and this was the McDonnell-Douglas F-4K Phantom fighter. Due to the increased size and weight of aircraft operated

ABOVE *Two Buccaneer S.1s demonstrate the different paint schemes employed by these aircraft. Flying from Lossiemouth over HMS* Tiger *during November 1963, XN691 and XK532 were both serving with 809 Squadron at the time.*

LEFT *Buccaneer S.2, XT283 111/E, of 800 Squadron, HMS* Eagle *in 1968. These aircraft served with the unit from 1959 to 1970.*

RIGHT *A Buccaneer
S.1 of 800 Squadron
displays the range of
bombs and under-wing
stores which it could
carry.*

OPPOSITE TOP *Not
the usual form!
A Buccaneer provides
in-flight fuel for one
of the RAF's Vulcan
V-Bomber Force.*

RIGHT *Buccaneer S.1 of
801 Squadron on HMS*
Victorious *with a nearby
Wessex operating as
planeguard.*

OPPOSITE BOTTOM
*Sea King HAS 1 of 814
Squadron with HMS*
Hermes, *early 1979.
The aircraft is using a
dunking sonar.*

by carriers by this time, *Ark Royal* and *Eagle* – which had originally been designed to carry up to 100 aircraft each – could accommodate less than half that number by the 1960s, including eight ASW helicopters. *Victorious*, despite her massive facelift, could by now only manage 25 fixed-wing aircraft and eight helicopters, while *Centaur* and *Hermes* each had room for only 20 of the former and eight of the latter. Thus the Royal Navy's five carriers between them now had a maximum capacity of some 145 fixed-wing aircraft and 40 helicopters.

Clearly it was time for some new vessels. The Navy Estimates of 1962–63 optimistically announced: 'There is no need to order a new carrier yet but the necessary design work has been put in hand.' On 30 July 1963, however, the Government announced that it had decided to order a new carrier to replace both *Ark Royal* and *Victorious*. *Centaur* was due to be withdrawn during the mid-1960s. *Eagle* and *Hermes* were both to be very extensively modernised in order that the Royal Navy would retain a force of three strike carriers until at least 1980.

The new carrier, initially known as CVA.01, was to be absolutely 'state of the art', despite being conventionally powered by oil-fired boilers

rather than by nuclear power, as were the large US carriers at this time. To have a displacement of about 53,000 tons, she was also to feature a parallel-line flight deck rather than an angled deck. This allowed a 'fly-through' to be achieved more easily in poor visibility since a pilot would be able to line up for a landing directly in line with the carrier, rather than having to position himself at a slight angle to line up with the angled deck.

The new vessel would carry the more powerful Buccaneer S.2 which was about to appear; the F-4K, acquired from the USA but powered by two Rolls-Royce Spey engines; and a new anti-submarine helicopter, the Westland Sea King, a licence-built Sikorsky S-61B. With this equipment the Royal Navy, although down to only three strike carriers, would achieve a major qualitative improvement.

The Buccaneer S.2 became available first, all four squadrons receiving this version between the end of 1965 and the start of 1968. The

Phantom was slower arriving. Efforts to maximise the involvement of British manufacturers in the construction and equipping of the aircraft achieved an input of more than 40 per cent, but this had the effect of increasing the ultimate cost to 50 per cent more than it would have been had a standard US-built version been purchased. Considerable modification proved to be necessary to allow the fitting of the Spey engines, which had originally been chosen in order to allow these aircraft to operate from *Hermes*-class carriers.

Initial orders had been for 143 F-4Ks for the Fleet Air Arm and 200 F-4Ms for the RAF. As deliveries began to arrive during 1968, the order was steadily reduced, for reasons which will shortly become apparent, dropping to only 48 F-4Ks and 120 F-4Ms. On arrival the F-4Ks were first subjected to intensive flying trials with 700P Squadron, a nucleus from this unit then enabling 767 Squadron to be re-formed to train both Fleet Air Arm and RAF pilots on the aircraft. The first operational unit was

ABOVE *Phantom FG 1 of 892 Squadron taking off from HMS* Ark Royal.

OPPOSITE *An RAF Handley Page Victor K.1, XA918, prepares to refuel a Royal Navy De Havilland Sea Vixen FAW 2 (XN685) and a Blackburn Buccaneer S.1 (XN976).* IWM T5927

ABOVE *Scimitar F 1 of 803 Squadron from HMS* Victorious *about to refuel from a Sea Vixen of 892 Squadron on 13 March 1962.*

892 Squadron, which had disbanded as a Sea Vixen unit in October 1968 and was re-formed to receive Phantoms the following March. It turned out to be the only Royal Navy Phantom squadron.

Soon after the unit had formed under the command of Captain Roy Lygo, himself a Second World War fighter pilot (and ultimately both an Admiral and a Knight), three aircraft and crews were entered in the *Daily Mail* Transatlantic Air Race, competing in the fastest-time section. On 11 May 1969 the third aircraft to go, in the hands of Lieutenant Commanders Brian Davies and Peter Goddard, won the race, breaking two records. One was the fastest-time section, the other was the New York–London Air Speed Record. Having been refuelled in the air three times by RAF Victor tankers, Davies and Goddard were picked up by a Wessex the moment they landed at British Aircraft Corporation's Wisley airfield in Surrey, and flown into Central London, completing the journey in 4 hours 46 minutes and 57 seconds. They received the 'Blue Riband' and a cash prize of £6,000.

Even before these events had taken place, however, and at a time when the US Navy was expanding its aircraft carrier fleet as a result of its experiences in Vietnam, the blow fell. The British Government announced that CVA.01 was to be cancelled and all existing strike carriers were to be phased out of service by the mid-1970s. In a White Paper entitled 'Statement on the Defence Estimates 1966' presented by the Secretary of State for Defence, Denis Healey, on 22 February 1966, the Paper stated:

'Experience and study have shown that only one type of operation exists for which carriers and carrier-borne aircraft would be indispensable; that is the landing, or withdrawal, of troops against sophisticated opposition outside the range of land-based air power. It is only realistic to recognise that we, unaided by our allies, could not expect to undertake operations of this character in the 1970s – even if we could afford a larger carrier force.'

ABOVE *Buccaneers of 809 Squadron and Phantoms of 892 Squadron on HMS Ark Royal.*

When one considers what was to transpire later, the sheer naivety of this statement nearly takes one's breath away. The Paper continued:

'Our plan is that, in the future, aircraft operating from land bases should take over the strike-reconnaissance and air-defence functions of the carrier. …Airborne early-warning aircraft will…[subsequently] operate from land bases.'

Apart from the fact that at this time the UK's only obvious ally was the USA, it also overlooked the fact that Britain had treaty obligations to 17 Asian and Pacific states. Almost in contradiction of its earlier statements, the White Paper went on to state:

'The aircraft carrier is the most important element of the Fleet for offensive action against an enemy at sea or ashore and makes a large contribution to the defence

of our seaborne forces. It can also play an important part in operations where local air superiority has to be gained and maintained and offensive support of ground forces is required.'

Instead, 50 US-built F-111K swing-wing fighter-bombers were to be acquired at a price which equated to the cost of CVA.01 and its aircraft. The theory was that these 50 aircraft alone were effectively to meet all Britain's international liabilities and any overseas operations.

The resultant outcry included the resignations in protest of Christopher Mayhew, the Minister of Defence for the Royal Navy, and Admiral David Luce, the First Sea Lord, and provoked a debate in Parliament. The Government remained obdurate, and Mr Healey stated:

'Those who are saying, for whatever reason, that the phasing out of the carrier force in up to ten years time means the end of the

Buccaneer launch

ABOVE *Buccaneers and Phantoms ranged on the flight deck of HMS Ark Royal.*

RIGHT *Buccaneer tensioned for launch.*

ABOVE *The pilot is given the signal to go.*

LEFT *The steam catapult strop falls away as the Buccaneer leaves the end of the carrier deck and becomes airborne.*

Royal Navy, are doing the Fleet a grave disservice. The fact is that the United States is the only country in the world which plans to maintain a viable carrier force around the world through the 1970s. Neither the Soviet Union nor China has carriers or plans to have them, nor does any of the countries with whom our commitments might have engaged us in hostilities over the last twenty years.'

BELOW *HMS* Ark Royal *sails from Gibraltar in November 1978 in full parade order, her crew lining the deck-sides. Aboard her can be seen Buccaneers, Phantoms, two Gannets and a Sea King.*

Subsequently, Major General J.L. Moulton, RM, in the publication *Navy*, presented an article entitled 'Aden and CVA.01'. In this he perceptively wrote:

'CVA.01 was lost because the case for maritime strategy was never properly presented to the public which has to pay

for defence. The Navy itself was far too slow in the 1950s to understand its role in modern limited war. It became seen by the public as an out-of-date relic of the past, thinking of fighting another Battle of the Atlantic, even another Jutland. Too often it was allowed to appear that the Navy demanded carriers to keep the Navy strong…the case for land-based air was that it claimed it could do the job better than a strong Navy.'

In the event, just two years later in January 1968 the Government was forced to cancel the order for the F-111Ks during a severe financial crisis. At that stage the country was left with no cogent strategy.

The three existing carriers, *Eagle*, *Ark Royal* and *Hermes*, soldiered on. *Hermes* was withdrawn in

July 1971 for conversion to the commando ship role, subsequently taking the place of *Albion*, which was decommissioned in March 1973 and sold. *Eagle* followed in 1972, then being scrapped. The departure of these two vessels resulted in three Buccaneer and the two remaining Sea Vixen squadrons all being disbanded. The arrival of a Conservative administration in Whitehall in 1970 did bring some respite, as the decision was taken to maintain *Ark Royal* in service at least until 1976.

809 Squadron with late model Buccaneer S.2c and S.2d aircraft and 892 Squadron with the F-4Ks remained as the sole operational Fleet Air Arm fixed-wing striking force, serving aboard *Ark Royal*. However, at the end of 1978 this vessel too went for scrapping and the two remaining squadrons were disbanded as the carrier force ceased to exist. Perhaps the cruellest cut of all occurred when these units were required to pass their remaining aircraft to the RAF. Indeed, by this time some 50 per cent of the pilots aboard were members of the latter service anyway. The cancellation of the training programme for fast jet pilots for the Navy and departures by way of early release programmes by those already trained but who now saw no future for themselves in their chosen service, had occasioned the need for this cross-service manning.

Thus it appeared at that stage that in future the Fleet Air Arm would be no more than a helicopter service, operating from commando carriers, cruisers and anti-submarine ships. Strangely, perhaps, it would be in the field of vertical take-off, until then the province only of the helicopter, that the Fleet Air Arm was to find its renaissance.

BELOW *Replenishment at sea: in Hong Kong waters, HMS* Hermes *(fourth from left) refuels from the RFA fleet tanker* Tideflow.

CHAPTER 28

A VERTICAL SERVICE

The Amazing Harrier

The Government's decision to abolish the carrier fleet arose principally from a change in its perception of Britain's strategic place in the world and its future likely military involvements. The intention to withdraw from commitments 'east of Suez' appeared to remove the need for carriers sporting fixed-wing aircraft. Now the North Atlantic route between Western Europe and the United States became the pre-eminent priority. The vast preponderance of North American air and naval strength appeared to indicate that the protection of NATO shipping from air attack on the Western side of the ocean could be left in the hands of US forces, while it was considered that over the Eastern basin cover would be provided by RAF high-performance fighters based in the north of the UK and guided, when necessary, by AEW Nimrod aircraft. All that appeared to be required of the FAA was to furnish anti-submarine protection for the shipping routes.

With this requirement in mind, the Royal Navy had been preparing studies of a fairly small 'flight deck ship' able to operate helicopters in this role. For political reasons the term 'carrier' had been studiously avoided, the design being referred to by a variety of alternatives such as TASS (Tactical Air Support Ship). In this way was born the 'through-deck cruiser'.

The Royal Navy remained concerned that

LEFT *Three Sea Harrier FRS 1s of 899, 800 and 801 Squadrons demonstrate each of the squadrons' individual markings, soon after the Sea Harrier's introduction to service.*

the distance between the mid-North Atlantic and the UK might leave vessels waiting too long for assistance in the event of a Soviet air attack, and with this in mind further trials had been undertaken with a pre-production Hawker Siddeley Harrier aboard *Bulwark* during 1966.

Already, in February 1963, tests had been undertaken aboard *Ark Royal* with the Hawker Siddeley P.1127 Kestrel vertical take-off jet fighter test vehicle. Initially it had been decided to go no further while conventional aircraft of equal, or superior, performance remained available as a viable alternative. By the mid-1960s, however, the P.1127 had been developed into the Harrier ground-attack aircraft, and had been ordered by the RAF as a replacement for its Hunter FRA 9s.

Meanwhile, as early as 1967 a new 12, 120-ton assault ship, HMS *Intrepid*, had been commissioned, capable of carrying six Wessex troop-carrying helicopters. During the decade which followed, the concept of the 'through-deck cruiser' had found favour with a more enlightened Government, and an order was placed for just such a vessel – actually to all intents and purposes a light fleet carrier. This new vessel was launched in 1977 as HMS *Invincible*, and would be commissioned in July 1980.

To provide a suitable aircraft for this new class of ship, the Harrier was again subjected to trials,

LEFT *Sea Harrier FRS 1 XZ454 250/N of 800 Squadron with HMS* Invincible *during 1980.*

BELOW *Down on the hangar deck on HMS* Invincible, *Sea Harrier FRS 1 XZ458 of 801 Squadron undergoes an engine change.*

ABOVE *A Sea Harrier FRS 1 of 800 Squadron receives maintenance inside the hangar on HMS* Hermes *while its pilot chats to the maintainers, 1983.*

OPPOSITE *Sea Harrier XZ492 123/H over HMS* Hermes.

this time aboard *Hermes* during February 1977, following which 24 were ordered. With *Intrepid* now on hand to take her place, *Hermes* was to revert from its commando ship role to embark the new aircraft until *Invincible* became available. The Sea Harrier differed from the RAF version in having a modified front fuselage and raised pilot's cockpit, plus improved avionics. As the FRS 1 it was to act as fighter, reconnaissance and strike aircraft, and was capable of carrying Sidewinder air-to-air guided missiles and/or a pod containing a pair of 30mm

Aden cannons, as well as a variety of bombs and other weaponry. However, given the role anticipated for them the need for any form of AEW aircraft aboard the new ships was at this stage not foreseen.

Tests were also being undertaken, at the Royal Aircraft Establishment at Bedford, of a 'ski-jump'-type structure from which the Sea Harrier could make a very short take-off, as an alternative to a fully vertical take-off which burnt considerable additional fuel. By 1978 it had been ascertained that a structure of this kind, at an angle of 20° to

the horizontal, so improved take-off that some 2,000lb of extra fuel or weapons load could be carried when using it. The first such device to be constructed aboard ship was fitted to the foredeck of *Hermes*, while such a ski-jump was incorporated in *Invincible* during construction. Meanwhile, a further *Invincible*-class vessel, to be named *Illustrious*, was launched in December 1978, although she would not be commissioned until June 1982. A third – a new *Ark Royal* – had also been ordered, and would be launched in June 1981, with commissioning due some considerable time later.

The first production Sea Harriers were supplied to 700A Flight at Yeovilton, which was to become the home base of these aircraft. Following intense trials, the flight formed the nucleus of a new 899 Squadron in March 1980, which was to be the Sea

Harrier Headquarters Squadron. At the same time 800 Squadron was also re-formed with four aircraft to commence service on the new *Invincible* during May. Fortuitously, the extension of *Ark Royal*'s life had allowed just sufficient of the experienced naval fast-jet pilots to be retained in the Service to ensure that a nucleus of these vital personnel was available on the formation of these new units.

801 Squadron was also re-formed at the end of January 1981 with five Sea Harriers, embarking on *Invincible* during May of that year, 800 Squadron having moved to *Hermes* a couple of months earlier. As it was to transpire, this had all happened in the very nick of time, for at the start of April 1982 the Argentinian military dictator General Galtieri launched an invasion of the British Crown colony of the Falkland Islands – long claimed by Argentina as rightfully her territory of the Malvinas.

CHAPTER 29

TASK FORCE

Operation 'Corporate' and the Falklands War

I n the face of this aggression an emergency session of the House of Commons was called on Saturday 3 April – the first since the Suez crisis of 1956. Here the Prime Minister, Margaret Thatcher, announced that a Task Force of naval vessels would be despatched at once to repossess the islands, by force if necessary. This operation was to carry the codename 'Corporate'.

At Yeovilton the two operational squadrons of Sea Harriers, 800 and 801, had their complements of aircraft and pilots increased by the expedient of dividing most of the establishment of 899 Squadron between them. At the time that squadron had a number of RAF Harrier pilots attached to it in order to gain experience with the fighter version of the aircraft, which the RAF did not have. Several of these pilots were to be included amongst those who sailed for the South Atlantic.

800 Squadron, with 12 Sea Harriers to hand, joined *Hermes*, together with nine Sea King anti-submarine helicopters of 826 Squadron, while 801 Squadron with eight Sea Harriers and 820 Squadron with nine Sea Kings went aboard *Invincible*. A further nine Sea Kings of 846 Squadron also joined *Hermes* as transports for a group of Royal Marine commandos which this vessel was to carry.

Just as the Task Force was about to sail, some of the commando Sea King crews were provided with

LEFT *Sea Harrier XZ499 of No 800 Naval Air Squadron takes off from the aircraft carrier HMS* Hermes *for Combat Air Patrol, 21 May 1982.* IWM FKD 2387

the first examples of a new type of Night Vision Goggles (NVG). Far more practical and effective than anything that had gone before, they were to prove invaluable for subsequent night operations – particularly those undertaken at low altitude when putting ashore Special Forces troops for clandestine operations. The NVG remains a very important element of helicopter crew equipment to the present day.

The Task Force set off on 6 April, heading first for Ascension Island; included were the two carriers, the assault ship *Fearless*, ten destroyers and frigates (all carrying Wessex, Lynx or Wasp helicopters) and four replenishment ships. The force thus had an air component of 20 Sea Harriers and 54 helicopters.

This small fleet would be faced, if hostile action commenced, by an Argentinian air force equipped with 16 French-built Dassault Mirage III fighters, 34 Dagger fighter-bombers (Israeli-built copies of the Mirage which operated mainly in the ground-attack role), 65 Douglas A-4 Skyhawks of US manufacture, nine elderly British-built Canberra bombers and 115 various propeller-driven or light aircraft including 25 Pucara ground-attack aircraft, Beech T-34C Turbo Mentors, Macchi 339s and a variety of helicopters.

The Argentine Navy had available an aircraft carrier, *25 de Mayo* (herself an ex-Royal Navy light fleet carrier, HMS *Venerable*), and a cruiser, *Generale Belgrano*, plus a force of 11 more A-4 Skyhawks, six Grumman S-2E Trackers, a pair of Lockheed SP-2H Neptunes, and five Dassault Super-Etendard fighter-bombers with five Exocet missiles. These latter aircraft were the most modern and the most dangerous to the British Task Force.

There were also a variety of transport aircraft available, including Fokker Friendships and F.28s, Lockheed Electras, Skyvans, Learjets, Boeing 707s, Lockheed C-139 and KC-130 Hercules, and other types. Total available aircraft to the Argentine Air Force, Navy and Army thus amounted to some 256, although a fair proportion of these were unserviceable at any one time. Because the French government had immediately supported the British reaction by placing an embargo on any aid or arms sales, the Argentine Navy would be obliged to use one of its few Super-Etendards for cannibalisation to keep the other four operational.

The Mirage and Dagger aircraft were capable of much greater speeds than was the subsonic Sea Harrier, but the latter was more manoeuvrable, and in theory at any rate had the advantage of VIFF (Vectored In Forward Flight) use of its adjustable jet effluxes. In practice this proved of less advantage than had been thought, and was used very little. Its greatest advantage was its equipment with the new AIM-9L Sidewinder heat-seeking missile, which could home onto a target aircraft from almost any direction, rather than just from the rear, as had been the case with earlier versions. The British pilots were also well trained for low-altitude flying, where much of the advantage of the faster jets was dissipated.

Possibly the greatest disadvantage faced by the Task Force proved to be its lack of AEW aircraft. Without a traditional carrier to operate from, such remaining Gannets as still existed had nowhere to fly from, and the range was too great for RAF aircraft from Ascension to undertake this role. Urgent attempts would be made to fit a Sea King for this duty, but the first of these would not be ready until well after the action had ended.

The Sea Harrier was thus very much the key to success for the Task Force, although it was hoped that the anti-aircraft missiles carried aboard the ships would go far to protect them from air attack. In Britain the remaining eight Sea Harriers on order were subjected to tremendous efforts to get them completed and fitted out for action as quickly as possible. To achieve this, infrared decoys and chaff-dispensers were acquired from US manufacturers, with supplies for the existing aircraft being rushed south to be fitted on arrival.

The only other potentially suitable aircraft available were the RAF's ground-attack Harriers. Consequently, 1 Squadron was ordered to Yeovilton to learn carrier operation with the aid of the ground-mounted practice 'ski-jump' installed there. Efforts were also made to fit them with Sidewinders before they were despatched to the combat area aboard the container ship *Atlantic Conveyor*. Unfortunately, unlike the RAF pilots from 899 Squadron, who had already joined the Task Force, 1 Squadron's men had not been trained for fighter operations, but specifically for ground attack.

Further efforts to strengthen the Task Force included the formation of three more helicopter units, mainly for transport duties. These were 825 Squadron with Sea Kings, and 847 and 848 Squadrons with Wessex aircraft, which had been in the process of being phased out of Fleet Air Arm service in favour of the Sea King.

RAF Nimrod 1 patrol aircraft reached Wideawake airfield on Ascension on 5 April, followed by more advanced Nimrod 2s by the 12th. On the 18th Victors arrived both for reconnaissance and for air refuelling duties. Vulcan bombers and Chinook heavy helicopters were also prepared for action.

Meanwhile, the British Government had declared a 200-nautical-mile exclusion zone centred on Port Stanley, the capital of the Falklands. This area was to be patrolled by Royal Navy nuclear-powered submarines. This was not able to affect

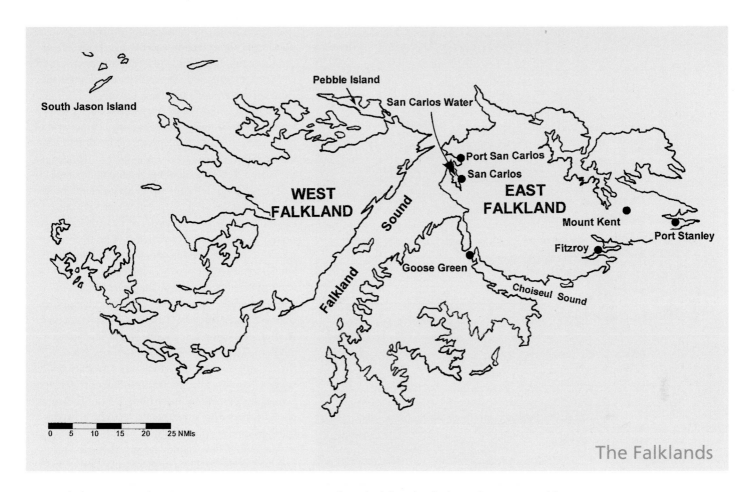

The Falklands

air supply, however, and Argentinian transport aircraft continued to fly in to Port Stanley with impunity. This was the only hard-surface all-weather airfield available in the islands, although there were grass strips at Goose Green and Pebble Island. Port Stanley airfield in particular was now heavily defended by ground-to-air missile batteries and considerable numbers of automatic anti-aircraft guns. In preparation for the support and movement of their troops garrisoned there, and already backed by a number of ground-attack aircraft, the Argentines now flew in 22 helicopters of various types.

Ascension Island is nearly 3,900 miles to the north-east of the Falklands, but 'only' 2,850 miles from South Georgia, another British dependency to the east of the Falklands which had also been occupied by Argentine forces. To investigate whether there were any Argentinian warships in the area of the latter island which might interfere with the Task Force, Victors from Ascension set off in the early hours of 20 April to reconnoitre. One of these aircraft completed the longest-range reconnaissance ever made to that date, remaining in the air 14 hours 45 minutes, and covering 7,000 miles. No hostile warships were reported.

By now, however, the Antarctic patrol vessel HMS *Endurance* had reached a point close to the north end of the island where she was joined by the destroyer HMS *Antrim*, the frigate *Plymouth* and the replenishment ship *Tidespring*. All these vessels carried helicopters, and were supported generally by the presence in the area of the nuclear submarine *Conqueror*.

Antrim now launched her 737 Squadron Wessex, flown by Lieutenant Commander Ian Stanley, to report on conditions on South Georgia in the area of the Fortuna Glacier. He returned to report that the landing of SAS troops could be achieved. He then returned to the area accompanied by two transport Wessex helicopters from *Tidespring* to deliver a party of these special forces. However, weather conditions were deteriorating, and by next morning the troops were suffering from exposure and would clearly have to be evacuated.

Initial trips by the three Wessex helicopters failed due to the adverse weather, but all three finally got down on their next attempt. On take-off first one and then the second of the *Tidespring* aircraft suffered 'white-out' conditions, and each struck the ground with a rotor blade, crashing as a result; fortunately, no serious injuries resulted in either case. Stanley flew back to the ship with his load, then returned with blankets and medical supplies. Forced away by the weather, he

nonetheless returned later, taking advantage of a pocket of calmer weather to land and take off all the survivors. He would subsequently be awarded a DSO for his outstanding performance on this date. He was by no means finished, however.

During the night of 22 April SAS parties were landed successfully by helicopter and Gemini rubber boats, still without the presence of the British ships having been spotted by the Argentinian troops on the island. Next day came intelligence information that the Argentinian submarine *Santa Fe* might be approaching the area. At this news, all the vessels except *Endurance* were ordered to withdraw to a point 200 miles to the north-east. Here they were reinforced by the guided-missile frigate *Brilliant*, which carried two Lynxes.

Further intelligence was then received that *Santa Fe* would be heading for Grytviken harbour on the 25th. At once the British warships moved south to seek an interception, and at first light Stanley's Wessex crew got a contact which led them to the submarine, which was travelling on the surface. Stanley called in aid, and *Brilliant*'s two Lynxes, accompanied by two Wasps from *Endeavour* and one from *Plymouth*, headed for the area, the three latter carrying AS 12 wire-guided missiles.

Meanwhile, Ian Stanley caught the submarine and dropped two 250lb depth charges, which,

ABOVE *A Wasp helicopter from the Ice Patrol Ship HMS* Endurance *touches down on pack ice during a survey operation in the Antarctic before the Falklands Conflict.* IWM FKD 720

RIGHT *The Royal Navy's Ice Patrol Ship HMS* Endurance *noses her way through pack ice in Antarctica. In the foreground is the ship's Wasp helicopter, XS539/434.*

exploding close to her port side, prevented her from submerging. Making tight turns, but trailing oil and smoke, *Santa Fe* made for Grytviken, but while the Wessex and the pair of Lynxes attacked her with machine-gun fire, one of *Endurance*'s Wasps obtained a direct hit on her conning tower with an AS 12, which went right through. She then reached harbour and grounded alongside the jetty, all of her crew leaping out.

With the presence of British forces now obvious, *Antrim* and *Plymouth* bombarded the area near the harbour in a demonstration of firepower, following which the Wessex and Lynx helicopters began flying in all available Marines and soldiers. Soon white flags were seen, and shortly after this South Georgia was in British hands again at a minimum cost in lives. The Royal Navy had struck the first blow.

The first aerial contact occurred on 21 April when a patrolling Sea Harrier of 800 Squadron intercepted an Argentinian Boeing 707 on reconnaissance. At this stage the British pilot had strict orders not to fire, so the two aircraft flew in formation, photographing each other. As more such flights were spotted, word was put out through diplomatic channels that if they continued the aircraft would be shot down.

As the Task Force closed on the area the first hostile action was taken early on 1 May when all

ABOVE *The Argentinian submarine* Santa Fe *was attacked and damaged by Royal Navy Wessex and Lynx helicopters on 25 April. She limped into Grytviken harbour on South Georgia, badly damaged and listing heavily.*

LEFT *Sea Harrier FRS 1 of 800 Squadron from HMS* Hermes *on the San Carlos airstrip in the Falklands. Flt Lt D. 'Mog' Morgan is at the controls.*

ABOVE *The Royal Navy nuclear submarine* HMS Conqueror *attacked and sank the Argentinian cruiser* General Belgrano *on 2 May, with the loss of 368 lives.*

available British fixed-wing aircraft attacked targets ashore. A single RAF Vulcan bomber, frequently air-refuelled on the flight down from Ascension, bombed the runway at Port Stanley during the pre-dawn darkness. At first light Sea Harriers undertook low-level bombing attacks. Nine of the 12 aircraft from *Hermes* (six flown by FAA pilots and three by RAF flight lieutenants) struck Port Stanley again, while three more – all flown by Navy pilots – hit Goose Green. 801 Squadron flew CAP while these raids were under way, maintaining four aircraft in the sky throughout. An Islander and a Pucara were destroyed on the ground at Port Stanley, the latter as it was preparing to take off. Having caught the defences relatively by surprise, the only damage suffered by the attackers was a single 20mm shell hole in the tail of the last Sea Harrier to cross the airfield. With the Argentines thus fully alerted, defence then became the order of the day for both fighter squadrons.

The commencement of action by the British had been expected, and in Argentina jet fighters were ready on the airfields nearest to the Falklands in anticipation of strikes on the mainland. The first Argentinian sorties over the Task Force were not long in coming, and were made by Mirage fighters. A pair of Sea Harriers on CAP were unable to make contact as the opposing fighters were flying at very high altitude and did not seek to come down.

During the latter part of the afternoon, however, hostile attackers arrived in some force, 40 sorties being made by Canberras, Skyhawks and Daggers, with Mirages as top cover. Flight Lieutenant Paul Barton (RAF) and Lt Steve Thomas of 801 Squadron were directed by the radars of HMS *Glamorgan* to intercept, engaging two Mirages which attempted to attack them head-on, but at too great a range. Barton turned in behind one, launched a Sidewinder and achieved a hit, the Mirage blowing up; the pilot managed to eject, but the Sea Harrier had gained its first success.

Steve Thomas, meanwhile, obtained a hit on a second Mirage, causing damage which resulted in the pilot trying to make a forced-landing at Port Stanley. As he went in, however, his aircraft was fired on by the defending AA batteries and crashed; the pilot was killed.

Ten minutes or so behind, three Daggers – each carrying a pair of 1,000lb bombs – attacked *Glamorgan*, *Arrow* and *Alacrity*, all these ships suffering slight damage. This highlighted an early shortcoming of the defences, for most of the shipboard radars controlling the missiles and AA guns suffered from 'ground clutter' interference during such low-level attacks.

Two of 800 Squadron's Sea Harriers were then attacked by three more Daggers, one of which fired a missile at Lieutenant Martin Hale's aircraft, which he had considerable difficulty in avoiding. Flight Lieutenant Tony Penfold (RAF) launched a Sidewinder at the leading Dagger at quite long range, but his target was hit and blew up, the pilot being killed.

The final success of the day occurred a few minutes later when six Canberras appeared overhead. Two 801 Squadron pilots intercepted and one of the bombers was shot down by Lieutenant Curtis. These initial results looked good – four shot down and two destroyed on the ground without loss. However, the Sea Harrier pilots felt at this stage that they were in for a long, hard battle which few of them anticipated surviving. They were surprised by the poor tactics employed by the enemy so far, and appreciated that the missiles used by the Argentinian fighters were considerably older and less efficient than their own 'state-of-the-art' Sidewinders.

The Argentinians were already suffering from a problem with the standard 'iron bombs' which they were using. In order to approach very low to allow them a fair chance of avoiding interception by the Sea Harriers, the fuses had to be set with a sufficient delay to allow the delivering aircraft to get clear before they exploded. This, however, was to mean that on frequent occasions when hits were obtained the bombs failed to explode, or only did so after passing through the vessel and plunging into the sea beyond.

More threats were on the point of appearing at this stage, for the aircraft carrier *25 de Mayo* was at sea and heading for the Task Force. This ship's Skyhawk pilots had the benefit of more specialist training in attacking surface vessels than their air force colleagues, and for this they were now preparing. The cruiser *General Belgrano* was also at sea, patrolling between the Islas de los Estados and Burdwood Bank, south-west of the Falklands. What concerned the Sea Harrier pilots more at this time was the prospect of the return of the Mirages to seek to wrest local air superiority from them. In the event, after this first day these aircraft were retained for the defence of the home airfields, and would not be encountered again over the Task Force.

At dawn on 2 May *25 de Mayo*'s Skyhawks were preparing to launch when a change in the weather presented the ship with too calm a wind to allow a normal unassisted take-off. The weight of the bombs and sufficient fuel to allow the aircraft both to attack and return were too great to allow the catapults to be employed. Consequently the carrier reversed course to await more favourable conditions. This was not a problem shared by the Sea Harriers, which, with their variable jet thrust and 'ski-jump' deck structures, were able to operate in virtually any conditions. Meanwhile, Sea Kings of 846 Squadron had flown a party of SAS observers ashore in the Falklands, and these would report on local Argentinian operations until invasion occurred.

During 2 May, in an attack which was later to provoke controversy as to its necessity, the nuclear submarine *Conqueror* sighted and sank the cruiser *General Belgrano* with the loss of 321 members of her crew. Following this, the Argentinian surface fleet retired immediately to mainland waters and would not sortie out again. *25 de Mayo*'s Skyhawks were disembarked and would later operate over the islands from land bases.

The first Sea Harrier loss was suffered on 4 May during an attack on Goose Green by three of 800 Squadron's aircraft. AA hit Lieutenant N. Taylor's fighter and it crashed in flames with the loss of the pilot. This was followed by a surprise attack made by two Super-Etendards, each carrying an Exocet missile. One of these hit the destroyer *Sheffield* before any evasive or defensive action could be taken – even the firing of chaff rockets. Twenty-one members of the crew were killed in this attack, although the second Exocet failed to find a target. Helicopters flew in fire-fighting teams and evacuated the wounded, but nothing could be done to save the vessel and she burnt out.

Next day dawned with heavy cloud and fog, but at 0900 hours two Sea Harriers were launched on patrol by 801 Squadron, operating about

20 miles apart. The stricken *Sheffield*'s radar gained a fleeting contact which appeared to be a fast-moving aircraft at very low level, and at once the two fighters were vectored onto this. Lieutenant Commander John Eyton-Jones and Lieutenant Al Curtis both dived through the murk almost to sea level, but both then disappeared and were not seen again. It was assumed that they had either both flown into the sea in the poor visibility, or (more likely) had collided and crashed. The loss of two Sea Harriers and their pilots at this critical time, and particularly following the previous day's loss, was extremely serious.

A lull in aerial activity followed, and it was 9 May before anything else of note occurred. On that date 800 Squadron's Lieutenant Commander Gordon Batt and Flight Lieutenant David Morgan (RAF) set off to undertake a high-level bombing attack on Port Stanley, each Sea Harrier carrying a pair of 1,000lb bombs. However, cloud caused the mission to be aborted although the pair could not land back on *Hermes* with their bombs still attached. They then spotted an Argentinian trawler, *Narwal*, well within the exclusion zone. Despite their bombs having seven-second fuses for high-level delivery, they attacked, gaining at least one hit on the trawler, which they then strafed. Sea Kings later landed a boarding party on the vessel and took it in tow, but it sank next day.

Despite the poor weather conditions two Skyhawks attempted to undertake a raid, but both flew into high ground on South Jason Island in cloud and were totally destroyed, the pilots being killed.

A good example of the problems being

ABOVE *Task Force commanders aboard the flagship HMS* **Hermes***: Major General Jeremy Moore, Commander of the Falklands Islands Land Forces, and Rear Admiral Sandy Woodward, overall commander of the Task Force.*

experienced by the Argentinians occurred on 12 May. Eight Skyhawks attacked the destroyer *Glasgow* and the frigate *Brilliant* as they lay on line. Of the three initial attackers, two were shot down by missiles and the third crashed into the sea. The pilot of one of the second flight obtained a direct hit on *Glasgow* with a 1,000lb bomb, but it passed straight through the ship with minimal structural damage, exploding in the sea well clear on the other side. Another bomb bounced on the surface of the water, passing right over *Brilliant*, and also fell in the water. The pilot who had gained the strike on *Glasgow* then passed over Goose Green, where his aircraft was shot down by the AA defences and he was killed – the second fatal Argentinian 'blue-on-blue' to occur.

The experiences of the last few days, meanwhile, had convinced the Task Force Commander, Admiral 'Sandy' Woodward, that daylight bombing attacks on a target as heavily defended as Port Stanley were too dangerous to risk. Any further attacks should be made only at night.

On 14 May two 846 Squadron Sea Kings put a party of 45 SAS troops ashore at Pebble Island, where they destroyed six Pucaras, four Turbo-Mentors and a Skyvan. Following this raid the airstrip was out of action for the rest of the conflict. Two days later the pilots of four Sea Harriers found two ships – the transport *Bahia Buen Suceso* and the merchant ship *Rio Carcarana* – in harbour at Fox Bay. These were strafed, following which both were abandoned.

Meanwhile, reinforcement of the Task Force's air strength was under way. At Yeovilton 809 Squadron had been formed on 8 April from the 'rump' of 899 Squadron, and was equipped with the eight factory-fresh Sea Harriers which had been rapidly completed. On 6 May these aircraft undertook the

Fleet Air Arm's longest flight to date, flying the 4,000 miles to Ascension in a single 'hop', refuelled under way by RAF Victor tankers. On arrival they joined the RAF Harrier GR 3s of 1 Squadron, which had arrived aboard *Atlantic Conveyor*.

All 809's aircraft were loaded on this vessel, which retained six of the GR 3s, six Wessex helicopters of 848 Squadron, a replacement Lynx and four RAF Chinooks. Four GR 3s were left at Ascension as that island's sole air defence. On arrival in the operational area on 18 May, four Sea Harriers were attached to 801 Squadron on *Invincible*, while the other four and the GR 3s went aboard *Hermes*. Next day the ammunition ship *Fort Austin* arrived, carrying four Lynxes fitted with special electronic equipment to serve as Exocet decoys; two flew aboard each carrier.

With the arrival of these reinforcements the Task Force had reached its maximum strength in operational aircraft. On *Hermes* it was decided to strip the Sidewinders and their launchers from the GR 3s, which would concentrate on ground attack when the invasion began. During the 19th a single 846 Squadron Sea King took off on a secret mission.

Flown by Royal Marine pilot Lieutenant Richard Hutchings (who had carried some of the SAS troops involved in other night operations), he now carried a small group of SAS who were to investigate the practicality of an attack on the Argentinian airfield at Rio Grande in the far south of the country. It was believed that the Super-Etendards and the remaining Exocet missiles were held here. A project had been advanced to force-land two C-130 Hercules transports full of SAS troops at the airfield to destroy these particular assets. This plan was codenamed Operation 'Mikado'.

The prior insertion of the reconnaissance group was Operation 'Plum Duff', and involved the long flight of the Sea King to Argentine territory, and then on to Chile at maximum range, since return to the Task Force was out of the question. En route, an unreported oil exploration platform was spotted directly ahead that required a fuel-consuming diversion, while arrival in the target area was met by fog. Uncertain that the helicopter had arrived at the right location, the SAS commander aborted the operation at that point, he and his men setting off to take cover and report.

The helicopter crew then flew on into Chile, landed the aircraft – now virtually out of fuel, and destroyed it. They then went into hiding in the countryside for eight days to protect the security of 'Mikado', should it go ahead. Finally, they announced themselves as having been forced to land after running short of fuel during a routine reconnaissance sortie. This made international

headlines for a time, but the true story remained secret and untold until many years later.

In the event the 'Mikado' operation would probably have been doomed to expensive failure since the Argentinian command, fully anticipating such an attack, had greatly enhanced the defences of the Rio Grande air base. For his part in the various Special Forces actions here and in the Falklands, Lieutenant Hutchings would subsequently receive the DSO.

Finally, during the evening of 20 May amphibious landings in Falkland Sound commenced, troops going ashore at San Carlos Water, which was only very lightly defended. At the same time 40 SAS soldiers were landed by helicopter to make a noisy diversion at Goose Green. By dawn on the 21st commandos and paratroops were well established ashore following brief fighting during which Argentinian soldiers had managed to shoot down two Royal Marine Gazelle light helicopters. These were aircraft of 3 Commando Brigade Air Squadron RM operating from the troopship *Sir Galahad*, the first of which rendezvoused with an 846 Squadron Sea King carrying mortar ammunition towards San Carlos. Both inadvertently flew too far inland, and were turning away when the Gazelle was hit by small-arms fire which struck the pilot, Sergeant Andrew Evans, in the chest and stomach. He managed to ditch in the sea and was helped out and ashore by his observer, Sergeant E.R. Candlish, but died soon afterwards.

Minutes later a second Gazelle, flown by Lieutenant K. Francis with Lance-Corporal B. Griffin as observer, took off to accompany another Sea King, seeking confirmation of the Argentine positions. Fire from the same unit which had just brought down the first Gazelle struck this helicopter also, and it crashed into a hillside with the loss of both men aboard.

Not surprisingly, this quickly became the busiest day of the war so far for the air forces, as both carriers launched Sea Harriers on patrol at first light. The intention was to maintain at least two Sea Harriers in the air at all times, with two more ready for immediate take-off on each of the carriers. The first action did not involve them, however, as a Falklands-based Pucara attempted to strafe the invaders, but was shot down by a shoulder-launched Stinger missile. Two GR 3s were off soon after dawn to provide initial support to the troops ashore. These had an important initial objective to fulfil.

It was realised that any Argentinian counter-attack would require the reinforcement of the area by troops likely to be carried there by helicopter – thus a search for such aircraft was instituted, the two RAF pilots spotting four in the Mount Kent area. They strafed these, destroying a Chinook and two Pumas. A second sortie by two more GR 3s ran into problems when the undercarriage of one, flown by the commanding officer, failed to retract, requiring the pilot to land again. The

BELOW *A Sea King helicopter stands by to take off survivors from the sinking Type 21 frigate HMS* Ardent, *which was hit by bombs and set on fire on 21 May.*

second aircraft proceeded alone, but while reconnoitring the area it was shot down by ground fire. The pilot ejected while flying at high speed which caused him to suffer a number of injuries; he was taken prisoner but was well looked after by his captors.

At 1035 hours the attacks on the Task Force really began. Six Daggers undertook an armed reconnaissance over the landing area, then attacked ships offshore. One Dagger was shot down by missiles and the rest were chased out by Sea Harriers. Shortly after midday a pair of Pucaras attempted to attack the ground forces ashore. Three Sea Harriers from 801 Squadron intercepted and one Pucara was shot down by Lieutenant Commander 'Sharkey' Ward using 30mm cannons.

Two Skyhawks launched a quick attack a little later, making good their escape, but as a further section of four approached two were intercepted and shot down by Lieutenant Commanders Blissett and Thomas of 800 Squadron. At 1420 four Daggers attacked, *Argonaut* being hit by two 1,000lb bombs, which failed to explode but nevertheless caused considerable damage. *Ardent* was also hit during this attack. 800 Squadron's Lieutenant Commander Frederiksen put a missile into one Dagger and the pilot ejected.

Skyhawks then strafed *Brilliant*, but as 801 Squadron Sea Harriers sought to intercept these their pilots spotted more Daggers and attacked them instead, with devastating effect. Lieutenant Steve Thomas shot down one and claimed a second as 'possibly destroyed', while Lieutenant Commander Ward sent down a third. Thomas's second victim had indeed gone down, all three Argentinian pilots safely ejecting from these aircraft.

At this stage *25 de Mayo*'s Navy Skyhawks appeared and attacked *Ardent* again. 800 Squadron Sea Harriers were swiftly upon them, Lieutenant Clive Morrell and Flight Lieutenant John Leeming (RAF) each shooting down one, while a third was hit by small-arms fire from *Ardent* and then struck by cannon-fire from Morrell's fighter. The pilot attempted to land his damaged Skyhawk at Port Stanley, but the undercarriage would not come down and he ejected instead. *Ardent* had been hit hard, however, and with 22 of her crew dead and 30 wounded she was to sink some hours later.

Two days after, during an early patrol in the Shag Cove area of West Falkland, Flight Lieutenant David Morgan spotted four helicopters low over the sea, the down wash of their rotors onto the water giving away their presence. These proved to be three Pumas and an Augusta 109A carrying munitions urgently required by the defenders. Attacking one of the Pumas at once, Morgan overshot and pulled up, but in seeking to evade his attack this helicopter crashed into the ground. The Augusta then landed and was at once destroyed with cannon-fire by Morgan and Flight Lieutenant John Leeming. Spotting another of the Pumas, now also on the ground a short distance away, Morgan fired on this with his remaining ammunition, obtaining hits before climbing away and announcing their find. A pair of 801 Squadron pilots immediately flew to the area and finished this aircraft off.

Early in the afternoon Skyhawks attacked HMS *Antelope*, one of these aircraft surviving a fleeting collision with the ship's mast, although a second was shot down by fire from several missile batteries and Bofors AA guns. *Antelope* survived hits by two bombs, both of which failed to explode and lodged in the vessel's hull. Two hours later Daggers appeared, but failed to cause any damage. They were intercepted over Pebble Island by a pair of 800 Squadron Sea Harriers and one was shot down by Lieutenant Martin Hale.

The next two days were to prove costly for the Argentinians. Dawn on 24 May saw an attack on Port Stanley airfield by two Sea Harriers of 800 Squadron and four GR 3s of 1 Squadron. Mid-morning two more 800 Squadron aircraft were on patrol when radar on the frigate *Broadsword* detected raiders coming in. The defending fighter pilots almost immediately spotted four Daggers and within seconds three of these were shot down, two by Lieutenant Commander Andy Auld and one by Lieutenant Dave Smith. One Argentinian pilot was killed, but the other two ejected and survived. A little later a Skyhawk fell to multiple weapons fired from *Argonaut* and *Fearless*. However, the day saw the loss of a further Sea Harrier when Lieutenant Commander Gordon Batt, 800 Squadron's senior pilot, crashed into the sea immediately after a night take-off and was killed.

The date 25 May proved to be a day of mixed fortunes. Over San Carlos Water and Goose Green three Skyhawks were brought down, two by the multiple weapons of the ground and sea defences, and one by Argentinian AA guns – yet another 'blue-on-blue'. It was Argentina's National Day, and following the losses of the morning a determined Skyhawk assault commenced by obtaining a hit on *Broadsword* just as her radar was guiding in a pair of Sea Harriers. The explosion broke the radar lock and no interception could be made. Moments later three bombs hit *Coventry*, causing severe damage to the destroyer which at once began to sink. Within moments at least a dozen Sea King and Wessex helicopters arrived overhead to assist in evacuating the crew, 19 members of which had been killed; 283 were successfully rescued.

At much the same time a pair of Super-Etendards, armed with the deadly Exocet missiles, had refuelled from a KC-130 Hercules tanker, then closed on the main British Fleet. Here the two carriers were sailing close to the *Atlantic Conveyor*, aboard which the remainder of her cargo of helicopters were being prepared for transfer to other vessels or ashore. Despite the presence of the decoy Lynx and the firing of chaff rockets, one Exocet impacted on the side of this ship, causing major damage and heavy fires. Twelve aboard were killed, including the captain, while three Chinooks, six Wessex helicopters and a single Lynx were all destroyed – a further Lynx was lost aboard *Coventry*. *Atlantic Conveyor* drifted for several days, but on 30 May she foundered and sank.

During the period 21–25 May the Argentine air forces had launched 180 sorties against the British warships, of which 117 had reached their targets. In doing so they had lost 19 Daggers and Skyhawks, at least 12 of them to the Sea Harriers. Although with only an average of 30 Sea Harriers and GR 3s available, the defenders had been able to launch 300 sorties in the same period. Apart from the losses of fighter-bombers, six helicopters and two Pucaras had also been lost by the Argentinians.

It would be several days before the Sea Harriers were to be successful in making further interceptions – in no small part due to the inclement weather. In the meantime, however, action continued. On 26 May Squadron Leader Jerry Pook of 1 Squadron destroyed another Puma helicopter on the ground near Mount Kent with a cluster bomb.

Next day a Skyhawk was shot down by AA fire, the pilot baling out over West Falkland, but a GR 3 was also brought down over Goose Green, probably by 35mm Oerlikon fire; Squadron Leader Bob Iveson ejected and evaded capture. On 28 May a Royal Marine shot down a Macchi 339 light aircraft using a Blowpipe shoulder-launched missile, while others shot down two Pucaras, a third of these crashing into high ground in bad weather while returning to Port Stanley. However, two more Pucaras from this unit – *Grupo 3* – achieved the only Argentinian aerial victory of the conflict when they attacked two Scout helicopters of 3 Commando Brigade Air Squadron RM and shot down one of them. Initially their fire wounded the observer, Sergeant A.R. Belcher, but a further burst then killed Lieutenant R.J. Nunn and the aircraft crashed at once. Belcher was thrown clear with terrible wounds and injuries, but was later recovered and survived.

On 29 May a Dagger fell to a Rapier missile, but a Sea Harrier was lost by 801 Squadron when it slid off the deck of *Invincible* while the carrier was turning in bad weather. Lieutenant Commander Mike Broadwater managed to eject as the aircraft went over the side and was rescued unhurt.

Another combined Super-Etendard/Skyhawk attack was launched on the 30th, the last remaining Exocet being carried. Refuelling again took place from a KC-130, and the missile was launched while the Skyhawks ran in at low level to attack. No hits were obtained, the crew of HMS *Avenger* claiming to have destroyed the Exocet at long range with 4.5in gunfire. Two of the Skyhawks were shot down by Sea Dart missiles fired from HMS *Exeter*; the surviving pilots returned convinced that the Exocet had hit *Invincible*; it had not.

By now the British ground forces were closing on Port Stanley, and during the day Squadron Leader Pook's 1 Squadron GR 3 was hit by ground fire in this area, causing him to eject over the sea during return to the carrier. A further Sea Harrier was lost two days later when hit by a Roland missile south of Port Stanley. Flight Lieutenant Ian Mortimer of 801 Squadron ejected and was picked up after eight hours at sea in his dinghy. The day was marked by an unusual success, however. A C-130 Hercules which had flown in to Port Stanley with supplies for the defenders during the night sought for British shipping during its return flight. While undertaking this very dangerous task,

BELOW *Two Sea King 4 helicopters of No 846 Naval Air Squadron, Fleet Air Arm, hover over the upturned hull of HMS* Coventry *searching for survivors. HMS* Coventry *overturned and sank after being hit by three 1,000lb bombs in an Argentine air attack. Twenty lives were lost, 25 May 1982.* IWM FKD 1274

FAR LEFT *Flt Lt David 'Mog' Morgan, DSC, was attached to 800 Squadron from the RAF during 1982. He accompanied the unit to the Falklands where he became one of the three most successful Sea Harrier pilots in aerial combat. Seen here with 'operational' whiskers, he subsequently transferred to the Fleet Air Arm, continuing to fly these aircraft for the rest of his time in the Service.*

LEFT *Lt Cdr Nigel 'Sharkey' Ward, DSC, commanded 801 Squadron during the Falklands War of 1982, flying from HMS* Invincible. *Here he was one of three Sea Harrier pilots to achieve three aerial victories against Argentinian aircraft.*

it was intercepted by a pair of 801 Squadron Sea Harriers and was damaged by one of the missiles fired by Lieutenant Commander 'Sharkey' Ward, who then finished the big aircraft off with his 30mm cannon. The Hercules crashed into the sea with the loss of its whole crew.

The helicopters were heavily involved during this period of the fighting, flying reinforcements, 155mm guns, ammunition and provisions to the advanced forces to the west of Port Stanley. From 5 June a strip became available at Port San Carlos for the Harriers to use as a refuelling base, allowing considerably longer patrols to be maintained over the battle area. By now Argentinian aircraft had become much rarer, although on 7 June a Learjet endeavouring to undertake a high-altitude photo-reconnaissance sortie was shot down over Pebble Island by a Sea Dart, again fired from *Exeter*.

On 8 June the troopships *Sir Galahad* and *Sir Tristram* anchored off Fitzroy to put ashore troops of the 5th Brigade. Aware of this, the Argentine air forces were ordered to launch a supreme effort. At once six Daggers and eight Skyhawks were sent off, the latter seeking to refuel with a KC-130 en route. Here three failed to link up to the tanker successfully, only five continuing to the

target area. Arriving first, the Daggers found their way blocked by HMS *Plymouth*, hitting this vessel with four bombs, all of which failed to explode. Five members of the crew were injured in this attack, but the Daggers now had to withdraw, pursued by Sea Harriers which were unable to catch them.

At this point the remaining five Skyhawks arrived and were able to climb to an altitude that would allow their bombs to arm properly. All five achieved effective hits, three on *Sir Galahad*, which was badly damaged and engulfed in flames. The other two hit *Sir Tristram* with less serious results. Nonetheless, the casualties on the two ships were little short of catastrophic and were the heaviest to be suffered by British forces in a single day in the Falklands; 51 men were killed and 46 more suffered injuries or burns, some of them severe.

Later in the day a follow-up attack by four Skyhawks failed to wreak further damage, two of the attackers suffering hits from AA defences. Finally, at dusk four more appeared, but on this occasion two 800 Squadron Sea Harriers were vectored to intercept them off Choiseul Sound. Before interception could be made the Skyhawk pilots managed to bomb landing craft F4 from HMS *Fearless*, hitting the vessel and killing six of those aboard. She later sank after the survivors had been taken off.

Meanwhile, incorrectly identifying these attackers as Daggers in the gloom, Flight Lieutenant Dave Morgan launched Sidewinders that took out two of the fighter-bombers, while Lieutenant Dave Smith brought down a third – all three pilots were killed. These proved to be the last victories for the Sea Harriers.

Fighting on the ground was now reaching a crescendo, and considerable support to the soldiers and Marines continued to be given by the GR 3s and helicopters. On 12 June a C-130 flew a number of the surface-to-surface version of the Exocet to Port Stanley. From here one was at once fired, gaining a hit on the destroyer *Glamorgan* at a range of about 18 miles. The missile did not explode, but its impact nevertheless managed to kill 13 members of the crew and injure 17 more, while the vessel's Wessex, an aircraft of 737 Squadron, was wrecked.

Still the Argentinians kept trying, and on 13 June they nearly achieved another major success. A dozen Skyhawks sought to attack positions on Mount Kent during the day, one formation finding the headquarters of 3rd Commando Brigade but missing the target with all their bombs. Others found an 846 Squadron Sea King in the air but were unable to shoot this down, despite inflicting some damage. The pilot, Lieutenant Commander Simon Thornewill described the action thus:

'I was about 120ft above the ground, and as the first pair of Skyhawks came in I turned to face their attack. I used our standard helicopter fighter evasion tactics, flying towards them then pulling round into their turn. The first aircraft opened fire and his rounds passed to our right as I pulled to the left. The second one obviously tightened his turn before he opened fire, and there was a loud bang as a cannon shell hit one of our rotor blades. The aircraft did not handle markedly differently, and I had to keep evading as the second pair were lining up for their attack. We managed to hide in a ravine, and they gave up and went away.'

Thornewill then landed to inspect the damage, finding a fist-sized hole in one blade about eight feet from the tip, which had destroyed part of the main spar. 'I'm surprised the blade didn't fold up – it speaks volumes for the strength of the aircraft,' he concluded. That night Canberras attempted raids on the British positions, but one was shot down by a Sea Dart from *Exeter* – the fourth such success for this vessel.

Next morning the helicopters enjoyed a rare opportunity to undertake an offensive operation when two Royal Marine Scout AH-1s joined two from 656 Squadron, Army Air Corps, to attack Argentinian bunkers with SS-10 wire-guided missiles, four of which were carried by each aircraft. Nine hits were obtained. Then, as resistance was crumbling, surrender of the Argentinian forces around Port Stanley occurred soon after midday. This fierce little war was at last at an end.

The fighting had been quite costly to both sides, but for the Sea Harrier force it had been a triumph. Air operations had been undertaken over greater distances than ever before, both sides making considerable use of air refuelling. Particularly, the Sea Harriers had proven to be extremely reliable and easily maintainable. The AIM-9L Sidewinder missile had done everything expected of it – and more; 26 had been fired, on three occasions pilots launching both of those they were carrying at a single target. This indicated that in 23 actual engagements in which missiles were used, 19 opposing aircraft had been shot down – a success rate of 82 per cent. Two more 'kills' had been made with cannon-fire and a third aircraft, already hit by missiles, had also been finished off with this weapon; one helicopter had crashed in combat without anything being fired. What might have been

BELOW *HRH Prince Andrew flew Sea Kings operationally during the Falklands War. He is pictured with Lt-Cdr R.J.S. Wykes-Sneyd, Commanding Officer of 820 Squadron (right) and other Sea King aircrew at Port Stanley in July 1982.*

achieved had AEW aircraft also been available may be left to the imagination.

The RAF GR 3s had also performed very well, while the Sea King, Wessex and Chinook helicopters had made the rapid advance of the ground forces on Port Stanley possible. Throughout the campaign, ASW Sea Kings had patrolled, protecting the ships from any possible submarine attacks. Bad weather had taken a substantial toll, four Sea Harriers, one GR 3, four Sea Kings and two Wessex being lost in weather-related accidents. Nine aircraft had fallen to Argentinian fire, including two Sea Harriers, three GR 3s, three Gazelles and a Scout. Thirteen more helicopters had been destroyed aboard the various ships which had been hit during the fighting.

While the claims for the Sea Harriers (and, indeed, for the Sea Darts) had been most precise, those made on behalf of ground and ship-borne missiles, anti-aircraft guns and small arms were typically inflated. Claims for 48 Argentinian aircraft shot down probably represented an actual loss to the opposition of about 16 aircraft. Captured on the ground at the conclusion of the fighting were some 30 aircraft at Port Stanley and two at Goose Green; many of these had suffered damage to varying degrees during the fighting. Total Argentinian losses therefore amounted to just over 100 aircraft, including 22 Skyhawks, 13 Mirages or Daggers and 25 Pucaras.

In due course a flight of RAF Phantoms were despatched to provide local air defence for the islands, allowing the carriers to return to a heroes' welcome at Portsmouth. There can be little doubt but that this was the high-water mark for the Fleet Air Arm. Under constant media scrutiny as never before, the force had gained the interest and affection of the public to a very high degree. With journalists and commentators aboard the carriers, the remark 'I counted them out and I counted them all back again' had captured the imagination of the nation.

Within days of the conclusion of hostilities, *Illustrious*, the second of the new *Invincible*-class vessels, now termed light aircraft carriers, was commissioned on 18 June 1982. Two months later the detachments of 809 Squadron on the other two vessels moved over to become the new ship's fixed-wing contingent, joining 815 Squadron which provided the helicopter element; the ship departed at once for a cruise down to the scene of the recent action in the South Atlantic. Meanwhile 899 Squadron resumed its headquarters and training function at Yeovilton, 800 and 846 Squadrons remaining aboard *Hermes*, with 801

ROYAL NAVY HELICOPTER UNITS OPERATING OVER THE FALKLANDS

737 Squadron	Lt Cdr M.S. Tennant
815 Squadron	Lt Cdr R.I. Money
820 Squadron	Lt Cdr R.J.S. Wykes-Sneyd, AFC
824 Squadron	Lt Cdr D.J.D. Acland
825 Squadron	Lt Cdr H.S. Clark, DSC
826 Squadron	Lt Cdr D.J.S. Squibb
829 Squadron	Lt Cdr M.J. Mullane
845 Squadron	Lt Cdr R.J. Warden
846 Squadron	Lt Cdr S.C. Thornewill
847 Squadron	Lt Cdr M.D. Booth
848 Squadron	Lt Cdr D.E.P. Baston
3 Commando Brigade Air Squadron RM	Maj C.P. Cameron

and 820 aboard *Invincible*. At the end of the year, however, 809 Squadron was disbanded on the return of *Illustrious* to home waters, the Sea Harriers being passed to the remaining three units.

Finally, in April 1984 *Hermes* was retired as an active first-line vessel, being laid up in Portsmouth for training purposes. Her place in the active fleet was taken somewhat later by *Ark Royal*, when the third of the *Invincible*-class, which had been launched in June 1981, was finally commissioned.

BELOW *Flying her paying-off pennant, HMS* Hermes *steams into Portsmouth on 22 November 1983 at the end of her sea-going life with the Royal Navy.*

CHAPTER 30

NEW WORLD ORDER

New Enemies, New Dangers

By this time, however, world events were rapidly changing the whole concept of defence needs. Unrest in Poland against the ruling Communist government had grown following the election of the Polish Pope John Paul II in 1978, the power of the workers' 'Solidarity' Union steadily increasing. From 1980 onwards a series of strikes shook the country from end to end.

In the Soviet Union the 1980s had seen a rapid economic decline occurring which weakened the hold of the Politburo. The liberating policies of President Mikhail Gorbachev's *Glasnost* were developed into *Peristroika* in June 1987. In Poland an election was forced upon the Communist government in 1989 in which they were obliged to allow representatives of 'Solidarity' to stand. The latter made sweeping gains and with these came the beginnings of a peaceful transition to democratic control.

Similar events in Czechoslovakia and Hungary followed, and then, without any violence, the Berlin Wall was suddenly breached and pulled down during the same year, rapidly leading to the fall of the hard-line East German regime and the beginnings of German reunification.

Against this background, efforts to preserve the Soviet Union between 1985 and 1991 steadily

LEFT *Sea King helicopter pilots dressed in full flying kit on board HMS* Invincible *during Operation 'Grapple', the British military deployment in support of the United Nations Peace Keeping Force in Bosnia (UNPROFOR) in 1993.* IWM HU92566

There were, however, new challenges rapidly appearing which would soon cause the 'Peace Dividend' to evaporate. These were to a considerable extent located in and around the ever-turbulent Middle East and in the similarly troubled Balkans.

During the period when Eastern Europe was in ferment, Iraq and Iran had been locked in a long and costly war. The balance of advantage had been mainly to the Iraqis, but this involvement had to a considerable extent reduced Iran's ability to be an irritant to the United States, which its fundamentalist government perceived to be an implacable foe. However, control of Iraq was in the hands of the dictator Saddam Hussein, an opportunist of the first order. In August 1990 he suddenly despatched his forces to overwhelm and occupy Kuwait. It will be recalled that Iraq had long considered this small oil-rich Sheikdom rightfully to be a part of that country.

When diplomatic attempts to correct this situation failed, a US-led coalition of nations invaded on 16 January 1991. While Saddam had been confident that his experienced army could deal with this threat, he had totally underestimated the power of modern US military technology, and by the end of February his forces had been totally defeated and mainly destroyed.

No doubt the USA had concerns connected with the need to maintain a balance of power to prevent Iran's potential dominance of the whole area if the threat of Iraq was removed. Coupled with this was

ABOVE *A similar view of three Sea Harrier FRS 1s similar to that on pp268–9, but a much later photograph, showing a completely different camouflage finish. 711 was from 899 Squadron, 000 from 801, and 127 from 800. 711 was ZA177 and would crash just two days later on 21 January 1983. Lt Fox ejected, but suffered spinal injuries.*

RIGHT *This is the view from the flight deck of HMS* Invincible *looking aft as she passes through the Suez Canal in early 1998. A Sea Harrier FA 2 (possibly from 800 Squadron) is on deck with two RAF Harrier GR 7s.* Invincible *spent a sizeable part of early 1998 operating in the region of the Persian Gulf, enforcing the No-Fly Zone over southern Iraq under the codename Operation 'Bolton'. She returned from the Gulf in April 1998.*
IWM SFPU N CO19022028

failed, the 15 constituent republics breaking away to form their own states – some democratic, others less so. Almost without a whimper the perceived Communist threat to the West had evaporated after some 70 years. For a short time the West seemed without significant enemies, and talk of a 'Peace Dividend' was rife with potential huge expenditure savings from defence budgets.

But life is never that simple, and already a new and quite different threat was appearing – that of militant Islam. As some of the old Warsaw Pact nations now sought to join the European Union and even NATO, the need and direction of the armed forces of the US, UK and other Western nations began to change. Initially, the performance of the carriers in the Falklands appeared to underwrite the need for the UK to maintain such a force in being. However, following its loss of the Falklands War General Galtieri's regime had swiftly fallen and Argentina had returned to democratic government. Increasingly, the Falklands began to be perceived as a probable 'one-off', unlikely to be repeated in a form in any way similar.

the possibility of a break-up of the latter country between the various conflicting religious orthodoxies and cultures should Saddam be removed from power. Whatever the reason, the coalition stopped short of forcing a change of regime. Thus Iraq was left in the hands of a weakened but still at least notionally independent Saddam.

During the brief campaign, known subsequently as the First Gulf War, twelve Royal Navy Sea Kings of 845 and 848 Squadrons had been carried to the area aboard *Atlantic Conveyor* (again 'called to the colours') and deployed to carry supplies and equipment to the 7th Armoured Brigade, which had formed the main British element of the coalition forces. Six Lynx helicopters of 829 Squadron, armed with Sea Skua ASV missiles, operated from four RN warships, achieving considerable success. The first such success occurred when HMS *Cardiff*'s Lynx '335' shared with a US Sea Hawk in the destruction of a vessel believed to have been either a minesweeper or a landing vessel. Aircraft from *Cardiff* and *Gloucester* were then despatched with US forces to destroy two anti-aircraft batteries on oil platforms off the coast of Kuwait where twelve Iraqis were captured, who became the first PoWs of the war.

On 24 January Lynx '335' was in action again, attacking three minesweepers and sinking two of them. An attempt to capture the third was thwarted when the crew scuttled the ship. Five days later a flotilla of seventeen landing craft were spotted carrying Iraqi troops for an amphibious assault on the town of Khafji. Flights of Lynx from HMS *Brazen* and *Gloucester* attacked and sunk one vessel, while the indefatigable '335' despatched another. The remaining vessels were then destroyed, damaged or dispersed by US Naval aircraft and RN Sea Kings.

TOP *Sea King HC 4 of 845 Squadron, painted white while operating under United Nations command in Bosnia.*

ABOVE *Lynx AH 1 XZ612 of 3 Commando Brigade Air Squadron, Royal Marines, at Yeovilton. This unit later metamorphosed into 847 Squadron.*

LEFT *Lynx HAS 2s XZ723 and XZ683 during a Trafalgar Day flypast in 2006.*

ABOVE *A lieutenant of 'A' Flight, 849 Squadron, at the early warning radar control panel of a Westland Sea King AEW helicopter, 1994.* IWM SFPU N 1994 CO 97 5

Next day a further convoy, consisting this time of three Polnochny-class landing ships, three TNC-45 fast attack craft and a Type 43 minelayer, were spotted also making for Khafji. *Gloucester*'s Lynx sank one of the TNC-45s while others from *Cardiff* and *Brazen* attacked the Type 43. Meanwhile, *Gloucester*'s aircraft sank two more TNC-45s. Several other vessels were damaged including one Polnochny, which was later finished off by an RAF Jaguar. Lynx '335' cemented its position as 'top scorer' when it attacked a Zhuk-class patrol boat on 8 February, and three days later achieved the sinking of one of these quite powerful ships. On 15 February *Manchester*'s Lynx sank the salvage vessel *Aka*, *Gloucester*'s aircraft completing this run of victories on the 16th when it destroyed another Polnochny.

No 826 Squadron was also active in supporting mine-sweeping of these coastal waters, allowing two US Navy battleships, *Missouri* and *Wisconsin*, to get in closer to provide gunfire support to troops ashore in the Basra area. Interestingly, during these various operations HMS *London* was acting as flagship for Commodore Chris Craig, the Senior Naval Officer, Middle East, while her Captain was Iain Henderson; both were qualified Fleet Air Arm pilots.

Following the return of Kuwait to independence, the Sea Kings, joined by Lynx and Gazelles

of 3 Commando Brigade Air Squadron, undertook a major humanitarian task aiding Kurdish refugees stranded in northern Iraq.

Even before the countries of the Warsaw Pact had reached the point where the continued existence of their Communist regimes became questionable, trouble was brewing in that historic political hotbed of Balkan nations which had been welded together to form Yugoslavia. In May 1980 Marshal Tito, the strongman who had held the heterogeneous collection of conflicting states together since the Second World War, had finally died. There had long been doubt regarding the continued stability of this country once his guiding hand had ceased to control events.

His death coincided with a period during which the Yugoslav economy had gone into decline. The country included the provinces of Croatia, Slovenia, Bosnia and Herzegovina, Macedonia, Montenegro and Serbia, the last including within its boundaries the semi-independent states of Kosovo and Vojvodnia. A substantial percentage of the population was Muslim, while the Christian elements were divided between Catholics – basically in Croatia in the north – and Orthodox Church, mainly centred on Serbia.

In such circumstances various provinces sought to break away to form independent countries, particularly those in the north (Croatia and Slovenia), which perceived themselves as potentially economically viable but held back by the poorer areas in the south. Serbian nationalism also came to the fore, to the discomfort of her immediate neighbours. In August 1991, just after the first Gulf War had been concluded, a series of extremely unpleasant civil wars broke out between these Balkan states, involving a considerable amount of what has become known as 'ethnic cleansing'.

The United Nations, NATO and the European Union became involved almost at once, but initially there was a distinct reluctance to become similarly involved on the part of the United States. Following the adoption of UN Resolution 836 by the Security Council during 1993, a small military presence known as UNPROFOR (United Nations Protection Force) was established in an effort to protect threatened minorities. At this stage NATO offered only close air support to this body, which soon proved to be quite inadequate to restrain the major 'players'.

With the Bosnian capital Sarajevo (which also had a substantial ethnic Albanian population) and other UN-designated 'safe areas' under constant threat, NATO began developing options for air strikes to help in lifting the siege of the city.

During February 1994 NATO created 'exclusion zones' in an effort to force a withdrawal of the

Bosnian Serb forces, or at least to control the heavy weapons they had established around Sarajevo. This initiative was extended to the Gorazde area during April, but on the 15th of that month came the first loss to hostile fire of a NATO/UN aircraft. Sea Harrier FRS 1 XZ498 of 801 Squadron was brought down while on a bombing sortie in the Gorazde area. Fortunately its pilot, Lieutenant Nick Richardson, was able to eject and was recovered safely.

Following the initial success of the air strikes in limiting Bosnian Serb actions, the warring factions began to neutralise the effects of NATO air power by taking advantage of the relative weakness and limited authority for action of UNPROFOR. The UN now requested NATO to assist in evacuating these forces.

In May 1995 Bosnian Serb forces took UN hostages and two months later overran the 'safe areas' at Srebrenica and Zepa. There followed a massacre of ethnic Albanian males which led finally to an enhanced US involvement. Late in August 1995, following a sustained mortar attack on Sarajevo, NATO launched a three-week campaign of air strikes against Bosnian Serb military targets under the codename Operation 'Deliberate Force'. This reduced the threat to both the city and other 'safe areas', allowing major diplomatic efforts to achieve a peaceful settlement to be pursued more forcefully.

Arising from this, in December 1995 NATO inserted an Implementation Force (IFOR) to take over from UNPROFOR. With more robust rules of engagement and considerably more military 'clout', IFOR completed its mission of separating the various factions during its one-year mandate. Thereafter it was replaced by a Stabilisation Force (SFOR) of about half the size to ensure that the relative peace was maintained.

The Fleet Air Arm had been active with the NATO force throughout its involvement. Bad weather over the Adriatic Sea during the winter had frequently limited the use of Italian-based NATO air power, but here the Royal Navy's carriers (together, increasingly, with those of the US Navy) were able to ensure that air cover requirements were maintained. Nos 800 and 801 Squadrons were rotated to the area with their Sea Harriers, frequently working-up aboard ship on the way out. The ability of the carriers to undertake this role was later to support arguments regarding the maintenance and re-equipment of the carrier force in the future.

The Commando Helicopter Force was also involved, with 845 and 846 Squadrons serving in rotation. Indeed, 845 Squadron and its Sea Kings remained deployed in the area for no less than thirteen years, first with UNPROFOR and then IFOR.

Trouble arose again during 1999. In 1991

ethnic Albanian leaders had declared unilaterally the independence of Kosovo. Following this, Albanian guerrilla forces became increasingly active, stepping up attacks on Serb targets. This escalation ultimately led to a brutal Serbian military crackdown. President Milosevic rejected international calls to halt these and consequently in March 1999 NATO air strikes resumed on Serbian targets in both Kosovo and Serbia, continuing until 10 June, by which time NATO aircraft had flown more than 38,000 sorties.

With Serbian forces withdrawn, NATO and the UN took over the administration of the province to prevent a reverse ethnic cleansing being carried out against resident Serbs by the Albanians. No independence referendum was to be permitted for three years, it was agreed. Milosevic was indicted for war crimes by the International Criminal Tribunal and he and his government were

ABOVE *Sea Harrier FRS 1 ZE698 of 801 Squadron undertaking a Deny Flight sortie over Bosnia from HMS* Ark Royal *in mid-March 1994.*

BELOW *Sea King AEW2.*

ABOVE *HMS* Brazen *and her Lynx helicopter on patrol off the Lebanon. Note the large Union flags painted on the helicopter and on* Brazen's *bridge as a quick means of identifying them as British units.*

BELOW *Merlin ZF649, the Fleet Air Arm's most modern helicopter in 2009. This is one of the prototypes, PP5, during tests.*

overthrown in the following year. On 17 February 2008, following several years of fruitless negotiations at the UN, Kosovo controversially declared independence again.

During this period the Fleet Air Arm had begun to take delivery of a new helicopter, the Augusta Westland Merlin. A large, but quite agile and fast aircraft, the main role of the Merlin is ASW (Anti-Submarine Warfare) and maritime support operations. It can also double up when required for the more traditional tasks of troop transporting, load carrying and Search and Rescue.

The first Merlins to be delivered went to a new 700M Squadron in December 1998 for service testing and development. Subsequently, the headquarters and training unit became 824 Squadron, based at Culdrose in Cornwall, which administers the three front-line units, 814, 820 and 829. The first two of these latter units

typically serve aboard the *Invincible*-class carriers and have taken part in patrolling the Persian Gulf area in connection with the pacification and reconstruction of Iraq. No 829 Squadron maintains flights on the Royal Navy's Type 23 Frigates that are frequently involved in similar work. As the Merlins approach ten years in service, a major programme has been put in place to update their electronics and keep them at the forefront of their tasks.

Meanwhile, based upon the experiences in the Falklands, the modifications necessary to create a Sea King AEW aircraft had borne fruit, culminating in the arrival in service during 2003 of the ASAC 7 version of this helicopter. This would see use in the Middle East when war broke out again in Iraq (of which more later). Here, the sensors developed for this aircraft proved so powerful and accurate that it was found to be possible to employ them for the identification of individual vehicles on land, as well as in the aircraft's main designed air defence duties.

The Sea Harrier had also been developed further with the introduction late in the 1980s of the FA 2 version. Initially supplementing and then replacing the ageing FRS 1s, the new aircraft carried the AMRAAM (Advanced Medium Range Air-to-Air Missile), the AIM-120, which featured 'Beyond Visual Range' capability, assisted by a new radar guidance system – 'Blue Vixen' – which replaced the FRS 1's 'Blue Fox'. This new equipment provided multiple target tracking and a 'look down-shoot down' capability. So equipped, the FA 2 was arguably the most capable and potent defence asset available to UK forces at the time. The increased weight of the AMRAAM over the previous Sidewinder was, however, to prove to be something of an Achilles heel to the aircraft, as will be seen.

It would be wrong to assume that the Fleet Air Arm was involved only in military and defence operations at this time. Already well known to the public for its Search and Rescue activities, the Navy's humanitarian services – provided free at the point of delivery – gave the taxpayer an excellent return while providing the Service with a very positive public image. Culdrose-based helicopters have been in the national news frequently for undertaking rescues of many types around the coasts and seas of south-west England. The three aircraft of Gannet Search and Rescue Flight based at Prestwick in Scotland (ex-HMS *Gannet*) have long covered an extensive coastline and have saved many lives. Some of the more high profile rescues occurred during the 1979 Fastnet yacht race, and the rescues of crews from stricken tanker vessels.

On the international front, Lynx helicopters from HMS *Manchester* assisted in evacuation operations when the volcano on the island of

Montserrat erupted in November 1999, while two helicopters from HMS *Chatham* were active during the Thai tsunami disaster in December 2004.

During the Israeli incursions into Lebanon in 2006, Sea Kings of 845 and 846 Squadrons, joined by RAF helicopters, assisted with the evacuation of more than 4,500 non-combatants from this country to the safety of Akrotiri in Cyprus. This was a strange reversal of earlier activities, for during 1974 helicopters from HMS *Hermes* had carried out similar evacuation flights, taking British subjects from the eastern area of Cyprus to the west during the Turkish invasion of that country.

Meanwhile, in 2001 the Royal Navy became involved in Operation 'Palliser'. Sierra Leone in West Africa was in a state of turmoil as savage and basically criminal insurgent forces threatened to bring down the elected government. UN presence had proved too weak and insubstantial to improve the situation, resulting in a governmental request for UK aid. A naval force arrived in the area that included HMS *Ocean* and *Illustrious*, with *Ocean* launching an amphibious demonstration. In short order the insurgents were dispersed and conditions created whereby reconstruction of the country to normal democratic stability could be achieved.

Following UN attempts to determine whether Saddam Hussein's regime in Iraq possessed 'weapons of mass destruction', a second invasion of the country was precipitated by US President, George W. Bush.

The main Coalition Forces to undertake this invasion were based in Kuwait, but in order to prevent the firing or destruction of the main oil-producing and exporting facilities on the Al-Faw

TOP *The successor to the Sea Harrier will be the Lockheed-Martin F-35B STOVL Joint Strike Fighter.* Lockheed-Martin

ABOVE *FAA pilots on-board* Invincible, *1994.* IWM SFPU N 1994 CO 0091

LEFT *Fast jet training flight. Two-seat Sea Harrier T 8 ZB603 is accompanied by BAE Hawk T1A XX168 in 2006, just before the former aircraft's withdrawal from service.*

OPPOSITE *HMS* Invincible *and HMS* Ark Royal *at sea in the Adriatic during Operation 'Grapple', the British military deployment in support of the United Nations Peace Keeping Force in Bosnia (UNPROFOR). Invincible sailed for the Adriatic on 22 July 1993 to relieve HMS* Ark Royal. *She remained in theatre until 20 December, with Nos 800, 814, 846 and 849A Naval Air Squadrons embarked. On 20 September 1993, the ship hosted unsuccessful warring parties peace talks, involving Lord Owen and Thorvald Stoltenberg.*

peninsula to the south of Basra, a direct invasion by seaborne and helicopter forces took place on 20 March 2003. Forces taking part included Royal Marine commandos and Special Forces of various types, quickly joined by US Marines and reconnaissance elements of the Royal Dragoon Guards from within Kuwait.

Elements of the Allied naval forces gathered at the head of the Arabian Gulf were HMS *Ark Royal* and *Ocean* carrying 42 and 40 Commandos respectively. *Ark Royal* was loaded with Sea King HC 4 and RAF Chinook helicopters, together with a number of the new ASAC 7 Sea Kings of 849 Squadron. *Ocean* brought 845 Squadron with its HC 4s, and 847 Squadron with six Lynx AH 7s and six Gazelles. This latter unit was the old 3 Commando Brigade Air Squadron which had become 847 during the mid-1990s; it was crewed mainly – though not exclusively – by Royal Marine personnel.

Codenamed Operation 'Houghton', the invasion was made in the face of some tough Iraqi resistance, but proved extremely successful in securing the oil installations undamaged and rapidly advancing to the outskirts of Basra. Here the main forces took over, moving north from Kuwait, while US armoured columns by-passed the area and headed direct for Baghdad.

From the outset 847 Squadron operated teams of one Lynx and one Gazelle in designated 'box' areas, providing close support to the advancing ground forces. This involved spotting targets for artillery fire, identifying defence locations ahead, calling in fast jet support, and when necessary providing direct fire support with the TOW (Tube-launched, Optically tracked Wire-guided) missiles and GPMG (General Purpose Machine Guns) carried by each Lynx (the smaller Gazelles being unarmed).

Sadly, on the third day of operations two of 849 Squadron's AWACs Sea King 7s collided in the air with the loss of both crews. During two sorties on 24 March, Lieutenant James Newton, a naval officer in the predominantly Royal Marine 847 Squadron, was able to employ his Lynx's TOWs to destroy three T-55 tanks which greatly outgunned the Scimitar light

tanks of the Queen's Dragoon Guards approaching them. On the second sortie, having destroyed two of the tanks, he and the pilot of the accompanying Gazelle were instrumental in spotting several more T-55s hidden amongst palm trees and guiding in two USAF A-10 'tank-busters' to attack them.

Six days later Lieutenant Newton was able to destroy an Iraqi armoured personnel carrier, and an important radio communications station. He and the Gazelle crew on their next sortie spotted a major artillery and headquarters bunker. They were able to direct artillery fire onto this, resulting in its almost total destruction. By the close of day 847 Squadron had achieved the largest armed helicopter action ever recorded by British forces. Lieutenant Newton was subsequently awarded a DFC (normally an RAF decoration) – a neat reversal of the Falklands situation when Flight Lieutenant Morgan had received a DSC from the Navy.

Immediately afterwards the main fighting was taken over by the 1st Armoured Division from Kuwait and 847's role virtually came to an end. The Sea Kings of the other Commando Helicopter

ABOVE *A pair of Sea Harrier FA 2s from 800 Squadron on HMS* Ark Royal.

BELOW *The future: an artist's impression of the new CVF design – two super carriers for the Royal Navy to be named* Queen Elizabeth *and* Prince of Wales.

Force units would remain active in Iraq for much longer, however. Not until November 2007 did their role finally end.

Prior to the Second Gulf War, so as to make best use of the Sea Harriers and the RAF's ground-attack Harriers, planning had begun to create what was initially known as 'Joint Force 2000', which would allow servicing and maintenance of the aircraft to be centralised. A joint RAF/FAA force, it would initially comprise two wings each of two squadrons, together forming a part of 3 Group at High Wycombe. To accommodate this arrangement 3 Group also became a Joint Service body and its initial commanding officer was Admiral Iain Henderson with an RAF 'one star' (air commodore) as his deputy. The RAF wing was to be formed with 1 and 4 Squadrons, while the Fleet Air Arm wing would comprise 800 and 801 Squadrons. Initially, the Sea Harriers would remain at Yeovilton with their 'parent' 899 Squadron.

By this time the Sea Harrier was seen to be in critical need of new and more powerful engines if it was to operate successfully in tropical climes. In such conditions the current engine power would only permit the aircraft to be landed back on-board safely if it was not carrying substantial under-wing stores. In practice this meant that if the extremely expensive AMRAAMs had not been used, they would have to be jettisoned before to landing. Clearly, this was an unacceptable situation – particularly on cost grounds.

By 2002 it had been accepted that it was simply not cost-effective to re-engine the FA 2. However, it was feasible to do so with the RAF's forthcoming GR 9. Consequently, a Joint Force Harrier Migration Plan was agreed whereby all FA 2 pilots would convert to the RAF aircraft. This would mean, of course, that the Fleet Air Arm pilots would effectively cease to be fighter pilots and instead become ground-attack 'mud movers'.

This was perceived as being only a temporary state of affairs until a replacement for the FA 2 could be introduced to service. The Eurofighter/ Typhoon, the French Rafale, and two US strike fighters, one produced by Boeing as the F-22 and the other by Lockheed-Martin, were considered. The choice was an adapted version of the latter – the F-35B Lightning II STOVL (Short Take Off and Vertical Landing) fighter, referred to in the UK as the Joint Combat Aircraft (JCA).

Meanwhile, the Royal Navy contributed £530 million of its defence allocation towards the cost of the GR 7/9 re-engine programme, while during 2006 the three FA 2 units were all stood down. In July of that year 800 Squadron was almost immediately re-formed, but at RAF Cottesmore

in Rutland, where the unit initially received the Harrier GR 7.

While Iraq and the Second Gulf War involved a substantial UK contingent in the southern part of the country, this had been in the main an Army and RAF operation. Since 2001, however, US forces had become involved in Afghanistan. Following an initial overthrow of the controlling Taliban, growing levels of insurgency had resulted in a steady build-up of coalition forces, with British and Canadian troops taking a particularly active part. It was here that elements of the Royal Navy were to assume a growing importance.

Initially, the range needed by aircraft to operate over Afghanistan was considerable since it had to be from the sea. Due to the difficulties experienced by Sea Harriers with hot weather operations, it meant the Royal Navy had no carrier capability available. At first cover had to be provided by US Navy carriers until adequate land bases for the Sea Harriers could be established. (Some air support is still provided in this manner, from the seas off the coast of Pakistan.)

During 2007 a Naval Strike Wing comprising 800 Squadron and the attached personnel of 801 Squadrons was formed from the Joint Force Harrier. This sailed to the area aboard *Illustrious* whereupon the wing operated from land bases, undertaking more than 1,200 sorties before being withdrawn late in 2008. By this time, more than 40 per cent of UK personnel in Afghanistan were of Royal Navy 'parentage', including some 2,500 Royal Marines of 3 Commando Brigade, and 160 Fleet Air Arm personnel with the Strike Wing or the Commando Helicopter Force which was itself sustained by elements of 845, 846 and 847 Squadrons with their Sea Kings and Lynx aircraft. At this stage more than half the fighting troops on the ground were Royal Marines. The Fleet Air Arm elements of the Joint Helicopter Force (RN, RAF and Army Air Corps) employed the Sea King for transport and equipment supply, while the Lynx 7s of 847 Squadron undertook reconnaissance and fire support spotting sorties.

As the centenary of British naval aviation approaches, HMS *Invincible* is now in reserve, but her two slightly younger sister ships, *Illustrious* and *Ark Royal*, remain in service, although both are now approaching their quarter-centuries. In the main they are still carrying helicopters for which they were originally designed, and on occasion the ground-attack Harriers of the Joint Force Harrier, but they no longer have any fighter aircraft aboard.

Against this background there was much rejoicing in the Service when in July 2008 the contract was signed for the two new aircraft carriers, the *Queen Elizabeth* and *Prince of Wales*. Successful development flights of the F-35B were also reported at this time, with orders placed for both the Fleet Air Arm and the RAF amounting to 138 aircraft at a total cost of £150 billion. The carriers are anticipated to enter service in 2015 and 2018 respectively. Orders were also confirmed for the AugustaWestland 'Future Lynx', scheduled for delivery during 2015. The future looked secure for the Fleet Air Arm.

Among the announcements emanating from the Admiralty at this time was an indication that the F-35B was to replace the Harriers in JFH. In turn this Force will join Joint Force Joint Combat Aircraft. It was also indicated that perhaps pilots from both Services might eventually fly from the new aircraft carriers.

The publication *Fly Navy 100* published a statement by the First Sea Lord, Admiral Jonathon Band, welcoming the rolling out of the first development aircraft:

'The Joint Strike Fighter will be operated by the RN and RAF crews from the UK's two new aircraft carriers due to enter service in 2014. With the announcement of the new carrier programme the Fleet Air Arm is poised to be the cornerstone of the UK's Future Combat Air Capability.' He added: 'The new aircraft carriers will be the largest and most potent warships ever designed and built in the UK. Together with their embarked aircraft they will provide the UK with a potent and powerful world-class joint expeditionary carrier force that will deliver air power in support of the full range of future operations at sea, in the air and on land.'

No sooner had these announcements been made than the UK and much of the developed world entered potentially the worst recession in 50 years. Inevitably, this has swiftly impacted on defence expenditure. The Prime Minister, Gordon Brown, anxious to maintain employment in capital projects at such a time, has not sought to cancel the carriers.

In the summer of 2009, the Joint Force Harrier will be withdrawn from Afghanistan to be replaced by an RAF Tornado force. The former is now receiving the very latest 'state-of-the-art' Harrier GR 9, which should stay in service for some considerable time since it is probably one of the best dedicated close-support aircraft in the world, although the US probably also rates its A0. It is also likely that the Wing will be scheduled for a further tour in the war zone in due course. There are hopes that it may be possible to maintain this new version of the aircraft until 2016, when it could represent the initial fixed-wing establishment on

the new carriers. Certainly, the GR 9 should survive until at least 2017 as a very cost-effective aircraft.

Unless the F-35B becomes available in less than eight or nine years, will the Fleet Air Arm be able to retain its precious lodestone represented by its experienced fast jet pilots? Meanwhile, its rotary-wing squadrons are due to receive their updated equipment and appear to have their immediate future satisfactorily resolved.

At the beginning of its second century of existence, the Royal Navy and its Fleet Air Arm are presented with problems and uncertainties no less daunting and challenging than those it faced one hundred years ago.

FLEET AIR ARM ORDER OF BATTLE, 2009

Operational Units

Naval Strike Wing	RAF Cottesmore, Rutland	Harrier GR 9
814 Squadron	RNAS Culdrose, Cornwall	Merlin HM 1
815 Squadron	RNAS Yeovilton, Somerset	Lynx HAS 3 and HMA 8
820 Squadron	RNAS Culdrose, Cornwall	Merlin HM 1
829 Squadron	RNAS Culdrose, Cornwall	Merlin HM 1
845 Squadron	RNAS Yeovilton, Somerset	Sea King HC 4 and 4+
846 Squadron	RNAS Yeovilton, Somerset	Sea King HC 4 and 4+
847 Squadron	RNAS Yeovilton, Somerset	Lynx AH 7
849 Squadron	RNAS Culdrose, Cornwall	Sea King ASaCS
854 Squadron	RNAS Culdrose, Cornwall	Sea King ASaCS
857 Squadron	RNAS Culdrose, Cornwall	Sea King ASaCS

Training and Ancillary Units

702 Squadron	RNAS Yeovilton, Somerset	Lynx HAS 3 and HMA 8
703 Squadron	Barkston Heath, Lincolnshire	T.67M Firefly
705 Squadron	Shawbury, Wiltshire	Squirrel HT 1
727 Squadron	RNAS Yeovilton, Somerset	Grob G.11SE Tutor
750 Squadron	RNAS Culdrose, Cornwall	Jetstream T.2
771 Squadron	RNAS Culdrose, Cornwall	Sea King HU 5 and HAS 6 (Search and Rescue)
792 Squadron	RNAS Culdrose, Cornwall	Mirach 100/5 (Missile Testing)
824 Squadron	RNAS Culdrose, Cornwall	Merlin HM 1
848 Squadron	RNAS Yeovilton, Somerset	Sea King HC4
Flying Officer Sea Training	Plymouth Airport, Devon	SA 564N Dauphin
Naval Flying Standards (Fixed Wing)	RNAS Yeovilton, Somerset	Hawk T.1 and T.1W
Fleet Requirements and Direction Unit	RNAS Culdrose, Cornwall	Hawk T.1 and T.1W
Gannet SAR Flight	Prestwick airport, Scotland	Sea King HU 5
RN Historical Flight	RNAS Yeovilton, Somerset	Chipmunk, Sea Hawk FGA 6, Swordfish II and Sea Fury FB 11

Note: 824 and 848 Squadrons have transferred from 'Operational' list to 'Training and Ancillary' list)

ABOVE *Radio mechanics work on a Swordfish.*

BELOW *A WREN at a plotting table on HMS* Urley *on the Isle of Man.*

RIGHT *Armourers, radio mechanics and fitters are pictured hard at work on a Grumman Hellcat.*

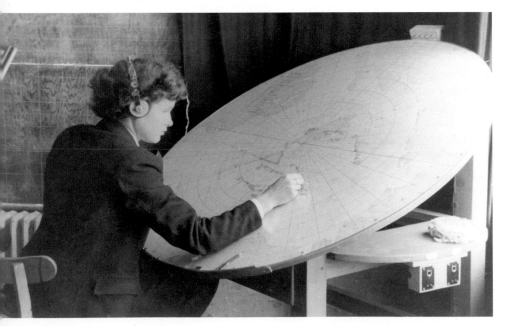

CHERCHEZ LA FEMME

Women in the Fleet Air Arm

While the latter part of the 20th century brought major changes in equipment and roles for the Royal Navy, perhaps the most fundamental change was the integration of women into the Service. The Women's Royal Naval Service had first been formed in 1917 as an aid and adjunct to the Navy. Women filled many of the roles considered suitable for them, such as those of clerks and domestic servants; however, some were allowed into more technical jobs. With suffrage still some time away, it is not perhaps surprising that the society of the twenties was generally more comfortable with those women returning to the home rather than continuing in military service.

Twenty years later the WRNS was re-formed, some of the more senior members picking up where they had left off in 1919. During the Second World War the WRNS grew to become a major element of the Navy, nearly 75,000 ladies responding to the call to 'Free a Man for the Fleet'. The range of their jobs was much greater this time. Little known until very recently were the 5,000 or so who operated the 'bombe' code-breaking machines at Bletchley Park which produced 'Enigma' intelligence and contributed substantially to victory, not least over the U-boats in the Battle of the Atlantic. Boats' Crew Wrens were able to demonstrate their pride in their jobs of operating small vessels in harbour. This task was not easily conceded by the traditional Navy, although large numbers of women became extremely competent in very technical roles, and nearly 15,000 Wrens served in areas specifically linked to the Fleet Air Arm.

At the end of the Second World War society had changed and it was agreed that the WRNS should remain in being, albeit at the much reduced level of 3,000 members. However, women were neither allowed to serve at sea nor learn to fly. Thirty years later, in 1977, the WRNS became subject to the Naval Discipline Act for the first time. Its personnel were still not allowed to serve at sea on warships, although members of certain branches did go to sea for short periods in support of trials, while others worked in support roles on ships of the Royal Fleet Auxiliary. These proved to be the first tentative steps towards full integration with the Royal Navy and full service at sea.

Changes in Britain's demographics led to a drop in naval recruits in the 1980s and one possible solution to the problem was to allow women to serve at sea. The then Captain Alan West led the study group looking at how to achieve this and in February 1990 the decision was announced in the House of Commons 'to extend the employment of members of the WRNS to include service at sea in surface ships of the Royal Navy'. For the first time WRNS were given the choice of going to sea or remaining shore-based. On 8 October 1990 HMS *Brilliant* became the first ship to carry women as members of the ship's company. On 2 November 1993 the Women's Royal Naval Service was disbanded and women were integrated into the Royal Navy. By this time there were 490 women serving at sea and their admission into aircrew training was also beginning.

Over the next few years female officers of the Royal Navy qualified as observers and began to fly in front-line helicopter squadrons; they were soon followed by the first ladies to qualify as pilots, and the process continues into the 21st century. Sadly, the first fatality occurred in June 2002 when Lieutenant Jenny Lewis was killed in the crash of HMS *Richmond's* Lynx when the aircraft suffered engine failure while flying off the US coast at Norfolk, Virginia.

LEFT *Lt Amy Grey trained at Britannia Royal Naval College, Dartmouth, and went on to specialise as a Lynx observer. She is now a qualified Observer Instructor on Jetstream aircraft.*

BIBLIOGRAPHY

Norman Polmar, *Aircraft Carriers* (Macdonald, 1969)

Hilary St George Saunders, *Per Ardua* (Oxford University Press, 1944)

Ray Sturtivant and Gordon Page, *Royal Navy Aircraft: Serials and Units, 1911–1919* (Air-Britain, 1992)

Brad King, *Royal Naval Air Service, 1912–1918* (Hikoki, 1997)

Chaz Bowyer, *Sopwith Camel – King of Combat* (Glasney Press, 1978)

Hugh Popham, *Into Wind: A History of British Naval Flying* (Hamish Hamilton, 1969)

Owen Thetford, *British Naval Aircrafts since 1912* (Putnam 1978)

Ray Sturtivant, *The Squadrons of the Fleet Air Arm* (Air-Britain, 1984)

Ray Sturtivant with Mick Burrow, *Fleet Air Arm Aircraft* (Air-Britain, 1995)

Ray Sturtivant, *Fleet Air Arm at War* (Ian Allan, 1982)

Seedie's List of Fleet Air Arm Awards, 1939–1969 *(Ripley Registers, 1990)*

David, Brown, *Carrier Operations in World War II, Vol 1: The Royal Navy* (Ian Allan, 1974)

David Brown, *The Seafire* (Ian Allan, 1973)

John Winton, *The Forgotten Fleet* (Michael Joseph, 1969)

Kenneth Poolman, *Illustrious* (William Kimber, 1955)

Lt Cdr Mike Apps, *Send Her Victorious* (Military Book Society, 1971)

John Winton, *Carrier Glorious: The Life and Death of an Aircraft Carrier* (Leo Cooper, 1986)

Peter C. Smith, *Eagle's War: The War Diary of an Aircraft Carrier* (Crecy, 1995)

Andrew Thomas, *Royal Navy Aces of World War 2* (Osprey, 2007)

Hugh Popham, *Sea Flight* (William Kimber, 1954)

Charles Lamb, *War in a Stringbag* (Cassell, 2001)

Gerard A. Woods, *Wings at Sea* (Conway Maritime, 1985)

Donald Judd, DSC, *Avenger from the Sky* (William Kimber, 1985)

Cdr R. 'Mike' Crosley, DSC, *They Gave me a Seafire* (Airlife, 1986)

David R. Foster, DSO, DSC & Bar, *Wings over the Sea* (Short Run Press, 1990)

Dunstan Hadley, *Barracuda Pilot* (Airlife, 1992)

Gordon Wallace, *Carrier Observer* (Airlife, 1993)

John Wellham, *With Naval Wings* (Spellmount, 1995)

A.H. Wren, *Naval Fighter Pilot: Lt Cdr R.J.Cork, DSO, DSC & Bar* (Heron Books, 1998)

Michael Hordern, *Memoirs: The Personal Account of a Royal Navy Officer, 1933–1958* (Hawke Productions, 2006)

John Lansdown, *With the Carriers in Korea, 1950–1953* (Crecy, 1997)

Jeffrey Ethell and Alfred Price, *Air War South Atlantic* (Sidgwick & Jackson, 1983)

Rodney A. Burdeon et al., *Falklands: The Air War* (Arms & Armour Press, 1986)

Cdr 'Sharkey' Ward, DSC, AFC, *Sea Harrier over the Falklands* (BCA, 1992)

David Morgan, *Hostile Skies: My Falklands Air War* (Weidenfeld & Nicolson, 2006)

And my own books in which detailed accounts of various actions and personnel may be found:

Fighters over Tunisia, with Hans Ring and William N. Hess (Spearman, 1975)

L'Aviation de Vichy au Combat: Tome 1 & 2, with Christian-Jacques Ehrengardt (Lavauzelle, 1985 and 1987)

Malta: The Hurricane Years, 1940–1941, with Brian Cull and Nicola Malizia (Grub Street, 1987)

Air War for Yugoslavia, Greece and Crete, 1940–1941, with Brian Cull and Nicola Malizia (Grub Street, 1987)

Above the Trenches: A Complete Record of the Fighter Aces and Units of the British Empire Air Forces, 1915–1920, with Norman Franks and Russell Guest (Grub Street, 1990)

Malta: The Spitfire Year, 1942, with Brian Cull and Nicola Malizia (Grub Street, 1991)

Fledgling Eagles: The Complete Account of Air Operations during the 'Phoney War' and Norwegian Campaign, 1940, with four colleagues (Grub Street, 1991)

Bloody Shambles: The First Comprehensive Account of Air Operations over South-East Asia, December 1941–May 1942, Vol 2: The Defence of Sumatra to the Fall of Burma, with Brian Cull and Yasuho Izawa (Grub Street, 1993)

Aces High: A Tribute to the Most Notable Fighter Pilots of the British and Commonwealth Forces in WW II, with Clive Williams (Grub Street, 1994)

Dust Clouds in the Middle East: The Air War for East Africa, Iraq, Syria, Iran and Madagascar, 1940–1942 (Grub Street, 1996)

Those Other Eagles: A Tribute to the British, Commonwealth and Free European Fighter Pilots who claimed between two and four victories in aerial combat, 1939–1982 (Grub Street, 2004)

Air War for Burma: The Allied Air Forces Fight Back in South-East Asia, 1942–1945 (Grub Street, 2005)

INDEX

Because of the size and complexity of an index suitable for a work of this nature, for greater ease of access it has been split between the various categories covered. These are: People; Places; Ships/Vessels; Aviation Units; Aircraft; Land and Sea Service Units.

PEOPLE

*Ranks given are generally (although not always) those appertaining at the date(s) when they are mentioned in the text. The application of a * following a decoration indicates the award of a Bar thereto.*

Acland, Lt Cdr P.J.D. 824 Sqn 291
Alexander, Flt Cdr W.M. 10 (N) Sqn 56
Appleby, Lt Cdr J.L.,OLM 808 Sqn 221
Armour, Lt Cdr J.O. 809 Sqn 225, *225*
Armstrong, Flt Cdr F.C. DSC, CdeG 3 (N) Sqn 56
Ash, Lt Cdr A.H.M. 805 Sqn 143
Ashbrooke, Sub Lt P.C.B. 803 Sqn 138
Asquith, Rt Hon Herbert, British Prime Minister 14,61
Atkinson, Cdr C.J.N. HMS *Formidable* 142
Auld, Lt Cdr A.D. 800 Sqn 287

Bailey, Lt Cdr J.E. 804 Sqn 221
Bailhache, Mr Justice 61
Baldwin, Lt Cdr G.C. CBE, DSC*, 801, 807 Sqns 174
BalFour, Rt Hon Arthur, 1st Lord Of Admiralty 61
Band, Adm Sir Jonathon, 1st Sea Lord 303
Bares, Col, French Air Service 61
Barnes, Lt W.L.LeC., DSC 806 Sqn 124, 129, 134
Bartlett, Sub Lt R.E. 803 Sqn 109
Barton, Flt Lt P.C. 801 Sqn 282
Baston, Lt Cdr D.E.P. 848 Sqn 291
Batt, Lt Cdr G.W.J. 800 Sqn 283, 287
Beggs, Sub Lt H.W. 151 Sqn (RAF) 113
Belcher, Sgt A.R. 3 CBAS RM 288
Bell-Davies, Flt Cdr R. VC 2 Wg 37, *37*
Bibby, Lt R.E. DSO 830 Sqn 148
Birrell, Lt Cdr M.A. DSC 79 Sqn (RAF) 113
Black, Lt Cdr A.F., DSC 805 Sqn, Cdr (F) *Ocean* 127, 133, 143, 221
Blake, Sub Lt A.G. 19 Sqn (RAF) 112, 113, *113*
Blissett, Lt Cdr M.S. 800 Sqn 287
Bloomer, Lt Cdr A.W., DSC 810 Sqn 221
Boddam-Whethem, Rear Adm E.K., DSC 159
Bolt, Capt A.S., DSO, DSC 812 Sqn 90
Booker, Sqn Cdr C.D., DSC, CdeG 56. *57*
Booth, Lt Cdr M.D. 847 Sqn 291
Borrett, Lt Cdr R.S. 811 Sqn 90
Bostock, Lt R.S., DSC, OLM 800 Sqn 109
Boswell, Flt Sub Lt H.G. Felixstowe 27
Bowles, Lt Cdr W.G. 805 Sqn 221
Bramah, Sub Lt H.G.K. 213 Sqn (RAF) 113
Brander, Lt Cdr T.L.M., DSC 807 Sqn 221
Brandon, Flt Sub Lt A.F. Manston War School *55*
Broadwater, Lt Cdr M. 801 Sqn 288
Brokensha, Sub Lt G.W., DSC 803 Sqn 102, 109
Bromet, Sqn Cdr G.R. 8 (N) Sqn 52
Brown, David NHB 7, 202
Brown, Lt Cdr E.M., MBE, DSC 802 Sqn *222/223*, 225
Brown, Rt Hon Gordon, British Prime Minister 303
Brown, Lt Cdr W.L.M., DSC 701 Sqn 90, 98
Bruen, Lt Cdr J.M., DSO, DFC 803, 600 Sqns 131, 134, 137, 138, 142, 144, 172, 175
Bryant, Lt Cdr J.P.G. 802 Sqn 90
Bulmer, Sub Lt G.G.R. 32 Sqn (RAF) 113
Bunch, Sub Lt S.H. 804 Sqn 113
Burnett, Rear Adm R.L. 159
Burrow, Mick, historian 9
Burton, N/A 806 Sqn 111
Bush, George W. US President 299
Butler, Flt Lt C.H. RNAS Westgate, Manston War Flt 35

Callingham, Lt G.R. 803 Sqn 100
Cameron, Maj. C.P. RM 3 CBAS RM 291
Camm, Sydney, Chief Designer, Hawker aircraft 78
Campbell, Capt D., Cco-inventor, angled deck 238
Campbell, Lt Cdr D.R.F. 803 Sqn 90
Campbell-Horsfall, Lt Cdr C.P. 806 Sqn 111
Candlish, Sgt E.R. 3 CBAS RM 286
CarmicHael, Lt P., DSC 802 Sqn *220*, 221
Carpenter, Sub Lt J.C. 229 (RAF), 46 (RAF) Sqns 113
Carter, Flt Cdr A.W., OBE, DSC, 3 (N), 10 (N) Sqns 56
Carter, Lt W.S. 809 Sqn *225*
Carver, Lt R.H.P., DSC 804 Sqn 113
Casson, Lt Cdr J. 803 Sqn 109
Chadwick, Flt Cdr A.J., DSC 5 Wg, 4 (N) Sqn 54
Charlier, Rear Adm S., Commander FAA 9
Charlton, Lt Cdr P.N., DFC, DSC RNFS 151
Chatterley, N/A H.T. 803 Sqn 109
Chiappe, M. Jean, French High Commissioner to Syria and Lebanon 126
Chilton, Cdr P.C.H., AFC 804 Sqn 113
ChurChill, Rt Hon Sir Winston (as 1st Lord Of Admiralty) 15, 19, 22, 41, 61, 64
(As British Prime Minister) 112, 128, 140, 141, 172, 175,178
Clark, Lt Cdr A.B.B. 899 Sqn 245
Clark, Lt Cdr H.S., DSC 825 Sqn 291
Clark-Hall, Lt E.A. pioneer aviator 19
Coates, Lt J.P. 808 Sqn 113
Cockburn, George 14
Cockburn, Cdr J.C., DSC 718, 804 Sqns 90, 94, 98, 113
Cockburn, Lt R.C., DSO 808 Sqn 113
Collishaw, Sqn Cdr R., CB, DSO*, DSC, DFC 3 Wg, 3 (N), 10 (N), 13 (N) Sqns 56, *57*, 68
Colmore, G.C. pioneer aviator 14
Colthurst, Cdr A.P., DSO 159
Compston, Flt Cdr R.J.O., DSO, DSC** 56, *57*
Connelly, Lt P.J. 801 Sqn 115
Corbett-Milward, Lt N.R. 820 Sqn 124
Cork, Lt Cdr R.J., DSO, DSC 242 Sqn (RAF), 880 Sqn 112, 113, *113*, 172
Coston, Pty Off F., DSM 803 Sqn 109
Cowdray, Lord, Minister of Munitions, President of Air Board 61, 63, 64
Craig, Cdr C. Snr Nav Off, Middle East 296
Crawford, Pty Off W. 800 Sqn 109
Crosley, Lt R.M. QCVSA, DSC* 800 Sqn 175
Cull, Brian historian 9
Culley, Flt Sub Lt S. Harwich Force 46
Cunningham, Adm Sir Andrew, Mediterranean Fleet 121, 123, 125, 135, 136
Cunningham, Pty Off H.G., DSM 800 Sqn 109
Curtis, Lt A. 801 Sqn 282, 283
Curtis, Flt Cdr W.A., DSC* 6 (N), 10 (N) Sqns 56
Curzon, Lord President of Council of Ministers 60, 61, *64/65*
Cuthbertson, Lt Cdr J.M. 812 Sqn 221

Dacre, Flt Lt G.B. HMS *Ark Royal (II)* 36, 37
Dallas, Sqn Cdr R.S., DSC* 1 (N) Sqn 56, *57*
Dalyell-Stead, Lt Cdr J., DSO 816 Sqn 92, 131, 136, 137
Davies, Cdr B. 892 Sqn 262
Davis, Lt G.B. 806 Sqn 142
Day, Mid A.G. 806 Sqn 112
Dearing, Susan FAA Museum 9
Debenham, Lt Cdr A.J., DSC 824 Sqn 90
De Frias, N/A F.J.L., DSM 800 Sqn 119
De Gaulle, Gen Charles Free French Leader 124
De Winton, Capt J. 9
Dickens, Capt B. RFC 17
Dickey, Flt Sub Lt R.F.L. Felixstowe 27
Dooley, N/A F.B. 803 Sqn 109
Drake, Flt Sub Lt E.B. Manston War Flt 33
Dubber, Pty Off F.B. 803 Sqn 113
Duncan, Lt Cdr G.M. 808 Sqn 90
Dundas, Lt J.H., DSC 814 Sqn 139, 140
Dunning, Sqn Cdr E.H. HMS *Furious* 44, *45*

Eden, Rt Hon Sir Anthony, British Prime Minister 245
Edmonds, Flt Cdr C.H.K. HMS *Ark Royal (II)* 36, 37
Elder, Capt W.L. 3 Wg 50
Enneccerus, Maj Walter II./StG 2 129, 144
Enstone, Flt Cdr A.J., DSC, DFC 4 (N) Sqn 56
Esmonde, Lt Cdr E., VC, DSO 825 Sqn 158, 159, *159*
Ethell, Jeffrey historian 9
Evans, Sgt A. 3 CBAS RM 286
Evans, Rear Adm C.L.G., CBE, DSO, DSC 806 Sqn, Cdr (F), HMS *Indefatigable* 93, 112, 123, 124, 138, 139, 142, 143
Eveleigh, Lt Cdr R.L., DSC 802 Sqn 245
Everett, Lt R.W.H. 804 Sqn 154
Eyton-Jones, Lt Cdr J. 801 Sqn 283

Falconer, Jonathan publisher's editor 9
Fall, Flt Cdr J.S.T., DSC** 3 (N), 9 (N) Sqns 52, 56, *57*
Fanshaw, Lt R.E. 803 Sqn 98, 109
Faragut, Sub Lt 803 Sqn 98
Fell, Rear Adm M.F., KCVSA, CB, DSO, DSC* Cdr (F), 21st CAG 221
Fenton, Lt Cdr J.E. 818 Sqn 90
Filmer, Lt C.H. 803 Sqn 109
Finch-Noyes, Lt G.E.D., DSC 800 Sqn 109
Firth, Lt Cdr K. 807 Sqn 141
Fleming, Lt Cdr A.H.T. 711 Sqn 90
Forbes, Lt Cdr J.H. HMS *Spearfish* 98
Fowler, Flt Cdr B.F. RNAS Grain 38, *39*
Francis, Lt K. 3 CBAS RM 286
Francke, Gefr Carl, I./KG 30 94
Franks, Norman historian 9
Franks, Capt R.D. HMS *Bulwark* 248
Fraser, Adm Sir Bruce, Eastern Fleet 191
Frederiksen, Lt Cdr R.V. 800 Sqn 287

Gallagher, Mid L.H., DSC 800 Sqn 109
Galpin, Flt Lt C.J. Yarmouth 26
Galtieri, Gen Leopoldo Argentinian dictator 274, 294
Gardiner, Pty Off H. 803 Sqn 109
Gardner, Lt Cdr J.R.N. 821 Sqn 221
Gardner, Lt Cdr R.E., OBE, DSC 242 (RAF) Sqn, 807 Sqn 112, 113, 141, 142
Gardner, Lt Cdr 98
Garnett, Lt Cdr J.N. 806 Sqn 143, 144
Gerrard, LT E.J., RM 14
Gibson, Vice Adm Sir David C.E.F., KCB, CB, DSC 109, 119, 138
Gilbert, Mid R.J. 111 (RAF) Sqn 113
Glazebrook, Dr Richard, Director, National Physical Laboratory 14
Glen, Flt Cdr J.A., DSC*, CdeG 3 (N) Sqn 56
Goble, Sqn Cdr S.J., DSO, DFC 1 Wg, 8 (N), 5 (N) Sqns 52
Goddard, Cdr P. 892 Sqn 262
Goodhart, Cdr N. co-inventor mirror landing aid 238
Gorbachev, Michail President Soviet Union 293
Gordon-Smith, Lt Cdr M.P., DSC 803, 807 Sqns 109, 221
Graham, Capt Q.D., HMS *Indefatigable* 199
GrAnt, Sub Lt D. 804 Sqn 113
Gray, Lt R.H., VC, DSC 1841 Sqn 198, *199*
Gray, Lt T.E., DSC 803 Sqn 105
Greenshields, Sub Lt H.F. 266 (RAF) Sqn 113
Gregory, R. pioneer aviator 14
Grey, Lt Amy, female RN air observer 305
Griffin, L/Cpl B. 3 CBAS RM 286
Griffiths, Sub Lt A.S. 803, 806 Sqns 109
Guthrie, Lt G.C.McE., OBE, DSO, 808 Sqn 113
Guy, Sub Lt P. 808 Sqn 113, 150
Haig, F M Sir Douglas, C-in-C, British Forces in France 52, 61
Haldane, Rt Hon R.B., Secretary of State for War 12
Hale, Lt Cdr J.W., DSO 825 Sqn 90
Hale, Lt M. 800 Sqn 282, 287
Hall, Lt Cdr S.J., DSO, DSC Cdr (F), 14th CAG 221
Hallett, Lt N.G., DSC* 807 Sqn 141, 148
Hamilton, Lt S.J. 713 Sqn 90
Hanson, Lt M.C.E., DSC 803 Sqn 105
Hare, Lt Cdr G., DSC 800X Sqn 145
Harris, Sub Lt J.A. 803 Sqn 109
Harris, Maj L.A., RM, OBE, DSC, 803 Sqn 105, 131
Hauck, Uffz 9./KG 26 101
Hay, Maj R.C., RM, DSO, DSC* 808 Sqn, Cdr (F) HMS *Victorious* 113, 138, 148, *194, 195*
Hayes, Cdr H.L., OBE 710 Sqn 90
Healey, Rt Hon Denis, Secretary of State for Defence 262, 263
HeAley, Lt Cdr M.W. 893 Sqn 245
Henderson, Brig Gen D. Military Aeronautics Directorate & Air Organisation Committee 59, 63
Henderson, Adm Iain, HMS *London* 302
Henley, Lt R.S., DSC 806 Sqn 129, 138, 142
Hitler, Adolf German dictator 127
Hobbs, Sub Lt B.D. Felixstowe 26
Hockley, Sub Lt F. 894 Sqn 198
Hodgkinson, Lt Cdr G.B., DSO 820 Sqn 90
Hogg, Sub Lt G.A., DSC 806 Sqn 111, 129, 138, 144, 145
Hort, Pty Off R.F. 800 Sqn 109
Hozzel, Hpt Werner I./StG 1 129
Humphreys, Lt Cdr P.N. 822 Sqn 90
Hunt, Lt Cdr J.G. 830 Sqn 150
Hussain, Sadaam Iraqi Dictator 294, 295, 299
Hutchings, Lt R., RM DSO 846 Sqn 284, 285
Hutchison, Sub Lt D.A., DSC 74 (RAF) Sqn, 804 Sqn 113

Iachino, Adm Angelo, Regia Marina 135
Inskip, Sir Thomas, Cabinet Defence Co-ordinator 87
Iveson, Sqn Ldr R. 1 (RAF) Sqn 288

Jackson, Lt Cdr P.B. Cdr (F), 13th CAG 221
Jacob, Lt Cdr J.C. 845 Sqn 245
Jago, Lt Cdr J.De F. 815 Sqn 132
James, Lt Cdr J.M. 895 Sqn 245
Jandley, Lt Cdr T.D. 800 Sqn 221
Jefford, Wg Cdr C.G., MBE map-maker 9
Jeram, Lt D.E. 213 (RAF) Sqn 112, 113
Johnston, Lt R.L. 806 Sqn 172
Johnstone, Flt Sub Lt E.G., DSC 8 (N) Sqn 56
Johnstone, Cdr M., DSC 810 Sqn 126
Jordan, Flt Lt W.L., DSC*, DFC 8 (N) Sqn 56
Judd, Lt Cdr F.E.C., DSC 880 Sqn 157

Kassem, Abdul Karim Iraqi dictator 248
Kearney, Lt R.E.N., OBE 718 Sqn 94
Keighley-Peach, Cdr C.L., OBE, DSO, 813 Sqn 117, 119, 120, 121, 137
Keirstead, Flt Cdr R.Mcn., DSC 4 (N) Sqn 56
Keith, Lt L.K., DSC 813, 805 Sqns 119, 120, 121, 143
Kennedy, Lt Cdr N., DSC 813 Sqn 90
Kerby, Flt Sub Lt H.S., DSC, AFC 3 (N) Sqn 33, *33*
Kestin, Sub Lt I.H. 145 (RAF) Sqn 113
Kettle, Lt Cdr R. von T.B. 804 Sqn 245
Kilroy, Cdr R.A., DSC 815 Sqn 122, 123
Kindersley, Lt A.T.J. 808 Sqn 113
Kinkead, Flt Cdr S.M., DSO, DSC*, DFC* 3 Wg, 1 (N) Sqn 56
Kitchener, Lord, Chief of Imperial General Staff 60
Koerner, Lt-zur-See Ernst German flying boat pilot 93

Lamb, Lt Cdr C.B., DSO, DSC 815 Sqn 130, 133
Lamb, Lt Cdr P.M., DSC* 810 Sqn 245
Lamb, Sub Lt R.R. 894 Sqn 113
Langmore, Lt Cdr D.E., DSC 828 Sqn 150
Latham, L/A A.C. 814 Sqn 139
Layard, Adm Sir Michael 9
Leatham, Lt Cdr A.G., CdeG 813 Sqn 137
Leckie, Capt R. 28
Leeming, Flt Lt J. 800 Sqn 287
Leggott, Pty Off R.T., MBE 808, 807 Sqns 142
Lemp, Kaptlt U-30 Commander 92
Lennard, Mid P.L. 501 (RAF) Sqn 113
Lewin, Lt Cdr E.D.L., CBE, DSO, DSC 718, 808 Sqns 94, 148
Lewis, Lt Jenny female RN pilot 305
Little, Flt Cdr R.A., DSO*, DSC* 8 (N) Sqn 56, *57*
Lloyd George, Rt Hon David, British Prime Minister 61, *64/65*
Logan, Lt Cdr B.E.W. 720 Sqn 90
London, Lt Cdr P.H., DSC 802 Sqn 221
Longmore, Air Marshal A.M. 14, 15, 36
Lowe, Sub Lt I.L.F., DSC 806 Sqn 124, 130
Luard, Lt Cdr N.S., DSC 814 Sqn 90
Luce, Adm David 1st Sea Lord 263
Lucy, Lt W.P., DSO 803 Sqn 94, 98, 100, 102, 105
Lunberg, Lt Cdr R.B., OLM 817 Sqn 221
Lydekker, Lt A.J.G., DSC 804 Sqn, 263 (RAF) Sqn 106
Lygo, Capt R. 892 Sqn 262
Lyons, Lt Cdr B.C. 827 Sqn 221
Lyver, Sub Lt S. 803 Sqn 100

Macdonald-Hall, Lt R. 806 Sqn 142, 144, 145
Mackinnon, Lt A.McL. 804 Sqn 113
Maclachlan, Lt Cdr I.M. 800 Sqn 221
Mahoney, Pty Off T.J. 804 Sqn 113
Malone, Sqn Cdr C.L.E. HMS *Engadine* 23
Marix, Flt Lt R.L.G. RNAS Antwerp 22, 23
Marmont, Lt J.F. 804 Sqn 102
Martin, Mid D.T.R. 800 Sqn 109
Martin, Sub Lt R.M.S. 808 Sqn 113
Massy, Lt P.W.V., DSO, DSC 813 Sqn 120
Masterman, Wg Cdr E.A.D. 24
Mayhew, Rt Hon Christopher Minister of Defence for the Royal Navy 263
McArthur, Gen Douglas US Commander, South-West Pacific 193, 217
McClean, Wg Cdr F.K. pioneer aviator 14
McEwan, Lt S.B. 803 Sqn 93
McKee, Mid T.A., DSC 803 Sqn 109
Mellings, Flt Cdr H.T., DSC*, DFC 2 Wg, 10 (N) Sqn 56
Milner-Barry, Lt P.J. 715 Sqn 90
Milosevic, Slobodan Serbian president 297
Minifie, Flt Lt R.P., DSC** 1 (N) Sqn 56
Mitchell, Cdr C.C., OBE designer of steam catapult 238
Moody, Rear Adm C. Rear Adm, Aircraft Carrier Squadrons 191
Moore, Maj Gen J. Commander, Falklands Land Forces *283*
Money, Lt Cdr R.I. 815 Sqn 291
Morgan, Lt Cdr D.H.S., DSC 800 Sqn *281*, 287, *289*, 290
Morrell, Lt C.R.W. 800 Sqn 287
Morrish, Flt Sub Lt C.R. Felixstowe 27
Mortimer, Flt Lt I. 801 Sqn 288
Moss, Sub Lt W.J.M. 213 (RAF) Sqn 113
Mottram, Graham Director, FAA Museum 9
Moulton, Maj Gen J.L., RM 266
Mullane, Lt Cdr M.J. 829 Sqn 291
Munday, Capt A.H. Killingholme 28
Murphy, Sub Lt G.J. 887 Sqn *192*
Mussolini, Benito Italian dictator 125
Mustafa, Kemal Pasha future Turkish premier 36

Nagumo, Adm Chuichi Commander Japanese Carrier Fleet 165, 166, *166*
Nasser, Gamel Abdul Egyptian President 241
Nation, Lt B.H.C. 882 Sqn 174
Newton, Lt Cdr J., DFC 847 Sqn 301
Newton, N/A 806 Sqn 112
Nicholls, Lt O.J.R. 806 Sqn 124
Nimitz, Adm Chester W. Commander US Pacific Fleet 193
Nowell, Sub Lt W.R. 804 Sqn 113
Nunn, Lt R.J. 3 CBAS RM 288
O'Brien, Lt P.E. 705 Sqn 90
O'Gorman, Mervyn , Member, Advisory Committee for Aeronautics 15, 17
Orr, Lt Cdr S.G., DSC**, AFC 806, 800 Sqns 123, 124, 127, 129, 138, 139, 186, 221
Osborn, Lt G.M.T., DSO, DSC 830 Sqn 148, 150
Owbridge, Mid 803 Sqn 98

Parke, Sub Lt T.R.V. 804 Sqn 113
Partridge, Maj R.J., RM, DSO 804, 800 Sqns 94, 101, *101*, 109
Paterson, Lt B. 804 Sqn 113
Patterson, Sub Lt N.H. 804 Sqn 113
Patterson, Mid P.J. 242 (RAF) Sqn 113
Pattinson, Capt T.C. Killingholme 28
Pattisson, Lt Cdr K.S., DSC 810 Sqn 221
Paul, Sub Lt F.D. 64 (RAF) Sqn 112, 113
Penfold, Flt Lt A. 801 Sqn 282
Phillimore, Lt Cdr R.A.B. 702 Sqn 90
Pickering, N/A H. 803 Sqn 109
Place, Cdr B.C.G. 801 Sqn 221
Polmar, Norman historian 7
Pook, Sqn Ldr J. 1 (RAF) Sqn 288
Pope, John Paul II 293
Porte, Cdr J.C. Felixstowe 26
Price, Alfred historian 9
Pudney, Sub Lt G.B. 64 (RAF) Sqn, 805 Sqn 113

Raleigh, Sir Walter historian 50
Ramsay, Lt Cdr A.R., DSC* 805 Sqn 143
Rawlinson, Capt M. 9
Rawbone, Lt Cdr A.R., KCVSA, AFC 897 Sqn
Rayleigh, Lord, Chairman, National Physical Laboratory 14
Reardon-Parker, Sub Lt J. 804 Sqn 113
Redgate, Flt Lt O.W., DSC 9 (N) Sqn 56
Reid, Flt Sub Lt E.V., DSC 10 (N) Sqn 56
Reitzenstein, Lt-zur-See Wilhelm Frederick von, German flying boat commander 93
Rice, Pty Off F.C., DSM HMS *Warspite* 98
Richards, Sub Lt D.H. 111 (RAF) Sqn 113
Richards, Lt L.G. 803 Sqn 109, 138, 144
Richardson, Lt H.J.C. 805 Sqn 143
Richardson, Lt N. 801 Sqn 297
Ridler, Pty Off T.F. 803 Sqn 109
Ritchie, Lt B., DSC* 800 Sqn 172, 175, 186, *187*
Roberts, Lt Cdr C.K. 825 Sqn 221
Roberts, Mid G.W. 808 Sqn 113
Robertson, Lt W.A. 803 Sqn 93
Rochford, Flt Lt L.H., DSC, DFC 3 (N) Sqn 56
Roe, Cdr A.J.T. OBE, DSO, 716 Sqn 90
Rommel. Gen Erwin Commander, Deutsches Afrika Korps 127
Roosevelt, Franklin D. US President 172
Rose, Lt C. HMS *Daedlus 234*
Rosevear, Flt Cdr S.W., DSC* 1 (N) Sqn 56
Rothermere, Lord, President, Air Board; Secretary of State for the RAF 64
Russell, Lt G.F. 804 Sqn 113
Russell, Lt Cdr J.D. 800 Sqn 245
Rutland, Sqn Cdr J.F. HMS *Engadine, Furious* 41, *41*, *42*, 42, 43

Sabey, Pty Off A.W., DSM 800X Sqn 148
Salisbury, Sub Lt H.H. 899 Sqn *184*
Samson, Cdr C.R., CMG, DSO, AFC pioneer aviator 14, 15, 17, *18*, 19, 20, 22, 35, 36, 37, 46
Saunders, Hilary St.G. historian 7
Saunt, Lt Cdr W.H.G., DSO, DSC 829 Sqn 131, 136, *136*, 144
Scholz, Kaptlt Wilhelm U-164 98
Schopis, Lt Hans 9./KG 26 101
Schwann, Cdr O. pioneer aviator 15
Scott, Adm Sir Percy Commander Air Defence of London 33
Seely, Rt Hon J.E.B. Technical Sub-Committee 17
Sergeant, Sub Lt E., DSC* 824 Sqn 137
Sewell, Lt A.J., DSC 806 Sqn 123, 124, 129, 138, 139, 144
Seymour, Pty Off B.M. 803 Sqn 93
Shaw, Pty Off F.J. 804 Sqn 113
Shilcock, Lt Cdr R.A. 809 Sqn 245
SholtO-Douglas, Cdr J.S., DSO 807 Sqn 141, 142, 148
Sholto-Douglas, Flt Cdr N. 4 Wg 28
Shook, Flt Cdr A.McD., DSO, DSC, CdeG, AFC 4 (N) Sqn 54
Shotton, Lt Cdr S.F., DSC 802 Sqn 221
Simpson, Capt W.C. OBE, DSC, 803 Sqn, Cdr (F) HMS *Ocean* 138, 221
Skeats, L/A J.G., DSM 818 Sqn 98
Skene, Capt N.R.M., RM, DSC 810 Sqn 90
Sleigh, Cdr J.W. OBE, DSO, DSC, 802 Sqn, Cdr (F) HMS *Glory* 113, 158, 221
Smart, Flt Sub Lt B.A. HMS *Yarmouth* 42
Smeeton, Lt B.J. 803 Sqn 98
Smeeton, Lt R.M. MBE, CB, 800, 800X Sqns 126, 145
Smith, Lt D.A.B., DSC 800 Sqn 287, 290
Smith, Sub Lt F.A. 145 (RAF) Sqn 113
Smith, Herbert Sopwith aircraft designer 49, 52
Smith, Ian Prime Minister Southern Rhodesia 256
Smuts, Lt Gen Jan Christian *60*, 60, 63, 64, *64*
Smylie, Flt Sub Lt G.F. 2 Wg 37
Somerville, Vice Adm Sir James, Commander, Force 'H', Eastern Fleet 115, 118, 165, 166, 167
Somerville, Lt M.F., DSC 808 Sqn 129, 141
Sopwith, T.O.M. aircraft designer and factory owner 15
Sparke, Sub Lt P.D.J., DSC** 806 Sqn 139, 143
Spurway, Lt K.V.V., DSC 800 Sqn 109, 142
Squibb, Lt Cdr D.J.S. 826 Sqn 291
Stackard, Flt Sub Lt H.F. 9 (N) Sqn 56
Stanley, Lt Cdr I. 737 Sqn 279, 280
Stevenson, N/A G.R. 803 Sqn 109
Stewart-Moore, Lt Cdr J.A. 820 Sqn 126
Stockwell, Pty Off W.E.J. 804 Sqn 113
Storp, Lt Walter I./Kg 30 93, 94
Stovin-Bradford, Capt F., CBE, DSC* Cdr (F), 17th CAG 221
Struthers, Flt Cdr J.G. 29
Stuart, Lt Cdr P.B., DSC 801 Sqn 221
Sturtivant, Ray historian 7
Sueter, Rear Adm Murray Commander, Naval Air Department 12, *13*, 15, 17, 18
Suthers, Lt Cdr S.H., DSC, DFC 824 Sqn 137
Swanton, Lt Cdr F.A., DSO, DSC* 812 Sqn, Cdr (F),14th CAG 221
Sydney-Turner, Lt Cdr P.G.O. 818 Sqn 98
Sykes, Lt J.H.C. 64 (RAF) Sqn, 805 Sqn 113

Taylor, Pty Off D.E. 808 Sqn 113, 137
Taylor, Lt N. 800 Sqn 283
Taylour, Lt E.W.T., DSC* 808 Sqn 113, 141
Tennant, Lt Cdr H.S. 737 Sqn 291
Terry, Lt Cdr G.N. 800 Sqn 90
Thatcher, Rt Hon Margaret British Prime Minister 276
Theobald, Pty Off A.W., DSM 800 Sqn 119
Thomas, Lt Cdr N.W. 800 Sqn 9, 287
Thomas, Lt S.R.T., DSC 801 Sqn 282
Thompson, Lt Cdr G.A. Cdr (F), 17th CAG 221
Thomson, Lt Cdr A.J. 807 Sqn 221
Thornewill, Lt Cdr S.C. 846 Sqn 290, 291
Tillard, Lt Cdr R.C., DSC 808 Sqn 113, 125, 126, 129, 141
Tilney, Lt Cdr G.A. 712 Sqn 90
Tito, Marshal Broz Yugoslav President 296
Torrens-Spence, Lt Cdr F.M.A., DSO, DSC, AFC 815 Sqn 133, 136, 147
Touchbourne, Lt P.S. 806 Sqn 142
Tremeer, L/A W.J. 800 Sqn 109
Trenchard, Marshal of RAF Lord 17, 50
Trewin, Asst Paymaster G.S/ HMS *Engadine* 41
Tribe, L/A D. 806 Sqn 129
Turner, Lt Cdr P.G.O.Sydney- (See Sydney-Turner, PGO)

Usborne, Cdr N.F. RNAS Kingsnorth 24

Vetter, Hptm 1./KG 26 93
Vian, Rear Adm Sir Philip Force 'H', 1st Aircraft Carrier Squadron *146*, 179, 192
Vincent-Jones, Lt D., DSC* 806 Sqn 129

Walsh, Sub Lt R.W.M. 111 (RAF) Sqn 113
Ward, Lt Cdr N.D., DSC 801 Sqn 287, 289, *289*
Warden, Lt Cdr R.J. 845 Sqn 291
Warneford, Flt Sub Lt R.A.J., VC *30/31*, *32*, 33
Watkins, Mid F. 803 Sqn 98
Watkins, Lt Cdr R.D. 823 Sqn 90
Wavell, Fld Marshal Sir Archibald C-in-C, Middle East 126, 140
Webb, Lt Cdr A.S. 714 Sqn 90
West, Capt A. 305
Whealy, Flt Cdr A.T., DSC*, DFC 3 (N), 9 (N) Sqns 56
Wightman, Mid O.M. 151 (RAF) Sqn 113
Wildman-Lushington, Lt G., RM 14
Wilhelm, Kaiser German monarch 31
Williams, Sub Lt G.P.C. 826 Sqn 136, 137
Williams, Sub Lt H.E., DSC 802 Sqn 158
Williamson, Lt H.A. aviation pioneer 19
Wilson, Rt Hon Sir Harold British Prime Minister 256
Winton, John historian 9
Wintour, Lt Cdr J.M. 802 Sqn 158
Wise, Sub Lt D.A., DSC 815 Sqn 147
Woodard, Vice Adm J. Commander, Falklands Task Force *283*, 284
Worrall, Sub Lt T.V. 111 (RAF) Sqn 113
Wright, Lt A.J., RM 803 Sqn 113, 138
Wright, Brothers (Orville and Wilbur) 11
Wykes-Sneyd, Lt Cdr R.J.S. 820 Sqn 291

Young, Lt A.N. 813 Sqn 121

Zeppelin, Count Ferdinand von, rigid airship constructor 12

PLACES

This section of the index lists specific locations together with the country (or in the case of England, the county) in which they lie. Spelling used is generally for the period at which they appear in the narrative – hence Sri Lanka is referred to as Ceylon, for instance. Individual nations are generally not included since reference to certain countries appear so often as to render listing them by page number impracticable.

Aandalsnes, Norway 99, 102
Aaransund, Norway *186*
Aboukir, Egypt 144, 145, 147
Adalia, Turkey 147
Addu Attol, Maldive Islands, Indian Ocean 165, 166
Aden 132. 137, 163, 165, 248
Aegean Sea 26, 187
Akrotiri, Cyprus 299
Alamein (see *El Alamein*)
Alexandria, Egypt 68, *88/89*, 91, 115, 118, 119, 121, 125, 126, 127, 129, 130, 133, 134, 135, 138, 140, 141, 142, 143, 144, 145
Al-Faw Peninsula, Iraq 299
Algiers, Algeria 118, 174, 175
Altenfjord, Norway *180/181*
Amawa, Iraq 140
Amiriya, Egypt 147
Anglesey, Isle of, North Wales 24
Andaman Islands, Indian Ocean 191
Anivorano, Madagascar 169
Antwerp, Belgium 22
Anzio, Italy 179
Archangel, Soviet Union 156
Arctic 157, 161, 181
Arrachart, Madagascar 169
Ascension Island, Atlantic Ocean 278, 279, 284
Askoy, Norway 98
Auchel, France 53
Augusta, Sicily 118, 119, 121, 150
Azores, Atlantic Ocean 156

Baghdad, Iraq 301
Bailleul, France *49*
Baku, Soviet Union 69
Baltic Sea 23, 24, 26, 43
Banak, Norway 102, 185
Bardia, Libya 121, 127
Bardufoss, Norway 102, 106
Barkston Heath, Lincolnshire 303
Barrow-in-Furness, Cumbria 12
Basra, Iraq 139, 248, 296, 301
Bathurst, Sierra Leone 128
Bedford, Bedfordshire 272
Beirut, Lebanon 147
Beisfjord, Norway 106
Bembridge, Isle of Wight 26
Bengal, Bay of, Indian Ocean 167, 169, 191
Benghazi, Libya 123, 127
Bergen, Norway 98, 99, 104, 106, 115
Bergues, France 55
Berlin, Germany 212
Bertangles, France 53
Bircham Newton, Lincolnshire 112
Bizerta, Tunisia 118, 129
Bjorne Fjord, Norway 115
Bletchley Park, 305
Blida, Algeria 174
Bodo, Norway 106
Bogenfjord, Norway 105
Bognor, Sussex 26
Bone, Algeria 178
Bonin Islands, Pacific Ocean 194
Bougie, Algeria 175
Bray Dunes, France 52, 53
Brest, France 118, 155, 156, 158
Brindisi, Italy 140
Brunei, Sultanate of, Borneo 249
Burdwood Bank, South Atlantic 283
Burray, Orkney Islands 98

Cagliari, Sardinia 121, 123, 125
Calais, France 24, 114
Calato, Rhodes 123
Calshot, Hampshire 18, 26, *28*
Cambrai, France 52
Canal Zone, Egypt (see *Suez Canal*)
Car Nicobar, Nicobar Islands, Indian Ocean 193
Caroline Islands, Pacific Ocean 194
Casablanca, Morocco 118
Caspian Sea 69
Castellorizo, Eastern Mediterranean 37, 132
Caucasus, Soviet Union 150
Cavendish Dock, Barrow-in-Furness 12
Cecil Hotel, London 61, 64
China Bay, Ceylon 165
China Sea/South China Sea 79, 91, 217, 248
Chinampo, Korea *220*, 221
Chipilly, France 53
Choiseul Sound, Falkland Islands 289
Clyde, Firth of/River, Scotland 97, 181
Cocos Islands, Indian Ocean 191
Cologne, Germany 22
Colombo, Ceylon 165, 166, 167
Constantinople, Turkey 26, 37
Copinsay Island, Scotland 94
Coral Sea, South-West Pacific 169, 178
Cottesmore, Rutland 302, 303
Coudekerque, France 49, 53
Crete 120, 121, 124, 125, 131, 132, 133, 134, 135, 140, 143, 144, 145, 146, 151, 165
Cromarty, Scotland 18
Culdrose, Cornwall *234/235, 254*, 298, 303
Cuxhaven, Germany 23, 94
Cyrenaica, Libya 138, 140

Dakar, Senegal 118, 119, 124
Dardanelles, Turkey 24, 35, *45*
Dar-es-Salaam, Tanzania 249, 250
Darwin, Australia 165
Decimommanu, Sardinia 125
Dekheila, Egypt 91, 115, 122, 126, 132, 133, 135, 140, 151
De Kooy, Holland 112
Denmark Strait, North Sea 155
Detling, Kent 111, 112
Devon, England 24
Diego Suarez, Madagascar 169
Dodecanese Islands, Aegean Sea 134
Dombas, Norway 99
Donibristle, Scotland 94, 126
Dover (and Straits of), Kent 22, 24, 55
Duhnen, Germany 94
Dunkirk/Dunkerque, France 24, 27, 33, 52, 53, *54*, 112, 114
Dusseldorf, Germany 22

Eastchurch, Kent 14, 17, 18, *40*
East Fortune, Scotland *38*
El Adem, Egypt 134
El Alamein, Egypt 174, 202
Eleusis, Greece 132, 133, 140
Elvenes, Norway 102
English Channel *16, 22*, 24, 26, 158
Euphrates, River, Iraq 139

Falkland Islands/Malvinas, South Atlantic 274, 278, 279, 282, 283, 286, 289, *290*, 294, 298
Farnborough, Hampshire 14, 61
Fauske, Norway 107
Felixstowe, Suffolk 18, 26, 27, 28
Ferejik, Gulf of, Turkey 37
Fishguard, South Wales 27
Fitzroy, Falkland Islands 289
Flanders, France 54
Flushing, Belgium 112
Folkestone, Kent 24
Formosa/Taiwan, China Sea 195
Fox Bay, Falkland Islands 284
Freetown, Sierra Leone 92
Furnes, France 52
Fuka, Egypt 147

Gadurra, Scarpanto 123, 138
Galite Island, Mediterranean 125, 126
Gallipoli, Turkey 35, 36, 37
Gardermoen, Norway 101
Gavdhos Island 135
Genoa, Italy 132
Gibraltar *88/89*, 97, 115, 117, 121, 124, 125, 128, 129, 137, 141, 142, 145, 146, 148, 149, 150, 151, 155, 158, 164
Good Hope, Cape of, South Africa 126
Goodwin Sands, English Channel 111
Goose Green, Falkland Islands 279, 282, 283, 284, 286, 287, 288
Gorazde, Bosnia 297
Gosport, Hampshire 69
Gozo, Malta 178
Grand Harbour, Valletta, Malta *7*, 130, *131, 134*, 148
Great Fisher Bank, North Sea 93
Great Yarmouth (see Yarmouth)
Greenock, Scotland 104, 121
Grimsby, Lincolnshire 31
Griz Nez, Cap, France 114
Grotli, Norway 101
Grytviken, South Georgia, South Atlantic 281, *281*
Guadalcanal, Solomon Islands, South Pacific 169, 178

Hagesund, Norway 115
Hal Far, Malta 118, 121, 130
Hammamet, Tunisia 138
Hammerfest, Norway 157
Harstad, Norway 99, 102, 106
Hartvigvan, Lake, Norway 104, 105
Hatston, Orkney Islands 94, 97, 98, 104, 105, 109, 115
Haugersund, Norway 106
Heligoland, Germany 23, 28
Heliopolis, Egypt *73*
Henstridge, Somerset *200/201*
Hepjangs Fjord, Norway *102/103*
Herzogovinia, former Yugoslavia 296
High Wycombe, Buckinghamshire 301
Hong Kong, China 199, *210/211*
Howden, East Yorkshire 26
Hoyer, Germany 38
Hudalen, Norway 104
Hull, Yorkshire 31
Humber Estuary, Yorkshire/ Lincolnshire 29
Hyeres, France 118

Irish Sea 24, 29
Islas de los Estados, South Atlantic 283
Isle of Grain, Medway, Kent 18
Isle of Man (HMS *Urley*), Irish Sea 304
Ismailia, Egypt 244

Jounie, Lebanon 147
Jutland, Danish/German coast 41, *41*

Kaalfjord, Norway 181
Kalafrana, Malta 117
Karachi, Pakistan 248
Kaso Strait, Greece 144
Kent, Mount, Falkland Islands 286, 288, 290
Kerkenah Bank, Mediterranean 148
Khafji, Saudi Arabia 295
Kiel Canal, Germany 23, 98
Killingholme, Lincolnshire 28
Kilya Bay, Turkey 68, 69
Kirkenes, North Norway 156
Kismayu, Somaliland 132
Kosovo, former Yugoslavia 296, 297, 298
Kurdistan/Kurds, Iraq 296
Kuwait, 248, 294, 295, 296, 299, 301
Kythera Island, Mediterranean 121
Kyushu, Japan 194

Lampedusa, Mediterranean 148
Landing Ground 109, Egypt 151
Land's End, Cornwall 93
La Senia, Algeria 174
Lee-on-Solent (HMS *Daedalus*), Hampshire *25*, 158, *182, 214/215, 224, 234/235*
Lesjaskog, Norway 99
Leuchars, Scotland 69
Listelles, France 52
Lofoten Islands, North Sea 106
London, England 31, 55, 63, 111
Lossiemouth, Scotland 102, *227, 256, 257*
Lydda, Palestine 147

Makra, Eritrea 137
Maldive Islands, Indian Ocean 165, 166
Maleme, Crete 135, 140, 143
Malta 29, *47, 113*, 117, 118, 119, 121, 123, 124, 125, 126, 127, 128, 129, 130, 132, 134, 128, 139, 142, 145, 146, *146*, 147, 149, 150, 151, 155, 159, 171, 172, 174, 178, 179, *187, 225, 226*
Manston, Kent *55*, 158
Margate, Kent 33
Mariana Islands, Pacific Ocean 191
Marmara, Sea of, Turkey 36
Marquise, France 24
Massawa, Eritrea 132, 137
Matapan, Cape, Greece *136*, 137, 156
Medway, River, Kent 15
Mersa Taclai, Eritrea 132
Mers-el-Kebir, Algeria 118
Messina, Sicily 149
Middlekerke, Belgium 54
Midway Island, Pacific Ocean 169, 178
Mindanao, Philippines 193
Minneriya, Ceylon 166
Mo, Norway 102, 106
Mogadishu, Somaliland 132
Montenegro, former Yugoslavia 296
Montserrat Island, Caribbean 299
Montevideo, Uruguay 94
Mosjoen, Norway 102, 106
Mozambique Channel, Indian Ocean 256
Mullion, Cornwall 26, 29
Murmansk, Soviet Union 57

Namsos, Norway 102
Narvik, Norway *96/97*, 98, 102, *102/103*, 104, 106
Nazari, Iraq 139
New Caledonia, South Pacific 178
New Georgia, South Pacific 178
Newlyn, Cornwall 27
Nicobar Islands, Indian Ocean 191
Nicosia, Cyprus 147
Nieuport, France 112
Nile Delta, Egypt 245
Nordalen, Norway 104
Norfolk Navy Yard, Virginia, USA 177, 305
Normandy, France *182*
North Front, Gibraltar 151
North Hinder Lightship, North Sea 27
North Sea 15, *22*, 23, 24, 46, 98, 106
North-Western Approaches, Atlantic Ocean 91
Noumea, New Caledonia 178

Oberndorf, Germany 52
Ofotfjord, Norway 98, 104
Okinawa, Pacific Ocean 193, 195
Onagawa Wan, Japan 198
Oran, Algeria 118, 119, 174
Orfordness, Suffolk *40*
Orkney Islands, North Sea 94, 97, 106, 111, 115, 155
Oslo, Norway 98
Ostend, Belgium 22, 26, 54, 112
Outram Road Jail, Singapore 193

Padstow, Cornwall *29*
Paestum, Italy 179
Palembang, Sumatra 193
Palermo, Sicily 130
Panama Canal 177
Pangkalan Brandon, Sumatra 192
Pantelleria, Mediterranean 150, 178
Paramythia, Greece 132, 133, 137, 140
Pearl Harbour, Hawaii 125, 163, 165, 207
Pebble Island, Falkland Islands 279, 284, 287, 289
Pembroke, South Wales 26
Persian Gulf, Indian Ocean 248, 298
Peterhead, Scotland 26
Petit Synthe, France 55
Petsamo, North Finland 156, 157
Piraeus, Greece 129, 130
Pladjoe, Sumatra 193
Plymouth, Devon 27, 303
Pola, Adriatis Coast 26
Polegate, East Sussex 24
Polyvestre, France 118
Portland (HMS *Osprey*), Dorset 26, *234/235*
Port Said, Egypt 137, 244
Port San Carlos, Falkland Islands 289
Portsmouth, Hampshire 291, *291*
Port Stanley, Falkland Islands 278, 279, 282, 284, 287, 288, 289, 290, *290*, 291
Prestwick (UMS *Gannet*), Scotland 298, 303
Pulham, Norfolk 26
Pusan, Korea 217
Pyongyan, Korea 217

Ramree Island, Burma 192
Ramsgate, Kent 33
Rangoon, Burma 169, 192, 193
Ratmalana. Ceylon 165
Red Sea 37, 132
Retimo, Crete 143
Rhodes, Mediterranean 120, 123, 127, 135, 138
Rio Grande, Argentina 284, 286
Rombaksfjord, Norway 105
Rome, Italy 135
Rosyth, Scotland 42
Russell Islands, South Pacific 178

Sabang Island, Indian Ocean 191
St Helena, Atlantic Ocean 131
St Pol, France 52, 53, 55
Sakishima Gunto Islands, Pacific Ocean 195, 196
Salerno, Italy 188
Salisbury Plain, Wiltshire 17
Salonica, Greece 37
Samawa, Iraq 139
San Carlos Water, Falkland Islands *281*, 286, 287
San Chiara Ula Dam, Lake Tirso, Sardinia 132
Sarajevo, Bosnia 296, 297
Sardinia, Mediterranean 121, 125, 132
Scapa Flow, Orkney Islands 41, 104, 106, 114, 158, 185
Scarpanto, Mediterranean 123, 144
Schelling Roads, North Sea 23
Scilly, Isles of, Cornwall 27
Sfax, Tunisia 127
Shag Cove, Falkland Islands 287
Shawbury, Wiltshire 303
Sheerness, Kent 15, 19
Sheppey, Isle of, Kent 15
Sicilian Narrows, Mediterranean 122
Sidi Barrani, Egypt 121
Sildvik, Norway 107
Sinai Desert, Palestine 37, 244
Singapore 117, 163, 165, 188, 193, 221, 239, 256
Skaanland, Norway 102, 106
Slovenia, former Yugoslavia 296
Soengi Gerong, Sumatra 193
Sollum, Libya 127
Somme, River, France 50
Sorfold, Norway 107
South China Sea (see *China Sea*)
South Georgia, South Atlantic 279, 281, *281*
South Jason Island, Falkland Islands 283
South-Western Approaches, Atlantic Ocean 91
Spartivento, Cape, Sardinia 126, 151
Spithead, Hampshire 19
Spitzbergen, Norway 158
Srebrenica, Kosovo 297
Stampalia, Mediterranean 127
Staring Bay, Celebes, Indonesia 165
Stavanger, Norway 99
Suda Bay, Crete 136, 138
Suez, Suez Canal, Canal Zone, Egypt 117, 126, 130, 133, 137, 145, 151, 171, 241, *242*, 244, *244*, 245, 246, 248, 249, 269
Sydney, Australia 193
Syracuse, Sicily 138, 150

Takoradi, Gold Coast 128, 146
Tangiers, Morocco 151
Taranto, Italy 23, *110/111*, 125, 136
Tenedos, Eastern Mediterranean 35, 37
Terschelling Light Vessel, North Sea 26
Teteghem, France 55
Texel, Germany 26, 112
Thourot, France 55
Tobruk, Libya 127, 151
Tokyo (and Tokyo Bay), Japan 198, 199
Tondern, Germany 38, 41, 45, 46
Torskenfjord, Norway 106
Toulon, France 118, 147, 178
Tranoy, Norway 105
Trapani, Sicily 129
Trincomalee, Ceylon 165, 166, 167
Tripoli, Libya 127, 132, 136, 140
Tripolitania, Libya 138
Tromso, Norway 99, 102, 105, 106
Trondheim, Norway 98, 100, 101, 102, 108, 109, 115
Truk, Pacific Ocean 188
Tunis, Tunisia 122
Turnhouse, Scotland *45*
Twatt, Scotland 233

Vaagsfjord, Norway 99
Vaernes, Norway 100, 101, 105
Valetta, Malta 130, *131*, 148
Valona, Albania 133, 140
Vert Galant, France 52, 53
Vlieland, Friesian Islands, Holland 26
Vojvodina, former Yugoslavia 296
Wales 24
Walmer, Kent 33, 55
Wei-Hai-Wei, China *68, 77*
Westende, Belgium 112
Western Approaches, Atlantic Ocean 26
Western Front 52, 53, *55*, 61
West Falkland, Falkland Islands 287, 288
West Indies 90, 164
Weymouth, Dorset 15
Wick, Scotland 94
Wilhelmsoord, Holland 112
Wisley, Surrey 262
Whitehall, London 19
Worthy Down, Hampshire 104, 106

Xeros, Gulf of, Turkey 37

Yarmouth, Norfolk 18, 26, 28, 46
Yellow Sea, Korea 217
Yemen, Arabia 249
Yeovilton (HMS *Heron*), Somerset 101, *184, 200/201, 253*, 274, 277, 284, 291, *295*, 302, 303

Zanzibar, Indian Ocean 249
Zeebrugge, Belgium 26, 52, 54, 55
Zepa, Kosovo 297

SHIPS/VESSELS

British and Commonwealth

Acasta, **HMS, Destroyer 107**
Achilles, HMS, Cruiser 94
Actaeon, HMS, Depot Ship 18
Activity, HMS, Escort Carrier 161, 175, 212
Adventure, HMS, Minelayer 156
Africa, HMS, Battleship 15
Africa (II), HMS, Aircraft Carrier (cancelled) 212
Ajax, HMS, Cruiser 94
Alacrity, HMS, Frigate 282
Albatross, HMS, Seaplane Carrier 87, 02
Albion, HMS, Light Aircraft Carrier *228, 234*, 238, 242, *242*, 248, 249, 266
Almirante Cochrane (see HMS *Eagle (I)*)
Ameer, HMS Escort Carrier 188, 192
Anne, HMS, Seaplane Carrier 37
Antelope, HMS, Frigate 287
Antrim, HMS, Destroyer 279, 281
Arabic, SS, Liner 26
Archer, HMS, Escort Carrier 159, 161
Ardent, HMS, Destroyer 107, *286*, 287
Argonaut, HMS, Frigate 287
Argus, HMS, Aircraft Carrier *46*, 47, 68, 69, 70, 76, *76*, 82, 91, 118, 121, 129, 137, *139*, 150, 157, 158, 172, 174, 175, 211
Ariguani, HMS, Fighter Catapult Ship 154
Ark Royal (II), HMS, Seaplane Carrier 24, 35, 36, 37, 68, 154
Ark Royal (III), HMS, Aircraft Carrier 82, 85, *88/89*, 89, 91, 92, *92*, 93, 94, 97, 99, 100, 101, 102, 104, 105, 106, 107, 108, 109, 114, 115, 118, 119, 122, 123, 124, 125, 126, *128*, 129, 132, 137, 139, 141, 142, 145, 146, 148, 149, 150, 151, 155, 156, 158, 171, 172
Ark Royal (IV), HMS, Aircraft Carrier 212, *230, 231, 232/233, 234*, 237, 238, *238/239*, 242, 246, *246/247, 250*, 256, 259, *261, 263, 264/265*, 266, *266*, 267, 271
Ark Royal (V), HMS, Through Deck Cruiser 274, *297, 300/301*. 301, 302
Arrogant, HMS, Aircraft Carrier (cancelled) 212
Arrow, HMS, Frigate 282
Atheling, HMS, Escort Carrier 188, 191
Athelstone, RFA, Support Ship 167
Athene, HMS, Aircraft Transport Ship 150
Atlantic Conveyor, SS, Container Ship 278, 284, 288, 295
Attacker, HMS, Escort Carrier 159, 179, 186, 211
Audacious, HMS, Aircraft Carrier (became *Eagle (II)*) 175, 211, 212, 237
Audacity, HMS, Escort carrier (previously *Empire Audacity*) *154*, 155, 158, 225
Aurora, HMS, Cruiser *253*
Australia, HMAS, Cruiser 124
Avenger, HMS, Escort Carrier 159, 160, *160*, 161, 174, 175
Avenger (II), HMS, Frigate 288

Barham, HMS, Battleship 90, 124, 130, 134, 134, 135, 144
Battler, HMS, Escort Carrier 159, 179, 188
Begum, HMS, Escort Carrier 188
Ben-my-Chree, HMS, Seaplane Carrier 24, *36*, 36, 37
Berwick, HMS, Cruiser 128
Biter, HMS, Escort Carrier 159, 161, 174, 212
Brazen, HMS, Frigate 295, *298*
Breconshire, HMS, Auxiliary 148
Brilliant, HMS, Frigate 280, 284, 287, 305
British Sergeant, SS, Tanker 167
Broadsword, HMS, Frigate 287
Bulwark, HMS, Light Aircraft Carrier 212, *231, 234*, 238, 242, *244*, 245, 248, 271

Campania, HMS, Seaplane Carrier 20, *23*, 41, 42
Campania (II), HMS, Escort Carrier 175, 212
Canton, HMS, Armed Merchant Cruiser 204
Capetown, HMS, Destroyer 120
Cardiff, HMS, Destroyer 295, 296
Centaur, HMS, Light Aircraft Carrier 7, 238, 242, 246, 248, 249, 259
Charger, HMS, Escort Carrier 159
Chaser, HMS, Escort Carrier 161
Chatham, HMS, 299
Colossus, HMS, Light Aircraft Carrier 199, 211, 213
Conqueror, HMS Nuclear Submarine 279, *282*, 283
Conte Rosso, became HMS *Argus*
Cornwall, HMS, Cruiser 167
Courageous, HMS, Aircraft Carrier 43, 44, 74, *74*, 77, 78, *80*, 81, 82, 85, 90, 91, 92, 93, *93*, 118
Coventry, HMS, Destroyer 287, 288, *288*
CVA-01, Aircraft Carrier Project (cancelled) 259, 262, 266

Dasher, HMS, Escort Carrier 159, 174
Devonshire, HMS, Cruiser 106
Diamond, HMS Destroyer 130
Dorsetshire, HMS, Cruiser 156, 167
Duke of York, HMS, Battleship *172/173*, 181

E-11, Submarine 23, 41
Eagle, HMS, Aircraft Carrier *47*, 47, 68, *70/71*, 70, *72, 73*, 73, *76*, 77, 82, 90, 91, *116/117*, 117, 119, 120, 121, 123, 124, 130, 131, 143, 156, 171, 172
Eagle (II), HMS, Aircraft Carrier 212, *226, 227, 228, 230, 232, 236/237*,237, 238, 242, *242/243* 245, 246, *251, 252, 254/255*, 256, *257*, 259, 266
Elephant, HMS, Aircraft Carrier (cancelled) 212
Emperor, HMS, Escort Carrier 182, *184*, 186
Empress, HMS, Seaplane Carrier 23
Empress (II), HMS, Escort Carrier 192
Empire Morn, SS, CAM ship 161
Endeavour, HMS, Frigate 280
Endurance, HMS, Patrol Ship 279, *280*, 280, 281
Engadine, HMS, Seaplane Carrier 20, 23, 41, *41*, 42
Exeter, HMS, Cruiser 94
Exeter (II), HMS, Destroyer 288, 289, 290

Fearless, HMS, Destroyer 148
Fearless (II), HMS, Assault Ship 278, 287, 289
Fencer, HMS, Escort Carrier 161, 182
Formidable, HMS, Battleship 24
Formidable (II), HMS, Aircraft Carrier 131, 132, 133, *133*, 134, 135, 136, 137, 138, 141, 142, 143, 144, 145, 146, 164, *164*, 165, 169, *170/171, 172/173*, 174, *175*, 175, 178, 179, 185, 194, 196, *197*, 198, 207
Foresight, HMS, Destroyer 141
Fort Austin, RFA, Ammunition Ship 284
Furious, HMS, Aircraft Carrier 43, *44*, 44, 45, *45*, 46, 47, 68, *69*, 70, 73, 77, 78, 81, 82, 87, 90, 91, 92, *93*, 97, 98, 99, 104, *104*, 105, 106, 114, 128, 141, 145, 146, 149, 156, 157, 171, 172, 174, 177, 182, 185, 211
Gibraltar, HMS, Aircraft Carrier (cancelled) 212
Glamorgan, HMS, Destroyer 282, 290
Glasgow, HMS, Cruiser 102
Glasgow (II), HMS. Destroyer 284
Glorious, HMS, Aircraft Carrier 43, 44, 74, *75*, 76, 77, 82, 85, 90, *90*, 91, 92, 97, 99, 100, 101, 102, 104, 105, 106, 107, *108*, 109, 117, 202
Glory, HMS, Light Aircraft Carrier 199, 219, *219*, 221, *229*, 242, 248
Gloucester, HMS, Cruiser 130, 135, 136, 138
Gloucester (II), HMS, Destroyer 295, 296
Hasty, HMS, Destroyer 137
Hector, SS, Merchant Cruiser 167
Hereward, HMS, Destroyer 138, 144
Hermes, HMS, Cruiser 19
Hermes (II), HMS, Aircraft Carrier 47, 68, *68,69*, 73, 77, 82, 90, 91, 92, 119, 132, 139, 140, 164, 165, 167, *168*, 169, 207
Hermes (III), HMS, Aircraft Carrier 211, 212, 238, 246, *250, 252, 258/259*, 259, 261, 266, *267*, 272, *272/273*, 274, *276/277*, 277, *281*, 282, *283*, 284, 291, *291*, 299
Hiburnia, HMS, Battleship 15
Hollyhock, HMS, Corvette 167
Hood, HMS, Battlecruiser 93, 94, 115, 118, 155
Hunter, HMS, Escort Carrier 179, 186

Illustrious, HMS, Aircraft Carrier 89, *110/111*, 112, 115, 121, 122, 123, 124, 125, 126, 127, 129, 130, 131, 144, 169, 175, 179, 181, 188, *190*, 191, 192, 193, 194, *194*, 196, 207, 211, 212, 225, 238, *240/241*
Illustrious (II), HMS, Through Deck Cruiser *274/275*, 274, 291, 299, 302
Imperial Star, SS, Freighter 150
Implacable, HMS, Aircraft Carrier 175, 186, 196, *198, 199*, 212, 224, *225*
Indefatigable, HMS, Aircraft Carrier 175, 185, 192, *192*, 193, 195, 196, 198, 199
Indomitable, HMS, Aircraft Carrier *162/163*, 163, 164, 165, 167, 169, 172, 175, 178, 179, 191, 193, 196, *196*, *197*, *204*, 207, 224
Intrepid, HMS, Assault Ship (Loading Platform Dock) 271, 272
Invincible, HMS, Through Deck Cruiser *270/271*, 271, 272, 274, 277, 284, *284/285*, 288, *289*, 291, *292/293*, *294* 298, *299, 300/301*, 302
Irresistable, HMS, Aircraft Carrier (built as HMS *Ark Royal IV*) 212, 237

Jaguar, HMS, Destroyer 130
Juno, HMS, Destroyer 130, 136

Khedive, HMS, Escort Carrier 186, 187
King George V, HMS, Battleship 192, 196

Leviathan, HMS, Aircraft Carrier (cancelled) 248
London, HMS, Cruiser 15
London (II), HMS, Frigate 296
Lucitania, SS, Liner 26

Magnificent, HMS, Light Aircraft Carrier 224
Majestic-Class, Aircraft Carriers 175, 211, 213, 248
Malaya, HMS, Battleship 90
Malta, HMS, Aircraft Carrier (cancelled) 212
Manchester, HMS, Light Cruiser 148
Manchester (II), HMS, Destroyer 296, 298
Manxman, HMS, Seaplane Carrier 24, 37, 42
Maplin, HMS, Fighter Catapult Ship 154
Matabele, HMS, Destroyer 105
Michael E, SS, CAM-Ship 154
Monmouth, HMS, Aircraft Carrier (cancelled) 212

Nabob, HMS, Escort Carrier 185
Nairana, HMS, Escort Carrier 175, *187*, 212, 213
Nelson, HMS, Battleship 90, 93, 149, 156, *172/173*
New Zealand, HMS Aircraft carrier (cancelled) 212
Nubian, HMS, Destroyer 130, 144

Ocean, HMS Light Aircraft Carrier 212, *218*, 219, *220*, 221, *222/223*, 242, 245, 248
Ocean (II), HMS, Helicopter Assault Carrier 299, 301
Ohio, SS, Tanker 172
Orion, HMS, Destroyer 130

Patia, HMS, Fighter Catapult Ship 154
Pegasus, HMS, Fighter Catapult Ship 154
Perseus, HMS, Ferry Carrier 234, 242, 248
Plymouth, HMS, Frigate 279, 280, 281, 289
Polyphemus, HMS, Aircraft Carrier (cancelled) 212
Pretoria Castle, HMS, Escort Carrier 212
Prince of Wales, HMS, Battlecruiser 149, 155, 163
Prince of Wales (II), HMS Planned New Aircraft Carrier *301*, 302
Pursuer, HMS, Escort Carrier 161, 182, 186, 187

Queen Elizabeth, HMS, Battleship 144
Queen Elizabeth(II), HMS, Planned New Aircraft Carrier *301*, 302

Raven II, HMS, Seaplane Carrier 37
Redoubt, HMS, Destroyer 46
Registan, HMS, Fighter Catapult Ship 154
Renown, HMS, Battlecruiser 93, 141, *172/173*
Repulse, HMS, Battleship 43, *43*, 163
Resolution, HMS, Battleship 90, 124
Richmond, HMS, 305
Riviera, HMS, Seaplane Carrier 20, 23
Rodney, HMS, Battleship 90, 93, 149, 150
Ruler-Class, Escort Carriers 211
Ruprena, SS, Freighter 115

Sagaing, SS, Freighter 167
Scylla, HMS, Cruiser 159
Searcher, HMS, Escort Carrier 182, 186, 187
Shah, HMS, Escort Carrier 188
Sheffield, HMS, Cruiser 156
Sheffield (II), HMS, Destroyer 283
Shropshire, HMS, Cruiser 132
Siretoc, HMS, Anti-Submarine Trawler 102
Sir Galahad, RFA, Troopship 286, 289
Sir Tristram, RFA, Troopship 289
Somali, HMS, Destroyer 93
Southampton, HMS, Cruiser 130
Spearfish, HMS, Submarine 98
Stalker, HMS, Escort Carrier 179, 186
Stuart, HMAS, Destroyer 120, 124
Suffolk, HMS, Cruiser 99
Sydney, HMAS, Light Aircraft Carrier 219

Tenedos, HMS, Destroyer 167
Theseus, HMS, Light Aircraft Carrier *216, 218*, 219, *226, 227*, 242, 245, 248
Tideflow, RFA, Replenishment Ship *267*
Tidespring, RFA, Replenishment Ship 279
Tracker, HMS, Escort Carrier *91*, 161, *186, 188/189*
Triumph, HMS, Light Aircraft Carrier 212, *213*, 214, *216*, 217, 219, 238, 242, 248
Trumpeter, HMS, Escort Carrier 185, *185*
Turpin, HMS, Submarine *251*

Unicorn, HMS, Repair Aircraft Carrier 179, 181, 211, 221
Utmost, HMS, Submarine 151

Valiant, HMS, Battleship 90, 121, 122, 123, 129, 135, 137
Vampire, HMAS, Destroyer 167
Vanguard, HMS, Battleship 175
Venerable, HMS. Light Aircraft Carrier 199, *200/201*. 213, 278
Vengeance, HMS, Light Aircraft Carrier 199, 225
Victorious, HMS, Aircraft Carrier 146, 150, 155, 156, 157, *157*, 158, 159, 172,
174, 175, *176/177*, 177, 178, 191, *191*, 193,
194, *195*, 238, *240/241* 242, 246, 248, *258*,
259, *262*
Vindex, HMS, Seaplane Carrier 24, 38, *40*, 41
Vindex(II), HMS Escort Carrier 161, 175, 212
Vindictive, HMS, Aircraft Carrier 47, 68, *76*, 77

Warrior, HMS, Light Aircraft Carrier 213
Warspite, HMS, Battleship 98, 123, 129, *131*, 134, 135, 136, 137
Whirlwind, HMS, Destroyer 105

Yarmouth, HMS, Cruiser 42, *42*
York, HMS, Cruiser 130

Other Nations

Admiral Graf Spee, German Heavy Cruiser 94
Aka, Iraqi Salvage Vessel 296
Akagi, Japanese Aircraft Carrier 165, *166*
Alfieri, Italian Destroyer 137
Amakusa, Japanese Escort Sloop 198
Andrea Gritti, Italian Freighter 149
Antietam, USS, Aircraft carrier 238
Aquila, Italian Aircraft Carrier 89
Arromannches, French Aircraft carrier 245

Bahia Buen Suceso, Argentinian Freighter 284
Bainsizza, Italian Freighter 150
Barenfels, German Troopship 99

Baro, Norwegian Passenger Steamer 158
Bearn, French Aircraft Carrier 89
Beveziers, French Submarine 169
Bismark, German Battleship 145, 155, 156, 158
Bolzano, Italian Cruiser 126, 135
Brarena, Italian Tanker 148
Bremse, German Training Ship 104
Bretagne, French Battleship 118

Caffaro, Italian Freighter 149
Caio Dulio, Italian Battleship 125
Caterina, Italian Freighter 150
Chevalier Paul, French Destroyer 147
Conte di Cavour, Italian Battleship 125

Daniele Manin, Italian Destroyer 137
Duca Degli Abruzzi, Italian Cruiser 151
Dunkerque, French Battleship 118, 119

Egadi, Italian Freighter 148
Elbe, German Freighter 156
Erich Koellner, German Destroyer 98
Essex-Class, US Aircraft carriers 177, 199

Fiume, Italian Cruiser 137

Generale Belgrano, Argentinian Cruiser 278, 282, 283
Gneisenau, German Battlecruiser *74/75*, 107, *107,108*, 158, *159*
Goeben, German Battlecruiser (see *Yaviz*)
Gonzenheim, German Supply Ship 156
Graf Zeppelin, German Aircraft carrier 89

Hannover, German Merchant Ship (became HMS *Audacity*) 155
Hermann Kuehne, German Destroyer 102/*103*
Hipper, German Cruiser 107, 128
Hiryu, Japanese Aircraft Carrier 165

Jean Bart, French Battleship 118
Jungingen, Norwegain Patrol Boat 104

Kaijo, Japanese Aircraft carrier 196
Koenigsberg, Gemran Cruiser 98, 105, 207

Lafayette, French Aircraft Carrier 245
Lanciere, Italian Destroyer 126
Le Heros, French Submarine 169
Leone Pancaldo, Italian Destroyer 119
Littorio, Italian Battleship 125
Lothringen, Gemran Tanker 156
Luciano, Italian Feighter 140
Luetzow, German Cruiser 98, 132

Madalena Odero, Italian Freighter 148
25 de Mayo, Argentinian Aircraft Carrier (ex-HMS *Venerable*) 278, 282, 283, 287
Merc Enterprise, Danish Coaster *234/235*
Midway, USS, Aircraft Carrier 238
Missouri, USS, Battleship 296
Moncalieri, Italian Freighter 132

Nazario Sauro, Italian Destroyer 137
Norviken, Norwegian Freighter 167

Panuco, Italian Freighter 148
Pietro Barbara, Italian Freighter 149
Po, Italian Hospital Ship 133
Pola, Italian Cruiser 136, 137
Polnochny-Class, Iraqi Landing Ships 296
Prinz Eugen, German Cruiser 155, 156, 158

Ranger, USS Aircraft Carrier 181
Rhybus, USS, Escort Carrier (became HMS *Emperor*) *184*
Richelieu, French Battleship 118, 119, 124
Rio Carcarana, Argentinian Freighter 284

Saint-Dizier, French Freighter 147
Santa Fe, Argentinian Submarine 280, 281, *281*
Santa Maria, Italian Freighter 133
Saratoga, USS , Aircraft Carrier *176/177*, 178, 191
Scharnhorst, German Battlecruiser *74/75*, *105*, 107, *108*, 108, 109, 158, *159*, 181
Scire, Italian Submarine 149
Shokaku, Japanese Aircraft Carrier 165
Soryu, Japanese Aircraft Carrier 166
Stampalia, Italian Freighter 140
Strasbourg, French battleship 118

Tirpitz, German Battleship 158, *180/181*, 181, 182, 185
TNC 45, Iraqi Fast Attack Craft 296
Trieste, Italian Cruiser 151
Type 43, Iraqi Minelayer 296

U-Boats, German Submarines 24, *152/153*, 153, 154
U-29, German Submarine *74/75*, 93
U-30, German Submarine 92, 93, 98
U-39, German Submarine 92
U-73, German Submarine 172
U-81, German Submarine 150
U-131, German Submarine 158
U-155, German Submarine 175
U-164, **German Submarine 98**
U-354, German Submarine 185
U-451, German Submarine 151
U-751, German Submarine *154*, 158
UB-20, German Submarine 27
UB-32, German Submarine 28
UC-6, German Submarine 27
UC-36, German Submarine 27

Valley Forge, USS, Aircraft Carrier 217
Vittorio Veneto, Italian Battleship 126, 134, 135, 136

Wasp, USS, Aircraft Carrier 171
Wisconsin, USS, Battleship 296
Wolf, German Surface Raider 37

Vaviz, Turkish Battlecruiser (ex-German *Goeben*) 37

Zara, Italian Cruiser 137
Zhuk-Class, Iraqi Patrol Boat 296
Zuikaku, Japanese Aircraft Carrier 165

AVIATION UNITS

These are arranged as: RNAS/RAF 1911-1920; Fleet Air Arm post-1920; Royal Air Force post-1920; Army Air Corps and others.

RNAS/RAF 1911-1920

Air Battalion, Royal Engineers 14, 17
Central Flying School 17, 18
Military Wing, RFC 15, 17, 18, 19
Naval Airship Section, RNAS 15
Naval Flying School, Eastchurch 14, 17, 18
Naval Wing, RFC 18, 19
Royal Air Force 31, 33, 37, 46.64, 65, 68
Royal Flying Corps 14, 17, 18, 33, 53, 61, 64, 67
Royal Naval Air Service 15, 17, 18, *18*, 19, 20, 26, *28*, 29, 31, 33, 53, 54, 55, 59, 61, 64, 67, 68, 87
War School, RNAS Manston *55*

1 Wing 52, 56
2 Wing *22, 34/35*, 56
3 Wing 50, 56
4 Wing 52
5 Wing 50, 52

1 (N)/201 Squadron 52, 53, 55, 56, 67
2 (N)/202 Squadron 52, 53
3 (N)/203 Squadron 52, 53, 55, 56, 69, 70
4 (N)/204 Squadron 52, 53, 54, 55, 56
5 (N)/205 Squadron 52, 53, 55, 69, 70
6 (N)/206/47 Squadron 52, 55
7 (N)/207 Squadron 52, 53, 55, 68
7a (N) Squadron 55
8 (N)/208 Squadron 52, 53, 55, 56
9 (N)/209 Squadron 53, 55, 56
10 (N)/210 Squadron 53, 55, 56
11 (N)/211 Squadron 53, 55
12 (N)/212 Squadron 53
13 (N)/213 Squadron 55, 56
14 (N)/214 Squadron *54*, 55
15 (N)/215 Squadron 55
16 (N)/216 Squadron 55
17 (N)/217 Squadron 55
18 (N)/218 Squadron 67

Summary of 219-274 RAF Naval Squadrons formed from RNAS Coastal Flights 67, 68
155 Squadron *38/39*
185 Squadron, RAF 69
186 Squadron, RAF 69

31 Training Depot Squadron 69
33 Training Depot Squadron 69
39 Training Depot Squadron 69
49 Training Depot Squadron 69
Walmer Defence Flight 55

Fleet Air Arm post-1920

Flights, 1920-1939
Summary on set-up 70
Renumbering, 1929 76
Order of Battle, late 1931 77
Re-organisation – Flights to Squadrons 79
Catapult Flight Renumbering, 19936 82
401 Flight 70, 77, 79
402 Flight 70, 77, 79
403/715 Flight 73, 77, 79, 82
404 Flight 73, 77, 79
405 Flight 76, 77
406/714 Flight 73, 76, 77, 79, 82
407/712 Flight 76. 77, 79, *79*, 82
408 Flight 76, 77, 79
409 Flight 79
420 Flight 70, 76
421 Flight 70, 73, 76
422 Flight 70, 76
423 Flight 70, 76
440 Flight 70, 73, 77
441 Flight 70, 73, *76*, 77, 79
442 Flight 70, 73, *76*, 77, 79
443/716/718 Flight 73, 76, 77, 79, 82
444/702 Flight 76, 77, *77*, 79, 82
445/713 Flight 76, 77, 79, 82
446 Flight 76, 77, 79
447/702/711 Flight 76, 77, 79, 82
448 Flight 76, 77
449 Flight 76, 77, *77*, 79
450 Flight 76, 77, 79
460 Flight 73, 77, 79
461 Flight 73, 77, 79
462 Flight 76, 77, 79
463 Flight 76, 77, 79
464 Flight 76, 77, 79
Flight 77, 79
Flight 77, 79

i) Squadrons 1933 to date
Summary, 700-799 Squadrons 87, 205
Summary, 800-899 Squadrons 205
Summary, 810-869 Squadrons 205
Summary, 870-879 Squadrons 205
Summary, 1700-1792 Squadrons 205
Summary, 1830-1853 Squadrons 205
Order of Battle, September 1939 90
700 Squadron 99
700M Squadron 298
700Z Squadron *256*
701 Squadron 90, 99, 107, *234*
702 Squadron 90, 303
703 Squadron 303
705 Squadron 90, *214/215*, 233, 303
707 Squadron *253*
710 Squadron 87, 90, 92
711 Squadron 90
712 Squadron 90
713 Squadron 90
714 Squadron 90
715 Squadron 90
716 Squadron 90
718 Squadron 90, 94
720 Squadron 90
728 Squadron *225*
737 Squadron 279, 290, 291
738 Squadron *227*
761 Squadron *200/201*
767 Squadron 118, 261
769 Squadron 87, 94
771 Squadron 155, 233, *234/235*, *254*, 303
778 Squadron 213, 236
788 Squadron 165, 166, 229
792 Squadron 226, 303
800 Squadron 79, 85, 87, 90, *92*, 93, 97, 98, 99, 100, 101, 102, 104, 105, 106, 108, 109, 121, 124, 125, 126, *128*, 129, 141, 156, 164, 169, 172, 174, 182, 186, 204, 213, 221, *226*, *227, 242, 250*, 251, *254/255, 257*, *268/269, 270/271, 272*, 274, *276/277*, 277, *281*, 282, 283, 287, 289, *289*, 291, *294*, 297, *300, 301*, 302
800X Independent Night Fighter Unit 145, 148, 151
800Z Squadron 155
801 Squadron *78*, 79, 85, 87, 93, 97, 99, 100, 101, 104, 112, 115, 145, 172, 174, 182, *198, 199, 206/207*, 221, *224*, 224, *258, 268/269, 271*, 274, 277, 282, 283, *284/285*, 284, 287, 288, *289*, 289, 291, *294*, 297, *297*, 302
802 Squadron *78*, 79, 85, 87, 90, 102, 106, 115, 117, *154*, 155, 157, 158, 174, 174, *210/211, 220*, 221, 223, *242*
803 Squadron 79, 85, 87, 90, *92*, 92, 93, 97, 98, 100, 101, 102, 105, 106, 108, 109, 119, *124, 128*, 131, 134, 135, 138, 142, 144, 147, 151, 165, 167, 171, 179, 223, 226, *227*, *250*, 251
804 Squadron 97, 98, 104, 106, 115, 153, 155, 174, 182, 192, 204, 221, *244*, 251,
805 Squadron 126, 127, 129, 130, 131, 132, 133, 134, 135, 140, 143, 145, *145*, 151, 171, *221*
806 Squadron 104, 106, 111, 112, 121, 122, 123, 124, 125, 127, 129, 130, 132, 134, 138, 139, 142, 143, 144, 147, 151, 165, 167, 169, 171, 172, 223, 224, 230
807 Squadron 141, 148, 1499, 150, 151, 172, *172/173*, 174, 178, 179, 186, *218*, 219, 221, *250*, 251
808 Squadron 125, 126, 129, 137, 141, 148, 149, 150, 179, 221
809 Squadron 156, 157, 172, 174, 179, 186, 225, *225*, 231, *236/237, 257, 262, 267, 274/275*, 284, 291
810 Squadron 79, 81, 90, 99, 194, 106, 121, 124, 125, 126, 169, 221, 223, 232
811 Squadron 79, 90, 118
812 Squadron 79, 90. 112, 114, 151, 156, 158, 221
813 Squadron 79, 90, 117, 119, 123, 130, 137, 172, 175, 178, *224, 225*, 229
814 Squadron 79, 90, 119, 139, 165, 230, 249, *258/259*, 298, *300*, 303
815 Squadron 112, 122, 130, 131, 132, 133, 135, 136, 137, 140, 145, 146, 147, 151, 230, *274/275*, 291, 303
816 Squadron 92, 98, 1056, 115, 151
817 Squadron 156, 157, 172, 174, 178, 221
818 Squadron 90, 92, 98, *100*, 112, 125, 179
819 Squadron 122
820 Squadron 79, *80*, 81, 90, 99, 104, 106, *114/115*, 119, 124, 125, 126, 146, 164, 174, 178, 179, 185, 193, 198, *229*, 230, 231, *234*, 291, 298, 303
821 Squadron 79, 81, 90, 108, 129, 151, 178, 221
821X Squadron 129
822 Squadron 79, 90, 118, 172, *172/173*, 174,
823 Squadron 79, 90, 106, 108
824 Squadron 79, 90, 123, 137, 172, 230, 232, 291, 303
825 Squadron 79, 90, 111, 112, 115, 146, 155, 158, 221, 223, 278, 291
826 Squadron 112, 114, 115, 131, 135, 136, 138, 144, 147, 151, 185, *229*, 232, *232*, 277
827 Squadron 156, 164, 169, 172, 182, 185, 221, 229
828 Squadron *146*, 150, 151, 155, 156
829 Squadron 131, 135, 136, *136*, 138, 144, 145, 147, 169, 182, *254*, 291, 295, 298, *303*
830 Squadron 118, 121, 129, 130, 132, 138, 146, 147, 148, 149, 150, 151, 182, 185, *228*, 229
831 Squadron 164, 169, 172, 182, *228*, 229, 230, 232
832 Squadron 157, 172, 174, 177
833 Squadron 174, 179
834 Squadron 179
835 Squadron *187*
842 Squadron 182
845 Squadron 234, 291, 295, 297, 298, 301, 302, 303
846 Squadron *185*, 277, 283, 284, 286, 290, 291, 297, 298, *300*, 302, 303
847 Squadron 232, 278, 291, 301, 302, 303
848 Squadron 234, 278, 291, 302, 303
849 Squadron 193, *229*, 229, 232, *232*, *233*, *296, 300*, 301, 303
853 Squadron *186, 188/189*
854 Squadron 193, 303
857 Squadron 193, *196, 197*, 303
878 Squadron 179
879 Squadron 179, 186
880 Squadron 155, 156, 164, *164*, 169, 172, 174, 178, 179, 182, 185, *198*
881 Squadron 169, 182
882 Squadron 169, 174, 177, 182
884 Squadron 172, 174
885 Squadron 172, 174, 178, 179, *182*
886 Squadron 179
887 Squadron 179, 185, *192*, 193, 198
888 Squadron 164, 167, 169, 174, 178, 179
889 Squadron 171
890 Squadron 179, 226, 231, 251, *252*
891 Squadron 174, 231
892 Squadron 231, *246/247*. 251, *251, 261*
893 Squadron 174, 178, 179, 251
894 Squadron 179, 185, 193, 198, 231
896 Squadron 177, 182
897 Squadron 179
898 Squadron 177, 182, *228*, *234*
899 Squadron 178, 179, 251, *251*, *252*, *268/269*, 274, 277, 284, 291, *294*
RN Fighter Squadron 151
RN Fighter Unit 171
1770 Squadron 185, 193
1820 Squadron 205
1830 Squadron *190*, 193
1831 Squadron 226
1832 Squadron 226
1833 Squadron 193, 226
1834 Squadron 182, *191*, 193
1836 Squadron 182, *191*, 193
1839 Squadron 193, 204
1840 Squadron 185
1841 Squadron 185, 198, *199*
1844 Squadron 193, 204
3 Commando Brigade Air Squadron RM 286, 288, 290, 291, 296, 301
Naval Joint Anti-Submarine School

ii) Wings
Naval Strike Wing 303
'D' Naval Fighter Wing 186
3 Naval Fighter Wing *182*
47 Naval Fighter Wing 182, *191, 195*

Royal Air Force Units post-1920

Bomber Command 102
Coastal Command 102, 104, 108, 109, 112, 114, 131, 155
Fighter Command 112, 113
Western Desert Air Force 186
2nd Tactical Air Force 182
3 Group 301
9 Group 154
201 Naval Co-operation Group 145
205 Group 147, 151
151 Wing 157
Merchant Ship Fighter Unit 154
1 Squadron 278, *284/285*, 287, 288, 302
3 Squadron 69, 284
4 Squadron 302
19 Squadron 113. *113*
30 Squadron 165
32 Squadron 113
33 Squadron 147
46 Squadron *90*, 104, 106, 113, 202
64 Squadron 113
73 Squadron 126
74 Squadron 113
79 Squadron 113
80 Squadron 147
111 Squadron 113
112 Squadron 121
145 Squadron 113
151 Squadron 113
210 Squadron 69, 73
213 Squadron 113
229 Squadron 113
235 Squadron 114
242 Squadron 113, *113*
254 Squadron 104
258 Squadron 165, 166
261 Squadron 165, 167
2163 Squadron 99, 104, 106, 107
266 Squadron 113
273 Squadron 165, 167
501 Squadron 113
617 Squadron 185
3 AACU 118
431 Flight 125

Army Air Corps and Other

Army Air Corps/ 656 Squadron 290
Commando Helicopter Force 297, 302
Joint Army/Air Force Experimental Helicopter Unit 242, 245
Joint Force 2000 301
Joint Force Harrier Migration Plan 302
Joint Harrier Strike Force 302, 303
Joint Helicopter Force 302
Royal Australian Navy Fleet Air Arm 219

AIRCRAFT AND AERO ENGINES

The brief description of each aircraft's nationality and use relates to its specific inclusion in the text. Thus, for instance, a Boeing 707 is described as 'Argentinian reconnaissance aircraft' rather than 'US-built airliner' because the former description depicts its particular use and ownership in the context of this book.

Comparison of Naval Aircraft Performances, 1939/40 95
Aichi D3A 'Val' – IJNAF dive-bomber 95, 166, 167
Aichi B7A 'Grace' – Japanese dive-bomber 198
Albatros – German fighting scout 52, 53
Arado Ar 196 – German catapult floatplane 98
Armstrong Siddley Double Mamba – aero engine 231
Armstrong Siddley Python – aero engine 229
Armstrong-Whitworth – Aircraft manufacturer 15
Astra Torres non-rigid airship 15, *16*, 17
Augusta A 109 – Argentinian helicopter 287
Augusta-Westland Merlin – RN helicopter 298, *298*
Augusta-Westland Future-Lynx – RN helicopter 287, 302
Avro Bison – RN reconnaissance aircraft *66/67, 72/73*, 73
Avro Lancaster – RAF bomber 185
Avro Vulcan – RAF bomber 282
BE 2C – RFC reconnaissance aircraft 24
Beech T-34 Turbo-Mentor – Argentinian trainer 278, 284
Boeing B-29 Superfortress – US bomber 219
Boeing 707 – Argentinian reconnaissance aircraft 278, 281
Boeing-Vertol Chinook – RAF helicopter 278, 284, 286, 288, 291, 301
Boeing F-22 Raptor – US experimental fighter 302
Blackburn Baffin – RN torpedo bomber 79, *79*, *80*, 81
Blackburn Blackburn – RN reconnaissance aircraft *66/67, 77,* 77
Blackburn Buccaneer – RN strike aircraft 253, *255*, 256, *256. 257, 258, 259, 260/261*, 261, *262, 264, 265, 266*, 267
Blackburn Dart – RN torpedo bomber *72/72*, 73, 76, 77, *77*
Blackburn Firebrand – RN torpedo fighter 224, *224*, *225*, 226, 229
Blackburn Ripon – RN torpedo-bomber 76, 77, *77*, 79
Blackburn Roc – RN turret fighter 86, *86*, 87, 90, 92, 102, 104, 112, 121, 126, 202
Blackburn Shark – RN torpedo bomber *80*, 81
Blackburn Skua – RN fighter-dive bomber *78*, 83, *83,84*, 85, 87, 90, 92, *92*, 94, 95, 97, 98, 99, 100, 101, 102, 104, 105, 107, 108, 109, 111, 112, 115, 119, 121, 122, 124, 126, *128*, 130, 137, 141, 202, *206/207*, 207
Blohm und Voss BV 138A – German flying boat 95, 106, 161
Boulton Paul Defiant – RAF turret fighter 86

Brandenburg W.29 – German seaplane *20*
Breguet – French aircraft manufacturer 49, 50, 52
Breguet/BAC Jaguar – RAF ground attack aircraft 296
Brewster Buffalo – RN fighter 95, 115, 133, 140, 143
Bristol Beaufighter – RAF heavy fighter 148
Bristol Beaufort – RAF torpedo-bomber 95, 102, 108, 109
Bristol Blenheim IV – RAF bomber and fighter 102, 108, 114, 136, 137, 148, 149, 165, 166, 167
Bristol Belvedere – RAF helicopter 249
Bristol Boxkite – RN trainer *14*
Bristol Centaurus – aero engine 224
Bristol Perseus – aero engine 86
Bristol Scout C & D – RN scout aircraft 38, *40*
Bristol Sycamore – RAF/Army helicopter 242, 245
British Aircraft Corporation – aircraft manufacturer 262
Brittain-Norman Islander – Argentinian light transport 282
Cant Z.501 – Italian flying boat 121, 122, 123, 124
Cant Z.506B - Italian floatplane 95, 119, 121, 122, 124, 125, 126, 137, 148, 150
Cant Z.1007Bis – Italian bomber 123, 138, 142, 148, 149
Caproni Ca 133 – Italian bomber/ transport 123
Caudron G-IV – RN bomber 49, *50*, 50, 54
Caudron Luciolle – French liaison aircraft 124
C-Class Airship – RN airship *25*, 26
Consolidated Catalina – RAF flying boat 95, 165, 167, 188
Curtiss H-4 'Little America' – RN flying boat 26
Curtiss H-12 'Large America' – RN flying boat 26, 27, *27*, *28*, 28
Curtiss H-16 – RN flying boat 27
Curtiss H-75A Hawk – French fighter 112, 119, 124
Curtiss SB2C Helldiver – RN dive bomber 205, 207, *209*
Dagger – Argentinian fighter-bomber 278, 282, 287, 288, 289, 290, 291
Dassault Mirage – Argentinian fighter 278, 282, 283, 291
Dassault Super Etendard – Argentinian fighter-bomber 278, 283, 284, 288
Dassault-Breguet Rafale – French fighter 302
De Havilland DH 4 – RN bomber 53, 54, 55
De Havilland DH 6 – RN trainer/ reconnaissance aircraft 29, *29*
De Havilland DH 9 – RN bomber 55, 67
De Havilland DH-9A – RAF bomber *66/67*, 69
De Havilland Hornet – RAF fighter 223, 224
De Havilland Sea Hornet – RN fighter *225*, *236/237*
De Havilland Nimrod – RAF AWACs aircraft 269, 278
De Havilland Vampire – RAF fighter 225, 231
De Havilland Sea Vampire – RN fighter *222/223*, 224, *226*, 226, *227*
De Havilland Sea Venom – RN fighter 225, *227*, 230, *230*, 231, 245, 251
De Havilland Sea Vixen – RN fighter *240/241*, 251, *251*, 253, 255, *260/261*, 262, *262*, 267
Dewoitine D.520 – French fighter 95, 147, 174, 175
Dornier Do 17 – German bomber 98, 105
Dornier Do 18 – German flying boat 95, 99, 157, 158
Dornier Do 24N – German flying boat 138
Douglas A-4 Skyhawk – Argentinian attack aircaft 278, 282, 283, 284, 287, 288, 289, 290, 291
Douglas AD Skyraider – RN AWACs aircraft 217, 219, *229*, 229, 232, *242/243*, 244, 245
Douglas SBD Dauntless – USN dive bomber 93, 95, 178, 191, 207, *209*
Douglas DB-7 – French bomber 174
Eurofighter Typhoon – RAF fighter 302
English Electric Canberra – RAF andArgentinian bomber 248, 278, 282, 290
Fairchild-Republic A-10 Thunderbolt II – USAF anti-tank aircraft 301
Fairey Albacore – RN torpedo bomber 95, *104*, 112, 114, *114/115*, 122, 131, 132, 135, 136, 142, 144, *146* 147, 150, 151, 155, 156, 157, *157*, 158, *162/163*, 164, 165, 167, 169, 172, *172.173*, 174, 178, 202, 203
Fairey Barracuda – RN torpedo/dive bomber 182, *183*, 185, 188, 191, 199, 203, 213, 230
Fairey F-17 Campania – RN seaplane *23*
Fairey Firefly – RN reconnaissance fighter 185, 193, 196, 203, 205, 213, 214, *216*, 217, 219, 221, 223, *229*, 230
Fairey Flycatcher – RN fighter 70, *70/71*, 73, *74*, 77, 79, 83
Fairey Fulmar – RN fighter 95, *120*, 121, 122, 123, 124, 125,126, *128*, 129, 130, 131, 132, 133, *133*, 134, 135, 136, 137, 138, 139, 140, 141, 142, 143, 144, 145, 147, 148, 149, 150, 154, 155, 156, 157, 158, 164, 165, 166, 167, 169, 172, 174, 202, 203
Fairey Gannet – RN anti-submarine & AWACs aircraft 230, 231, *231*, 232, *232*, *233*, 234, 244, 256, *266*, 278
Fairey Sea Fox – RN Catapult floatplane 81, 90, 92, 94, 203
Fairey Seal – RN reconnaissance aircraft 79, *80*, 81
Fairey Swordfish – RN torpedo bomber *80*, 81, *81*, *82*, 87, *88/89*, 90, 91, 92, 93, 95, 98,99, 100, 101, 104, 105, 106, 107, 112, 114, 115, 117, 1178, 119, 121, 122, 123, 124, 125, 126, 127, 129, 130, 132, 133, 135, 136, 137, 138, 139, 140, 144, 145, 146, 147, 148, 149, 150, 151, 155, 156, 158, 159, 161, 164, 155, 166, 167, 169, 174, 182, 185, 186, 202, 203, 213
Fairey IIIC-F – RN reconnaissance aircraft/seaplane 68, *72/73*, 76, *76*, *77*, 77, 79, *80*, 81
Farman, Maurice, Shorthorn – RN training aircraft *10/11*, 37
Farman F-40 – RN bomber 52
Farman, 223-4 French civil airliner 126
Felixstowe F.2A – RN flying boat *20/21*, 27, 28
Felixstowe F.3 – RN flying boat 27, 28
Fiat BR 20M – Italian bomber 148, 149, 150
Fiat CR 32 – Italian fighter 123
Fiat CR 42 – Italian fighter 123, 126, 127, 129, 133, 135, 136, *141*, 141, 144, 149, 150
Focke-Wulf FW 190 – German fighter 159, 179, 186, *187*
Focke-Wulf Fw 200 Kondor – German reconnaissance bomber 99, 153, 154, 158, 161
Fokker Eindekker – German fighting scout 49
Fokker Friendship – Argentinian passenger aircraft 278
Fokker F-28 – Argentinian passenger aircraft 278
Friedrikschafen – German seaplane 22
General Dynamics F-111K Aardvark – USAF bomber 266
Gloucester Gladiator – RAF fighter 85, 99, 104, 106, 107, 121
Gloucester Sea Gladiator – RN fighter *78*, 85, *85*, 87, 90, 92, 97, 101, 102, 104, 117, 118, 120, 121, 122, 124, 126, 130, 132, 134, 135, 140, 143, *143*, 155, 202
Gloucestershire Mars (see *Nieuport Nightjar*)
Gotha G.IV – German bomber 33, *33*, 55, *55*, 60
Grumman G-36/F4F Wildcat/Martlet and Goodyear
FM-1/FM-2 Wildcat V & VI – RN/USN fighter 95, 115, 122, 145, *151*, *153*, *154*, 155, 157, 158, 161, 164, 165, 167, 169, 171, 172, 174, *176/177*, 177, 178, 179, 182, *185*, 185, 186, *188/189*, 191, 192, 202, 203, 204, 213, 225,
Grumman F6F Hellcat – RN/USN fighter 182, *184*, 185, 186, 191, 192, 193, 196, 198, 203, 204, *204*
Grumman F9F Panther – USN fighter 217, 226
Grumman TBM Avenger – RN/USN torpedo-bomber *7*, 161, 177, 178, 182, *185*, 185, 186, *186*, 191, 192, 193, 196, *196*, *197*, 204, 213, *229*, 230, 232, 244, 245
Grumman S-2E Tracker – Argentinian anti-submarine aircraft 278
Halberstadt – German fighting scout 52
Handley-Page O/100 - RN heavy bomber 53, 54, *54*, 55
Handley-Page O/400 – RN heavy bomber 55
Handley-Page Victor – RAF aerial tanker aircraft *260/261*, 278, 279, 284
Hawker Fury – RAF fighter 78
Hawker Fury (II) – experimental fighter 224
Hawker Hurricane – RAF/RN fighter 83, 86, *90*, 104, 107, 112, 115, 120, 121, 122, *122*, 125, 126, 128, 130, 137, 139, 143, 145, 146, 147, 149, 150, 141, 154, 155, 156, 157, 158, 65, 166, 167, 171, 202, 203
Hawker Hunter – RAF fighter 248, 271
Hawker Nimrod – RN fighter 78, *78*, 79, 83, 85
Hawker Osprey – RN reconnaissance-fighter 78, *79*, 85
Hawker P.1040 – experimental fighter 230
Hawker P.1052 – experimental fighter 230
Hawker P.1081 – experimental fighter 230
Hawker Sea Fury – RN fighter-bomber 7, 213, *214*, *218*, 219, *220*, 221, *224*, 224, 230
Hawker Sea Hurricane – RN fighter *122*, 148, 154, 156, 157, 159, 160, 161, *162/163*, 164, *164*, 169, 172, 174, 175, 186, *187*, 202
Hawker Sea Hawk – RN fighter-bomber 226, *228*, 230, *230*, 231, *242*, *243*, 244, 245, 250, 251,
Hawker Tempest – RAF fighter 230
Hawker-Siddeley P.1127 Kestrel – experimental VTO aircraft 271
Hawker-Siddeley Harrier – RAF ground attack aircraft 271, 277, *284/285*, 284, 286, 287, 288, 290, 291, *294*, 301, 302, 303
Hawker-Siddeley Sea Harrier – RN fighter *268/269*, *270/271*, 272, *272*, *272/273*. 274, *274*, *274/275*, *276/277*, 277, 278, 281, *281*, 282, 283, 284, *284/285*, 286, 287, 288, 289, *289*, 290, 291, *294*, 297, *297*, 298, *299*, *301*, 302
Heinkel He 111 – German bomber 93, 94, 95, 98, 99, 101, 102, 104, 105, 106, 108, 130, 132, 134, 139, 142, 144, 158, 160, 161
Heinkel He 115 – German floatplane reconnaissance aircraft 95, 99, 100, 102, 106, 161, 186
Hispano-Suiza – Aero engine manufacturer 60
IA 58A Pucara – Argentinian ground attack aircraft 278, 282, 284, 287, 288, 291
Ilyushin Il 28 – Egyptian jet bomber 245
Junkers Ju 52/3m – German trimotor transport aircraft 98, 100, 104, 138
Junkers Ju 87 – German dive-bomber 100, 102, 123, 129, 130, 152, 144, 145, 151, 156, 172
Junkers Ju 88 – German bomber 93, 04, 99, 101, 102, 105, 112, 115, 134, 135, 137, 138, 139, 142, 144, 145, 161, *178/179*
Kawanishi H6K 'Mavis' – IJNAF flying boat 95, 169
Learjet – Argentinian executive jet employed for reconnaissance 278, 289
Lc Rhonc, aero engine manufacturer *58/59*
Lockheed C-130 Hercules – British and Argentinian transport aircraft 278, 284, 288, 289, 290
Lockheed C-139 – Argentinian transport aircraft 278
Lockheed Electra – Argentinian transport aircraft 278
Lockheed Hudson – RAF patrol bomber 95, 99, 102, 108, 122
Lockheed SP-2H Neptune – Argentinian anti-submarine aircraft 278
Lockheed-Martin F-35B Lightning II Joint Combat Aircraft – RN/RAF future fighter-bomber *299*, 302, 303
Loire 130 – French catapult flying boat 124
LVG – German reconnaissance aircraft 52
Macchi 339 – Argentinian reconnaissance aircraft 278, 288
Martin 167F Maryland – French & RAF reconnaissance-bomber 95, 125, 138, 189, 155
'Mayfly' – HM Rigid Airship No. 1 12, *12*, 15
McDonnell F2H Banshee – USN fighter 226
McDonnell-Douglas F-4 Phantom – RN/ RAF fighter *246/247*, 256, *261*, 261, 262, *263*, *264*, *266*, 291
Meridionali Ro 43 – Italian catapult floatplane 126, 136
Messerschmitt Bf 109 – German fighter 102, 108, 112, 115, 143, *146*, 156, 179, 186, 202
Messerschmitt Bf 110 – German heavy fighter 102, 105, 108, 142, 156, 157
MiG-15 – Egyptian fighter 219, *220*, 226, 245
MiG-19 – Iraqi fighter 248
Mitsubishi A5M 'Claude' – IJNAF fighter 95
Mitsubishi A6M Zero-Sen – IJNAF fighter 95, 166, 167, 198, 203
Mitsubishi G4M 'Betty' – IJNAF bomber 95, 191
Mitsubishi Ki 21 'Sally' – IJAAF bomber 191
Morane 406 – French fighter 169
Morane-Saulnier MS 3 – RN scout *31*, 33
Nakajima B5N 'Kate' – IJNAF torpedo-bomber 95, 166, 167
Nakajima Ki 43 'Oscar' – IJAAF fighter 191, 192
Nieuport 11 – RN fighting scout 52
Nieuport 12 – RN fighting scout *34/35*, 37
Nieuport 17 – RN fighting scout 52
Nieuport Nightjar – RN fighter 69, *69*, 70, 73
North American F-51 Mustang – USAF fighter-bomber 219
North American F-86 Sabre – USAF fighter 219, 226
Panavia Tornado – RAF fighter-bomber 303
Parceval – early RN non-rigid balloon 15, *16/17*. 17
Parnall Panther – RN Spotter-reconnaissance aircraft 69, 73, *73*, *76*
Parnall Plover – RN fighter 73
Pfalz – German fighting scout 53
Potez 63 – French reconnaissance-bomber 169
Pratt & Whitney Twin Wasp – aero engine 151, 178, 203
Pucara (see IA 58B)
Rolls-Royce – aero engine manufacturer 60
Rolls-Royce Eagle – aero engine 26, 27
Rolls-Royce Eagle(II) 229
Rolls-Royce Griffon – aero engine 185, 203, 223, 224
Rolls-Royce Kestrel – aero engine 78
Rolls-Royce Merlin – aero engine 86, *120*, 122, 203
Rolls-Royce Nene – aero engine 226
Rolls-Royce Spey – aero engine 261
Savoia S.79 – Italian bomber 119, 120, 121, 123, 124, 125, 126, 129, 130, 132, 134, 138, *140*, *141*, 141, 142, 148, 149, 150
Savoia S.81 – Italian bomber 123, 144
Savoia S.82 – Italian transport aircraft 123
Savoia S.84 – Italian bomber 149
SE 5/5A – RFC/RAF fighting scout 53
Short S.27 – RN floatplane 15
Short 184 – RN floatplane *25*, 36, 37, 38, 41, *41*, 44, 50, 54, 68
Short Sunderland – RAF flying boat 95, 102, 125, 126, 135, 139, 156
Short Skyvan – Argentinian light transport aircraft 278, 284
Sikorsky R-4 Hoverfly – RN/US helicopter 233
Sikorsky S.51 Dragonfly – RN/USN helicopter 217, *218*, 233
Sikorsky S.55 – USN helicopter 234
Sikorsky S.58 – USN helicopter 253
Sikorsky S.61B – USN helicopter 261
Sopwith Baby – RN seaplane scout 28
Sopwith Bat – flying boat 26
Sopwith Camel – RN/RFC/RAF fighting scout 28, 45, *45*, 46, 47, 53, 55, *55*, 69
Sopwith Cuckoo – RN torpedo-bomber *38/39*, 47, 69, *73/74*
Sopwith Pup – RN/RFC fighting scout 28, 33, 42, *42*, *43*, 43, 44, 45, 52, 53, *59*
Sopwith Sneider – RN seaplane scout *22*
Sopwith 1½ Strutter – RN/RFC fighting scout/bomber 49, 50, *50*, 52, 53, 54
Sopwith Tabloid – RN seaplane scout 49
Sopwith Triplane – RN fighting scout *48/49*, 52, 53, 55
Spad S.VII – RFC/RAF fighting scout 53
SS non-rigid airship 24, *24*, 26, 29
Supermarine Attacker – RN fighter *226*, 226, *227*, *236/237*
Supermarine Scimitar – RN fighter-bomber 250, *250*, 251, 253, 256
Supermarine Seafang – RN experimental fighter 224
Supermarine Seafire – RN fighter *170/171*, *172/173*. 174, *175*, 178,179, 182, *182*, *184*, 185, 186, 191. 192, *192*, 193, 196, 198, *198*, *199*, 202, 203, *210/211*, 213, *213*, 214, 217, 219, 221, 223, 224, *227*
Supermarine Seagull V – RN catapult flying boat 79
Supermarine Sea Otter – catapult flying boat 203, *203*, 205, 213
Supermarine Spiteful – RAF experimental fighter 224
Supermarine Spitfire – RAF fighter 83, 86, 111, 112, 158, 159, 171, 172, 174, *178*, 179, *200/201*, 202, 203, 224
Supermarine Walrus – RN catapult amphibian 69, 81, 87, 90, 92, 99, 106, 107, 124, 130, 135, 136, 167, 193, 202, 203
Supermarine E.10/40 – experimental fighter 226
Vickers Wellington – RAF bomber 132, 138, 150, 151, 178, 188
Vought F4U Corsair – RN/USN fighter 182, 185, 188, *190*, 191, *191*, 192, 193, *194*, *195*, 196, 199, 204, 213, 217, 219, 245
Vought-Sikorsky OS2U Kingfisher – RN/USN catapult floatplane 204, *205*
Westland Dragonfly – RN helicopter 219, 233, 245
Westland Gazelle – RN helicopter 286, 291, 301
Westland Lynx – RN helicopter 278, 280, *280*, 281, 284, 288, *295*, 295, 298, *298*, 301, 302
Westland Scout AH-1 – Army Air Corps helicopter 288, 290, 291
Westland Sea King – RN helicopter *8/9*, *235*, *258/259*, 261, *274/275*, 277, 278, 283, 284, *286*, 287, *288*, 290, *290*, 291, *292/293*, 295, *295*, 297, *297*, 298,299, 301, 302
Westland Walrus *66/67*, 69, 70, 73
Westland Wasp – RN helicopter 253, *254*, 278
Westland Wessex – RN helicopter *233*, 249, *249*, 253, *254*, 256, 278, 279, 280, 281, 287, 288, 290, 291
Westland Whirlwind – RN helicopter 234, *234*, *235*, *240/241*, 242, 245, 256
Westland Wyvern – RN torpedo-fighter 226, *228*, 229, *242/243*
Westland/Aerospatiale Puma – Argentinian helicopter 286, 287
Wolseley – aero engine manufacturer 12
Wright Cyclone – aero engine 151, 177, 203
Yak – North Korean fighter 217
Zeppelin – German Rigid Airship 15, 19, 22, 23, 26, 28, 31, *32/33*, 33, 38, 41, 42, 45, 46

LAND AND SEA SERVICE UNITS

Admiralty (Board of Admiralty) 11, 15, 17, 19, 20, 38, 46, 60, 61, 63, 64, 73, 74, 83, 87, 89, 202, 203, 224, 231
1st Aircraft Carrier Squadron 192
Allied Expeditionary Force, Norway, 1940 98
1st Armoured Division 301
7th Armoured Brigade 295
14th Army 192
Battle Fleet 74
1st Battle Squadron 135, 137, 140, 143, 144
2nd Battle Squadron 79, 82
Battlescruiser Squadron 82, 90
Beira Patrol 256
5th Brigade 289
British Expeditionary Force, 1914 17, 20
British Expeditionary Force, 1940 111
British Falklands Task Force 277, 278, 281, 282, 283, *283*, 284, 287
British Pacific Fleet 192, 193, 194, 195, 196, *197*, 199, 204
CAM ships 154, 161
3 Commando Brigade, RM 302
40 Commando 301
42 Commando 301
1st Cruiser Squadron 79, 82, 90
2nd Cruiser Squadron 79, 82, 90
3rd Cruiser Squadron 79, 82, 90
4th Cruiser Squadron 79, 82, 90
5th Cruiser Squadron 79, 82, 90
6th Cruiser Squadron 79, 82, 90
8th Cruiser Squadron 79, 82, 90
15th Cruiser Squadron
Deck Landing Control Officer (Batsman) 82
Eastern Fleet 165, 166, 167, 169, 191, 192
East Indies Fleet 192, 204
Fleet Air Arm Museum, Yeovilton 101
Fighter Catapult Ships 154
Force 'B' 135, 144
Force 'F' 169
Force 'H' 115, 118, 119, 121, 124, 125, 126, 127, 128, *128*, 129, 131, 132, 141, 142, 145, 148, 149, 150, 155, 156, 165, 172, 174, 178, 179
Force 'M' 157, 1`58
Force 'R' 135
Force 'V' 179
Gannet, HMS, Prestwick, Scotland 298
Gemini rubber boats 280
Grand Fleet 38, 41, 42
Home Fleet 44, 93, 98, 102, 115, 155, 156, 158, 172, 181
MAC ships 161, 202
Mediterranean Fleet 117, 118, 119, 121, 123, 124, 125, 126, 129, 134, 138, 141, 156
Queen's Coronation Review of the Fleet 231
Royal Australian Navy 219
Royal Canadian Navy 213, 248
Queen's Dragoon Guards 301
Royal Engineers
Royal Marines 22, 245, 248, 249, 277, 288, 301, 302
Royal Navy Armoured Car Force 22
Royal Naval Volunteer Reserve *170.171*, 205, 226, 231
Special Air Service 284, 286, 301
Task Force 14
Task Force 57 194
Task Force 58 194
Task Force 77 219
TG 38.3 199
TG 77.3 217
Womens' Royal Naval Service *304*, 305

Want to be a
high-flyer?

There's a huge range of career and job opportunities for women who join the Royal Navy's Fleet Air Arm as Observers or Pilots in Harrier fast jets or Lynx, Merlin and Sea King helicopters. And along with an exciting career, there's the satisfaction of knowing that you've got a secure job and an exceptional way of life. Here's an insider's view:

Name: Amy Grey
Age: 27
Job: Qualified Observer Instructor – Jetstream Aircraft

Why did you join the Royal Navy?
I was still in the sixth form at school when I found out that not only do you get paid the whole time you're training for a career flying fast jets and helicopters, you get to fly them during training as well – I jumped at the chance!

What about getting a degree?
You get a degree as well as being paid to train as a Pilot or Observer with the Royal Navy Fleet Air Arm. So, unlike a lot of my student friends, I got a flying start to a fantastic career with no money worries!

How did you get to become an Observer?
After initial training at Britannia Royal Naval College in Dartmouth, I went on to specialise as a Lynx Observer.

What do you enjoy most about your job?
The fact that it's more an amazing lifestyle than just a job. Every day is different and exciting. I get to travel all over the world and have the kind of experiences other people only dream of.

What's the most rewarding thing about your job?
The fact that I have already accomplished so much more already than I ever thought I would be capable of. The training really motivates you to make the most of your potential in a way that I can't imagine happening in any other job.

What interests do you have outside work?
I take full advantage of the amazing social life and loads of sports opportunities on offer in the Royal Navy.

Lynx helicopter in action,
launching a Sea Skua
anti-surface missile

Join the Royal Navy
royalnavy.mod.uk/careers
or call 08456 07 55 55

ROYAL
NAVY

**LIFE
WITHOUT
LIMITS**